D1378617

NEW TESTAMENT HOURS

*   *

THE ACROPOLIS, ATHENS.

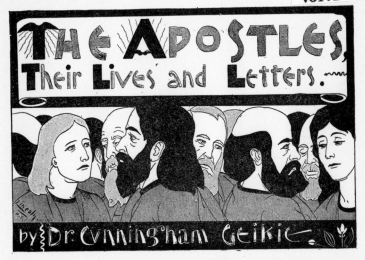

THE APOSTLES,
Their Lives and Letters.

by Dr. Cunningham Geikie.

A.D. 55 TO A.D. 64, WITH THE EPISTLES TO THE GALATIANS, FIRST AND
SECOND CORINTHIANS, ROMANS, COLOSSIANS, PHILEMON,
EPHESIANS, PHILIPPIANS, FIRST AND SECOND
TIMOTHY, AND TITUS.

NEW YORK:

JAMES POTT & CO., PUBLISHERS,

119 WEST 23D ST.

1901.

Press of J. J. Little & Co.
Astor Place, New York

TO

THE REVEREND AUGUSTUS JESSOPP, D.D.,

RECTOR OF SCARNING, NORFOLK.

AN IDEAL PARISH PRIEST ;

AN AUTHOR, WHO, LIKE GOLDSMITH, ADORNS WHATEVER

HE TOUCHES :

A FRIEND LOVED AND HONOURED MOST, WHERE

MOST INTIMATELY KNOWN.

THAT SUCH A MAN HAS NOT LONG SINCE BEEN AT

LEAST A DEAN, MAY BE NO LOSS TO HIM,

BUT IT IS A GREAT ONE TO

THE CHURCH.

PREFACE

AMERICAN EDITION

THE series of which this is a volume is a continuation of the Hours with the Bible, to which so much favor has been shown in America. New Testament Hours, beginning with The Gospels: a companion to the Life of Christ, and now followed by the first part of The Apostles: their Lives and Letters, are designed on the same lines, so far as possible, as those on which the Old Testament Hours were written. It is not, indeed, practicable for me, after having published my Life of Christ, to go through the Evangelists again, systematically; but there were so many side-lights on the Great Story, which escaped notice in that Life, or could not be introduced without making it too large, that I felt able to compose "The Gospels," with such a freshness of material as must make it an indispensable companion to the "Life," for all who wish to see their Lord's earthly existence in full and glorious clearness.

The Apostles: their Lives and Letters necessarily form an expanded narrative of the "Acts," with the insertion of the Epistles at the proper places, and will, if I be spared to complete my design, carry out the history of the Early Church to the close of the Canon. The translations given of the Apostolic Letters, duly expanded for greater clearness, and the narrative of their travels and doings, will, I hope, be found just such an aid to the full understanding of the New Testament as I aimed to create in Old Testament Hours.

My knowledge of the various countries through which the Apostles wandered, will, I believe, be found to bring the story of the New Testament, in these "Hours," with vivid distinctness before the Reader. That my books may be of true use to them, and thus serve my Master, is my heart's prayer.

Meanwhile, to the multitude of my American friends, I send all good wishes, and a world of love and gratitude.

CUNNINGHAM GEIKIE.

CONTENTS

LIST OF ILLUSTRATIONS

NEW TESTAMENT CHRONOLOGY

YEAR.	CHRONOLOGY.	CONTEMPORARY EVENTS.
B.C. 27	ACCESSION OF AUGUSTUS.	
25	Northern Spain and Western Gaul subdued.	
19	Death of Virgil. Herod's Temple begun.	
12 to 7 A.D.	Campaigns in Rhætia, Vindelicia, Noricum, Pannonia, and Moesia under Tiberius and Drusus.	
7	Death of Horace.	HIGH PRIESTS.
7 to ?	BIRTH OF CHRIST. Ideler gives B.C. 7 as the date, Sulpicius Severus B.C. 4, Clemens of Alexandria B.C. 3, Eusebius and others B.C. 2.	Joazer, son of Boethus (H. P.).
A.D. 1 Year of Rome 750	DEATH OF HEROD. Archelaus, Philip, and Antipas get nearly all his dominions. Friedländer gives the date as B.C. 4.	Eleazer, son of Aretas (H. P.). Boethus (H. P.).
A.D. 6	ARCHELAUS BANISHED. JUDÆA AND SAMARIA (TOGETHER) PUT UNDER ROMAN PROCURATORS. Famine in Rome, A.D. 5–8.	Joshua (H. P.). HANNAS, son of Seth (H. P.). PROCURATORS OF JUDÆA.
7	Germanicus, son of Drusus, on Danube and Rhine.	Coponius (6–9 ?).
9	Varus defeated, with loss of the legions, in Germany. End of war in Dalmatia.	Marcus Ambivius (9–12 ?).
10–11	Tiberius again in Germany.	Annius Rufus (12–15 ?).
14	DEATH OF AUGUSTUS, 76 years old. TIBERIUS IS EMPEROR (14–37), 56 years old.	Ismael, son of Phabi (H. P.).
14–16	Germanicus again in Germany.	Valerius Gratus procurator, 15–20.
16	Germanicus recalled. Rise of Sejanus.	Eleazer, son of Hannas (H. P.).
17	Germanicus sent to the East. Great earthquake in Asia Minor. Twelve cities destroyed.	Simon (H. P.).

Year.	Chronology.	Contemporary Events.
18	Ovid dies (18), and Livy (17).	Joseph (Caiaphas) (H. P.).
19	Germanicus dies, poisoned at Antioch. Jews banished from Italy. Drusus poisoned by Sejanus.	
22–31	Sejanus is vice-emperor. Tiberius at Capri (27–37).	
26	Pontius Pilate, Procurator of Judæa (26–36). Tiberius leaves Rome (26). Goes to Capri (27).	
28 or 29	John the Baptist. The crucifixion of Christ is assigned to 29 by the majority of ancient sources. Christ baptized.	
30 (?)	Christ crucified (30, Schürer; 35, Keim and Hausrath). Sejanus falls and is put to death.	31, Philo in Egypt. Vitellius (father of the emperor) Proconsul of Syria.
34	Philip the Tetrarch dies. His dominions annexed to Syria.	
35–36	Parthian war threatened. Antipas is on the Euphrates with Vitellius.	Caiaphas (H. P.) deposed.
35	Stephen stoned. James, brother of Christ, head of the Jerusalem Church. Conversion of St. Paul (Ramsay and Weiszäcker).	
36	Aretas defeats Antipas. Josephus born in Jerusalem	Jonathan, son of Hannas (H. P.).
37	Tiberius dies 16th March. Caius Caligula is Emperor (born, A.D. 12; killed, A.D. 41). Pilate is deposed before Easter. Agrippa I., grandson of Herod, made King of North Palestine, that is, of Philip's domains and those of Lysanias.	Theophilus, son of Hannas (H. P.). 35 or 36, Pilate massacres Samaritans at Gerizim. Marcellus procurator, 37–41.
39	Paul is in Arabia and Damascus. Antipas deposed and banished. His territory given to Agrippa.	Petronius Proconsul of "Syria."
39–40	Fierce resistance to the attempted desecration of the Temple by Caligula. Paul's first visit to Jerusalem after returning from Damascus. He is in the Holy City only fifteen days, then goes to Syria and Cilicia. Ramsay gives the time as in the "early spring."	
40	Philo's embassy to Rome on behalf of Alexandrian Jews. Baptism of Cornelius.	

YEAR.	CHRONOLOGY.	CONTEMPORARY EVENTS.
41–Jan. 54	CLAUDIUS is EMPEROR.	Simon, son of Boe-thus (H. P.).
41	HEROD AGRIPPA made King of all Palestine.	Matthias, son of Hannas (H. P.).
43	Claudius begins "the conquest of Britain."	
44	NEW PERSECUTION in JERUSALEM. James, son of Zebedee, killed. Peter imprisoned. Itinerates outside Judæa. AGRIPPA DIES after the Passover. JUDÆA AGAIN MADE a ROMAN PROCURATORSHIP under Fadus. Fadus fights the revolutionist Theudas. Herod, brother of Agrippa, grandson of Herod the Great, made King of Chalcis in Lebanon, with superintendence of the Temple and Temple treasury, and nomination of high priests.	Eljonai, son of Kantheras (H. P.). Joseph, son of Kami (H. P.). CUSPIUS FADUS, PROCURATOR OF JUDÆA, 44.
45	Famine in Judæa.	
46	Thrace made a Roman province, as also Lycia and Mauretania. QUEEN HELENA in Jerusalem. Long famine continues.	TIBERIUS ALEXANDER, procurator to 48.
48–49	PAUL in ANTIOCH a whole year with Barnabas. PAUL'S SECOND JOURNEY TO JERUSALEM with Barnabas, to hand over alms for poor brethren. Paul, however, does not go the whole way, and does not actually visit the Holy City, but returns to Antioch. Late in the year 48, or in spring of 49, Paul sets out on his FIRST MISSIONARY JOURNEY with Barnabas and Mark. Journey lasted till 51 (Ramsay). Jews driven out of Rome. Herod of Chalcis dies. Berenice his widow henceforth lives with her brother Agrippa. Agrippa (II.), hitherto living privately in Rome, is made King of Chalcis, with all the offices lately held by his uncle Herod.	VENTIDIUS CUMANUS, procurator, 48–52. Ananias, son of Nebedaius (H. P.) (c. 48–59). Rich, but hated for his greed. Murdered by the people at the beginning of the last war.
49	Claudius marries Agrippina. Adopts Nero, her son.	
51	Ramsay brings Paul to Antioch about July 51. He remained there about a year. PAUL'S THIRD JOURNEY TO JERUSALEM. In autumn of 51 or the following winter, 51–52 (Ramsay), the DELIBERATION of the JERUSALEM CHURCH	

YEAR.	CHRONOLOGY.	CONTEMPORARY EVENTS.
	respecting the bearing of the Mosaic Law on heathen converts. Peter at Antioch.	
52	Cumanus involved in trouble with Jews about the Samaritans. Jonathan, formerly high priest, murdered by plot of FELIX. EPISTLE OF JAMES (Meyer). Paul's SECOND MISSIONARY JOURNEY, lasting 2½ or 3 years. Ramsay makes it begin in April 52	52–60 FELIX made procurator on the disgrace of Cumanus.
53	Agrippa obtains Philip's dominions instead of Chalcis, securing also some other territories. PAUL in CORINTH from autumn 53 to early spring 55 (Ramsay). GALLIO is Proconsul of Achaia from April 53 to April 54.	
54–68	NERO, born A.D. 37. Accession, 13th October 54. FIRST EPISTLE TO THESSALONIANS. Wieseler assigns it to 52 or 53, and SECOND THESSALONIANS to 53–54.	Brückner assigns the FIRST EPISTLE of PETER to A.D. 54. Many, however, think its date c. A.D. 63–64.
55	Spring. PAUL'S FOURTH JOURNEY to JERUSALEM on his return from Corinth. He is at Antioch through the summer, and thence writes EPISTLE TO THE GALATIANS. Wieseler says 54–55. In the late summer Paul set out on his THIRD GREAT MISSIONARY JOURNEY. PAUL in EPHESUS from winter of 55 to early in 58 (Ramsay).	
57	FIRST EPISTLE TO CORINTHIANS. Wieseler assigns it to 57, and thinks TITUS and SECOND CORINTHIANS date from the same year. Ramsay assigns CORINTHIANS and ROMANS to 56–57.	
58	PAUL visits MACEDONIA and GREECE. SECOND EPISTLE TO CORINTHIANS. EPISTLE TO ROMANS.	
59	In autumn of 58 or in 59 PAUL makes his FIFTH JOURNEY to JERUSALEM, and is made prisoner for two years at Cæsarea.	
60–62	PORCIUS FESTUS procurator. PAUL SENT to ROME from Cæsarea. Felix had been dismissed in the winter of 60–61.	Ismael, son of Phabi (H.P.) (c. 59–61).
62	Poppœa is empress. PAUL in ROME. EPISTLE TO EPHESIANS, COLOSSIANS, PHILIPPIANS (Wieseler), and PHILEMON.	Joseph (H. P.) (c. 61–62).

YEAR.	CHRONOLOGY.	CONTEMPORARY EVENTS.
62–64	ALBINUS is procurator (Schürer, i. 488).	
63	JAMES the JUST, brother of our Lord, KILLED at Jerusalem. EPISTLE to HEBREWS written in 64, after his martyrdom (Wieseler).	Hannas, son of Hannas (H. P.). Joshua, son of Damnai (H. P.).
64	FIRST EPISTLE TO TIMOTHY. TITUS. Paul's journey to Spain. Burning of Rome, 19–25th July. SECOND EPISTLE TO TIMOTHY. SECOND EPISTLE OF PETER. PETER CRUCIFIED.	Joshua, son of Gamali (H. P.) (c. 43–45).
64–66	GESSIUS FLORUS procurator.	
65	PAUL BEHEADED. Seneca dies.	
66	JUDE written. Poppœa dies. Jewish war breaks out. Vespasian intrusted with the command. Cestius Gallus badly defeated. The Zealots in power in Jerusalem. Josephus in Galilee.	
67	Vespasian in Galilee.	Phannias, son of Samuel (H. P.).
68	NERO dies, June 9. GALBA is emperor. Rising of John of Gischala. Vespasian in South Palestine.	
69	OTHO is emperor in January. VITELLIUS is emperor in April. Vespasian, then at the gates of Jerusalem, leaves for Rome by way of Egypt. VESPASIAN is emperor in December. Proclaimed by troops in Alexandria, July 1. APOCALYPSE written (Düsterdieck).	The EPISTLES of ST. JOHN appear to have been written in the old age of the Apostle. His death is supposed to have taken place about A.D. 100 : possibly some years later.
70	Eleazer the priest, a "Zealot," in power. Titus in Palestine. JERUSALEM and TEMPLE DESTROYED in harvest time, September 8.	
73	Masada falls at Easter.	
79	TITUS is emperor. Eruption of Vesuvius. Pompeii and Herculaneum destroyed, August 21.	
81	DOMITIAN is emperor.	
96	Nerva is emperor.	
98	Trajan is emperor.	
115	Rabbi Akiba stirs up the Jews. Great Jewish revolt everywhere in Africa and Asia.	
117	Hadrian is emperor in August.	
132	Revolt of Bar Cocheba.	
135	End of Jewish War. Akeba beheaded.	
138	ANTONINUS PIUS emperor.	

NEW TESTAMENT HOURS

CHAPTER I

THE DAYS AFTER CALVARY

To realise the influences affecting the infant Society left without a Head by the catastrophe of Calvary, the intense excitement prevailing in Judæa, both before and after the death of Christ, must be kept in mind. Assuming that the date of the crucifixion was the year 30,[1] it took place when the abhorred rule of Pilate had stirred up the bitterest feelings for years.[2] The fierce revolt of Judas the Gaulonite, in the boyhood of Christ, had kindled a fanaticism which steadily increased, till the Zealots, as his party were called, in the end became uppermost in the State, and forced on the final war against Rome, in which Jerusalem perished. The overpowering popular excitement, roused by the preaching of the Baptist, had been followed by that attending the ministry of Christ. Men everywhere expected the appearance of a Hero-Messiah, raised by God to crush the alien, and expel him from the sacred territory of the people of Jehovah. The

---

[1] This is Schürer's date. Keim and Hausrath fix on A.D. 35, but as Christ was born several years before our era commences, and His death appears to have happened when He was as yet only about 33, it seems as if A.D. 30 must be nearer the proper date than 35.

[2] Pilate was procurator from A.D. 26 to 36.

air was electric. The one thought of all Jews was that, at any moment, this divinely commissioned Restorer of the Kingdom to Israel might reveal Himself. Samaria was no less agitated by an expectation of His appearing on Mount Gerizim, than was Judæa by the belief that He might, any day, unfurl His banner on the Temple Hill, in the Holy City. Storm after storm of wild excitement broke over the land. In the year 34, Philip, the tetrarch, died, and his dominions were, for the time, incorporated with the province of Syria. Somewhere about the same time, Pilate massacred a great many Samaritans who had made Gerizim a place of pilgrimage, in hopes of meeting on it the Messiah. Then came the downfall of Pilate and his recall to Rome; the deposition of Caiaphas the High Priest under whom Jesus had suffered; the defeat of Antipas of Tiberias, by Aretas of Petra, whose daughter he had dismissed, years before, to marry Herodias; the death of Tiberius;[1] the temporary gift of Damascus to Aretas by the new emperor, Caius Caligula;[2] the downfall and banishment of Antipas, and the elevation of Agrippa, the son of Aristobulus, and grandson of Herod the Great and Mariamne, to the throne of Palestine, and, finally, the insane command of Caius, that his statue should be erected for worship, in the temple at Jerusalem, and the frightful sufferings of the Jews in Alexandria, from the heathen community of the city. All these events were crowded into the years immediately following the death of Christ. But, indeed, this was not all, for the years 35 and 36 were filled with wars and rumours

[1] March 16, A.D. 37.
[2] This is Wieseler's theory of the occupation of Damascus by Aretas (2 Cor. xi. 32). Art. *Aretas* in Herzog.

of wars, between Rome and the terrible Parthians, beyond the Euphrates, whither Antipas had gone, with the
Governor-General of the province of Syria, Vitellius,
father of the emperor of the same name. Amidst such
universal commotion, the little band who believed Christ
to be the Messiah had additional excitement of their own.
He had promised to return, and, now, when nation was
rising against nation, must not this be the birth-throes of
His Kingdom? Now, when the Man of sin was revealed,
would He delay? The tension of mind in the Christian
community must have been extreme. We know how a
modern revival may rouse the whole spiritual nature of
multitudes to an enthusiasm almost beyond belief, and
the disciples lived amidst such a condition of things as
no religious movement of our day can remotely parallel;
their emotional and demonstrative nature, as Orientals,
being, moreover, much more susceptible of excitement
than our colder tempers.

The immediate followers of Jesus, with the exception of
Iscariot, were exclusively Galilæans. Judas indeed owed
his byname to his former home, for "Iscariot" means
"the man from Kariot;" and this marked him as a
stranger amidst the little band from the North.

Bereft so suddenly, and in a way so awful, of their
beloved Master, His alarmed and helpless followers, safe
for the time, only from their obscurity, must have been
sorely perplexed as to the future. The intimation by
some of the women of their little company, however, on
the morning of the Jewish Monday—our Sunday—that
they had seen a vision of angels at the garden tomb, and
had been told by them that Jesus was no longer in it, but
had risen from the dead and would meet them again in

Galilee, to which He was going before them, and, still
further, the statement of some of them, that they had
afterwards seen their Lord Himself, and that He had
repeated the words of the angels, determined their duty,
on the instant.[1] To return to their own district ensured
their temporary safety, and the hope of once more beholding Him whom they so passionately loved, quickened
their retreat to its friendly and familiar scenes. The
saying of Jesus, in appropriating to His followers the
words of Zechariah, "Smite the Shepherd, and the sheep
of the flock will be scattered abroad," [2] had been fulfilled.
On the "mountain" He had named to them, and, in the
gray of the dawn, on the shore of the lake so dear to the
Eleven, the promise that He would once more meet them
was realised, and it was, we may imagine, at one of these
hallowed interviews, that He directed them to go back
again to Jerusalem, and wait till they received the great
gift of the Spirit promised by the Father, of which He had
spoken while still with them.[3] To hear was to obey.
Pentecost was approaching, when great multitudes of
pilgrims from all lands would gather in the Holy City, and
a supreme opportunity would thus offer itself of announcing the Risen Jesus as the Messiah, not only locally, but,
in effect, to the whole Jewish world, while they themselves
might feel safe amidst the enthusiastic throngs, from the
keen eyes of the enemies of their Master. But, indeed,
personal considerations weighed, after all, very little with
minds roused to such impassioned fervour, for nothing less
than an engrossing ardour and devotion, could have induced a band of Galilæan families to forsake their homes,

---

[1] Matt. xxviii. 7–10.

[2] Zech. xiii. 7 ; Matt. xxvi. 31 ; Mark xiv. 27.　　[3] Acts i. 4.

their property, their connections and friends, and exchange their pleasant life-long occupation on the clear waters of their lake, for some mean labour in Jerusalem; to abandon its shores, so dear to them, for the bare hills of Judæa; and give up their free life in the charming landscapes of Galilee, with its breezy hills, for the close stone walls of the city of priests and Levites, abhorrent to them, beforehand, as the scene of their Master's sufferings and death. All that was of weight or value to men in ordinary circumstances, and, indeed, what ordinarily appeals to them as duty, lay far behind, and was no longer a care. He whom they loved had told them, "There is no man that hath left house, or brethren, or sisters, or mother, or father, or children, or lands, for My sake, and for the gospel's sake, but he shall receive an hundredfold, now, in this time, houses, and brethren, and sisters, and mothers, and children, and lands, with persecutions; and in the world to come eternal life."[1] With such words treasured in their hearts, they had no second thought about obeying His parting instructions. There was nothing, indeed, in the attitude of Galilee towards the New Society, that made the removal to Jerusalem desirable, for we have no grounds for thinking that any abiding hostility to the little band of Christians, was felt by their neighbours, while, on the other hand, judged by all maxims of worldly prudence, the choice of the fanatical Temple City as a home, was rash and unadvisable. But Christ had directed them to remove to it, and make it the centre of their activities in His cause, while, on His part, He would there gratify their longing for the fulfilment of the promises He had left them, and this was more than enough to decide them

[1] Mark x. 29

unhesitatingly to abandon all their past and thenceforth,
make the Holy City, their home.

It was, indeed, meet that the new Kingdom of David
should be set up on Mount Zion; Jew and Christian
assuming as a fixed decree of Jehovah that it should be
so.   Believing that Jesus was speedily to return, the most
fitting place, even apart from direct instructions, in which
His followers could await His appearance, was the city in
which during His life He had revealed Himself most fully
to them.   Besides, it was the centre of the Theocracy, in
which, when "clothed with power from on high," [1] the
sound of their witness for the Messiahship of Jesus would
in the words of the prophet, go out into all the earth, and
their words unto the ends of the world.[2]

He had chosen Twelve Apostles, that the spiritual Israel
he was founding might proclaim itself the true perpetua-
tion of the Twelve Tribes of "Israel after the flesh." [3] But
now, when the treachery of Judas had left a vacancy in
that number, the Eleven showed their realisation of the
commission imposed upon them to announce the new
Kingdom of God and the soon-returning Messiah, to al
sections of their race, by choosing one of their number
"who had companied with them, all the time that th·
Lord Jesus went in and out among them, beginning from
the baptism of John, unto the day that He was received up
from us," [4] to become a witness with them of His resurrection, in the place of the traitor.

From the time of the return of the little Christian com·
munity to Jerusalem, Galilee almost disappears from the
story of the Church; the only mention of it, as a scene of

---

[1] Luke xxiv. 49.   [2] Rom. x. 18 from Psalm xix. 4 (LXX.).
          [3] 1 Cor. x. 18.   [4] Acts i. 21.

Christian life, being a passing notice, in the closing years of the first decade after the crucifixion, that " the Church, throughout all Judæa, and Galilee, and Samaria, had peace, and was built up." [1] All who clung to their faith in our Lord joined in the Exodus to the Holy City. Not only did the Apostles, with their wives, set out to it; others accompanied them, who had been their close associates since the days of the Baptist, and, along with these friendly Capernaum families, went the brethren and relations of Christ, hitherto settled at Nazareth with His mother. How many, in all, took part in this pilgrimage of love is not said, but we find no fewer than one hundred and twenty gathered in the first recorded assembly, though some of these were, no doubt, from Jerusalem itself, or its neighbourhood.[2] The Galilæan pilgrims, however, formed the central strength of the little community, and the living germ of the whole Church of the future. They had committed themselves, finally and enthusiastically, to the brave enterprise of spreading abroad the claims of their Risen Lord, on the fulfilment of whose promise, to help them with power from above, and Himself ere long to return, they waited with a patient but glowing fervour.

Among these venerable Coryphæi of Christianity, the foremost place is assigned, in the glimpses we have of these early days, to Simon Peter, who appears in the Gospels as one of a numerous Capernaum household, two members of which, at least,—his wife, and his brother Andrew,—had come to Judæa with him.[3] The ardent impulsive nature that had revealed itself so often in the lifetime of his Master, still gave him the place of honour, as

---

[1] Acts ix. 31. [2] Acts i. 22, 14 ; xii. 12 ; Gal. ii. 9 ; 1 Cor. ix. 5.
[3] Acts i. 13 ; 1 Cor. ix. 5.

head of the little band.[1]　With Peter and Andrew,
James and John,—the sons of Zebedee and Salome. who,
in her passionate devotion to Jesus, had followed Him
from Galilee to Jerusalem, on His last journey, after
"ministering" to Him in the past, and had kept near
Him even at Calvary, and sought His tomb by the gray
light of the Resurrection morning,—were most prominent.
The two had already been called Sons of Thunder, from
their stormy and energetic zeal for their Master, but the
smoke and flame of youthful enthusiasm was, in John, at
least, to be softened hereafter, into the calm glow of that
love which had endeared him, beyond all the rest. to
Christ.[2]　Besides these, others are mentioned of whom I
have already spoken in my Life of Christ; Levi-Matthew,
the publican acquainted with letters; Judas-Lebbæus-
Thaddæus, brave and good-hearted, and Simon the Zealot,
formerly a member of that sect of fierce fanatics, which,
in the last days of Jerusalem, degenerated into mere
bloodthirsty dagger-men.　But, already, by the side of
the Apostles, stood the brothers of Jesus, James, Joseph,
Simon, and Judas, who, in Christ's lifetime, had looked
on His claim to be the Messiah as a mere delusion. They
had come to Capernaum with their mother to take Him
back, by force, to Nazareth, their home, as "beside Himself,"[3] and they evidently did not yet believe in Him,
when He visited Nazareth, for the hostile population
spoke in that tone of them, and Jesus retorted with the
proverb that "A prophet is nowhere without respect

---

[1] Acts i. 15 ; ii. 14, 37 ; iii. 1, 12 ; iv. 8 ; v. 3, 15, 29 ; ix. 32, 38 ; x.
5, 25, &c.
[2] Mark xv. 40 ; xvi. 1, 3, 17 ; Luke ix. 54 ; Mark ix. 38 ; Matt. xx. 20 ff.
[3] Mark iii. 21.

except in his native place, and among his own relations, and in his own home."[1] After the crucifixion, however, matters changed, for we find Jesus appearing to them, as part of the company who saw His ascension, and met together, in their upper chamber, immediately after.[2] They had, therefore, settled in Jerusalem, with the Twelve, having brought their wives from Galilee;[3] James, "the Lord's brother," to whom individually, Jesus had shown Himself, being, thenceforward, with Peter, a leader of the community.[4]

Of the private members of the New Society we know only a few. It cannot be doubted that, if he were still alive, Simon, the leper, and Lazarus, who had been raised from the dead, and the sisters of Bethany, would be found in the upper room with the Galilæans. We learn incidentally, moreover, that the two sons of the cross-bearer, Simon of Cyrene,—Alexander and Rufus,—were well known in the Christian brotherhood.[5] Of the old companions of the Apostles from the days of John's baptism, two appear in these first days after Calvary; Joseph Barsabas, called the Just, and Matthias; both selected as fit to fill up the vacant place of Judas, though the lot actually fell on Matthias.[6] Mary, the mother of John Mark, and her maid Rhodope, are, also, mentioned in the story of these times; her house, it seems, offering the brethren a refuge and hiding place from the authorities.[7] Round her, in fact, there gathers a whole family circle of adherents of Jesus, for the Levite Joses, from Cyprus, was a brother, or brother-in-law of this Mary; hereafter a companion of Paul, and already so

---

[1] Mark vi. 4.   [2] Acts i. 14.   [3] 1 Cor. ix. 5.
[4] Gal. i. 19 ; 1 Cor. xv. 7.   [5] Mark xv. 21.   [6] Acts i. 23
[7] Acts xii. 12, 13 ; xiii. 13.

noted for persuasive discourse as to have gained the name
of Barnabas, "The son of prophesying."[1] His generous
nature is, moreover, indicated by the fact recorded of
him, that, having a field at or near Jerusalem, he sold it,
and handed over the price he received to the Apostles, for
the good of the little community.[2] But he was not the
only speaker in the Christian assembly, for we read of
one Agabus, a prophet, that is, primarily, gifted with
power of forcible and fluent speech; meeting him in the
opening years of Claudius, at Antioch, whither he had
gone to announce "by the Spirit" an approaching famine.
Later, also, he appears at Cæsarea, warning St. Paul, by
a symbolical act, like an old prophet, not to go up
to Jerusalem.[3] Silas, moreover, who afterwards accompanied St. Paul in his missionary journeys, was one of the
Jerusalem brotherhood, and there was Philip, who was
soon to be chosen as one of the seven so-called "deacons,"
and, later on, did a great work in Samaria and in the towns
of the sea-coast, earning the honourable title of Evangelist,
for his long itinerant labours.   His enthusiasm for Christ
seems, indeed, to have glowed warmly to the end, for we
have a glimpse of his household at Cæsarea, which shows
us four daughters, who had so fervently caught the inspiration of their surroundings, that they one and all
"prophesied."[4]   But, before all these, stands the first
martyr Stephen, one of the "deacons," a man full of faith
and of the Holy Ghost, and full, also, "of grace and power,
and working great wonders and signs among the people;"
one, moreover, so skilled in Scripture, as it bore on the
Messiahship of Jesus, that those with whom he disputed

---

[1] Col. iv. 10.   [2] Acts iv. 36, 37.   [3] Acts xi. 27 ; xxi. 11.
[4] Acts xv. 22 ; xxi. 9 ; vi. 5 ; viii. 5, 40.

felt him their superior, while his bearing even before
a court bent on his death proved him no less brave
than able.[1] We have, besides, the names of five others,
chosen as deacons, all Greek, and thus, apparently, those
of foreign-born Jews, but not necessarily so, as many
Palestine Jews,—called in Acts "Hebrews," in contrast
to their brethren of outside lands, who were known as
"Hellenists,"—also bore Greek names. But their names
are all we know of them.

The feeble stock from which Christianity thus spread
abroad over all lands shows itself, even from the little
told us respecting it, to have glowed with the enthusiasm,
energy, and aggression which the Acts and Epistles reveal in its apostolic missionaries, in after years, throughout
the whole inhabited globe. It had, moreover, in its small
numbers, a wealth of varied individuality. From its
bosom we find Philip, Barnabas, Silas, and Mark, going
forth to nearer or more distant lands; it opened the
glorious roll of martyrs for the faith in the persons of
Stephen, and James the son of Zebedee, and it reveals
the high-wrought fervour of prophets, in Agabus and the
daughters of Philip. It is equally true, indeed, that, from
Jerusalem, there went forth also swarms of fanatical
Judaizers, seeking, as Paul puts it, to "pervert" the
infant churches;[2] men whom he denounces as "false
apostles" and "deceitful workers," "fashioning themselves
into apostles of Christ," as Satan fashions himself into
"an angel of light;"[3] but no great movement of free
thought, like Christianity, can escape from having shadow
as well as brightness. These disturbers and destroyers of
the churches cannot be said, however, to have in any way

[1] Acts vi. 5 ff.   [2] Gal. i. 6, 7.   [3] 2 Cor. xi. 13, 14.

represented the legitimate apostolic spirit of the Jerusalem community.

Of the simple internal economy of this mother-church of the new faith, only a few hints are left us. In the first enthusiasm of their settlement in the capital, the Galilæans, pressed to maintain themselves in their new conditions, were met, we are told, by a spontaneous movement on the part of those among their adherents who had more or less property, to sell their "possessions and goods," and hand over the proceeds to the Apostles, for the common good.[1] But from the first, this was carried out to the full extent, only by some, for though individual brethren gave up everything for the poor of the community, and all, doubtless, aided with loving freehandedness, human nature still asserted itself, more or less, since we find the Hellenists, or foreign Jews, presently, murmuring, that the Palestine Jews, or "Hebrews," favoured the widows of their own party, at the expense of those of the Hellenists, in the "daily ministration." Nor did the mother of Mark part with her house, the retention of which involved that of the means to live in it,[2] while Dorcas was able to dispense bounty freely, and St. James, in the earliest of the Epistles, speaks of "rich" brethren in contrast with poor.[3]

At Antioch, Ephesus, Corinth, and Thessalonica, also, we find members of the local Christian communities enjoying their private means,[4] while Ananias was free to keep or withhold the price of his property,[5] and it is

---

[1] Acts ii. 45.   [2] Acts vi. 1.   [3] Acts ix. 36 ; Jas. ii. 1–4 ; v. 1-5.
[4] Acts xi. 29 ; Ephes. iv. 28 ; 1 Tim. v. 8 ; vi. 17 ; 1 Cor. xiii. 3 ; xvi. 2 ;
2 Cor. viii. 14 ; 1 Thess. iv. 11 ; 2 Thess. iii. 7–12.
[5] Acts v. 4.

recorded as an act worthy of special note, that Barnabas handed over the price of his land to the Apostles.[1] This impulsive experiment in Christian Socialism, therefore, was not only partial, but very short-lived. A spirit of generous brotherhood, however, long survived. The care of the poor, and the sick, or imprisoned, continued, permanently, a characteristic of the Christian communities. Thus, it was in connection with the delivery to the Church in Jerusalem, of monies gathered by him among the Gentile Christians, that Paul was arrested, and consigned to long imprisonment at Cæsarea and Rome. A noble interest in all the sufferings of the poorer brethren shows itself, indeed, in all the Epistles. "Labouring as I have done," says St. Paul, "ye ought to help the weak, and to remember the words of the Lord Jesus, how He Himself said, *It is more blessed to give than to receive.*"[2] And this is only one out of many similarly tender utterances. The example of our Lord and the Apostles, who had a common bag, doubtless influenced the earliest days of the Church, and the whole tone of Christ's language, from first to last, tended to similar conceptions of life. "Lay not up treasures on earth," He had said. "Ye cannot serve God and Mammon." "Be not anxious for what ye shall eat, or what ye shall drink, nor yet for your body, what ye shall put on." "Consider the birds of the heavens, that they sow not, neither do they reap, nor gather into barns; yet your heavenly Father feedeth them." "Mark the lilies of the field: they toil not, neither do they spin." "Be not,

---

[1] Acts iv. 36, 37.
[2] Acts xx. 35. See also, among other passages, Gal. ii. 10; vi. 10; 2 Cor. viii. and ix.

therefore, anxious, saying, 'What shall we eat, or what shall we drink, or wherewithal shall we be clothed?' for after all these things do the heathen seek; but your heavenly Father knoweth that ye have need of all these things. Seek ye first His kingdom and His righteousness, and all these things shall be added unto you. Be not, therefore, anxious for the morrow, for the morrow will be anxious for itself." "Get you no gold, nor silver, nor brass, in your girdles; no wallet for your journey, neither two coats, nor shoes, nor staff." "The kingdom of heaven is like a merchant, who, having found one pearl of great price, went and sold all that he had, and bought it." "Sell that thou hast, and give to the poor, and thou shalt have treasure in heaven." "It is easier for a camel to go through a needle's eye, than for a rich man to enter into the kingdom of heaven." "There is no man that has left house, or brethren, or sisters, or mother, or father, or children, or lands, for My sake, and for the gospel's sake, but he shall receive an hundredfold, now, in this time, houses, and brethren, and sisters, and mothers, and children, and lands, with persecutions; and in the world to come, eternal life." "Sell that ye have, and give alms; make for yourselves purses which wax not old, a treasure in the heavens that faileth not."[1] Believing "the end of all things at hand,"[2] these words must have dwelt in the minds of the Galilæans as a resistless impulse towards such a communistic life as they attempted to carry out, especially since the Palestine Jews, as a rule, were very poor, the avenues to money-making being shut up from

---

[1] Matt. vi. 19 ff., 24, 25; vi. 26–34; x. 9; xiii. 46; xix. 21, 22; Mark x. 29; Luke xii. 33.
[2] 1 Pet. iv. 7.

them, in great measure, from the rich being, largely, Roman officials or their adherents, to work for whom, or for the objects they sought, would have defiled the " Hebrew." The moderate wants of humble Orientals, and the mildness of the climate, moreover, made extreme self-denial less trying than it would be in regions where the actual wants of life are much greater. Yet, with all this, and in spite of the glowing excitement and enthusiasm of the moment, human nature proved incapable of maintaining such an ideal organisation for any length of time, even in Judæa.

One feature of this common life, however, continued longer than the rest ; the custom of the whole brotherhood having special meals together. In the first days after the arrival of the little band of Galilæans, one " upper chamber" was enough, we are told, for their "abiding" place ; the "alijah" of some friendly private dwelling— a large chamber immediately under the flat roof, used for prayer and social gatherings of any kind. There were, doubtless, from the first, other houses of local Christians which offered shelter to the brethren, by night, but the central upper room was their "meeting place." There we find not only the Eleven, but "the women, and Mary, the mother of Jesus, and His brethren," assembled, on their return from witnessing the Ascension from the Mount of Olives. One mind pervaded all ; as yet, no jarring note disturbed their unanimity, in waiting for the promise left them by their Master. By day, they must have separated to pursue their daily callings, as soon as work had been found, but day by day saw them in the Temple, at the hours of prayer, as far as possible, and, towards evening, they gathered to the upper room, to

share a common meal, the most important of the day
together; "gladness and singleness of heart" marking
their simple table, and each meal, after the example of
Jesus at the last supper He ate with them, closing with
the " breaking of bread," in remembrance of Him, as He
had commanded. What we now call Holy Communion
was thus celebrated every evening, the sacred rite accom-
panying the meal, as it still did in the first apostolic
churches ; as when the brethren at Troas, for example, at
Paul's visit, are seen " breaking the bread, and eating "
their common meal, during the night. As, moreover, in
this case, the meal thus closing with " Holy Communion "
was followed by Paul's " talking with them a long while,"
so, the Jerusalem assembly listened, after supper, to the
teaching of the Apostles, and joined them in devotion.[1]
Meals in common were already in use among the Pharisees
and Essenes, as an expression of close religious relations,
and, hence, were natural among the Christians, who, for
the time, were only one of many similar brotherhoods
among the Jews ; their sole distinction being that they
honoured Jesus as the Messiah. Nothing is disclosed of
any detailed ecclesiastical organisation, in the fulness of
our modern sense. We may, indeed, compare them to
The Brethren of the Common Life, in the Middle Ages, and
it was, doubtless, this relation to each other as forming
one great family, which made a temporary common purse
easy ; all being so enthusiastically " of one heart and soul,"
that separate interests would seem treason and coldness.[2]
But, that they did not all live together, is shown from
Paul having to go into house after house, in his search for
victims.[3]

[1] Acts i. 14; ii. 42, 46 ; xx. 11.   [2] Acts iv. 32.   [3] Acts viii. 3.

Besides the daily "breaking of bread" and suppers in common,—the Agapæ or "love-feasts" of St. Jude,[1]—we find, in the first days, only the rite of Baptism. As John had baptized into the "kingdom of heaven," the Christian community baptized into the faith of Jesus as the Messiah. From its association with the broken body and shed blood of our Lord, "the Lord's Supper"[2] was justly regarded as raising the soul to a spiritual communion with Christ Himself, so that Paul speaks of disrespect shown towards it, as being virtually shown to their Master, and thus entailing "judgment;" a warning eminently needed, as abuses of gluttony and drunkenness had crept into the Agapæ of the Corinthians to such an extent, that not a few brought on illness by their excesses, and some even died.[3] Baptism was the symbol of the washing away of the former sinful life, and the precursor of the gift of the Holy Spirit, which was communicated by the laying on of hands, as when Paul, having baptized disciples of John at Ephesus, "and laid his hands on them, the Holy Ghost came on them, and they spoke with tongues and prophesied."[4]

In all our attempts to bring before us the earliest Christian assembly, however, the exceptional poverty of the Jerusalem community must be kept in mind. The "Saints," as they called themselves,[5] were always in need of outside help, which was, therefore, sent to them from Antioch,[6] from Asia Minor,[7] Macedonia, and Achaia,[8] and, indeed, from all the little Christian communities everywhere, however poor they might themselves be.[9] The

[1] Jude 12.   [2] 1 Cor. ii. 20.   [3] 1 Cor. ii. 29, 30.   [4] Acts xix. 5.
[5] Acts ix. 13, 32, 41 ; xxvi. 10, &c.   [6] Acts x. 29.   [7] Gal. ii. 10.
[8] Rom. xv. 26 ; 1 Cor. xvi. 1, 15 ; 2 Cor. viii. 4 ; ix. 1.   [9] 2 Cor. viii. 2.

most unbounded liberality was, in truth, inculcated even after the strictly apostolic age, for in the Epistle of Barnabas, which was written early in the second century, we read,[1] " Thou shalt share with thy neighbour in all thou hast, and must not call anything thine own : for, if ye share together in incorruptible things, how much more should you do so in corruptible things." [2]

But extreme poverty is a sore trial even to the worthiest, and, as we have seen, a suspicion of unfairness in the distribution of the daily help to the widows, soon rose; the Greek-speaking Jews, or " Hellenists," murmuring against the native Aramaic-speaking Jews, or " Hebrews," for their alleged wrongdoings in this matter. It was the first open sign of a bitter party spirit, destined to develop into the fierce opposition which we find between the two classes, in the missionary work of Paul. To mix in such sordid strife was clearly beneath the dignity of the Apostles, and led to the introduction of a special office, for the care of the daily meals, and the various details of general charity. The disciples, as a whole, were, therefore, summoned together by the Twelve, and directions given them, to look out from among their number " seven men of good report, full of the Spirit and of wisdom, whom the Apostles might appoint over this business." The proposal, we are told, " pleased the multitude," who, forthwith, selected the appointed number, among whom we know none beyond their names, except the famous martyr Stephen, and the evangelist Philip. The seven were then " set before the

[1] Barnab. Epistle c. 19.

[2] The great edition of the Apostolic Fathers by Gebhardt, Harnack and Zahn, assigns the Epistle vaguely to the period between A.D. 71 and 132. Pat. Apos. Opera, Fasc. 1, Part 2, p. lxviii.

Apostles, who, when they had prayed, laid their hands upon them." Henceforth, all the mechanical duties of the little community were confided to these officers; the Apostles confining themselves to "the ministry of the word and prayer."[1]

We must beware, however, of transferring to those days, the well-defined organisations of later ages. Subdivision of work is the result of growth and development. At first, the care that the daily public meals were impartially distributed was all, so far as we are told, for which the "seven" were set apart, but, of course, other duties would be added as they rose, for while the principles of the new faith were unchangeable, the machinery and modes of presentment, by which these might be most effectually established and extended, were left to the wisdom and practical experience of successive generations; those which, in the beginning, sufficed for then existing conditions, being inevitably inadequate and unfitted, for ages and countries in which all the social ideas, institutions, and even necessities of life, were widely different. Adaptation and modification of non-essential details, to meet the requirements of human advancement, is not only unavoidable, but is imperative in any great organisation.

---

[1] Acts vi. 1, 6. Our word deacon is the Greek word for a "servant" or "waiting man,"—its Latin equivalent being "minister." Its derivation seems to point to "one who is dusty from running" or "one who sleeps in the dust and ashes." In Phil. i. 1, and 1 Tim. iii. 8, 12, it is used of the Christian officers, associated, in a subordinate way, in the text, with the "bishops" or "overseers," but, in eighteen cases, it is used of the Apostles and public ministers of the higher class. It is also used of "Phœbe, a 'servant' (or 'deacon') of the church at Cenchræa" (Rom. xvi. 1).

CHAPTER II

PENTECOST

A.D. 30 (?)

THE enthusiastic band of Galilæans, as we have seen, had migrated to the Holy City in obedience to the instructions of their Master, who had charged them to wait there "for the promise of the Father;" for, as John had baptized with water, they, in fulfilment of the heavenly promise, "would be baptized with, or in, the Holy Ghost not many days hence." These mysterious words, following the remembrances of the wondrous life they had been privileged to see; the awful experiences of the Passover week; and the transcendent wonders of the Resurrection and the Forty Days, must have wrought the simple minds of the Pilgrims, as, indeed, they would those of any men, to an almost inconceivable fervour of excitement and expectation. Two weeks had passed since the Eleven had returned from the Mount of Olives, with the amazing report that they had seen Christ rise, from amidst them, into the sky, and vanish out of their sight in the upper heavens. What could it be which they had been told was to happen next? They were soon to learn. Pentecost, the great harvest feast of the nation,[1] was held, as its name implies, on the fiftieth day after the first day of the Passover, and, as

---

[1] Exod. xvi. ; Num. xxviii. 26.

six weeks had passed since that, before Christ left them,
it was now only seven days off. The death scene on Calvary
had made the Friday of the Passover week for ever memorable to the disciples, and Pentecost fell, that year, striking
to say, on the day of the Resurrection, the Sunday.
Would that be the day on which the mysterious promise
of their Lord would be fulfilled? On that morning the
whole body of disciples then in Jerusalem, including not
only the Apostles, but also the Galilæan company, and
local believers in Christ, had met in their upper chamber
before the hour of morning prayer—nine o'clock—"the
third hour." [1] Suddenly, a great uproar, like that of the
rushing of a mighty storm-wind, filled all the house—
perhaps the very scene of the farewell supper with the
Master. The hundred and twenty, or more, present,[2]
were sitting "at the feet" of their teachers,[3] for the hour
of prayer, when they would have risen, since they prayed
standing, had not yet come. Presently, they saw what
seemed flames, lighting on the head of each of the company, and resting on it like a tongue of fire. Fire
had, always, among the Jews, been the symbol of the
Divine presence; they were forthwith to learn the
vivid symbolism of this tongue-like shape. God had,
indeed, visited them, for, instantly, their souls were
"filled with the Holy Spirit." Similar communications
had been granted during the life of Christ to the leaders
and to favoured saints,[4] but, compared to what had now
been given, they had been momentary and partial, as if
anticipations of that full, abiding endowment, which could
only be vouchsafed after Christ had been glorified.[5]

[1] Acts ii. 15.　　　　[2] Acts i. 15.　　　　[3] Acts ii. 2.
[4] Luke i. 41 ; John xx. 22.　　　[5] John vii. 39 ; xvi. 7.

The effect, we are told, was extraordinary. The simple, unlearned, company, forthwith began to " speak with other tongues, as the Spirit gave them utterance ; " these tongues proving to be the real languages of the various nationalities represented in the world-wide gathering of the pilgrims attending the feast. The roar of what seemed a storm had caused a multitude to rush to the spot whence it came, and of this crowd many made their way to the spacious upper chamber, to find, to their amazement, that they were being addressed, " every man in his own language." It was astounding! " Are not all these who speak, Galilæans ? " was, as St. Luke tells us, the instant remark. " And how is it we hear, every man in our own language, wherein we were born ? " The narrative, beyond question, declares that these inspired ones began to speak in languages different from their own—the mother-tongues of men from every part of the then civilised world—Parthians, and Medes, and Elamites, from north of the Persian Gulf, beyond the Tigris ; pilgrims from the Euphrates' countries ; men speaking the dialect of the Jews of Judæa, which was a different one from that of the Galilæans, now using it ; men from Cappadocia, north of Aramaic-speaking Syria—the head-quarters of the slave-trade in those days, a " Cappadocian " being equivalent to our " negro," or to " slave ; " men from Pontus, stretching from the north of Cappadocia to the Black Sea ; men from the whole western coast-lands of Asia Minor,—Caria, Lydia, Mysia ; men from the countries behind these—Phrygia and Pamphylia ; men from Egypt, and from the far west parts of Lybia, reaching towards Cyrene, the population of which was one quarter Jewish, and so many of whom lived in Jerusalem that they had a synagogue of their own;[1] Jews from Rome, visiting the Holy City, for the feast, or other objects,—with many from the Roman lands of the West, both Jews, and proselytes from heathenism ; men from the island of Crete, and men from far off Arabia. The only explanation, in the opinion of not a few of the amazed and perplexed listeners, was to declare the speakers had taken too much wine, but this, Peter, the leader of the Christians, at once showed to be ridiculous. "No," said he, "this miracle is the gift to us, of the Spirit of God, from heaven, through that Jesus whom you lawlessly crucified, but whom God has raised from the dead."

It would be worse than idle, to attempt any explanation of what must have been intended to be viewed as distinctly miraculous, but the fact that while "the gift of tongues" was one of the peculiarities of the earliest church, the description of this power, in the Epistles, points to characteristics very different from those of the endowment at Pentecost, and makes it desirable to realise what is thus said of the subsequent extra-natural use of language in the Christian communities.

Two cases of "speaking with tongues" are mentioned in the Acts ; the one, at the visit of St. Peter to the centurion Cornelius ;[2] the other at the baptism by St. Paul of some who, till then, had only heard of the baptism of John.[3] St. Mark also tells us, that our Lord, before He left the earth, said that those who believed in Him should "speak with new tongues,"[4] but in none of these passages is any explanation given of what is meant by these expressions. Circumstances, however, arose in the Church at Corinth which, happily, led St. Paul to speak

[1] Acts vi. 9.   [2] Acts x. 46.   [3] Acts xix. 6.   [4] Mark xvi. 17.

at some length of this "gift," in his notice of the various special endowments of the members of Christian com· munities in that age.[1] The gift of tongues had proved in Corinth, as, no doubt, elsewhere, a source of difficulty. That the apostle valued it less than any other "gift," is shown by his putting it at the close of his list,[2] and ranking it as belonging rather to the childhood than the maturity of Christian life.[3] In themselves, he says, "tongues" have no religious value, since, if one could speak not only any human tongue, but even the tongues of angels, and had not love, the speaker would be no better than one who clatters a cymbal, or blows a trumpet;[4] adding that, while faith, hope, and love, are eternal, with love as foremost of the three, tongues, and all other merely external endowments, will pass away. "He who uses tongues," says he, "speaks not to men but to God. No one understands what he says. He speaks, in the Spirit, to himself and to God. His meaning is beyond the hearers, and, thus, even if he build up his own spiritual life, he contributes nothing to that of the community.[5] He is of benefit to the brethren, only when some one can interpret what he has been say-ing.[6] Without this, he is no better than a confused noise, from harps or flutes. In prayer, his understanding is passive, whatever his spirit may be. It is impossible to answer 'Amen' after his utterances, for no one knows what he has been saying." On this ground, the apostle who had the gift more abundantly and variedly than all the other Corinthian Christians, would rather speak five words that were intelligible, in the assembly, than ten

[1] 1 Cor. xii., xiii., xiv.   [2] 1 Cor. xii. 10.   [3] 1 Cor. xiv. 20.
[4] 1 Cor. xiii. 1.   [5] 1 Cor. xiv. 2-4, 28.   [6] 1 Cor. xiv. 5.

thousand in tongues. This gift, then, as shown in the apostolic churches, was not that of speaking regular languages, of this nation or that, without previous knowledge of them, but an ecstatic flow of sounds, in uttering which, the understanding of the speaker was in abeyance.[1] It could only be compared by St. Paul, in its inarticulate confusion, to meaningless intermixed whirls of sounds from an instrument blown or struck blindly, so that no one could dream what was intended. The Jews, like all ancient nations, regarded the speech of other races as mere stuttering and stammering,[2] and, no doubt, this idea made utterances of the "tongues" often thought real foreign dialects, as happened when the same gift was fancied to have been bestowed in the Irvingite Church, fifty years ago. But this is distinctly contrary to the words of St. Paul. Excitement, in every age, is apt to vent itself, in some temperaments, and, especially in the East, in this way, as we see in the case of the prophets, of whom Micah is pictured by himself, as "howling like the jackals, and roaring like the ostriches."[3] How, in any case, such strange outbreaks of religious emotion could be interpreted is hard to imagine, even if a confused mingling of words, singly intelligible, was employed. The whole subject, in fact, is mysterious, and as such, may well excuse one from any attempt at explanation.

It is striking to find that Jewish tradition has pictured the giving of the Law on Mount Sinai, very much as the narrative in the Acts paints the giving forth of the new Christian Covenant, which was to supersede that of Moses. According to the rabbis, the Law was given on Pentecost, and the Talmud explains the words of one of

[1] 1 Cor. xiv. 14.   [2] Isa. xxviii. 11.   [3] Micah i. 8.

the Psalms.[1] "The Lord gave the word: great was the
company of those that published it," thus—"When the
word went forth from Sinai, it was divided into seven
voices, and these were again divided into seventy tongues,"
the number of languages in the world in the opinion of
the Jews. "These sprang forth like sparks of fire. hither
and thither, as when one beats an anvil, and, therefore,
were the announcing voices of God a great company."[2]

The effect of this wonder, followed as it was by effective
words, from Peter, to the crowd that thronged, in ever-
growing numbers, to the scene of such a marvel, was worthy
of the first proclamation, after the Crucifixion, of the new
Kingdom of God. Standing up from before the sitting
rows of the disciples, and hushing their strange utterances,
Peter, stepping forward from among the Eleven, as their
mouthpiece, flouted the explanation of what had happened being only the noisy babbling of a drunken mob, as
some before him affirmed. It was too soon for the "new
wine" of the season, though, indeed, the secret was then
known by which wine could be long kept sweet, and it
was then very intoxicating. But, apart from it not being
yet even nine o'clock—the hour of morning prayer and
of the morning sacrifice — they knew that men in the
East drink only in the evening, so that no drunken person is ever seen by day.[3] As Jews, his hearers had an
awful reverence for their ancient Scriptures. He would
show them from these, so that they would not have his
word only for it, but that of a holy prophet, what the
sights and sounds that had amazed them really meant.
They were a fulfilment, he told them, of the words of the

[1] Ps. lxviii. 11.   [2] Gfrörer, Urchr. i. 390.
[3] Arabian Nights, "Story of the Sleeper Awakened."

prophet Joel. They, themselves, believed that the Kingdom of the Messiah, which they recognised as ushering
in the "last days" of the then existing state of things,
was at hand. What they had seen was clearly what Joel
had predicted as the sign of these last days having begun,
and of the Messiah having appeared! It was the beginning
of the pouring out of God's Spirit on all flesh, of which
the prophet had so long ago spoken, as marking this
anxiously waited, and supreme event! That Spirit would,
from this time, be poured out on all the true Israel of
God, as they had seen it poured out on those before them!
Could the prediction that "your sons and your daughters
shall prophesy" be more literally fulfilled than in what
they had witnessed? Was not this the pledge of further
revelations of God, in the future, in visions by day and
dreams by night, as with the prophets of old? Was not
this a fulfilment of the prediction of man and woman
alike, so far as they were the true people of God, being
filled with His Spirit? And if so, was not this a sign
that the Messiah had come? And were not these times,
so full of wars and rumours of war,—tumult after tumult,
as they knew, filling the world, while the heathen reigned
in the land of Jehovah,—just such as the prophet had
declared would usher in the great and notable day of the
Lord? Did not Nature itself, as he had foretold, appear
to feel the close approach of the dissolution of the existing economy,—that day when the Messiah would be manifested as judge of all, and they only who had called
beforehand, that is, now, on the name of the Lord, could
have a hope of being saved! Having thus fixed their
attention by invoking their Scriptures, Peter turned, with
great skill to prove that Jesus, the man of Nazareth, who

had been crucified, had been shown to be the Messiah, by
God having raised Him from the dead; a wonder, he adds,
likewise foretold by no less a hero of the ancient church
than the "patriarch David," to whom he ascribes a clear
prediction of the Resurrection of Christ, in language which
he quotes from one of the Psalms.[1]   In accordance with
this, Jesus had been raised from the dead, and, in fulfilment of another prophecy, had ascended into the heavens,
and sat down on the right hand of God, till the Eternal
had made His enemies His footstool.[2]   Could there be a
doubt, after such sacred proof, that "God had assuredly
made both Lord and Messiah, this Jesus whom ye
crucified"?[3]   An argument driven home by appeal to
prophets was irresistible.   Many, forthwith, cried out for
counsel, by following which they might escape the wrath
of this awful Messiah when He appeared, as they believed
He presently would, to take vengeance on His enemies,
and raise His servants to honour in His Messianic Kingdom, to be set up in Jerusalem.   The result was, that
before the throng broke up, "about three thousand souls"
had professed faith in Christ, and readiness to be baptized
in His name.   That so great a multitude, from the most
widely separate countries, should have joined the new
faith, and been admitted to its communion, by its solemn
rite of initiation, was of signal moment, for it secured
that "Christ" would be preached far and wide over the
earth.

This illustration of the earliest apostolic preaching is
of surpassing interest, since it must have been a virtual
prototype of all the preaching of those early days.   At
the outset there could hardly be said to have been any

[1] Ps. xvi. 8 ff.   [2] Ps. cx. 1.   [3] Acts ii. 14–37.

organised mission-work, such as we find after the persecution which began with the martyrdom of St. Stephen, and at no time was there anything like an attempt to spread the faith by rhetorical arts. The Apostles had caught from their intercourse with Christ a grand enthusiasm for God and for humanity, as, in all its races, His children and members of a common family, and this animated them with a passion of universal love, which was wiser than all human philosophy. The great love of Christ, as shown not less in His life and death than in its still shining down on the world, now, when He had ascended to the right hand of God, kindled a divine love, in return, which reflected His image from the depths of their souls, in all its heavenly brightness. It was this touching love, so new in that age of Jewish narrowness and hatreds, and heathen contempt for alien races, that attracted men from the temples of the gods, and the chambers of the synagogue, to the upper room of the Nazarenes. When they addressed their fellows, it was not in " wisdom of words "—so dear to the vainglorious rhetoricians of the schools—but " in demonstration of the Spirit and of power." [1] Ten times, in his letters, we hear Paul " beseeching " those he addresses, with loving entreaty, and we may be sure that the simple men of the Galilæan lake resembled him in these tones of affectionate appeal. Their homilies, in keeping with the usage of their race, and, indeed, of all Orientals, would be brief and vivid; delivered with the enthusiasm of intense conviction, and revealing minds filled with one overmastering theme. The words of Peter to the lame man at the gate " Beautiful " in the Temple,[2] would often be those of the forefathers

[1] 1 Cor. i. 17 ; ii. 4.   [2] Acts ii. 6.

of the Church, in similar cases. "Silver and gold have
I none; but what I have give I thee. In the name of
Jesus Christ of Nazareth, walk!" . The gift of Pentecost
had not only kindled their whole nature to an ardour
which expressed itself in "new tongues," unable to keep
within the bounds of common utterance, but urged them
to a deadly warfare with all the forms in which the
kingdom of Satan showed itself around. We see them
exorcising evil spirits, healing the sick, and, in all ways,
reproducing the daily works of their Master, till, we are
told, the excitement grew so intense, that "men carried
out the sick into the streets, and laid them on beds and
couches, that, as Peter came by, at the least his shadow
might fall on some one of them. And there, also, came
together the multitude from the cities round about Jerusalem, bringing sick folk, and them that were vexed with
unclean spirits; and they were healed every one." [1]

The usual place of assembling, among the Christians,
at this time, is said to have been the arcade, on the east
side of the Temple grounds, known as Solomon's porch.
There they met, with a unity of heart and spirit, which,
as yet, nothing disturbed; scoffers and the insincere keeping aloof from them, but the people at large holding them
in high esteem, so that "multitudes of new believers, both
men and women, were added to the Lord." [2] Such practical recommendations of the new faith as its miracles
of healing, made anything like doctrinal reasoning superfluous, nor do we find any trace of the elaborate theology
of later days in these first moments of the Church.

It would seem that some years of comparative peace,
before the outbreak of the formal persecution in which

[1] Acts v. 15, 16.   [2] Acts v. 13, 14.

Stephen fell, enabled the new movement to strike its
roots to some depth in Jerusalem, in spite of intermittent
opposition from its opponents, the Pharisees and Sadducees,
who frowned on it from different grounds. The Pharisees
would not hear of Jesus being the Messiah, as this would
overthrow their whole teaching that the " Anointed of
God," when He came, would found a Jewish world-empire,
before which that of the Romans would be swept away.
The Sadducees were fierce against the Christian doctrine of
the Resurrection and the Judgment, which they denounced
as the preaching of social tumult and revolution.   Hence,
when they found the Apostles habitually frequenting the
Temple grounds, where Christ had so often disputed with
both parties, the police in charge of the great Temple
" Close," who had laid hands on Jesus in the garden of
Gethsemane, were equally rough towards His followers,
whom even Calvary, to their disgust, had not silenced.
The Sadducean Church dignitaries, alarmed by the ferment
of the popular mind about the expected Messiah, and in
dread of the movement assuming uncontrollable force,
could not permit the excitement which they had com-
bated in connection with Jesus, to break out afresh.   It
would never do to allow the charge to go abroad that the
high priestly family—Hannas, Caiaphas, and the others
—had put the Messiah to death.

Fortunately for the Apostles, the great advance of the
Pharisaic party since the death of Herod, had already
forced open the doors of the Sanhedrim to some of its
chiefs, much to the chagrin of the Sadducees, whose
aristocratic blood shrank from this admixture of ecclesiastical Radicalism.   Among others, Rabbi Gamaliel, a
man of proverbial mildness, dignified the popular party,

in this, the supreme church court, and marked its policy for the moment, by advising that the new movement should be disregarded, since, if it were no better than the many other cases of Messianic fanaticisms they had seen in past years, it would, like them, speedily die out. Otherwise, they might find themselves opposing the divinely ordained fulfilment of the promises. The fact was that some of the Pharisees had rather a kindly feeling to the proclaimers of the new Kingdom of God, as, in a measure, allied to them in their views. To offer an uncompromising opposition to the "Kingdom of God," even when thus set forth, was dangerous to themselves, for such a policy might be turned, presently, against their own hopes and aims. The Apostles, therefore, were protected from serious consequences, for the time, though it was thought well to teach them caution, by the infliction of the cherished punishment of the synagogue, forty stripes save one. The concession, however, as might have been expected, had no effect on men so enthusiastic for the Master, whose claims as the Messiah they believed to be so fully attested by God Himself. "They, therefore, departed from the presence of the Council, rejoicing that they were counted worthy to suffer dishonour for the Name. And every day, in the Temple, and at home (in their own meeting place), they ceased not to teach and to preach Jesus as the Christ."[1]

The central argument against the new faith, on the part of the Jews at large, is seen, from both the Gospels and the Acts, to have been, that Christ had suffered such a shameful death, instead of "redeeming Israel" from its heathen oppressors, as a triumphant Hero-King. On the

[1] Acts v. 17–42.

Cross, the dying Saviour had heard the priests and rabble shouting to Him, "Physician, heal Thyself!" "Thou that destroyest the Temple, and buildest it in three days, save Thyself!" "Let the Christ, the King of Israel, now come down from the Cross, that we may see and believe!" 'Let us see whether Elias cometh to take Him down!" But Elias did not come, and Jesus did not free Himself from the Cross, so that these scoffs still held good with the multitude. All this, however, did not disturb the disciples, since they believed that Jesus had risen from the dead. The story of the body having been stolen, which was circulated to meet this, is a sample of the answers offered to the declarations of the Christians, though, of course, the Resurrection was of no weight as a proof of Christ being the Messiah, where the fact was treated as a ridiculous invention.

Apart from the evidence of their own senses, however, the Christians were triumphantly confirmed in their faith, by their rendering of the prophecies of the ancient Scriptures. From their unchallengeable words they were convinced that it behoved the Christ to suffer as Jesus had done, and then to enter into His glory, as He had by His Ascension to the right hand of God.[1] To them it seemed incontestable, that Moses, and all the prophets, spoke of a Messiah rejected by the nation, and abandoned to suffering and a shameful death.[2] Ignorant of all other writings, they, like all their race, were profoundly versed in every part of the oracles of God, and drew from them a hundred texts quite as applicable to the Messiah as those applied to Him by the rabbis. Hence it was their invincible conviction, that " the testimony of Jesus was the

---

[1] Luke xxiv. 26.   [2] Luke xxiv. 27.

spirit of prophecy," alike in Moses, the prophets, and the Psalms,[1] yet this was only the Christian rendering of the unanimous voice of the rabbis, that, "All the prophets prophesied of nothing else than of the days of the Messiah."[2] Hence the Apostles did not introduce controversy on unfamiliar lines, when they reasoned in the synagogues that Scripture proved Jesus to be the Messiah, but only sought to show that they were right in their application of it to Him.

Among those sacred testimonies, that to which the greatest prominence was given, was the grand prophecy respecting the Servant of Jehovah, in Isaiah.[3] Even the rabbis, indeed, while referring it primarily to the suffering people of Israel, in their captivity at Babylon, did not hesitate to apply it, in a still higher sense, to the Messiah. If these two chapters, as Christians believe, spoke of Him, Jesus had unquestionably fulfilled their predictions with a marvellous completeness. Of whom could it more fitly be said[4] than of the meek and lowly man of Nazareth, "He shall not cry aloud, nor lift up, nor cause His voice to be heard in the street. A bruised reed shall He not break, and the dimly burning wick shall He not quench. He shall not blanch nor be discouraged, till He has planted the right on the earth, and the isles shall wait for His teaching."[5] Or what could the eunuch of Candace reply to Philip, when he pointed out how exactly Jesus had fulfilled the words, "He was led as a lamb to the slaughter, and as a sheep before her shearers is dumb, so He opened not His mouth"?[6] The

[1] Rev. xix. 10 ; Luke xxiv. 44.   [2] Gfrorer ii. 198.
[3] Isa. lii., liii.   [4] Isa. xlii. 2–4.
[5] Matt. xii. 18–20.   [6] Isa. liii. 7.

whole story of the Cross could be reproduced from the far-off visions of the prophet. "Through oppression and a (criminal) judgment He was taken away, and who considered that He was cut off out of the land of the living, and stricken, for the transgression of My people? And they made His grave with the wicked, and with the rich, in His death, though He had done no violence, neither was any deceit in His mouth."[1] Believers in Him could, also, confidently ask which it better suited,— the conquering Messiah they expected, or Him who had died on Golgotha,—when the prophet says,[2] "He has no form or comeliness; and when we see Him there is no beauty that we should desire Him. He was despised and rejected of men; a man of sorrows and acquainted with grief: and as one from whom men hide their face; He was despised, and we esteemed Him not. Surely He has borne our griefs, and carried our sorrows: yet we esteemed Him stricken, (and) smitten, and afflicted, of God. But He was wounded for our transgressions, He was bruised for our iniquities; the chastisement of our peace was upon Him, and with His stripes we are healed." If Isaiah, the greatest of the prophets, spoke thus of the Messiah, who could doubt that "the Anointed of God" was to suffer and to die, and, if so, whom could this wondrous picture more perfectly point out than Jesus? Nor were the lineaments of the Man of Nazareth, or the minutest details of His story, set forth by this prophet only; a hundred texts from all parts of the Canon were urged as enforcing the words of St. Paul, that "Christ died for our sins, and was raised again from the dead, according to the Scriptures."[3] Or, as St. Peter

[1] Isa. liii. 8, 9.   [2] Isa. liii. 2–5.   [3] 1 Cor. xv. 3, 4.

expressed it, that "God foreshowed by the mouth of all the prophets, that His Christ must suffer."[1]

The appearance of John the Baptist was, rightly, in the opinion of the Apostles, that of the forerunner of the Messiah, of whom Isaiah had spoken, as the voice of one "crying in the wilderness, Prepare ye the way of the Lord, make straight in the desert a highway for our God."[2] He had been, also, the "Messenger" announced by Malachi, as sent to "prepare for the coming of the Lord.[3] It was ordained that Jesus should move in the regions of despised Galilee, on the lake of Tiberias, and in the obscure Capernaum, for had not Isaiah said that "Zebulon and Naphtali, and the way of the sea, the Galilee of the heathen, should see a great light."[4] No one could deny that Jesus had been meek and lowly; pitying, helping, and healing, all who were in trouble, but had not the prophets noticed this long before? Had not His entry into Jerusalem in His last week been exactly painted by Zechariah[5] centuries before: "Behold, thy King cometh unto thee; He is just and having salvation; lowly, and riding upon an ass, and upon a colt, the foal of an ass."[6] Had not Jesus, Himself, told them that the passage in Isaiah, about the Messiah preaching the gospel to the poor, had been fulfilled when he read and commented on it in the synagogue at Nazareth?[7] If the rabbis demanded where it was written that the Messiah would be rejected by His nation, the Apostles were ready with the passage from the Psalms,[8] "The stone which the builders refused is become the headstone of the corner," and had not

---

[1] Acts iii 18. [2] Isa. xl. 3 ; Mark i. 3. [3] Mal. i. 3 ff. ; Matt. xi. 10.
[4] Isa. ix. 1 ; Matt. iv. 14 f. [5] Zech. ix. 9.
[6] John xii. 15. [7] Luke iv. 17-21 ; Isa. lxi. 1. [8] Ps. cxviii. 22.

Isaiah said, "Who hath believed our report?"[1] and
Habakkuk, "I will work a work in your days, which you
will not believe, though it be told you."[2] If mockers
taunted the Twelve with their craven flight on the arrest
of their Master, they turned the edge of the reproach by
showing, from the words of the prophet,—"Smite the
shepherd, and the sheep shall be scattered,"[3]—that it had
happened in accordance with divine prediction. If the
treachery of Judas were added to the sneer at their
cowardice, this, also, was only in fulfilment of the divine
decree, for David, a thousand years before, had spoken of
the betrayer who ate bread with the Messiah and lifted
up his heel against Him.[4] Even the exact amount of the
blood-money paid to the traitor had been foretold by
Zechariah : "They weighed for my price thirty pieces of
silver," and so had their being "cast to the potter in the
house of the Lord."[5] Had the whole scene of Calvary
not been painted by inspiration, long ages before, in the
Psalms ? Was not the twenty-second Psalm, throughout,
all about their Master, from its opening words, "My God,
my God, why hast Thou forsaken me;" the very words He
had uttered on the Cross. Listen, they would say. What
could be more literally an anticipation of the facts than
the words, "All they that see me laugh me to scorn; they
shoot out the lip, they shake the head, saying, He trusted
in the Lord that He would deliver him : let Him deliver
him, seeing He delighteth in him." "Dogs have compassed
me ; the assembly of the wicked have enclosed me ; they
pierced my hands and my feet." "They part my garments
among them, and cast lots upon my vesture."[6] Had not

[1] Isa. liii. 1 ; John xii. 38.   [2] Hab. i. 5; Acts xiii. 41.   [3] Zech. xiii. 7.
[4] Ps. xli. 9.   [5] Zech. xi. 12, 13.   [6] Ps. xxii. 1, 7, 8, 16, 18.

the women, and John, who were by the Cross, seen and heard all this, just as the sacred words told it, and had not the Roman soldiers divided the garments of Jesus among them by lot? And had not another Psalm described still another of the touching incidents of that closing scene : " They gave me also gall for my meat, and in my thirst they gave me vinegar to drink."[1] He was the Passover lamb, none of whose bones could be broken,[2] and had not Zechariah seen afar off the spear that should pierce His sacred side, when he said, "They shall look on him whom they pierced."[3] Was not His Resurrection foreseen in the words of the Psalm, " Thou wilt not leave my soul to Sheol ; neither wilt Thou suffer Thine Holy One to see corruption."[4] Was it not pointed out by prophecy, that He should ascend to the heavens, in the interval before He returned, on the clouds, to judge mankind, and set up His unsuffering kingdom? "The Lord said unto my Lord, Sit thou on My right hand, until I make thine enemies thy footstool."[5] The proof was, indeed, overwhelming to the Christians, that every detail of their Master's story had been marked out by divine decree, from the earliest dawn of inspiration, by all the holy men, in succession, who spake as they were moved by the Holy Ghost. It seemed to them so inconceivable that their countrymen should question this, that even Paul, once the bitterest of persecutors, could explain it only by regarding their minds as " blinded ; a veil covering them, in the reading of the Old Testament. For even to this day, when Moses is read, the veil is upon their heart."[6]

[1] Ps. lxix. 21.
[2] John xix. 36 ; Exod. xii. 46 ; Num. ix. 12 ; Ps. xxxiv. 20.
[3] Zech. xii. 10 ; John xix. 37.　　[4] Ps. xvi. 10.
[5] Ps. cx. 1 ; Acts ii. 34.　　[6] 2 Cor. iii. 14, 15.

That such a blindness in the synagogues, as a whole, led to all this Scripture proof making little impression, is at once certain and easily explained. Belief in Christ as the Messiah, was, in fact, not a question of the meaning of texts. Those who had not been won over by the words of Jesus Himself, or by His miracles, were only, in a limited number of cases, to be convinced by Christian applications of any number of verses. That the rabbis explained them differently was enough. The Christians were not, like them, trained theologians, but only fishermen, publicans, and despised " common people." To take the law from such teachers was impossible to their illimitable pride. They might not be able to answer them, but they could at least drag them before the San-hedrim, and beat them with rods, or scourges, before the door of the synagogue. And this the Pharisees and Sadducees did, till Christianity drew more and more away from them, and a final breach divided, for ever, the Christian from the Jew.[1]

[1] Hausrath Neutest. Zeitgesch. II., sect. 4, ch. 4.

CHAPTER III

THE infant Church appears to have enjoyed comparative
peace for the next few years after the Crucifixion; the
limited numbers and humble position of its members,
with the fact that they still devoutly attended the Temple
worship, combining to screen them from any organised
persecution. Public affairs, moreover, were stirring, and
must have tended to withdraw notice from them. In the
year 34, Philip, the Tetrarch of Batanæa and other districts beyond the Jordan, the only worthy son of Herod
the Great, died, and as he left no children, his dominions,
much to the mortification of Antipas and Herodias, who
had hoped, through the marriage of Salome to the old
man, to have inherited them when he passed away, were
incorporated with the great Roman province of Syria.
Pilate still ruled over Judæa and Samaria, hated and hat-
ing. He had shown himself mean, greedy, bloodthirsty,
and utterly unprincipled, in his relations to Judæa: he
was now to exhibit himself in colours as revolting to the
people of Samaria, who had always been loyal to Rome,
and, on that account, if on no other, deserved generous
treatment.

The intense religious excitement, which, just before the

40

death of Herod the Great, had torn down the reputedly
idolatrous figure of a golden eagle, set up by the king in
the sacred Temple bounds, had been, if possible, increased,
by the burning alive of a number of the students of the
Law who had taken part in the bold deed.   Then, in
the year A.D. 6 or 7, had come the Census ordered by
Augustus; a measure hateful beyond endurance to an
Oriental people, but especially so to the Jews; so hateful,
that it roused Judas of Gamala, known as the Gaulonite,
or the Galilæan, to head a wild revolt against Rome, which
scourged the land, for years, with fire and sword, never,
indeed, quite dying out, but, ever and anon, breaking out
in new despairing efforts against the heathen lords of
"the heritage of Jehovah," till it finally, as I have said,
flamed up in the furious crimes of the later " Zealots,"
whose excesses at last made even the kindly Titus remorseless, in the war in which the nation perished.   The
entire Jewish race, indeed, since the time of Herod, "the
Edomite's," accession to the throne of David, had been,
more and more, absorbed in dreams of the deliverance of
their country, as rightfully that of Jehovah alone, from
foreign domination.   Amidst such a state of public feeling John had appeared on the Jordan, proclaiming the
immediate revelation of the Messiah, rousing the entire
land by the announcement, so that the whole population
flocked to him from every quarter.   Then had come the
preaching of Jesus, the Galilæan, who, after a brief but
great popularity, had been cast off by the people, and put
to death by the priests, because He would not preach a
political revolution, to crush the Roman and give the Jew
the empire of the world in his place.   The universal excitement which all this indicated, had, naturally, extended

beyond the strictly Jewish population, to their rivals, the
Samaritans, who, indeed, claimed that they, and not the
so-called Israel, were the true "people of God." [1] Already,
in the lifetime of Christ, the woman at the well, who regarded Gerizim as the sacred mountain, had shown the
common expectation of her people that the Messiah would
very soon appear on it. [2] The Samaritans claimed that
they, not the Jews, possessed the true Holy Land promised to Abraham, over which the patriarchs had pas-
tured their flocks. Gerizim, they maintained, was the
real Temple Mount. They only, they affirmed, had the
pure Law, uncorrupted by any prophet; on their holy
mountain Moses had buried the vessels used in the Tabernacle, which the Jews claimed to have had in the Temple
of Solomon, and to have lost when it was destroyed by
the Chaldæans. On this supposed possession of the sacred
vessels, moreover, they grounded the assurance that Samaria would be the centre of the kingdom of the Messiah,
and Gerizim the scene of His manifestation, to honour
which the long lost Ark of the Covenant, and the ancient
holy vessels, would be again brought to light. [3] Jeremiah
had, according to the Jews, hidden all these in Mount
Nebo, and had announced that the spot should remain
unknown "till the time that God shall gather His people
again together, and receive them unto mercy. Then
shall the Lord show them these things, and the glory of
the Lord shall appear, and the cloud also, as it was shown
to Moses, and as when Solomon desired that the place

[1] See "The Gospels," a companion to my Life of Christ—chapter on
the Samaritans.

[2] John iv. 20, 25.

[3] For the Jewish tradition on this subject, see 2 Macc. ii. 5.

might be honourably sanctified." Another tradition,
assigned to Baruch, the scribe of Jeremiah, told that,
before the first destruction of Jerusalem, an angel descended to the Holy City and alighted in the Temple, to
save the holy things. Packing up the sacred tent, the
high priestly ephod, the Ark, the two stones of the Law
from Mount Sinai, the high priestly robes, the altar of
incense, the Urim and Thummim, and the sacred vessels,
he bore them away to a secret place, and cried with a
loud voice, "Earth, Earth, Earth, hear the word of the
strong God, and receive what I have entrusted to thee,
and keep it till the end of the times; then to give it up
when thou art summoned to do so, that the alien may not
get possession of it. For then will come the day when
Jerusalem will be restored, never more to fade! Then
the earth opened its mouth and swallowed up all." [1] A
third and more dignified tradition is embodied in the
Apocalypse, describing the holy vessels as hidden in
heaven. The "hidden manna" is to be given to the
faithful, and "the ark of the covenant" is seen in "the
temple of God." [2] In opposition to all this, the Samaritans
maintained that all the sacred vessels had been concealed
on Gerizim, and had never been in Solomon's Temple
at all.

Not to be behind the hated Jews, in their confidence
that the Messiah was about to come as a Jewish representative of Jehovah, the Samaritans caught the spirit
of unrest which agitated the neighbouring districts. "A
man," says Josephus,[3] "appeared, who stirred up the multitude, spreading abroad among them whatever flattered
their taste, however untrue it might be, and gradually

[1] Apoc. of Baruch, vi.   [2] Rev. ii. 17; xi. 19.   [3] Jos., *Ant.* xviii. 4, 1.

working them into a wild excitement. Sending messengers
through the Samaritan territory, when the minds of all
had been wound up to a sufficient pitch of fanaticism, he
summoned them to come, in their multitudes, on a fixed
day, to Mount Gerizim, for, on that day, a new prophet
would reveal to them the holy vessels buried there, ages
before, by Moses. This was equivalent to announcing
that the Kingdom of the Messiah would, then and there,
be set up, for the holy vessels were to come to light only
at His advent. The evident object of the agitation was
to take the wind out of the sails of the Messiah-expecta-
tions of the Jews, and forestall them in the setting up of
"the Kingdom of God." The "lying prophet" had craftily
availed himself of the passionate faith of the race, that
they held possession of the true Temple Mount, and of the
only uncorrupted version of the Law, and that all the
sacred memorials of the Tabernacle would be disclosed,
from their concealment on Gerizim, at the appearing of
the Messiah. With such anticipations, the summons of
the prophet roused the Samaritan thousands, as the
preaching of John had stirred up the population of Palestine at large. Vast throngs crowded the little valley
of Shechem, and overflowed into the wide plain of the
Mukhnah, outside. The now unknown village of Tirathana, "near the holy mount," had been appointed as the
spot where the prophet would meet them, and thither,
therefore, multitudes streamed, day after day. As, however, if Josephus be right, they came armed, and had the
chief men of the land and the elders of the people at their
head, the jealousy of the authorities, which had seen a
political aim in John's assemblages, felt still more reason
for the same suspicion respecting this new Gerizim agita-

tion.   Pilate was ruler over Samaria, and had suffered
much from past Messianic excitements. This, of the
Samaritans, might be only a pretext to hide illegal inten-
tions, though the announced object was merely to obtain
the restoration of the holy vessels.   They proposed to
ascend Gerizim in all their thousands to see them when
found.   Might not the real object of the leaders be to
proclaim the advent of the Messiah, when they had

Colonnade of Herod, at Samaria.

gathered the population round them, and give forth that
His Kingdom was set up?   The Procurator had already
been so harsh that the Samaritans had concentrated at
Tirathana, as they afterwards said, to be able to protect
themselves from his violence.[1]   Altogether, it looked to
Pilate's cold suspicious nature, as if there were treason in
the wind, so that, before the day of the final grand ascent

[1] Jos., *Ant.* xviii. 4, 2.

of the mountain, he forbade it, and barred the approaches
to Gerizim with posts of infantry and patrols of horse.
But the Samaritans were in great numbers at Tirathana,
and in their wild fanaticism would not turn back when
ordered by the troops to do so. Roman soldiers, however,
were not the men to give way before a mob, however
fierce, numerous, or audacious. The order was given to
fall on the rioters. Many were cut down, many trampled
to death, in the tumultuous flight from the charge of the
troops; many, also, were taken prisoners, and of these the
chief men were executed as traitors. But the Samaritan
elders would not submit to all this without a protest.
Betaking themselves to Vitellius, father of the emperor
of that name, now governor-general of the great province
of Syria, which included Palestine, they admitted having
sought to protect themselves against the violence of
Pilate, but repudiated any thought of revolt from Rome.
The suit dragged on its slow length for two years, and
ended by the deposition of Pilate by Vitellius, who came
to Jerusalem. The fallen man was ordered to Rome to
give an account of his government, but he reached it only
after the death of Tiberius, in March A.D. 37, though he
had been deposed before the Easter of A.D. 36. Beyond
the fancies of tradition, the arrival of the judge of our
Lord at the Tiber drops the curtain on his story. Nothing
is certainly known of him after.

The visit of Vitellius to Jerusalem was fatal, also, to
another of the actors in the tragedy of Calvary; Caiaphas,
the high priest who condemned Christ. He was a son-in-
law of Hannas, the head of the priestly aristocracy, but
had now to make way for Jonathan, a son of Hannas, who
however, was allowed to hold his great office for only

one year; Theophilus, another son of Hannas, succeeding
him in A.D. 37. To mitigate the bitterness of the Jewish
feeling at the hateful rule of Pilate, Vitellius, moreover,
abolished the impost hitherto levied on market stuff, in
Jerusalem, and granted to the new high priest and his
successors, the keeping of the high priestly robes, which
for thirty years had been laid up in the castle of Antonia,
on the north-west edge of the Temple grounds, and given
out only a week before each of the three great feasts,
and of the Day of Atonement. Still more, he definitely
ordered that the troops should not bear with them the
standards with the imperial likeness on them, when they
marched through Judæa, and went the length of presenting a sacrifice, of course through the priests, in the
Temple.

But local affairs, however engrossing to Judæa itself,
were mingled, in these days, with matters of far more
momentous interest. The great Oriental State of Parthia,
which for generations had been an abiding trouble to
Rome, and also to all Western Asia, was now, again, the
source of wars and rumours of war, which kept all the
nations in restless anxiety. The appearance of the Parthians in Palestine, in the year B.C. 38, as allies of the
exiled Asmonæan prince, against the intrusion of Herod
on their Jewish kingdom, had filled the land with a terror
which two generations could not abate. Even in the
Apocalypse, indeed, St. John uses them as the symbol
of the four destroying angels, loosened from their dread
prison in the bed of the Euphrates, to destroy the third
part of men. Two hundred thousand horsemen, in fiery,
blue and brimstone-coloured, mail, rode forth, after these,
from the dried-up river bed, an army of hell, to destroy

mankind; just as the Parthians had swept over the western lands when they invaded Judæa.[1] The Roman historians use language hardly less striking, of the endless rushing swarms of wild cavalry—their terrible shouts, like the bellowing of wild beasts, and the hideous clamour of their countless drums, like the noise of thunder; their horses covered with brass and steel trappings, glittering like lightning, the faces of the soldiers painted, and their shaggy hair gathered in a mass on their foreheads, after the Scythian fashion. Their dreadful lances, their feigned retreats, their resistless arrows, the clouds of dust raised by their charges, hiding the battle-field,— their spears, their slings, their blazing banners, gleaming with gold and silver, are all recounted. These awful enemies, of whom the men of Christ's day had so often heard, threatened to waste the land once more, swarming over it on their lean and untiring steppe horses, murdering, violating, burning, and plundering; the embodiment of treachery, rapine, and wild brutality.[2] The never ending, ever beginning, alarms respecting them, seemed to have good ground at this time, for Vitellius had been ordered, in A.D. 35, to bring the Parthian Sultan to reason; his intrigues with Armenia, a country closely related to his own kingdom, giving Rome fresh trouble. The threatenings of Vitellius, however, and the revolt of his own subjects, drove Artabanus, the Parthian king, to flight. The Romans then advanced, taking with them a Pretender to the throne, whom they had adopted, as the British did Shah Soojah, fifty years ago, and setting him over the empire, as we set our puppet over that of Dost Mahomed, in Afghanistan—with the same ridiculous result. For, before the

[1] Rev. ix. 13-20. [2] Geikie's Life of Christ, i. 389.

year was out, a counter-revolution restored Artabanus to his throne, and drove out the Roman nominee, Tiridates. But, now, peace was to be made with the old king, who, like Dost Mahomed, protested his loyalty to the foreign power. An interview was arranged between Vitellius and him, on the Euphrates, and his son Darius was given over to the Romans, as a hostage for the faithful observance of a friendly treaty, there concluded. This interview was of special interest in Palestine, from Herod Antipas being present at it. He had gone with Vitellius, and even acted the host to him and Artabanus, in a costly tent which he caused to be set up, on a bridge over the great river.

But Antipas had, in these days, trouble of his own, nearer home, which must have given abundant matter for popular excitement. His marriage to Herodias brought him little happiness. The Arab king, Aretas, could not forget that Antipas, on her account, had divorced his daughter. The grudge simmered on till, in A.D. 36, disputes respecting boundaries in Galaaditis gave an opportunity of revenge. War was declared between the two, and the army of Antipas was utterly defeated, leaving no hope for the beaten "fox,"[1] except in accusing his conqueror before Tiberius. That Aretas had dared to attack a vassal of Rome, without permission, was a supreme offence, for which it was ordered that Vitellius should seize Aretas, dead or alive. But the Syrian Viceroy, having little friendship for Antipas, was in no mood to hurry his execution of the command. Setting his army in motion towards Petra, the capital of Aretas, he had to march round Judæa, through which he could not carry the imperial standards, bearing the image of Tiberius.

[1] Luke xiii. 32.

II.   D

Vitellius, however, himself, visited Jerusalem, apparently at the Passover season, and during his stay there of four days, having heard of the death of Tiberius, found in this an excuse for recalling his army, with which he returned to his headquarters at Antioch.

Pilate had been degraded before Easter 36, and was succeeded by the Procurator Marcellus. On the 16th March, 37, Tiberius had died, and a youth, Caius, known better from his byname Caligula, the grand nephew of the dead emperor, ascended the throne of the world, at the age of twenty-five. His accession was hailed with the wildest joy, since he was the son of Germanicus, a name honoured over all the empire; the son of such a father seeming to promise a reign in happy contrast to that of his misanthropic predecessor; an anticipation to be only too terribly disappointed. Vitellius, being in Jerusalem when the news came of his accession, the Jews were enabled to be the first of the Syrian populations to take the oath to him, and to offer sacrifice for his prosperity; an eager loyalty which, for a year and a half, they had no reason to regret. With the opening reign, however, a new actor in the political history of Judæa came before the world;—Herod Agrippa I.,whose connection with Palestine began, forthwith, by the grant to him, from Caius, of the former Tetrarchy of Philip, and of that of Lysanias,— Abilene,—a district on the eastern slopes of Anti-Lebanon, the title of king being given, with these principalities. The previous history of this personage, who was hereafter to play a prominent part in the story of the early Church, had been a strange commentary on the character of the times.

More than twenty years older than Caligula, Agrippa

had been named after the great minister of Augustus.[1]
He was the second son of Aristobulus, son of Mariamne,
who, with his brother, her other son, had been put to
death by their common father, Herod the Great; the last
victims of the tragic family life of that strange compound
of good and evil. The widow, Berenice, was sent, shortly
before Herod's death, to Rome, with her children, that
they might join the band of princes without dominions,
who, in that age, formed a court nobility round the new
Cæsardom, which it could play off against the haughty
aristocracy of the capital.   In this crowd of royal depen-
dents, Berenice, with her two daughters and three sons,
took a prominent place, securing intimate relations with
the highest circles of the imperial house, so that her sons
grew up as companions of the imperial heirs, and might
thus hope for a splendid future. To the Roman world,
this intimacy of the Herod princes with the young Cæsars
was a trouble; the aristocracy hinting, not perhaps without grounds, that it was through them that the imperial
lads caught ideas of Asiatic despotism, and demanded
Oriental obsequiousness from those round them.   But, on
the other hand, the Herods learned little good from their
august associates. The young Drusus, son of Tiberius
was, like Agrippa, passionately devoted to gladiators,
whom he urged on to fight each other with doubly
sharpened swords, named after him; taking such pleasure
in their murderous battles that it was said Tiberius must
want his son to be hated, since he let him do so completely as he liked.   After a time, however, Agrippa
became intimate with Sejanus, the infamous favourite of
Tiberius, who had a deadly hatred of Drusus for having

[1] He was born B.C. 10.

been struck by him, and, in revenge, having seduced his wife, won her over to poison her husband. But the Herods were, also, far from patterns. Agrippa was a spendthrift, and his sister Herodias left her husband, Herod Böethos, for Antipas, who could make her a princess, instead of merely a private lady. In the circles amidst which these people moved, such exchanges of wife or husband were daily occurrences, and it was only among the Jews in their home-land, where she and her young daughter Salome had now to live, that a stricter morality was asserted. After Berenice's death, things grew still worse. Agrippa, seeking to emulate the extravagance of the young Cæsars, but not having their resources, ere long sank into ruinous debt. So long, however, as he had his imperial friends to help him, this was no great trouble, but, unfortunately for his peace, the son of Tiberius died, by the poison of Sejanus, in the year A.D. 23, when Agrippa was thirty-three, and Tiberius forbade the friends of the dead man to approach the court, on the pretext that the sight of them would increase his grief.

The creditors of Agrippa, forthwith, mercilessly levied writ after writ on him. Moreover, the dreadful times of the sole reign in Rome of the favourite Sejanus began, and continued till the year 31. In those years, the imperial house was the scene of a succession of the most shameful murders. Germanicus, like his father, had died, as his widow believed, through the orders of Tiberius, against whom she, consequently, began a series of intrigues, which ended only in her own ruin and that of her associates. To escape her, Tiberius betook himself to Capri, leaving Sejanus to wreak his vengeance as he chose. Her supporters speedily received the emperor's

commands to put themselves to death, and the widow,
Agrippina, was banished to the small island of Panda-
taria, about fifty miles west of Vesuvius. There she was
cruelly ill-treated, and left to the solitude of the barren
island, where, after three years, she refused to take food
any longer, and died apparently of starvation. Her son,
Nero, the eldest son of Germanicus, killed himself at the
little island of Pontia, off the coast, by order of Tiberius,
who had banished him thither. Another son, Drusus,
died of hunger in the dungeons of the palace at Rome.
Then, in the year 31, when, at last, the iniquities of
Sejanus, as vice-emperor, were full, the cup of his
wickedness was put to his own lips, and what remained
of his body, torn limb from limb, by the populace,
after his ignominious execution, was hurled over the em-
bankment of the Tiber, to find its only burial in the
thick, yellow, waters. But now came to light his seduc-
tion of the sister of Germanicus, wife of the poisoned
Drusus, son of Tiberius, and her complicity in her husband's murder. Roman in the purest sense, Antonia,
her mother, a daughter of Mark Antony, demanded her
punishment by the emperor, and she was shut up in
her palace and left to die of hunger. One intended
victim only, out of her desolated home, was saved to
Antonia, her grandson Caius, our Caligula, son of the
murdered Germanicus, the splendid son of the afflicted
matron. But she already saw in this his last male
descendant, a bestiality which foretold her, before Rome
dreamed of it, what kind of a ruler was growing up in
the women's room of the palace.

Meantime, while blood was raining down on his former
friends at Rome, Agrippa was fighting a hard battle with

his creditors. His wife's means—she was his cousin,
Cypros—could not keep his head above water, so that
nothing remained for him but to return to Palestine,
with her and her children. To keep out of the reach
of bailiffs, he there buried himself in the loneliest places,
taking up his abode, finally, in his castle, Malatha, in the
wild desert of Judæa, half-way between Beersheba and
the south end of the Dead Sea; a miserable spot, en-
livened, at most, by an occasional visit of a Roman
detachment, sent as a protection against the Arabs. The
contrast between this refuge and the splendour of Rome
almost maddened him, and it was only by the shrewdness
of his excellent wife, that deliverance came in time to
prevent him from committing suicide. Writing to her
brother-in-law, Antipas, she described Agrippa's miserable position, and obtained an invitation to Tiberias, the
new capital on the charming Lake of Galilee. Thither,
therefore, he betook himself, and was once more in the
midst of the "great ones," "gorgeously apparelled in soft
clothing, and living delicately in king's courts,"[1] whom
our Lord contrasted with the rude simplicity of His own
great forerunner, the Baptist, as He saw them flashing by
from the palace of Antipas, visible, day by day, when
He looked from Capernaum towards the neighbouring
Tiberias. But Agrippa had come to an indifferent patron.
A small income was granted him, and after the custom
of Rome, where the nearest connections of the court did
not disdain to accept municipal offices, he was appointed
clerk of the market of the town. The boon companion,
in brighter days, of the Cæsars, thus found himself super-
intending the weights and measures, the buying and

[1] Luke vii. 25.

selling, the price and quality of the contents of the hucksters' stalls, and keeping law and order among the motley market crowds of a provincial town, the centre of the local fishing industry!. But he could not long endure the degradation of the post, which, though profitable enough at Rome, was, at best, a paltry affair in the petty capital of Antipas. The haughtiness of his sister, Herodias, and the reproaches of his host, did not add to the comfort of the position. A great dinner at Tyre, at which both were present, brought matters to a head; Antipas denouncing him, at it, as a beggar! Agrippa could stand his ignominy no longer, but forthwith went off to Antioch, where his friend Flaccus was Proconsul, to be followed, ere long, by the energetic Vitellius. Flaccus received his old acquaintance kindly, though Agrippa's brother, Aristobulus, with whom the new guest was at variance, was also at court. But the brothers could not live in peace. In his stress for money, Agrippa had received bribes from the authorities of Damascus, to serve them by his access to the Proconsul, and this, coming to the ears of his brother, and being disclosed by him to Flaccus, at once ended the friendship between them.

Agrippa had, therefore, to seek, once more, for help, and as the East offered no prospect, he had to return to Rome, where he arrived in the spring of 36, having raised the money needed for the journey, from a freedman at Ptolemais, who allowed him a sum equal to about seven hundred pounds of our money, on his note for eight hundred, and that, only because he trusted to his sister Berenice, and his mother's friend Antonia, widow of Drusus, son of Tiberius, to see him repaid. Agrippa did

not escape to Italy, however, without much trouble.
Fleeing by night to his ship at Anthedon, a long forgotten place of departure for vessels, near Gaza, he was
arrested when embarking, by the Roman local procurator,
for debt due to the imperial treasury, and only got free,
by new borrowing, on the credit of his wife, from the
chief man of the Jews of Alexandria. On reaching
Puteoli, the crafty debtor at once sought an audience of
the gray-haired Tiberius, at Capri, and was received by
him kindly, as an old family friend. A generous loan
from Antonia, moreover, saved him from a legal judgment
that was hastening after him. Presently we find him
"governor" of the son of Drusus—grandson of Tiberius;
but he cared a great deal more for his old companion
Caius, the grandson of Antonia and son of Germanicus,
whose favour he gained by inducing his grandmother to
pay some of his debts, and getting a Samaritan freedman
to advance him a large amount. Caius, as the wily Jew
saw, was the popular favourite for the near approaching
vacancy in the imperial succession, and had, also, the
secret favour of Tiberius as his heir. Such sowing, he
thought, should yield a rich harvest, but for this he
waited only too impatiently. Venturing one day, while
on a private carriage ride with Caius, to whisper to him
that he wished the happy day for the world were come,
when he could greet him as emperor, instead of the old
man now reigning, he was overheard by the driver, who,
when brought up soon after for pilfering from his master's
wardrobe, sought to serve himself by telling the story to
the city prefect. Tiberius was not long in hearing it,
but, though already displeased with Agrippa for his neglect
of his grandson, only took action against him when the in-

criminated man had foolishly importuned for an audience. The charioteer's testimony, however, was too clear, and, to his horror, Agrippa was thrown into chains, in which he lay for six months, till the death of Tiberius. A few days after the accession of Caius, the new emperor, with the good-will of Antonia, set a diadem on the prisoner's head, hung chains of gold on him instead of the iron ones he had worn, and, as already stated, made over to him, with the title of king, the two principalities of his dead uncle Philip, and of the long dead Lysanias.[1] Tiberias had joined his grandson with Caligula in the succession, but the poor lad was at once murdered, just before this grand liberality to the adventurer! Had Agrippa a hand in the removal of the victim? The Senate, in obedience to the imperial hint, added to the honours of the now fortunate one, by giving him the dignity of a prætor! Such was the strange story of Agrippa, "the Great," as Josephus calls him, before his appearance in Palestine as a ruler.

[1] Jos., *Ant.* xviii. 6. 4-10.

CHAPTER IV

AFFAIRS IN JUDÆA (*continued*)

A.D. 30–37

AMIDST all the changing lights and shadows of the world drama, there had, however, been, for some years, a calm spot in the centre of all its wild commotions; the little sphere of the infant Christian movement at Jerusalem. Yet, even in it, there were, from the first, the elements of strife which would inevitably break out, sooner or later, into open hostility. The Jew of those ages ranged himself in one of two widely differing camps. Between the Israelite born in Palestine, and clinging to its rude Aramaic language, and his brother living in foreign lands, speaking Greek, and more or less affected by Greek modes of thought, there was a marked contrast which could not be put aside permanently, even in the infant Church at Jerusalem. It had shown itself very early, in the alleged unfair treatment of the widows of the Hellenist, or Greek-speaking section, by the Hebrews, or native Aramaic-speaking brethren, and was to burst into a flame, a few years later, between the Christian Hellenists and those of the synagogue.[1] At Jerusalem, above all other places, as the headquarters of the "Hebrew" party, there was a

[1] Gal. i. 13; 1 Cor. xv. 9; Phil. iii. 6; 1 Tim. i. 13; Acts viii. 3; ix. 1; vi. 12.

special dislike of the Greek version of the Scriptures, and
of the use of Greek in any form, as we see incidentally,
but strikingly, in the readiness of the infuriated Temple
mob to listen to Paul on hearing him speak "in the
Hebrew language," when they had supposed him to be
a Hellenist.[1] But this contrast was not limited to prejudice against the language of the Gentiles. The Hellenists,
who used the Greek Bible, put a far more generous interpretation on the divine promises and sympathies than the
Hebrews. They were willing to dispense with obligatory
observance of the Law by the heathen, while the fanatical
Jews of Palestine had no deeper wish, than that the Holy
Land should be purged from the defilement of the presence
of heathen. The Hellenists, living far from the narrowing
influences of the Temple City, had, in fact, come to regard
the moral precepts of their religion as alone essential, and
to think the merely historical and ritual as more or less indifferent. When, moreover, we see that even among the
Judaizing Christians who spoke Greek, the thought of an
announcement of the Messiah to the heathen kindled
their animosity; that the Hellenist, Stephen, was seized
and stoned for hinting, as was thought, at the future
abolition of the Temple service; when we find envoys
from the Judaizers in the Jerusalem Church itself, travelling everywhere in the track of St. Paul, stirring up his
converts to think zeal for the Temple worship, circumcision, and the Law, essential for their favour with God,
and when we find the Epistle to the Hebrews warning
the Jerusalem Judaizers against setting too high a value
on the services of the Temple, for speaking against which
Hellenists like Stephen were stoned, it is abundantly

[1] Acts xxi. 40.

clear, that the difference of views which separated the Hebrews from the Greek Jews long survived, with momentous consequences, in the Christian community. In every age, and in all questions that greatly interest men, there must, indeed, from our mental constitution, be the rigidly conservative, and the progressive; the Tory, and the Radical; the wide minded and the narrow; the immovable and the reforming; the national and the cosmopolitan, and these opposites revealed themselves almost from the first in the infant Church; developing, ultimately, into the two great contrasted aspects of Christianity represented by St. Peter and St. Paul.

Among the Hellenists of the Jerusalem congregation two stand out as specially active in propagating the new faith—Philip and Stephen. Both were in the list of "deacons," but both were also zealous preachers of "Christ." Of Philip we are informed that he visited Samaria, as a Christian envoy, with so much success, as to induce Simon, the Magian, from interested motives, to seek baptism; that he baptized the eunuch of Queen Candace of Ethiopia; then laboured on the Phœnician coast of Palestine, and finally settled down at Cæsarea, after thus leading the way in the foreign missionary activity of the Church.

St. Stephen, "a man full of faith and of the Holy Spirit;" "full," also, "of grace and power, and working great wonders and signs;" [1] with a special gift in the effective statement and defence of the new faith, devoted himself to its spread among his fellow-Hellenists in Jerusalem. Using the privilege, open to all, of speaking in the synagogues, he selected from among the alleged

[1] Acts vi. 5, 8.

48C in Jerusalem the three frequented by foreign-born Jews—the one that of freedmen—descended, probably. from Jews carried off as slaves by Pompey or others in the wars, and afterwards manumitted — the others, of zealots for the Law, from various provinces of the empire —Alexandria in Egypt, Ephesus, Cilicia, and Cyrene. As Hellenists, they might have been expected to listen sympathetically to such generous renderings of the promises as Stephen might propound, but the contentiousness of all Orientals, who cannot resist wordy disputes and discussions, "their mouths," as Josephus says of the Greeks of his day, "being always wide open, and their tongue ready for controversy," led to noisy scenes, which grew ever more heated. Some of them, moreover, were, no doubt, more bigoted and fanatical than others, and all must have been more so than the Hellenists outside Palestine; the narrowing influence of Jerusalem, and the very fact that they had come to it from religious motives, implying an approximation to the gloomy straitness of the " Hebrews."

There must, moreover, have been something in the addresses of Stephen different from the teaching till now heard from the Apostles, for it is expressly said that, in the outbreak of persecution which presently desolated the local church, its leaders, the Apostles, were left undisturbed, in Jerusalem, when their flock, at least so far as it was identified with the teaching of Stephen—that is, the Hellenists in it—had to flee for their lives.[1] To credit the Apostles with special courage does not explain this, for no bravery could have protected them from the tipstaffs of the priests, urged by a soul so fiery as that of

[1] Acts viii. 1.

Paul. The only satisfactory solution of the phenomenon is, that while the Apostles were honoured "by all the people" for their strict compliance with Jewish forms and rabbinical precepts, and were zealous in their attendance at the Temple services and devotions,[1] Stephen was accused of having spoken against the Fathers, the Temple, and the Law. It is to be noticed, moreover, that these charges are exactly similar to those with which Christ was assailed The witnesses against Stephen declared they had heard him say that "Jesus of Nazareth would destroy this place (the Temple), and change the customs which Moses had delivered to the nation,"[2] thus repeating the words ascribed to our Lord, "I will destroy this Temple that is made with hands, and, in three days, I will build another made without hands."[3] The charge from which Jesus defends Himself, that He came "to destroy the Law and the Prophets,"[4] is also identical with that made against the first martyr. The accusation is, indeed, called "false witness," but it was only so in the perverted sense in which the impugned words were quoted. It was false and treacherous in its insinuating against the accused, in either case, violent and revolutionary designs, or a fundamental hostility to the law. Such feelings in the case of Stephen would, in fact, have hindered him from ever attaining the honourable office he held in the Christian community. But in another sense it had some foundation. The zealous and eager disputant of the synagogue must, it is clear, have penetrated more deeply into the meaning of Christ, in many of His sayings, than the mass of his brethren, and have realised His distinctions

---

[1] Acts ii. 46, 47.
[2] Acts vi. 14.
[3] Mark xiv. 58 ; Matt. xxvi. 61.
[4] Matt. v. 17.

between the Law of Moses and that of His own new
" Kingdom of God," and, especially, of His famous words
about the new Temple which should take the place of the
existing one—a saying which had been altogether mysterious to the disciples at large, and no less so to the
populace.[1] Can it be questioned that he saw the impossibility of uniting the Mosaic institutions with the spiritual
genius of the Gospel, and its instinctive alliance with
liberty and cosmopolitan charity? A convincing proof
that he did so is seen in his defence before his accusers.
He shows historically what gracious arrangements God
had made for His people, from the days of Abraham, and
how, notwithstanding this, the nation had always " resisted the Spirit," and displayed, throughout their whole
history, that hardness of heart and refractoriness which,
at last, had reached its worst, in the rejection of the
Messiah, Jesus, and, therefore, must entail a breach between them and the new " Kingdom of God," for preaching
which he was accused. After having pointed out, in his
opening, how all the promises were designed, not for the
patriarchs themselves, but for the race which entered
into the enjoyment of them under Moses, he finds the
national relations to Christ foreshadowed and indirectly
described in those of his brethren to Joseph, but more
forcibly still in those assumed towards Moses.[2]

The building of the Temple by Solomon—no advance,
in Stephen's opinion, on the old movable Tabernacle—
serves to carry the speaker from the reproach he has
urged against the idolatry of the previous ages, to a
still keener accusation of bigotry against the generations since, whose fierce zeal for the material sanctuary,

[1] John ii. 20   [2] Acts vii. 35.

went hand in hand with the murdering of God's
messengers, the prophets, and now demonstrated its
unholy contradiction of both Law and Prophets, by the
rejection and crucifixion of the Messiah, of whom both
Law and Prophets bore witness throughout. The close of
the address seems to have been lost in the wild howls of
the crowd, whom its whole tenor had infuriated. But it
is clear that Stephen knew his certain fate, and concerned
himself less, in what he said, with his defence and the
saving of his life, than in giving a dying protest against
the perverseness of his race, and exalting the glory of his
Master. Nothing of the same tone could have been
heard before, from the Apostles, otherwise the authorities
would have made short work with them, and Gamaliel,
the oracle of the Pharisees, would, assuredly, have been
the last to protect them from the Sadducees, who sought
to kill them for their tenacious loyalty to Pharisaic ideas
and hopes. Yelling aloud, the hearers rushed upon the
victim, and in wild tumult, which would not allow itself
to be delayed by the legal forms, requiring permission
from the Roman authorities to carry out its murderous
purpose, dragged him outside the town, and stoned him
to death as a blasphemer—the martyr, like his Master,
dying with a prayer for his foes. He had perished
because he had openly uttered convictions opposed to the
religious sentiments of the masses; that is, anti-Phari-
saic, and contrary to the ultra legalism of the day. One
Pharisee, a scholar of Gamaliel, took a prominent part in
the hideous tragedy, as, probably, he had been among the
foremost in keen disputes with Stephen, in the synagogues
—the future Apostle Paul. But it is still more worthy
of note, that the funeral of the saint was followed, not by

Jewish Christians, but by "devout men," the name for still uncircumcised frequenters of the synagogues,[1] who filled the air with their loud wailings over him, as they bore him to his tomb; expressing, we may believe, their sorrow for one whose wide charity had won them for the Gospel of Christ.

The passions of the mob, once roused, and whetted by blood, the cry for the rooting out of the new heresy rose on every side, so that all who feared they would be identified with the views of the martyr—that is, we may assume, all the Hellenists and, no doubt, many of the "Hebrews"—fled for their lives; some of them as far as Phœnicia, Cyprus, and Antioch.[2]   Nor need we wonder, when we find the future Paul, as one of the leaders of the crusade against the "heretics," "laying waste the church, entering into every house, and haling off both men and women to" the horrors of an Oriental "prison."[3]

Among those thus driven from Jerusalem, Philip, the Deacon, showed himself a worthy associate of St. Stephen, and, like him, a worthy precursor of St. Paul, by throwing aside his Jewish narrowness, and going " down " to the country of the intensely hated Samaritans, to preach the wide charity revealed in the message to all mankind, of salvation in the name of Jesus Christ.   A great effect was produced, we are told, by the labours of the missioner, "the multitude giving heed with one accord" to what they heard, accompanied as it was by striking "signs." With others who sought baptism at his hands, a famous local representative of the "magic" then much in repute —that is, a Cagliostro of the day, claiming to do wonders by spells, incantations, charms, and the like, Simon by

[1] Acts viii. 2.   [2] Acts xi. 19.   [3] Acts viii. 3.

name. according to Josephus, a Jew born in Cyprus, but
said by others to have been a Samaritan, educated in
Alexandria,[1] came to him. Professing belief in Jesus as
the Messiah, Philip baptized him, and he, thenceforth,
connected himself with him. But it soon proved that
even the miracle-working Philip could be over-reached
by smooth hypocrisy, for on Peter and John coming to
Samaria, some time after, Simon, noticing that the Holy
Spirit, with the miraculous powers it conferred in that
age, was given to converts by the laying on them of the
hands of the Apostles, offered money to them if they
would confer it on him, and thus secure him the same
wonderful endowments. The secret was out. Christianity
had proved a serious rival to his magic, in the popular
esteem, and this meant loss of gain, but he might hope to
win back his former prestige, if, like the Christian leaders,
he could do miracles. His *Simony*, however, met its deserved punishment, and we hear no more of him in the
New Testament. Could it be, that he was the chief of
that movement which Pilate trampled out so bloodily at
Tiranatha ? Tradition appears to show that he really was
so; and that he had set himself to initiate a counter
movement to that of Christ, and exalt himself by thus
taking advantage of the popular ferment respecting the
Messiah, in the mind of the Samaritans.

From Samaria Philip passes, in the narrative of the
Acts, to "the way that goes down from Jerusalem to
Gaza, which is desert," words that do not now admit of
easy application, since there were several ways to the old
Philistine city from Jerusalem,—one by Ramleh, another
by Beth-Shemesh, and the third by Hebron and Beit

[1] Jos., *Ant.* xx. 7, 2 ; Just. Mart., *Apol.* i. 26 ; *Clement. Hom.* ii. 22.

Gebrin, a great part of which, as I can testify, is down rough hill-tracks, where there is profound loneliness and no population. By whatever route he travelled, however, his journey yielded an indication of the mighty future before Christianity, in the baptism of an Ethiopian magnate—the head treasurer of Candace, queen of the Ethiopian kingdom of Meroë. This may be said to have been in the district of Khartoum, though its capital, Napata, stood somewhere about the site of the present Dongola; the two places thus marking the beginning and end of the great bend of the Nile, about half-way on which, Berber stands. The name Candace was that of the royal line, being borne by successive queens; for the kingdom was governed by female rulers as late as the time of Eusebius of Cæsarea, who died about the year A.D. 340.

Being a eunuch, the traveller could not have been a full member of the Jewish community,[1] but only " a proselyte of the gate; " that is, he could not go inside the gate of the Temple. He had come to Jerusalem, however, to worship; thanks, perhaps, to the teaching of some far - wandered Jew, in his home at Napata. He had with him a roll of the great prophet Isaiah, and was reading it as he sat in his chariot, no doubt from the Greek version, which was made in Egypt, in which Greek was the current language of the ruling class, and thus must have made its way up the Nile. Gaza, to which he was going, is still the largest town in the south of Palestine, and the road to Egypt still runs through it.

Orientals are accustomed to read aloud, even when they are alone, and it was usual for a Jew, or one who had

[1] Deut. xxiii. 1.

virtually become so, to read from the Scriptures when
travelling, to beguile the way; for the sacred writings,
in some part of them, were, we may say, the one book a
Jew of that age would open; all others being proscribed
as heathen, or concerned with subjects related to heathen
studies.

Going alongside the chariot, therefore, Philip, with the
freedom of Eastern manners, having heard what he was
reading, asked him if he understood it. Seeing, from the
air of the questioner, and perhaps from his being a Jew,
that he could probably help him, the great man, forthwith, begged him to come up into the chariot. A rabbi
was regarded as one to be honoured above all men, however poor he might be, as, at present, a *hakeem*, or savant,
is free to all circles in the East, on the ground of his
assumed knowledge.

Ere long, the comments of Philip were, we are told, so
effective in applying the words of the prophet to the
crucified Jesus of Nazareth, that the eunuch asked to be
baptized in His name; baptism having been appointed by
Christ as the formal expression, by all who might join
His new society, of their having done so, and being
henceforth publicly known as His followers. Washing,
or bathing, had always had a place in Judaism, in its
many purifications, but the use of these had greatly
increased since the return from Babylon. A bath was
required from the strict Jew before private devotion and
before entering the house of public prayer, or the Temple,
or a synagogue, and, hence, places for religious uses were
built beside flowing water.[1] The adoption of baptism by
John, and afterwards by Christ, was, therefore, natural,

[1] Acts xvi. 13.

and would excite no opposition on the ground of novelty. In the pass by which Gaza is reached from Hebron there is a fine spring, flowing out of the limestone on the right hand of the track, and now offering grateful refreshment to the traveller. Perhaps it was at this they stopped, for, seeing water, the eunuch asked Philip if he could not be, there and then, baptized. The stream may, perhaps, have been dammed back at the time, to collect the means of irrigation; and, indeed, there are, even now, dams across the little valley to retain the surplus water of the rainy months.

This triumph of wide Christian charity won, Philip seems to have devoted himself to missionary work in the Phœnician towns on the sea-coast plains, for we find him presently at Azotus, or Ashdod, and, afterwards, permanently settled in Cæsarea.

Another incident of a little later date shows Peter to have been no less active in widening the door of hope for other races than the Jew, though his hereditary narrowness required special enlightenment, before it could rise to the Christian liberality in which Stephen and Philip found their natural sphere, and ere long seems to have, once more, in some measure, shrunk into its old limits.[1] St. Paul had been won for Christ about the time when Caligula ascended the throne,[2] and the peace which followed for a time, after his accession, the flight from Jerusalem of the hated Hellenist Christians, the agony of the closing half of the reign, and, possibly, also, the conversion of the chief agent in the persecution,[3] gave the Christians a fresh breathing time, during which they spread their congregations over a number of the towns

---

[1] Acts ix. 32 ff.   [2] March 16, A.D. 37.   [3] Gal. i. 13, 14.

and villages of Judæa. Matters had at last prospered so greatly, that Peter, who, with the other Apostles, had till now remained unmolested, as unoffending Jews, in Jerusalem, set out on a short tour through the district within easy reach of the city, and thus came "down" to Lydda, among other places.

The Hebrew name Lod[1] had taken the Greek form Lydda, then a half-town-like village, though it now has, by the last numbering, only about 1300 inhabitants. It stood, and still stands, nine miles from Jaffa, the ancient Joppa, on the road from Jerusalem to Cæsarea. Orchards, of the poor kind one meets in the East, encircle it, with an intermixture of gardens, on all sides but the east, for more than a mile, the hills coming close on the east side; but the village is squalid and decaying. Its great feature is the ruined church of St. George, built during the Crusades, most of the site of which has been taken for a mosque. Palm-trees, bearing no dates so far north, rise gracefully over it; and there is a large well at the edge of the houses, while the fine plain around, looks, in summer, with its varied crops, like the rich landscapes of an English county. In Peter's day, the village was, no doubt, more thriving than it is now, and among its charms for the apostle, it could boast one of the earliest Christian congregations.

Curiously, Lydda is now especially marked by the great number of blind persons in it, the common saying being that in Lydda every man is blind, or has at most only one eye. Here, Peter, we are told, healed a man with the Greek name Æneas, though doubtless a Jew, of a palsy, by which he had been helplessly bedridden for

[1] Neh. vii. 37.

eight years; a miracle so wonderful as to lead to a great
spread of the faith in the neighbourhood.

It had already taken root in the old seaport of Joppa,
and now, while Peter was still at Lydda, was visited by
a trial which led to the apostle's going to that place.
Among the little band of Christians found in its very
mixed population, there had been one Tabitha, a Jewess,
of course, worthy of the name she bore, which means
"the Gazelle," or, in Greek, "Dorcas." Whether she was
a widow or a spinster is not told us; but, in either case,
she had a loving heart, which delighted in deeds of tenderness worthy of a follower of Christ.

Most of the little Christian community in Joppa would
be from the very humblest of the town; for St. Paul tells
us that everywhere they were, mainly, such as the higher
classes called "weak," "base," "despised," and as only
deserving contempt. There was ample room, therefore,
for pitying love, in making garments for both men and
women, including both outer and inner clothing, and to
this grateful charity Dorcas gave herself. But now this
benefactress, perhaps the only well-to-do member of the
little community, had died.

Peter was at Lydda, only a few miles off, and had just
raised Æneas from an eight-year-long palsy. Might not
he bring back the dear one to them? They would try.
Coming at once, at their urgent request, the lost one was,
we are told, presently restored to life.

Such a miracle would soon spread through the little
town, and naturally led to many joining the Christians.
Anxious to follow up the impression made by the raising
of Dorcas, Peter was in no haste to leave Joppa, but
stayed "many days" there It was the single natural

port of Palestine, though only a poor one at any time, owing to the ledges of rock which run out across the mouth of the little harbour, making it necessary, even now, that anything larger than a boat, lie out in the roads, exposed to sudden storms.

The town stands on the slope of a little hill, up which

The (so-called) House of Simon, the Tanner, at Joppa.

its flat-roofed houses rise in terrace after terrace, separated only by the narrow, windowless lanes, which, in the East, serve for streets. Along the shore, other streets were more open, but, in Peter's day, one spot, at least, was looked upon as to be avoided by strict Jews; a tannery having been established at it, making it ceremonially "unclean."[1]

---

[1] A tanner was, from his trade, almost an outcast. "Woe to him," says the Talmud, "who is a tanner!"

It was now occupied by one Simon,—a namesake, it will be noticed, of the apostle,—and, with him, of all men, in spite of his despised trade, Peter took up his abode. His narrow Jewish ideas were evidently relaxing, through the loving influence of his new creed, which—as he was, in the end, to learn - taught that God was no respecter of persons, but accepted every one, of any race or calling, who feared God and wrought righteousness.

As in India, at this day, tanneries were not allowed among the Jews inside a town, a space of fifty cubits' distance from the walls being imposed on "corpses, graves, and tanneries." Nearness to the sea was, moreover, an advantage for the easy removal of offensive waste.

About thirty miles north of Joppa, and a little over fifty, north-west of Jerusalem, lay the famous port of Cæsarea, built by Herod the Great, and named after the Emperor Augustus, or, rather, in honour of him. It was the Roman capital of the sub-province of Judæa, and the residence of the procurators, or, as we should call them, lieutenant-governors, who held office under the viceroy, or, as we might say, governor-general, of the great province of Syria.

Till Herod's day, there had been no fitting port to receive the fleets coming from the west, or south, to Palestine, now a part of the world-wide empire of Rome; but the energy and ability of the Jewish king had, in twelve years, created a splendid city, with a double harbour, where there had been only a useless ledge of rock, washed by the waves. Broad quays, fine bazaars for trade, noble public buildings, commodious streets, lofty barracks for sailors, and a palace used by the procurators when they afterwards appeared; a huge open-air theatre

on the hills north of the city, and a circus a thousand
feet long in its ellipse, on the east of the town; the whole
adorned with many statues and lavish ornamentation,—
showed what despotic power could do, in the hands of a
strong intellect and splendid energy.

The population, as was to be expected, was very mixed;
half of it being Jewish, and the other half made up of
Greeks, Syrians, Phœnicians, and a motley gathering from
all parts of the Roman and Eastern world. It had, also,
a garrison of considerable size, of which, when St. Peter
was at Joppa, on the death of Dorcas, a cohort known
as the "Italian," and numbering, apparently, about six
hundred men, formed a part. Most of the troops in
Palestine were local levies, just as, in India, native troops
form the bulk of the imperial forces; but this cohort
seems to have consisted of Italians, perhaps to form a
more imposing bodyguard to the procurator.

The officers of such a regiment would naturally be, in
keeping with its standing, men of substance and family.
Among them was one Cornelius, a member, that is, of the
aristocratic "gens Cornelia," a noble and distinguished
family of Rome. Like many others in that age, he had
become dissatisfied with heathenism, and attracted by the
Jewish doctrine of the one God; yet he had not joined
the Mosaic faith, but, while still, in other respects, a
heathen, simply worshipped Jehovah instead of idols.
He was "a devout man," we are told, "and one that
feared God with all his house, who gave much alms to
the people, and prayed to God alway,"—traits which
needed little theology, but were mighty with heaven.

The spread of Christianity had, in all probability, been
a frequent topic in the religious atmosphere such a man

would prefer. In any case, his mind was so full of what he had heard of the new faith, from whatever source, that, while at his evening prayers, in his private chamber, a vision seemed to direct him to send for Peter, from Joppa: the wonderful story of Æneas and Dorcas, having, we may suppose, made him familiar with the name of the apostle, as that of a chief man among the followers of the new Messiah.

Calling two of the soldiers of his household, the centurion ordered them, therefore, to go to Joppa and bring Peter, joining with them a third soldier, his body-servant, who. as he knew, was of his own feelings in religious matters. Thirty miles are more than one day's journey in the East, so that the three had to sleep by the way; but the next day, before they actually got to the town, Peter, having gone up to the quiet of the flat roof, to pray, about noon, a set time of devotion with pious Jews, suddenly fell into a trance, or " ecstasy ; " that is, according to the Greek word, " was beside, or out of, himself," —so raised above his ordinary condition, in fact, that his senses were suspended,—he having, apparently, like many Jews, fasted for some time before. He had indeed asked that food should be prepared, but while it was preparing this exaltation of the faculties came on him.

Presently, it seemed as if a great sheet, filled with " all manner of fourfooted beasts and creeping things of the earth and fowls of the heaven," clean and unclean, were being let down to him from the sky, by cords from the fom corners, and that, with it, there went out a voice, saying, " Rise, Peter; kill and eat." To a strict Jew like him this was a monstrous thought. " Not so. Lord," murmured back the faithful soul ; " for I have never eaten

anything that is common and unclean." But the voice
replied a second and a third time, "What God hath
cleansed, make not thou common." And then the sheet
was drawn up to heaven again.

The arrival of the messengers of Cornelius, presently
threw light on what, in itself, was quite beyond Peter's
comprehension. He was clearly to go and preach the
gospel to the centurion. It is hard for us to understand
the fanatical narrowness of the bigoted Jew, who could
not conceive God as more than the head of his own little
nation, and indifferent toward the whole world beside.
It never entered his mind that a Gentile had any place
in the divine regards, and as to their being accepted by
the Almighty without first becoming Jews,—the very
thought was blasphemy. In the Epistles, the amazement which filled the mind even of St. Paul at a Gentile
being put on the same footing, before heaven, as a Jew,
continually breaks out. It was only, he tells us, by a
special revelation that it was brought home to him " that
the Gentiles are fellow-heirs and fellow-members of the
body, and fellow-partakers of the promise in Christ Jesus,
through the gospel . their being so having been a mystery,
which in other generations was not made known unto the
sons of men." [1]

In due time the apostle, unable to disobey such a
summons, arrived at the quarters of Cornelius, who met
him at his door, with grand politeness, but had to listen
to Peter's apology, as a Jew, for entering his house at
all. It was contrary to the Law, he said, for a Jew to
have anything to do, beyond what was unavoidable, with a
person of any other nation, but in the present case, he came

[1] Eph. iii. 3–6.

in obedience to the evident will of God. The attitude of the Jew toward other races in those times was most insulting. They would not eat with any one but a Jew, or be alone with him, or travel with him, or bring home anything of his that had been lost. All the world, in fact, was rigorously boycotted by a race which, in return, all races alike despised and hated. Peter, the fisherman, would not have crossed the threshold of this illustrious Roman till taught better by a vision from heaven; and the dignitaries who were hounding our Lord to death would not enter the Roman court of justice lest they should be defiled.

In the end, we are informed, Cornelius was brought to see in Jesus of Nazareth, though crucified, the true Messiah of God, and was baptized as an open confessor of faith in Him; Peter thus, with Philip, and others, illustrating the essential universalism of Christianity, in contrast to the narrowness of his ancestral faith.

Yet, strange to say, the apostle was far from maintaining this wideness of mind as a final principle, for we find him "withstood to the face" by St. Paul, for taking the side of bitter Judaizers at Antioch, by refusing to eat with heathen converts, for fear of "the circumcision."[1] Did Paul remind him of the vision at Joppa, or of the incident of Cornelius, or of his own defence of his conduct at Cæsarea, before "the circumcision," that is, the "Hebrews," —in the Jerusalem conference?[2] What could he have said if thus confronted with his past? And how strange that Paul did not refer to the story in his letter to the Galatians, when they were so fiercely rent by the agitation of Judaizing teachers, who claimed to represent St. Peter and the Apostles of the Mother Church of the Holy City?

[1] Gal. ii. 11, 12.   [2] Acts xi. 5 ff.

CHAPTER V

THE appearance of St. Paul marks a new epoch in the advance of Christianity. St. Stephen and St. Philip, among others, had realised its underlying principles, and, in a measure, had nobly carried them out, but it remained for the genius of St. Paul, formally, and for ever, to proclaim its essential distinction from Judaism, of which it had, at first, been silently assumed to be only a new offshoot. He it was who first announced, far and wide, that participation in the new kingdom of God depended solely on spiritual union with Christ, and fearlessly followed this out to the inevitable result, that the Jewish Law was, consequently, not only superfluous, but hurtful. Still more, it was he who first showed how Christianity linked the present life to the life beyond, by revealing Christ as the Great Reconciler of our race to God, as Him through whom men, of all races indifferently, might become members of one great family in heaven and on earth. The universality of the religion of Christ, as opposed to the particularism of the systems of the past, became, through him, an accepted characteristic of Christianity, while his exposition of the relations of man to God, through Christ, gave a permanent outline to Christian theology.

"I am a Jew," said Paul, to the Jerusalem mob, "born
in Tarsus of Cilicia," and this place is elsewhere repeatedly
named as that where he first saw the light.[1] Jerome,
indeed, speaks of him as having been born at Gischala, in
Galilee, and carried by his parents, in infancy, to Tarsus,
but as he connects with this migration a war which can
only be that in which the Jews were finally crushed, the
mention of a birthplace in Palestine must have been an
afterthought of a later age, when such an honour was
created for different Palestine localities, by linking them
with the various leaders of the Apostolic Church.   Though
a Cilician by birth, however, he was able to speak of
himself as "a Hebrew of the Hebrews," that is, of the
purest Hebrew descent, and, as such, one of a household
still using the language of their fathers, and maintaining
a zealous fidelity to the views and observances of "the
straitest sect of their religion."[2] The retention of Aramaic by the Cilician Jews was the more easy, as the
general population spoke a dialect akin to it,[3] enabling
them, without disadvantage, to avoid much use of the
hated heathen Greek, though they needed it for ordinary
intercourse and business.   Like other Jews who lived
among Gentiles, he seems to have had two names given
him ; a Hebrew name, Saul, and a Roman one, Paul ; the
former being always used of him, in the Acts, till he
finally committed himself to missionary work, among
Jews and Gentiles alike.   Similar modifications of names
were indeed common in those days, as we see in that
of Jesus into Jason, or Eliakim into Alkimos, or Simon
into Peter, and in the Greek names of the seven

---

[1] Acts ix. 11 ; xxi. 39 ; xxii. 3.   [2] Acts xxvi. 5.
[3] Pauly's R. Ency., &c., vi. 2, 1616.

"deacons," who must, also, have had Jewish names originally.

The date of the future apostle's birth is not exactly known, but it seems most probable that it was somewhere about the tenth year of our era. He was put to death in A.D. 65, and had spoken of himself, three years before, to Philemon [1] as "Paul, the aged," so that it is hard to imagine him as not at least between fifty and sixty when he died. On the other hand, he is described as a "young man" at the time of the stoning of Stephen, in A.D. 35, and, as that expression meant any age between twenty and thirty, to suppose that he was born not earlier than A.D. 10, would make him twenty-five when he took part in the death of the first martyr. At best, there must be an element of conjecture in the matter, but we cannot be far wrong, one way or other, in fixing on A.D. 10 as the year that saw his birth.

Tarsus, Paul's birthplace, was, in his day, "no mean city." [2] Had the boy delighted in the beauties of nature, of which, however, his letters give no sign, its situation must have made it a Paradise to him Twelve or thirteen miles to the north of the town, rise the great masses of the Taurus chain, towering, huge and dark, peak beyond peak, to 11,000 feet above the level of the sea. From a deep valley in the depths of these gloomy heights the Cydnus river bursts down the southern slopes, rushing in headlong tumult, over rough, descending, ledges, in foaming whirls, till its icy-cold waters, clear as crystal, reach the rich plain at the foot of the mountains, to make their way over it to the sea. Tarsus lies in this magnificent land scape, on the banks of the river, rolling luxuriance of

[1] Ver. 9. [2] Acts xxi. 39.

TARSUS.

M. & N. WILLIAMS'

wood and many-coloured fields stretching far and wide,
girdling, close at hand, a broad reach of multitudinous
orchards and fertile gardens, watered by countless run-
lets from the stream, and never losing their beauty even
in the sultry heat of summer.   In Paul's day, the mouth
of the Cydnus was, moreover, ceaselessly astir with arrivals
and departures of larger and smaller craft, and the passage
of huge rafts of timber from the mountain forests, for
Tarsus was the port of Cilicia.   The waters of the Cydnus
had borne Cleopatra in her gilded barge, with its purple
sails, and silver oars, beating time to flutes and harps, to
beguile the lower nature of Mark Antony, whom she had
come to visit, in the city.   The harbour has long, however, been silted up, and is to-day a marsh, from the
stagnant waters of which, the south wind, in summer,
wafts the terrors of malaria on every side.   Still fair in
its surroundings, Tarsus was much more flourishing two
thousand years ago.   It was then the seat of a great
general commerce; the headquarters of a widely known
guild of weavers, who manufactured the finer and coarser
fabrics, known as "Cilicium," from the softer or rougher
hair of countless goats fed on the mountains; the capital of
the province and a "free city," allowed, through the favour
of Cæsar and Augustus, to govern itself by its own laws,
under magistrates of its own selection.   It was, moreover,
the seat of a celebrated school of philosophy and general
culture; a whole list of distinguished teachers in its
schools, in the apostolic age, being preserved to us by
Strabo.   One writer speaks of its citizens as devoted to
dress, buffoonery, and pride, and spending their lives as
idly as the sea birds over the river waters, but another
extols them as zealous for knowledge: opposing charac-

teiistics, each, no doubt, true of many. The Jewish colony—a large one—in the town, must have been warmly attached to their old mother-city, Jerusalem, for they sent aid to her, when pressed by the Roman legions, in the last great war.[1]

Here, then, on the road which leads from the central plateau of Asia Minor, through the snow-covered summits of the Taurus, rising black below, and glittering with winter above, when I saw them, in the month of April,— in the gay, busy, school-loving Tarsus, amidst a very mixed population of many races, surrounded by keen, trading Hebrews and Gentiles, lean artisans, rich burghers, throngs of students, a Roman garrison with its military music and marchings, a local court, and plentiful folly and display of the gay and idle—grew up the boy Paul. The mountains rose in their bold masses, before his young eyes, seamed by profound gorges; their sides often strangely heaved up at all angles, into a wild confusion and savage roughness. On their upper slopes, full of gloomy caverns, and abounding in wild creatures, hung great oak forests, passing, far above, into sombre stretches of fir and pine; the whole landscape, with its woods, cliffs, glens, frowning peaks, far up the sky, and leaping torrents, hurrying noisily down the ravines and precipitous descents, showing, in its whole character of rude grandeur, why the province had received its name Cilicia, "the rough." Towards the south, the mountains sink, as they approach Tarsus, into picturesque terraces, which thrust their steep walls far out into the plains. "The pass," says Xenophon, "which leads from Cappadocia to Cilicia, is very steep and only wide enough for a single

[1] Furrer, in Schenkel, Art. *Tarsus.*

waggon to get through.   Descending from it, you come to
a great plain, beautiful, rich in water, adorned with trees
of all kinds and countless vineyards, and varied by a succession of fields of sesame, millet of different kinds, wheat,
and barley.   A lofty mountain-chain forms a great natural
fortress round it, on every side.   About twenty-five miles
from the pass, lies Tarsus, a great and flourishing city,
through which flows the Cydnus, in a stream two hundred
feet wide."   Asia Minor, like Italy, is, as a rule, mountainous to the edge of the sea, but Tarsus stands in
open country exceptionally extensive; rolling landscapes
stretching away from it, east and west, for about forty
miles; while, at its broadest, on the east, the plain is nearly
twenty-five miles deep.

The busy community, with its colony of his own people,
for wherever there was trade there were sure to be Jews,
and with its numerous "schools" of different sects of
philosophy, was still intensely heathen, when Paul was
a child.   It had its oracle, and Apollo, whose sword was
shown, miraculously kept bright, was seen on many of its
coins.   A statue held to represent Sardanapalus, the reputed founder of the city, at Anchiale, fifteen miles to the
west, on the sea-shore, must have been well known to the
boy, for it was a local boast,—showing the Great King,
snapping his fingers, while underneath his figure was the
inscription, "Eat, drink, and make love; nothing else
is worth while,"—but the image was, in fact, that of the
local god of war and fire.   Idolatry, indeed, was rampant
in Tarsus, and, doubtless, kindled that abhorrence for it,
in the Jewish quarter, which was caught by Paul, and
marks his letters on every page.   The Sun-god was the
central object of worship; the wildest and most lascivious

orgies marking his festivals. A "king of the feast" led the processions, and, at their close, was, in some places, burned alive to the god, though, in Tarsus, a lay figure was substituted. Everything which the prophets had most bitterly denounced, was constantly thrust on the sight of the Jewish citizens, quickening their zeal for their own faith, and putting far from them any thought of assimilation to the Gentile. There were no Hellenists among them, as there were in other places. Hence Paul only reproduced the spirit of those among whom he grew up, when he declares that he was "exceedingly zealous for the traditions of his fathers."[1] That a community thus intensely Jewish, should have supplied many pilgrims to the feasts at Jerusalem; that so many of them should have removed to the Holy City as to have a synagogue of their own; that the sister of Paul should have married there, and that Paul should, himself, have been sent there, to be trained up as a rabbi, was only what might have been expected. The atmosphere which the child breathed is, indeed, seen in the proud repetition by him of the glories of his race, as he must often have heard them vaunted under his father's roof. "They were Israelites;" the proudest of names; theirs were the adoption by Jehovah as His sons; the glory that had covered the peaks of Sinai; the Covenants of everlasting love made with them by the Eternal; the Giving of the Law, by the hand of angels, amidst the blasts of the trump of God; the holy ordinances of the Temple worship and ministrations, appointed according to the direct instructions of the Eternal, by the mouth of prophets; the Divine Promises, vouchsafed to Israel alone, of all the

[1] Gal. i. 14.

nations of the earth, that God would ever bless it—that
the Messiah would come from the root of David, and that
the sun and the moon would fail before Israel would be
forgotten by the Most High, or cease to be His peculiar
regard ; theirs, finally, were the Fathers—Abraham, with
whom Jehovah spoke in the door of his tent; Jacob-
Israel, who wrestled with the angel of the Lord and
prevailed, and all the illustrious names of a splendid
history, adorned by prophets, mighty warriors, kings, and
famous priests; men among whom they could name, beside others hardly less exalted, heroes of God like Moses,
and Aaron, and David, and the noble roll of the Maccabees.[1]
But, if enthusiastic pride of race thus swelled up in the
heart of Paul, passionate love of one's nation could not rise
higher than when, in after years, forgetting the long relent-
less proscription and persecution by which his countrymen
had embittered his life, he to whom Christ was all in all
for time and eternity, cries out in sublime self-sacrifice, "I
could wish that I, myself, were anathema for Christ, for
my brethren's sake, my kinsmen according to the flesh."[2]
A reflection, this, of the love " that passeth knowledge ! "

Brought up in a circle so intensely national, alike in its
aspirations and religion, the early training of Paul must
have been sedulously Jewish.   He would learn to speak
Greek, from its being the language of all around, but we
cannot fancy his being sent to any school taught by a
heathen.   That he wrote his Epistles in Greek, is no
evidence to the contrary, for his Greek is not that of a
regular educated scholar, but, rather, such as one would
use who had caught the language from conversation.   It
has ever been thought that his constant use of an

[1] Rom. ix. 4, 5.   [2] Rom. ix. 3.

amanuensis may have risen from his want of skill in
writing the Greek characters, and that he apologises for
the rudeness of those in the paragraph he personally added
in his letter to the Galatians, when he says, "See with
how large letters I have written to you, with my own
hand." [1]   Whereas, moreover, he is lavish in quotations
from the Scriptures, the only ones he gives from Greek
authors are mere proverbial expressions, which needed no
acquaintance with the literature of the language.   There
are, indeed, only three, " A prophet of their own said,
Cretans are always liars, evil beasts, idle gluttons" [2]—
" As certain even of your own poets have said, For we
are also His offspring " [3]—" Evil company corrupts good
manners." [4]   Had he been at home in the wondrous
literature of Greece, is it conceivable that he would never
have availed himself of the many passages in the trage-
dians or poets, which would have enforced the lessons of
Christianity?   Greek, in fact, was detested by the strict
Jew, except as an unavoidable medium of general intercourse, or in the form of the Greek Bible, which even
such households as those of the Jews of Tarsus used, or in
the apocryphal books of Jewish literature, then in fashion.
Of Greek literature in the ordinary sense they were
proud to know nothing; the abhorrence of it, as heathen,
leading, in the end, during the last war, to its formal prohibition; the rabbis issuing a command that no child
should learn Greek.[5]   We may, therefore, take in a literal
sense, his declaration to the Corinthians, that his absorp-

---

[1] Gal. vi. 11.   [2] Titus i. 12.   [3] Acts xxvii. 28.

[4] 1 Cor. xv. 33.   Callimachus, Hymn, *in Jov.* 8 ; Cleanthes, Hymn, *in
Jov.* 5.   Alexander, *Thais.*   The quotations are found, even now, in each
case, in two poets, and were mere commonplaces of the day.

[5] Hamburger ii. 315.

tion in the great interests of the faith made all things
else indifferent, and gave him a dislike to all rhetorical
"speech or wisdom;" determining him to know nothing
among them but his crucified Lord.   In this, however,
the child must have been the father of the man, for if he
had been enriched by wide Greek culture in his early
years, it would have been a help, rather than a hindrance,
to his effective presentation of the claims of Christianity.

We may be sure, therefore, that he was sent to some
Jewish school, perhaps in the synagogue or, at least,
beside it, where, as Eastern children are taught now, he
would learn, from the recitation of his master, line after
line of the Law and the Prophets, writing them down as
they were spoken on a slate-like board, as, along with the
other children, he sat on the floor of the schoolroom; all
the scholars repeating, over and over, with fearful din,
what they had thus set down, till it was for ever fixed in
their memory.   I watched the little folks in just such a
school, at "Cana of Galilee," and could readily understand
that, if the Law, instead of the Koran, had been the text-
book, the scholars would inevitably have known it for life
as Paul knew it, word by word.   The passion for educat-
ing their children, in their own sense of education, was
absorbing, among all Jews.   They believed that the breath
of school children was sweeter to God, than the odours of
sacrifices on the smoking altar.[1]   Every synagogue, as far
as possible, had a schoolroom connected with it.   The
reader of the synagogue was often the teacher.   The
teaching given is implied in one name for the school
being, "The house of the Book," that is, of the Law.
As soon as the child could speak, it was to be taught

[1] Hamburger ii. 1103.

sentences of the Prayers, but it was not to be sent to school
before it was six years old.   Yet when school attendance
began, at last, it was a serious matter, of at least five
hours a day.   Little Paul had a weekly holiday, however,
on Fridays, and there was no school on the day before a
feast.   Fathers held it their daily pleasure, to lead their
sons to school; a sweet custom, to which, in after years,
Paul looks back, where he speaks of the Law having been
our conductor to Christ.[1]   It throws a curious light on
these old days, to read that scholars were forbidden to
overwhelm the teacher with questions, especially with
such as were outside the instruction of the school, or to
argue points with him; a prohibition that shows what disputing and challenging there must have been in the synagogues, when all the tongues of such loquacious Orientals
were let freely loose.   It was a law that rich and poor
should be treated absolutely alike by the teacher.

The son of a father of the tribe of Benjamin, proud of
his pure Jewish blood; all that was fitting, in a household
firm in the traditions of Judaism, would be carried out
towards Paul.   He would, of course, be circumcised on
the eighth day,[2] for he was the son of a pure Jewess
mother, and no half Jew.   He would first speak "the
tongue of Paradise," not that of the heathen, and be carefully trained at the knees of his father and mother, in all
the "righteousness" of the Pharisees, which they and he
then thought the highest aim in life, but which he was to
regard in later years as worse than worthless.[3]   He would
thus grow up, from childhood, a zealot for the extremest
Judaism.   "I advanced," says he, to the Galatians, "in
the Jews' religion, beyond many of mine own age, among

---

[1] Gal. iii. 24.   [2] Phil. iii. 5.   [3] Phil iii. 8.

my countrymen, being more exceedingly zealous" (than
they) "for the traditions of my fathers." [1]   His whole life,
indeed, from the first, would be netted over by religious
observances.   There were services in the synagogue every
day, but those on Monday, Thursday, and Sabbath, when
the Law was read, were especially sacred.   He had already, when five years old, been made to read what he
could of the Law, at home, and not much later would be
brought to the synagogue, at the three hours of prayer,
which took the place, among the Jews out of Palestine,
of the three daily offerings in the Temple.   Gradually, at
school, and in the family, he would grow more and more
versed in the minutest details of Pharisaic theology and
rules of life, by reading the Law, seeking explanations of
its every line, and taking part in the endless discussions
thus raised.

In such a strenuously orthodox household, the supreme
ambition of the parents was to see one of their sons a
rabbi, and the bright, energetic, and disputatious boy, who
was their pride, seemed, alike in his tastes, and special
mental and moral characteristics, destined by nature for
a "master in Israel."   It was, therefore, determined that
he should be sent to Jerusalem, the centre of rabbinical
education, and the sacred home of that Temple, in
which the Jew believed Jehovah still sat between the
cherubim, in the awful darkness of the Holy of Holies.
Had not the prophet said that "out of Zion should
go forth the Law, and the Word of Jehovah from Jerusalem"? [2] and what could this mean, but that it should
be the great seminary of the faith, whence duly trained
rabbis should go out to all the dispersed of Israel over the

[1] Gal. i. 14.   [2] Micah iv. 2.

world, and even proclaim, triumphantly, to the heathen, the glories of Judaism, and bring them, as captives to it, to worship on the holy mountain ? The family could afford the outlay, and to Jerusalem, therefore, Paul must go, to win his degree as a teacher of the Law, in the great university of the Jewish race. He had been born, as I have said, apparently, in the first decade of our era, perhaps about A.D. 10, and the fitting time for his being entered in the rabbinical schools was at the close of his twelfth year, so that he would probably leave his father's house on his long journey, in charge, we may suppose, of some of the many friends who went up from Tarsus to the great feasts. He had a married sister in the Holy City, and it may be the boy found a home under her roof;[1] his future Lord being then an obscure villager, working, day by day, in His lowly carpenter's arch, at Nazareth. The incident of the visits of Jesus to the rabbinical schools in the Temple grounds, fourteen years before throws light on Paul's daily life in them. Seated, with his fellows, in half-moon rows, on the floor, with a cluster of rabbis on seats or cushions before them, he would read prescribed passages from the Law, listen to the exposition of them from the masters, and freely ask explanations, or even enter into discussions with them and his fellow-scholars, on what was said. Instruction was given by catechetical exercises and frank discussions, as I saw in the Arab university at Cairo; old and young, alike, being questioned, and answering with a republican indiscriminacy which would horrify our professors. The transcription of the holy writings would, moreover, occupy much time daily, while a record of the opinions of the rabbis of the past,

[1] Acts xxiii. 16.

announced as the grounds of every exposition advanced in the schools, would leave very little time for relaxation. Diligence in such studies and labours had, for their prospective reward, the possible obtaining some office in the community, and a seat and vote in some local sanhedrim, if not even in that of Jerusalem. A specially successful student, might, indeed, rise to be the ruler of a synagogue, or, possibly, to see himself head of the local Jewish community, while his highest promotion left him unaffected in his relations to his father's house, his special lay calling, or his own household. In the eager circle round him, the young lad would necessarily be absorbed in the school life, which was their world, just as Oxford or Cambridge, in one interest or other, monopolises the existence of the beautiful young life that gives such a charm to both. Even the Puritans, though hard Western men, caught the spell of the inspired writings on which their thoughts habitually dwelt, till their spoken and written language, and the whole cast of their life, were coloured by the imagery and sacred incidents of the old Hebrew seers and poets, and it was, inevitably, in the highest degree thus, with Paul. Living, moreover, among a people to whom the sacred books were the only literature deemed worthy of their regard, and whose religious services continually carried them back to the great forefathers of their race, all nature gradually became an aid to devotion, for the stars in every land recalled the vision of Abraham, and a chance grove, the tamarisks he planted, and under which he pitched his tent and entertained angels, at Beersheba. Their memories dwelt with intense self-complacency on the long roll-call of worthies, and the transcendent events of their past history—the venerable patriarchs, the great Lawgiver, who spoke with Jehcvah, "as a man talks with his friend;" the wonders of Sinai, the dividing of the sea before the footsteps of their fathers, the marvels of the forty years in the wilderness, and all the amazing story from that day, through century after century. Paul's mind must have been saturated with every detail of the history of his people, and written over, as it were, like a palimpsest, with the words which had come from the very lips of God, to his race, alone, among men. It was only to be expected, then, that when he came to write, his reminiscences of Scripture language and events, and of the rabbinical glosses and exposition, which, from childhood, had been their scarcely less Divine accompaniments, should continually mark his style.

These constantly recurring quotations and allusions are taken, with equal frequency, from the Law and from the Prophets, and he also delights in citing from the Psalms. As a rule, he uses the text of the Greek Bible, as was natural, since, in his day, the original Hebrew needed, everywhere, to be translated, for almost all Jews, in this, resembled Josephus, who, though a Jew of Jerusalem, uses the Septuagint. Yet Paul shows that he knew the old Hebrew text, by turning to it when the Greek version is defective, and the Hebrew serves his purpose better.[1] But he did not confine his studies to the

[1] Examples of this are seen in 1 Cor. xiv. 21, where the Epistle reads, "By men of strange tongues, and by the lips of strangers will I speak to this people; and not even thus will they hear Me, saith the Lord;" the Greek rendering being, "By reason of the contemptuous words of the lips, by means of another language . . . but they would not hear" (Isa xxviii. 11). So, Gal. iii. 11, Sept., "The righteous shall live by faith;" Heb., "The righteous shall live by my faith." So, Rom. ix. 17, he has, "Did I raise thee up?" instead of the Sept., "Hast thou been preserved?" the emendation of Paul supporting his doctrine of predestination. But in

canonical books, in Hebrew and Greek; the religious
writings of the time, in Greek, composed by Hellenistic
Jews, were familiar to him, as is shown, especially, by
frequent correspondences in expression with the Book of
Wisdom, composed in Alexandria, according to Schürer,
somewhere between B.C. 190 to 170, but, according to
others, immediately before our era.[1]

But, conscious or unconscious imitation of rabbinical
writings, phrases, modes of thought, and turns of expression, were only a small result of his long attendance in
the schools of Jerusalem. His mind, as was inevitable,
had, like the fuller's hand, been subdued to what it had
so long "worked in." The Epistles, once and again, show
the influence of rabbinical teaching, by the adoption of
some of its amplifications of the narrative of Scripture,
and by the use of rabbinical allegories; a form of argument much in favour among the Jewish doctors. Thus

2 Cor. iv. 13, he quotes the incorrect text of the Greek (Ps. cxvi. 10), "I
believe, and therefore did I speak," instead of the Hebrew, "believe, for
I will speak" (R.V., which is correct).

[1] Compare Wis. ii. 24 and Rom. v. 12, Wis. iii. 8, and Matt. xix. 28, 1 Cor.
vi. 2. In Wis. v. 17 we have, " He shall put on righteousness as a breastplate, and true judgment instead of a helmet. He shall take holiness for
an invincible shield, and whet His wrath for a sword ;" words reminding
us of Eph. vi. 14, and 1 Thess. v. 8. So, Wis. xv. 7 says, "For the potter
. . . of the same clay maketh both the vessels that serve for clean uses,
and also all such as serve to the contrary ; but what is the use of either
part, the potter himself is the judge." Comp. Rom. ix. 21. I have
translated the Greek for the benefit of the general reader. The noble passage, "Things which eye saw not, and ear heard not, and which entered not
into the heart of man, whatsoever things God prepared for them that love
Him," is attributed by Origen to an "Apocalypse of Elias," now lost
(1 Cor. ii. 9) ; the only verse at all resembling it in the Old Testament
doing so very faintly (Isa. lxiv. 4). Parallels between the Epistles and
the words of the rabbis, moreover, as might have been expected, abound
(see Eisenmenger ii. 239).

we read[1] that the rock which Moses struck in Sinai,
bringing water from it, to supply the tribes, was not a
natural but "a spiritual rock;" in fact, was the Messiah,
and that it followed them, thenceforward, through their
long wanderings; an embellishment of the sacred story
borrowed from the rabbis, but a physical impossibility,
since the country rises some thousand feet between Sinai
and Palestine. In the same way he speaks of the law,
when given at Sinai, having been "ordained through
angels;" a rabbinical addition to Scripture.[2] Like the
rabbis, he speaks, also, of the third and the seventh
heavens—the "paradise" of the Jewish schools.[3] Alle-
gorising interpretation, which had risen originally among
the Alexandrian Jews, but had been adopted by those of
Palestine, is also introduced by him, to illustrate and
prove his arguments, apparently on the principle, held
by the rabbis, that any spiritual "accommodation" of Scripture was valid, however foreign to the natural sense. In
this way, he turns the strife between Sarah and Hagar,
into an allegorical picture of the relations between the old
Covenant and the new. "Which things," says he, "contain an allegory: for these women are two covenants;
one, from Mount Sinai, bearing children unto bondage,
which is Hagar. Now, this Hagar is Mount Sinai, in
Arabia, and answereth to the Jerusalem that now is; for
she is in bondage with her children. But the Jerusalem that is above, is free, which is our mother."[4]
He does not even say that these words may be
used as an allegory, but treats the hidden sense he
draws from them as divinely embodied and intended.

[1] 1 Cor. x. 4. [2] Gal. iii. 19.
[3] 2 Cor. xii. 2, 4. [4] Gal. iv. 24, 26.

"These women," he says, "*are* two covenants" In support of his reference to the heavenly Jerusalem, moreover, he quotes, just as a rabbi would have done, words
which, as they stand in the text from which they are
taken, have no apparent connection with the subject.
They are addressed by Isaiah,[1] in anticipation, to the then
ruined and desolate Jerusalem, ere long to be rebuilt
by the returning exiles, but have no reference, so far as
appears, to the Jerusalem above. " Rejoice," says he, "thou
barren, that bearest not; break forth and cry, thou that
travailest not: for more are the children of the desolate
than of her who has the husband,"—the version quoted
being the Greek, not the inspired Hebrew. Isaac and
Ishmael are, further, used as types of Christians and unbelieving Jews respectively, and the duty of putting away
hurtful Jewish influence from the Galatian churches is
urged as required by Scripture, since it says, respecting
Ishmael—the verse being given freely, and not strictly
according to either the Greek or the Hebrew—"Cast out
the handmaid and her son, for the son of the handmaid
shall not inherit with the son of the free woman." In
quite rabbinical style, moreover, he sees divinely designed
types of Christian truth in the incidental events of old
Jewish history. Melchisedec is an ordained foreshadow
ing of Christ; the Wilderness journeys furnish many
parallels to the Christian life, not merely illustrative, but
predestined; the whole Old Testament history, in fact, is
a series of ordained prefigurations of the new economy
But perhaps we may regard the constant allusions to
Jewish history in the epistles as, in some cases at least,
rather illustrations confirmatory of his statements than

[1] Isa. liv. 1.

II.   G

inspired prototypes of the distant future, just as we use
references to historical parallels in the writings of to-day.

The rabbi whose teaching the young Paul especially
sought was, he tells us, Gamaliel.   But he must have
attended other rabbis than one so mild and reasonable in
his relations to Christianity, to have preserved the zealot
fanaticism he had brought from Tarsus so perfectly as his
bearing in the death of St. Stephen, and the subsequent
persecution, manifests.   Young men change their feelings
very much in changing their teachers, and the gentleness
of the man who taught that the doctrine of tithes was not
to be pushed too far, and kept the Sadducees from killing
the Apostles, since their teaching would come to nothing
if it were not from God, may well have been exchanged,
at a later time, for the bigotry of the opposite school, to
which heresy-hunting was the most imperative duty of
religion.   The liberal spirit of the grandson of Hillel may
have played its part in moulding the future apostle, but
he would easily have his furious narrowness roused again
by a passing intimacy with the school of Schammai.   The
hatred between the two parties—the liberal Pharisees of
the school of Hillel and Gamaliel, and the gloomy zealots
of the school of Schammai—need not have hindered him
from catching features of character from both.

How long Paul stayed at this time in Jerusalem is not
known, but he must have been out of Palestine during
the public life of the Baptist, since he never even alludes
to him, and, also, during the public life and the fatal
close of the career of our Lord.   We know this, from his
ascribing to those who had seen Christ "after the flesh,"
a privilege of which he could not boast.[1]   In the laments

[1] 2 Cor. v. 16.

of his later years over his furious hatred of the religion
he subsequently so zealously embraced, we find, moreover,
that he bewails only his hostility to the Christian congregations, while he speaks of Christ Himself as unknown
to him, till divinely revealed in the vision on the way to
Damascus.[1]

Is it too much to suppose that, before John had
appeared, Paul, then in the fiery glow of early youth,
may, like other Pharisees, have returned to Tarsus, in his
eagerness to carry out the idea so dear to his party, of
gaining converts to Judaism from the heathen of his
native city ? We know that many of his party passed
feverishly from land to land, eager to win even a single
proselyte; that, by the enthusiastic labours of many such
emissaries, bodies of allies might be created in all the
provinces of the Empire, to rise in universal insurrection,
when the hour came for a world-wide outbreak which
should overthrow Rome, and make Jerusalem, in its stead,
the capital of an all-embracing empire, under the conquering glory of the daily-expected Messiah.   It was perhaps
at Tarsus that Paul learned the trade of tent-making,
which he afterwards practised; in accordance with the
rule that all Jews, but especially rabbis, should secure
their future independence by having a recognised calling.
Weaving tent-cloth from the hair of the goats fed in
great numbers on the mountains behind Tarsus, has been
thought the craft to which the eager young Pharisee gave
himself, but it appears more probable that he rather made
tents from cloth already woven, as we find him at work
in places where the raw hair would hardly have been

[1] Gal. i. 13, 15 f.; 1 Cor. xv. 8, 9 ; Phil. iii. 6 ; Acts ix. 5 ; xxii. 8 ;
xxvi. 15 ; 1 Tim. i. 13.

plentiful: as, for example, at Corinth,[1] Ephesus,[2] and elsewhere.[3] If he left his Jerusalem "college life," after spending four or five years at the "schools" he would have been absent from Palestine during the ministry of the Baptist and of our Lord, and in such an outburst of early missionary enthusiasm, would have been carrying out the work which would most strongly recommend him to the favour of his party. We see, indeed, how, in his riper years, he shows an inability to settle down in any one spot; his restless yearning for the wide spread of the faith, constantly leading him, when he had broken ground in any fresh locality, and sown what he so earnestly believed " the good seed," to go off and renew the same course elsewhere, as soon as his labours had taken root, and in some measure promised future independent vigour. We find, in keeping with this, traces in his epistles,[4] of his having been an eager preacher of Judaism in his youth, and we know that he was among the foremost of its defenders in the Hellenist synagogues of Jerusalem, through the heated months of discussion with St. Stephen, which ended in that hero's martyrdom. Tarsus, as his mother city, was always near his heart, and there was a more inviting field for proselytism in the varied population of Cilicia than at the centre of Judaism, under the shadow of the Temple, where the religion of his fathers was upheld and championed by so many teachers, and by the traditions of so many past generations of rabbis. The towns and villages dotting the great landscape, from the foot of the mountains to the sea, would give him ample fields for his

---

[1] Acts xviii. 3. [2] Acts xx. 34.
[3] 1 Cor. iv. 12; 1 Thess. ii. 9; 2 Thess. iii. 8.
[4] Gal. v. 11, with Meyer's remarks.

youthful ardour as " a Pharisee of the Pharisees," in trying
to win converts to Judaism. and, little as he thought it,
such missionary efforts would be an admirable preparation for the time when he would as zealously strive to
pull down the idols of his youth, as he now was to secure
their wide triumph.

His prolonged absence from Palestine had the further
quite inestimable advantage, of keeping him from any
share in the awful scenes of Pilate's judgment-hall and
Golgotha.   Thanks to this, he was not among the rabble
of high and low who cried " Crucify Him! crucify Him!"
and had not the intolerable reproach on his conscience,
of having had any share in the condemnation of Him
whom he so soon after recognised as the glorified Messiah.
Had he been guilty of the blood of his Lord, we must
have found him uttering the bitterest self reproaches for
the awful offence, but instead of this, he turns against
" the rulers of this world" with the fearful accusation
that they had "crucified the Lord of Glory." [1]   Moreover, even had he dared to speak thus, while yet a party
to the death of the Baptist or our Lord, his enemies
would assuredly have exposed his hypocrisy, in assailing
others for what he himself had approved and promoted.
That such a reproach was never cast at him, is a con-
clusive proof that he had borne no part either in the
opposition to the Baptist, or in the deadly strife between
Jesus and the Pharisees.

That Paul should have been a child of cities, rather
than of a country hamlet or village; that he should,
moreover, have grown to manhood, first in a great heathen
community, among the families of the Dispersion, and,

[1] 1 Cor. ii. 8 ; 1 Thess. ii. 15.

then, in the close atmosphere of the rabbinism of Jerusalem, inevitably coloured his modes of thought, as well as
his whole moral and mental nature. On every page, his
letters show traces of his having lived, habitually, amidst
the stir of city activities. Contrast them with the Sermon
on the Mount, and it is at once felt, that, while Christ
draws His imagery from a life spent amidst the hills, and
in the open country, with its pastures, fields, and gardens,
and its simple rural communities, or amid the varied
landscapes of the Sea of Galilee, Paul writes as one bred
in the streets of a great town, amidst the busy concourse
drawn to them from all parts. As Jesus speaks to the
crowds, from the mountain or the waters of the lake
beside which He lived, or in the lonely " desert," Paul
chooses, through life, like a true townsman, the synagogue, the upper chamber, or some quiet retreat in the
humble " Jewish quarter," where he is in the bosom of his
friends. Christ assails the leaders of the nation, and the
sins of the great; Paul wrestles with the sins of the
general community. Jesus avoided Jerusalem; Paul
sought the great cities, wherever he went. As Jesus
draws endless images from nature, so that the lilies of
Galilee shed their perfume, the birds of the air flit past,
the morning red glows, in His discourses, and the fresh
air from the Sea of Gennesareth blows as we read them,
so Paul draws a wealth of illustrations from the daily life
of a Jewish household. The unleavened cakes, and the
lamb, of the Passover ; the nursing mother, and the leaven
on the hearth, furnish him with the comparisons in which
he delights. His town modes of thought are seen in his
allusions to the sentinel at his post, so familiar to one who
must often have seen the military quarters in a great city ;

to the armour and weapons of the soldiery, or the scenes of
the amphitheatre, to which he compares his life, as watched
by angels and men, whom he makes spectators,—like the
great banks of eager lookers-on at the tragedies of the
arena.[1]   Had he been a Palestine Jew, he would scarcely
have compared the Christian life to a race in the circus,
or have reproduced, so minutely, the various details of the
long temperate training of the competitors, in the different
struggles of the public games, or the self-denial, in hopes
of the crown, which, after all, only one could obtain ; or
the eyes of the runners fixed on the judge ; or the boxing-
matches, in which men fought with their eyes covered up,
amidst the laughter of the multitude ; or the herald calling aloud, with all his voice, the laws of the struggle ; or
the runner pressing on to the winning-post ; or the name
of the victor shouted out, and his being led up to receive
the prize.[2]   In such allusions he shows the influence of
familiarity with the practices and ways of the heathen
population of the cities in which the Dispersion found
themselves.   Instead of introducing references to anything heathen, a Jew of Palestine would have shrunk
from it with horror.   But the very fact that it was otherwise with St. Paul, was one of his special helps to success
as the Apostle of the Gentiles !

[1] 1 Thess. v. 6, 8 ; 1 Cor. iv. 9 ; Eph. vi. 14 ; 2 Tim. ii. 4.
[2] Gal. ii. 2 ; v. 7 ; Phil. ii. 16 ; iii. 14 ; 2 Tim. iv. 7 ; Eph. vi. 12 ; 1 Tim.
vi. 12 ; 2 Tim. ii. 5.

CHAPTER VI

PALESTINE UNDER CALIGULA—PRECEDED BY THE CONVERSION OF PAUL

A.D. 37–41 ; PAUL'S AGE, c. 27–31

THE return of Paul to Jerusalem appears to have fallen some time before the death of Tiberius and the accession of Caius Caligula; that is, somewhere about the year 34, when he was in the springtide of his early manhood; it may be, twenty-four or twenty-five years of age. The focus of Judaism was, doubtless, to his ambitious and fervent nature, the spot at once most congenial, and most promising. Stirring events crowded on each other in Judæa, in those days. Pilate, the horror of the Jew, was at last ignominiously dismissed, apparently before Easter 37, and another procurator, Marcellus, put in his place. Caiaphas was set aside from the high priesthood, which he had held for eighteen years, from A.D. 18 to A.D. 36, and Jonathan, a son of Hannas, raised to the office, instead of the dishonoured son-in-law. Henceforward, change, at short intervals, was to be the rule, for Jonathan gave way in A.D. 37, to another son of Hannas, Theophilus, who was deposed in 41; and no fewer than three high priests followed, in the next three years, under Agrippa I. With the departure of Pilate, had come the great concession to national sentiment, of the surrender of the high priestly robes to the keeping of the Jews, the

Romans having hitherto guarded them in their castle, Antonia, and the equally great favour of the Roman soldiery being forbidden to march through Judæa with the image of the Emperor on their standards. The oppressive market-tax in Jerusalem, moreover, had been abolished. War with the terrible Parthians was, however, in the air, and had been for some years; they might cross the Euphrates again, at any moment, as in the last century, filling the land with despair. Nor was this the only cause of uneasiness, for the invasion of the territory of Antipas, by Aretas of Petra, spread a war-cloud over the regions beyond Jordan.

But, now, Tiberius was dead. He had been justly execrated by the Roman aristocracy, but his memory was respected by the Jews. Bad as the state of things had been under his procurators, they had been immeasurably worse in the provinces generally, under Augustus, and were destined to be no less wretched in times to come. Tiberius had at least discriminated between good and bad rulers, and had kept the former in their places as long as the hunt for office by the Roman aristocracy allowed him. Moreover, he had punished misgovernment where he could, and had, himself, been a pattern of unselfishness as a ruler. Even the terrible permission of secret and irresponsible accusation, which had been so fatal to the unspeakably corrupt and vile nobility, seemed to the provincials, in the absence of public prosecutors, better than nothing, as a means of justice to the provinces they outraged. As to the actual or suspected murders in the imperial circle, which had almost extirpated the Julian line, the guilt was laid far less on Tiberius than on the unscrupulous members of his family, who constantly availed themselves of the dagger or the poison cup, to remove their enemies or rivals, and were accustomed to ascribe every death to secret murder. The Emperor, it was felt, had suffered more than any one else from the corruptness of the imperial house, and from the hideously depraved morals of the day.

But, now, at the age of twenty-five, Caius, the son of the honoured Germanicus, held the sceptre of the world, and whatever had been wrong was sure to be put right! All lands were in raptures. Thanks to the gods for his accession rose to the heavens, in the first nine months of his reign, from the smoke of, it is reckoned, 160,000 victims, burnt on the altars of every province. As he rode in the funeral procession of Tiberius, the multitude almost blocked the way, in their zeal to bring to his presence their countless thank-offerings, and to strew incense before the new god. His boundless extravagance and profligacy were overlooked, in the contrast they offered to the moroseness of his predecessor. His excesses having brought on an almost fatal illness, Rome hardly breathed lest it might disturb him on his sick-bed. On his recovery, new clouds of offerings rose through the Empire, and deputations hastened to express the joy of the nations. But a strange disillusion awaited their members, when ushered into his presence, for, instead of their winning ideal of what the son of Germanicus must be, they were shocked to see a youth whose very features betrayed gross sensuality and cruelty of nature, and a temper at once irritable, malevolent, and furious. Still, an excuse was found. His illness had disturbed his mind. Presently, murder succeeded murder, by his orders. The grandson of Tiberius had to kill himself; no one being

worthy to shed sacred imperial blood. On every side, all
from whom he feared anything, or to whom he had, in
the past, been under obligations, disappeared before his
headsmen, but the necessities of public order were, still,
advanced as an explanation. People had suffered so much
in the old civil wars ended by Augustus, that desire for
peace made any violence of the ruler to the leaders of
the great world, seem, very possibly, a security against
commotion. So long as the mass of the population were
left free to trade and pass quiet lives, the Emperor might
do much as he chose in destroying the old nobility. Ere
long, however, his insane ferocity spread in such ever-
widening circles, that, even in the provinces, and among
the common people, terror and hatred took the place of
former idolatry. One province, in particular, found the
personal vanity of the Cæsar a stupendous public calamity,
though it had been the first to hail his accession with
the warmest loyalty. It was Judæa, which had already
suffered so terribly, under Sejanus.[1]

Meanwhile, Agrippa, set free from the prison into
which his incautious treason had thrown him, under
Tiberius, had passed, on the accession of his boon-com-
panion, Caligula, into the full sunshine of imperial
favour, with ornamental fetters of gold hanging up in his
chambers, instead of the iron ones in which he had lain
for months. The young Antiochus—son of Antiochus,
King of Conmagene—who, like Agrippa, had now been
raised to royal dignity by Caligula, among his first acts
as emperor, was, with the Herodian, the intimate associate
of their common patron; the blame of the ever-increasing

---

[1] The fullest picture of Caligula is that given by Philo, in his *Leg. ad
Gaj. ed. Mangold.* The narrative of Suetonius is simply appalling.

love of Eastern state, on the part of Caius, being ascribed to their influence; to which, also, was set down his ever-growing tyranny and profligacy. Antiochus was made king of his father's principality—the part of Syria bordering Cilicia—receiving, with the throne, the repayment of all the revenue obtained from the kingdom by the Romans, during the twenty years they had held it. Agrippa was, moreover, credited with having prompted Caius to the murder of his possible rival, the grandson of Tiberius. The poor young fellow, only seventeen, having been brought out into a hall, was surrounded by soldiers, and told that he must die. Baring his neck, he offered it to his murderers, but they handed him a sword, and showed him where he should stab himself with it—for a Cæsar's blood could only be shed by himself—and thus he died. Then followed the murder of Macro, colonel of the Prætorian Guard, the man to whom Caius owed everything, and Agrippa much. Silanus, the father-in-law of the Emperor, was next forced to cut his throat with his razor. Eunuchs, Phœnician and Egyptian buffoons, play-actors, and astrologers, ruled the court, but, in Rome, it was believed that Agrippa was even more dangerous than they. Sharing, as he did, in all the follies and enormities of these months, people were furious at the Jewish adventurer, who, in cold blood, and with crafty calculation of his own interests, led on the already half-mad Caius to excesses, which brought him to the verge of the grave, from sleeplessness and physical exhaustion, in the summer of A.D. 38. Yet Agrippa managed to save himself, while all round were falling; even Antonia, his patroness, the widow of Drusus, and grandmother of Caius, having paid, with her life, for an attempt to bring the monster to a

wiser course.   At last, however, Agrippa felt it prudent
to withdraw to his Palestine kingdom, for which, therefore, he set sail, by way of Alexandria, in the autumn of
the year 38, a year and a half after Caligula's accession.
His arrival in Egypt was the signal for bitter outbreaks of
the standing hatred of the population towards the swarms
of their Jewish fellow-citizens, who flattered their own
vanity, and that of the royal good-for-nothing, by noisy
rejoicings at his elevation; loudly boasting of him as a
Jewish king, in the city which he had left, some years
before, a penniless bankrupt.   At last, in the autumn of
A.D. 38, he reached his little capital, Julias, at the north
end of the Lake of Galilee, the burial-place of Philip, his
predecessor.   His dominions, stretching away to the east,
had, in old times, been the prey of robbers and marauders,
but Herod the Great had crushed these outlaws, and
Philip had maintained the peace and security thus
brought about.   Not till two years before—in A.D. 36—
had war invaded the land, but, then, the Bedouins of
Petra, under Aretas, had administered a deserved defeat
on Antipas, for his baseness in dismissing their king's
daughter, to marry Herodias.   Since that humiliation,
the tetrarch had striven to efface his disgrace, by seeking, if possible, a post in the army intended to meet the
Parthians, but peace having been kept, he had nothing
left but to scheme how he might recommend himself
in any way, to Caligula.   To enable him to take a prominent part in the next war that might break out, he
began to collect arms beyond his means, and coined
money with the name of the emperor on it, instead of
Jewish emblems, for bribery at Rome.   But it was useless.
The 70,000 stand of arms he gathered, and his attempt

to push himself forward, in connection with the Parthian imbroglio, proved his ruin, for his arsenal seemed, or might be made to seem, intended for revolt from Rome. Herodias, his evil genius, was, however, the direct means of his fall. She had stirred him up to murder the Baptist, and had caused the troubles with Aretas, and now brought banishment on him. It was intolerable to her, to see her brother, who had been a slighted inmate of her palace, and had held the humble post of overseer of the Market of Tiberias, ruling dominions she had always coveted, and made a king, while her husband was only a tetrarch. When, therefore, at the Feast of Tabernacles at Jerusalem, in A.D. 38, she found herself overshadowed by the new "king," and forced to take the second, instead of the first place, nothing would do, but that Antipas and she should go to Rome, where Agrippa had been so successful. In vain "the Fox" strove to dissuade her. It was, he urged, too dangerous. His wife was determined, and the weak man and she finally landed in Italy in the summer of 39, settling, for the time, at the warm baths of Baiæ, near Naples, now, for ages, only a local wonder from the fierce volcanic heat, which rises, through the old chambers in the rocks, from subterranean depths. But their journey had roused the fears of Agrippa, and he hastened to poison the mind of the Emperor against them. Caius was then at Baiæ, full of his insane dream of riding over the sea, by building a bridge of ships across the bay. In the midst of the excitement, Antipas was allowed an audience. He and his wife rejoiced to find themselves kindly received, but, unfortunately for them, the indictment of their loyalty, by Agrippa, was put into the hands of Caligula while they were still in his presence. Reading it quietly

the Emperor asked him if he really had collected 70,000
stand of arms, and on his admitting having done so,
thought he had been deceived, and forthwith sent him
into exile at Lugdunum, the modern Lyons, in France;
Herodias refusing his offers of favour, as the sister of
Agrippa, and, for once in her life, acting nobly, by refusing to leave her husband in his eclipse.   Thus passed
from the scene of Palestine life, the man who had beheaded
John, and arrayed the Saviour in robes of mockery !
Agrippa, meanwhile, profited by his brother-in-law's ruin,
being granted his dominions, in addition to those of Philip,
which he already held.   Hereafter he was to be made king
of all Palestine, in A.D. 41, by the Emperor Claudius !

While these events were succeeding each other with
startling rapidity, the madness of Caligula had taken a
turn which threw Judæa into the wildest commotion.
Rome had always worshipped Jupiter Capitolinus, during
the Republic, as the idealisation of the State, and, hence,
when a single ruler became the one recognised power, the
same worship was more and more paid to him, as, now,
the embodiment of what Jupiter had formerly been.
Augustus had been deified on his death, and Caligula, ere
long, convinced himself that the Julian line, as such, was
divine, so that in his madness, he, in all earnestness,
believed he was a god.   He had opened his reign well,
affecting to have burned the documents which incrimi-
nated those who had acted as the instruments of the late
Emperor against his family, releasing prisoners condemned
by Tiberius, recalling exiles, and granting important re-
forms in the municipalities.   But the evil in his nature,
fanned by vile companions, had soon changed him for the
worse, while his illness added the caprices of madness to

the violence of ungovernable passions and remorseless cruelty. One example may suffice. Too few criminals having been procurable on one occasion, to fight with the wild beasts at the public games, he ordered victims to be taken, at random, from the benches of spectators, directing that their tongues should be first cut out, to prevent their cries, or their cursing him. But, now, the edict went forth that he should be everywhere worshipped as a god. Forthwith the smoke of sacrifices in his honour, rose in every province; hymns were chanted to him as divine; hecatombs smoked on altars raised to him, and men began to swear by his godhead. He dressed himself, moreover, like, now, one, now, another of the gods, and took his stand before the multitude, while they offered prayer, made vows, and burnt incense to him. Terror, or hope of advantage, made him, presently, adored by more worshippers than any other divinity. The temples were almost deserted for his shrines. Over the provinces, officials and municipalities competed in building temples to him, except in Judæa. There, no Jew would have anything to do with this blasphemous craze, or suffer the Holy Land to be polluted by its abominations. Where Jews lived amidst a heathen population, their position was exceptionally difficult, for, though they had been tacitly allowed to avoid an altar to the local gods, it was a graver matter to refuse to honour the altars of the deity on the throne.

The first open sign of the rising storm was at Jamnia, a town on the Philistine plain, half Jewish, half Phœnician, and, hence, divided into bitterly opposed factions; for wherever Jews were numerous in a heathen community, they were alike hated and full of hate; treating their neighbours with the most contemptuous scorn, and bearing themselves as the favourites of Heaven. One sees their counterpart, still, in the scornful and supercilious bearing of fanatical Mahomedans in some parts of the East. In Persian bazaars and town streets, for example, mollahs, scribes, traders or merchants, claiming descent from Mahomed, pass through the crowd as if they were superior beings, expecting to have their hand and their very clothes reverently kissed as they go by. Even a Jew beggar bore himself thus, in Paul's day, to all mankind, outside his own petty race, for was he not a son of Abraham, with whom Jehovah spoke in the door of his tent? And were not all mankind made for the glory of Israel, and born under the curse of God, as not knowing the Law? As soon, therefore, as it was heard at Jamnia that the Emperor required personal homage at altars raised in his honour, the mixed population, encouraged by the Roman fiscal officer, so bitter a Jew-hater that he had arrested even Agrippa when seeking to flee from his creditors, hastily put together an altar of coarse materials, that every one might burn incense on it, in honour of the man-god Caius. Amidst indescribable uproar, however, the Jews, forthwith, threw down the "abomination," and thus took the first step toward a religious war. At Alexandria, things were even more serious. The hatred of the Jews was there intense, and the tumults between them and the citizens continual, even in ordinary times. Nothing would induce them to submit to the edict; but the rabble, excited to the uttermost by terrible rioting and bloodshed in the streets, infuriated them more than ever by dragging a statue of Caligula into the synagogue. The irritating enthusiasm with which Agrippa had been welcomed by his race, had caused the com-

motions culminating in this outrage, even before he left
the city. The Jews, being too numerous to find accommodation in their own "quarter," had gradually taken
possession of the neighbouring streets. But their houses
there were now burned down; ships owned by the hated
Semites were plundered in the harbour, as they arrived;
Jew labourers were hounded from the wharves, and if a
Jew showed himself in a heathen "quarter," he was instantly hunted down and murdered. Others were forced
to prove their loyalty by eating "unclean" food. The
trees before the synagogues were cut down, and one
synagogue was set on fire. In the largest, an immense
building, a colossal bronze statue of the imperial man-god
was set up, and a great temple was dedicated to him in
the city, that he might be roused to order the annihilation
of the Jews, who affected to despise it. Nor were matters
bettered by a Hebrew embassy sent to Rome. Caligula
had agreed to give its members an audience, but, instead
of doing so, he set off to France, to extort money from the
provincials; then to Germany, on a pretended campaign.
After his return from this, however, he, at last, in August
40, allowed the deputation to approach him. They were
received in the gardens of one of his Roman villas; their
opponents from Alexandria being also present. "Are
you the people," asked the Emperor, or entering, "who
refuse to acknowledge my divinity?" Then he burst into
wild blasphemies, which the Egyptians and court parasites
received with shouts of laughter. Presently, after some
more profanities, he left, to examine what was wanted in
a neighbouring room; the embassy being all the time the
butt of jokes from those round. Suddenly turning, he
asked them why they did not eat swine's flesh; a question

greeted with fresh laughter by those around him. Before an answer could be given, he was off, from hall to hall, ordering white glass for a window in one, and a painted table in another. The deputation expected death, every moment, but, at last, Caligula dismissed them as rather to be pitied for not recognising his godhead, than punished as wilful criminals. The tumults of Alexandria were destined to continue till he was murdered, a year later !

But the wildest storm broke out in Judæa. The peace in the province under Claudius before the first eighteen quiet months of the new reign, had permitted the zealous Stephen to bring forward his generous conception of Christianity in the Hellenistic synagogues of Jerusalem, but the result had been, to disclose to the bigots of Judaism, and, among others, to Paul, the essential difference between the new and the old faith. Till then, Christianity had been regarded, from the exact compliance of its adherents with all the details of Jewish worship and daily life, as, certainly a new, yet, still, an orthodox sect ; but, now, the cry rose, that the old faith was in danger, and the fanatics of the Law, headed by such as Paul, broke out into the violence of which the stoning of Stephen was the first expression. In the calm interval in political affairs then prevailing, the fury of persecution found its opportunity, and it was now that Paul busied himself in hunting down the dreaded heresy, by following the scattered Christians even to Damascus ; that journey which was to see him changed from the bitterest of enemies into the foremost of the confessors of Christ. But Caligula was speedily to give Judæa other occupation for their religious fervour, than bating poor Christians. In the year 39, Petronius, the Proconsul of Syria, received at Antioch, a command to march to Jerusalem with three legions of the army of the Euphrates, and set up in the Jewish temple, a statue of the Emperor, bearing the inscription, " Caius, the new incarnation of Jupiter." What was he to do ? No people were so unmanageable as the Jews. The command meant the kindling all the deadly ferocity of a religious war. He could not disobey, but he could gain time by delay. To get a new statue cast would put the matter off for some months, so he ordered one to be prepared in the metal foundries of Sidon. In the autumn, the three legions were marched to Ptolemais, now Acre, and the dignitaries of the Temple summoned thither, to bring about some arrangement in reference to the imperial command. But the only answer of the Jewish officials was that such an outrage could not be carried out except over the dead bodies of the citizens. Meanwhile, as news of the hideous proposal spread through the land, the whole population streamed towards Ptolemais, covering the country, far and near, and raising, continually, such cries and wailing, as made the town's people declare they would lose their hearing. Finally, the vast throng, arranged in six columns, of old women, matrons, maids, old men, men in their strength, and boys, gathered before the palace of the Proconsul, and threw themselves on the earth, with wild and piteous outcries of despair, when he showed himself on the balcony. Petronius was deeply moved, and determined to do what he could to help them. The artificer, in Sidon, was told to take his time ; what was slowly done was well done. In the spring of 40 the Proconsul moved to Tiberias, the capital, now, of Agrippa, who, however, had prudently gone to Rome, to be out of the way. His brother

Aristobulus, meanwhile, with others of the family, held
counsel with Petronius, and, as the brother was the
very opposite of Agrippa, the people feared the worst.
The plain of Gennesareth was, therefore, covered with
new multitudes, who repeated to the Proconsul what they
had told him before at Ptolemais, that they would die but
never give way. Sowing, ought to have kept them at
home, but they stayed round Tiberias, week after week,
till the idle soil offered the welcome excuse for fresh
delay, in the affected dread of a famine, if the command
of Caius were carried out at that time. The Emperor
received the despatch of Petronius while he was in France,
and turning pale with fury, threatened to behead the
Proconsul, but presently shrank from this, remembering
that Petronius had the army of the Euphrates behind
him. Nothing further could be done till he reached
Rome, which he did on the last day of August 40, his
birthday.

It now depended on Agrippa, at once a Jew and a close
friend of Caius, to solve the terrible difficulty, but when
an audience was granted him, the Emperor stormed so
fearfully against the Jews, that Agrippa made-believe
to fall in a dead swoon, in which, it was asserted, he
lay unconscious for thirty-six hours. Yet the utmost he
could obtain was a command to Petronius not to interfere with the Temple; every one, however, being free to
raise altars to the Emperor outside its gates. Forthwith, many, dedicated to him, were raised by enemies of
the Jews, to spite them, keeping alive all the popular
troubles as acutely as before, while news came, making
confusion worse than ever, that, gradually, all the synagogues of Alexandria had been turned into temples to

Cæsar. But the scene changed with the opening of
A.D. 41, for, on the 24th of January of that year, he who
had so terribly afflicted the world lay murdered.[1]

Such were the agitations that held men breathless in
the years following Paul's return to Judæa. He had used
the calm of the new reign to carry ruin far and wide
among the poor Christians, against whom, we are told, he
"breathed out threatenings and slaughter." But before
the people had been turned away from thoughts of harrying
the Nazarenes, by their agony at the approaching dese-
cration of the Temple itself, by a statue of their supreme
enemy, whom they were required to worship instead of
Jehovah, Paul the persecutor had become Paul the passionate adorer of the Man of Calvary!

The year in which this great change, so momentous in
the history of Christianity, took place, is so uncertain
that, in thirty-five opinions of scholars which I have
collated, there are ten different dates assigned to it,
ranging from A.D. 31 to A.D. 41. To many it appears that
it must have occurred in the later months of the year
38, which saw the ominous change for the worse in the
relations of Caligula to the Jews. Agrippa had then,
just come from Rome, to his little capital, Bethsaida-
Julius, to take up the government of what had been
Philip's tetrarchy, granted him by Caligula, eighteen
months before, on his accession; Antipas had still a
few months of royalty, before his final disaster, and Marcellus, who had been appointed by the friendly or politic
Vitellius, was ruling at Cæsarea, as procurator of Samaria
and Judæa. I think Paul's conversion happened in 35.

[1] The authorities for the story of Caligula are mainly Philo and
Josephus.

Fanatically devoted, as by a hereditary passion, to the extremest Judaism, he had eagerly thrown himself into the struggle in its defence, which raged in the synagogues of foreign Jews in Jerusalem. To these, Hellenists by birth or descent, but gloomily bigoted, as their having settled in the Holy City showed, Stephen became the object of the fiercest hatred, as leader in the new attitude of the Nazarenes towards the old faith. No feud is so bitter as that associated with so-called religion, and Jews, of all men, could least brook the questioning of even the minutest of their customs or scruples. The strife of words, as we have seen, broke, before long, into acts of violence, till the zealots for "Moses" lost all self-control, and rushing on an opponent whom they could not confute, dragged him outside the town-gate, and beat his life out with stones, for the glory of God and the Temple! At this shameful scene Paul was not only present, but showed so eager a sympathy, that the rabble who hurled the stones at the martyr, laid their outer clothing, stripped off to make their blows the easier and heavier, at the feet of the noted young Pharisee rabbi, whose presence no doubt increased their murderous ferocity. Blood once tasted, the partisans of Things-as-they-were thirsted for more. The pestilent heresy must be extirpated which accused them of having crucified the Messiah, and threatened to change the customs delivered to them by Moses, and even to destroy the Temple—for popular fury had invented all these charges against the Christians since Stephen's preaching. In the war of extermination thus begun, Paul took the lead, "laying waste the Church, entering into every house" thought to be Christian, now quite a large number, and,

haling out men and women alike, dragging some off to
the Jewish prison,[1] and getting others flogged or beaten
with rods, in all the synagogues.   It sounds strange to
read of legal scourgings in a synagogue, but the synagogue officials were the Jewish police magistrates, and
their beadle or verger, the warder, who inflicted the forty
stripes save one on the naked backs of the victims.   The
synagogues were in fact the "police-courts."[2]   But, Jerusalem exhausted, Paul sighed for fresh worlds to conquer.
Intensely sincere, he would be content with no half-mea-
sures where he believed his God affronted and His will
defied.   All the Christians who could, had fled for their
lives, to this or that place of safety; many to Damascus,
where Jews abounded; Nero having, at a later time, put
no fewer than ten thousand to death there, in an outburst of fury.   Theophilus, son of Hannas, was now high
priest, and a commission from him, authorising a repetition, in the Syrian capital, of the vigorous enforcement of
orthodoxy which had so scattered the heretics of Jerusalem would at once be honoured by the local synagogue
authorities.   Nor would there be any opposition from the
Romans, who then held Damascus, for they always supported the jurisdiction of the high-priestly Sanhedrim,
even in criminal matters; the sentence of death alone
requiring confirmation by the Roman governor.   For
such an authorisation Paul applied, and the necessary
document was at once granted, directing all synagogue
rulers in Damascus, to aid him in his search for Christians, whether men or women, that he might bring them
in fetters to Jerusalem, for punishment by the High

---

[1] Acts v. 18–23 ; viii. 3 ; xxii. 5 ; xxvi. 10.
[2] Matt. x. 17 ; xxiii. 34 ; Mark xiii. 9 ; Acts xxii. 19 ; xxvi. 11.

Court; the scourgings permitted to synagogue officials not being now thought enough for such flagrant offenders. That they were rapidly increasing is shown by a special name—"The Way"—apparently standing for "The Way of the Lord"[1]—being given them in the narrative; as if they had now, finally, separated from the synagogues.

Attendants sufficient to guard and lead back expected prisoners, having been assigned him, Paul lost no time in setting off at their head, on his odious mission; the men apparently on foot; he, possibly, indulging in a riding ass—the usual beast of travel in Palestine even now. At the slow rate of Eastern journeys, the 150 or 160 miles between Jerusalem and Damascus would take about a fortnight, for Paul would not stir on the Sabbath. If he and his bailiffs took the road I followed, he would go straight north, from the Damascus gate, past Bethel; then by Shechem and Samaria to En-gannim, on the plain of Esdraelon. Next, keeping on, across the plain, he would pass by Nazareth, and make for the Lake of Galilee, at Hattin and Tiberias. Thence, the road lay north, to the Lake Merom, above which he would cross the Jordan at Cæsarea Philippi. From this lovely spot, the road stretched north-east, in a straight line to Damascus, but he may have gone as I did by the much frequented route over the Hermon mountains—the nearest way to the Syrian capital, then, as now; a slow but grand ascent of seven or eight thousand feet, to the edge of the snow level, and then, across tne black lava fields of ancient volcanoes, till the descent begins, down a rough lava track like frozen waves, covered with innumerable boulders large and small, towards the great plain extending from

[1] **Acts xviii.** 25.

the base of the mountains, to far beyond Damascus. He would no doubt travel only at the ordinary rate of Orientals, which seems always to have been as it is still, about three miles an hour; the rate, in fact, at which an ass walks, for no other pace than walking is possible, as a rule. The road, after descending from the mountains, is a slow and often imperceptible decline, to the lower level of the so-called "Pearl of Cities." The road, in Paul's day, must have been studded along its whole length with towns and villages, for the soil is wonderfully rich, and the great commerce, east and west, must have made it very busy. Villages are, now, quite scarce, and there are few trees, but the landscape is always charming; the grand heights of farther Lebanon shutting in the view, at a distance, on the north, while other hills and mountains rise here and there, in various directions. To the south lies the strange volcanic plateau called the Ledja, and beyond, as well as on the north of it, hills higher and lower.

Somewhere in this region, as he "drew nigh unto Damascus, suddenly," we are told, "there shone, round about Paul, a light, out of heaven: and he fell upon the earth, and heard a voice saying unto him, 'Saul, Saul, why persecutest thou Me?' And he said, 'Who art Thou, Lord?' And he said, 'I am Jesus whom thou persecutest: but rise, and enter into the city, and it shall be told thee what thou must do.' And the men that journeyed with him stood speechless, hearing the voice, but beholding no man. And Saul arose from the earth; and when his eyes were opened, he saw nothing; and they led him by the hand, and brought him into Damascus. And he was three days without sight, and did neither eat nor drink."[1]

[1] Acts ix. 3–9.

Such is the account given by the compiler of the Acts, and often repeated by himself, with such natural variations as must always be found in recapitulations of any event, under varying circumstances, and before different audiences; requiring at each delivery, prominence to some special points and omission of others, in the condensed story, which was not intended to be critically minute.[1] Thus, in the first account, the men are said to have heard the voice, and in the second, not to have heard it; but the one may very naturally mean that they heard the voice, not the words—the light and the terror overpowering them. The third account speaks of the men with the apostle, all falling to the earth; the first, describes them as standing speechless, but surely they may have done both; rising, after sinking down before the splendour!

That the vision cannot be explained on natural grounds, is clear; but while the direct action of Heaven is to be recognised without hesitation, and in the fullest sense, there were, beyond question, influences at work in Paul's mind, which prepared it to profit by the amazing incident. He had heard of Gamaliel's caution, to take care, lest, in fighting against Christianity, men should find they were opposing the counsel of God. He had taken part in the disputes with Stephen, had listened to his arguments for the Messiahship of Jesus, and had, with the crowd, seen his heroic end, with its quenchless charity and sublime faith and devotion. Still more, he had seen the bearing of the poor men and women he had since been dragging to prison, and, just as the moral dignity of some of the martyrs waked sympathy, in later days, even from those leading them to death, his sensitive nature may well

[1] Acts xxii., xxvi.

have been touched by such experiences. Though once a
disciple of the temperate-minded Gamaliel, his fiery spirit
had apparently sat also at the feet of harsher masters,
and now urged him, for the time, to take sides with the
extreme party of his sect, and launch out on the career
of persecution which he lamented so deeply in later
years[1] Yet it had been his deep religious sincerity;
his zeal for the glory and honour of God, which had
driven him to this fanaticism, and this rare conscientiousness tended ultimately, without his knowing it, to
lead him to that very Gospel he was seeking to destroy.
For, in his intense earnestness and honesty, which made
him the least Pharisaic of all Pharisees, he was as zealous
to honour the Law in his inner life, as to enforce its
outward observance on the Nazarenes, who ventured to
be broader-minded than himself. To attain perfect righteousness, by a laborious fulfilment of all its demands, as
he understood them, was his one thought. But the effort
must have roused, in a nature like his, a suspicion of the
essential worthlessness of all formal acts and rites, before
God, with His awful standard of holiness in thought and
heart. Even after he had long been a Christian, he
speaks of internal struggles which must also have agonised
him, while formerly chasing the phantom of possible
self righteousness. "With his mind he served the Law
of God; but with his flesh the Law of sin."[2] The
chapter from which these words are taken reveals a
spiritual chaos, over which, as yet, shone no faintest
morning light of internal peace and hope. The conflict
must have been very similar to that of Luther in his

---

[1] 1 Cor. xv. 9; Gal. i. 13; Phil. iii. 6; Acts xxii. 4; xxvi. 10.
[2] Rom. vii. 25. See the chapter throughout.

monastery.[1] Both were equally zealous for external religion, and both equally torn by secret doubts of its value
as a means of salvation. Paul confesses that, for a time,
he did not feel "the sting of the Law," and lived in
peaceful self-satisfaction with his own righteousness. But
he adds that he realised the full meaning of the deep
and all-embracing command, "Thou shalt not covet" (or
"lust"). The Law rose against him like an accusing
judge, and kindled a struggle within him, between his
moral nature and his desires, or, as he expresses it,
between his spirit and his flesh, in which the will to do
right constantly succumbed to the indwelling power of
his worst tendencies, and left him only the despairing
cry for deliverance from this bondage, by some salvation
of which, as yet, he did not know. Thus, finding no
peace in the most exact observance of the Law, his tender
conscience was driving him, without his suspecting it,
to that Gospel which he persecuted. He was destined,
as he himself says, "Through the Law, to die unto the
Law, that he might live unto God."[2]

The conversion of the most violent enemy of Christ
into His most devoted servant, while the greatest and
most wonderful event of the apostolic age, was, thus, in
some measure a natural development of influences secretly
at work beforehand, in his deepest moral being. Hence, the

---

[1] "Verily," wrote Luther to Duke George of Saxony, "I was a devout
monk, and followed the rules of my Order so strictly that I cannot tell
you all If ever a monk entered into heaven by his monkish merits, certainly I should have obtained an entrance there. All the monks who
knew me will confirm this; and if it had lasted much longer, I should
have become literally a martyr, through watchings, prayers, reading, and
other labours."—D'Aubigné, History of the Reformation, vol. i. p. 162.

[2] Rom. vii. 9–24; Gal. ii. 19.

calming of his inner conflict, by the disclosure of a Divine
Saviour in Jesus, when it broke on his soul in heavenly
light, seemed as if, indeed, scales which till then blinded
his eyes, had fallen from them.[1] All the accounts of the
revelation on the way to Damascus, and all the allusions
to it in the Epistles,[2] show that he firmly believed he had
seen Jesus, in the glory of His spiritual body, as the older
Apostles had seen Him, after the resurrection. This overpowering experience, moreover, of the exalted majesty of
the once cruc fied One, settled an overwhelming conviction in his mind, henceforth, for ever, that, in spite of
all its utter contradiction of the ideas of the Messiah,
which he, in common with every Jew, previously held,
Jesus was, in very deed, the " Christ ;' while it scattered
to the winds the fine-spun web of Pharisaic theology,
in which, till then, he had trusted. What had happened
could not be a mere mental illusion, for he often had
experience of ordinary visions, and recognised them as
such, however highly he valued them.[3] Had there not,
indeed, been grounds, recognised by him as decisive, for
regarding the incident on the Damascus road as something absolutely real, and no mere vision, it could neither
have been to him the demonstration which he held it, of
the bodily resurrection of Jesus, nor the warrant on
which he habitually based his apostolic claims.[4] He felt
that the risen One had actually appeared to him, in the
midst of that splendour of God, in which He now stands,
at the right hand of the Majesty in the heavens. That
Majesty, the pledge of a Divine appearance, which may
well have dazzled the men with him, so that, though

[1] 2 Cor. iv. 6.   [2] 1 Cor. ix. 1 ; xv. 8 ; 2 Cor. iv. 6 ; Gal. i. 1, 15, 16.
[3] 2 Cor. xii. 1 ff.   [4] 1 Cor. ix. 1 ; xv. 8.

they heard a voice while not catching its words, they saw no one, was to Paul, in the strictest sense, a revelation of the Saviour, which stamped itself on his soul for ever. What else, he always urged, could it be, which, at high noon of an Eastern day, eclipsed its brightness by a still greater glory, and how could he question the words of Him who looked down from its midst, proclaiming Himself no other than Jesus whom he persecuted.

CHAPTER VII

RISING, after a time, from the earth, which had in some measure obscured the blinding light, so suddenly bursting on him from the heavens, Paul was for a moment able to look up, but the awful glory had passed away, and the Divine form on which he had for an instant gazed, had disappeared. The next moment his eyes grew dark, and he only reached Damascus, led, helpless, by his men. Safely housed at last, nature sank, overpowered by all he had seen and heard; no food or drink crossed his lips for three days; and his sight, scorched out of his eyes by the heavenly glory, was, apparently, permanently gone.

A street bearing the name of that in which he lodged—"Straight"—still exists at Damascus, running east and west across the southern part of the city. It was then a great parade, with covered sideways for passengers, under rows of arches and pillars; but the one side has long since perished—though a gate, of two small side arches and a large centre one, still remaining at one end, shows the original width and splendour of the whole. This road, still honoured by the old name, may well have been the street where Paul lodged; for it is near the Jews' quarter. Presently, Ananias, a local Christian, instructed in a vision

—that is, a dream, sought him out, and found the change in the feelings of the former persecutor profound. The enthusiasm he had shown for Jehovah, however blind, had been sincere; and his submission to Him who had deigned to stop him by the way, and reveal the truth to him, was no less earnest. Humble, grateful love to Jesus, the Messiah, had become the consuming passion of his soul.

Ananias, on his arrival, deepened this, if that were possible. " Brother Saul," said he, " Jesus has sent me, that thou mightest receive thy sight, and be filled with the Holy Ghost." Then, laying his hands on Paul, scales fell from the blind eyes, and sight came back, the Holy Spirit also falling on the penitent; seeing all which the envoy of his new Master, hailed in him a brother, and forthwith baptized him in the name he had till so lately blasphemed, but now supremely adored. Erelong, being able to take food, his strength began to return. Now " in Christ," he was, indeed, a " new creature; old things had passed away," or. rather, " they had become new," in the different light in which he saw them. He had accepted Jesus as the Messiah, and also as his personal Saviour, who had reached forth His hand from heaven, to stop him in his mad career, and lead him to Himself. This belief, openly confessed by his baptism, gave him, instead of the unsatisfying " righteousness " of the Law, which had left his heart so troubled, and so eager for something better,— the peace of assured forgiveness, and an inner impulse and sustaining power to live a true life towards God, such as he had never hitherto known. Filled with an overpowering sense of the unspeakable love of Christ, in His atoning death for man ; a love which, to his adoring soul, seemed,

alike in its "breadth, and length, and height, and depth,
to pass all knowledge," [1] from the moment of his great
change, "to live was," henceforth, "Christ." [2]   In a very
real sense he could say that as regarded any personal
interests or ambitions, "he no longer lived, but Christ
lived in him." [3]   Forthwith, therefore, he felt constrained
to use the privilege of the Jew, and especially of a rabbi,
of rising in the synagogues of Damascus, to proclaim that
Jesus, whom it was known he had come to blaspheme, so
far from being the impostor he had hitherto declared
Him, was, in very deed, the Son of God. [4]   The wonder of
Christians and Jews alike, knew no bounds.   What could
have happened, that he who, after having made his name
terrible to all in Jerusalem who honoured Jesus as the
Messiah, had come to Damascus for the very purpose of
dragging off the local Christians in fetters, as prey for
their fierce enemies in the Temple city, should now
preach that very faith which he had hitherto sought so
furiously to stamp out?

But he soon found that the new world of religious
experience into which he had passed, as by a lightning
flash, raised questions requiring the profoundest reflection
and excogitation.   It had taken him long years to master
the Pharisaic theology ; that of Christianity was infinitely
wider in the considerations it involved.   Seeking the
retirement thus imperative, therefore, he tells us " he
went away into Arabia;" [5] a vague term in those days,
indicating, it may be, only a sojourn in the steppes of the
Hauran near at hand, or a journey to Petra, or to Mount
Sinai, or even to the peninsula still known as Arabia,

---

[1] Eph. iii. 19.   [2] Phil. i. 21.   [3] Gal. ii. 20.
          [4] Acts ix. 20.   [5] Gal. i. 17.

over the wide extent of which large numbers of Jews
were settled at that time.[1]   Arabia-proper continued,
indeed, to be much sought by Jews, even so late as
the days of Mahomed, before whose appearance it had
saturated the native population with Jewish tradition, as
we see in the Koran, besides, of course, accumulating the
wealth which tempted the prophet to plunder and massacre
them so remorselessly.   In this retreat, Paul, no doubt,
pondered over and elaborated with much travail of soul
that Christian system which appears in his Epistles,
especially in "Romans" and "Galatians," but which, it
is clear, he had substantially reached before they were
written, from his attitude in the dispute with St. Peter,
at Antioch.[2]   The special experience he had gone through
with the Law,—in its impelling him, on the one hand, to
what had really been a war against God,—now stopped
by the revelation of His Son; and, on the other, in its
rousing a discord within him which it had proved unable
to calm, must have furnished a convincing key to the
Divine purpose of the work of Christ.   The older Apostles
had hitherto regarded the Gospel simply as a realisation
of the Law and the Prophets, and, thus, as the crowning,
and glorious rounding-out and perfecting, of Judaism.
But Paul, starting from the opposition between the Law
and the Gospel, by this distinct separation of Christianity
from Judaism, became not only the originator of the first
scheme of Christian doctrine, but of such a scheme, as, by
its disclosure of the universal charity of the new faith,
separated it fundamentally from that of the Jew, and by
showing that it was designed to meet the spiritual wants

[1] Jos., Ant. xiii. 13, 3 ; 15, 4 ; xiv. 1, 4 ; xv. 4, 1, &c.
[2] Gal. ii. 11.

of all humanity, prepared the way for its acceptance by the heathen world. He came to see clearly, and henceforth taught, that while the Law could not secure for man that true righteousness which is the basis of all complete spiritual deliverance, God, of His free grace, had made provision for this in Christ.[1] In the "delivering up for us all" of His " own Son," to the death of the Cross, the Father had given a supreme manifestation and pledge, that, through Him, He would, of His free "grace," put within man's reach a perfect judicial righteousness. No conception could have stood in more acute contradiction to the Jewish ideas of the moral government of the world; the Cross being the very opposite of their dream of the Messiah "restoring the kingdom to Israel."[2] To Paul, now, however, the Cross was the highest expression of eternal love, seeking to win back to itself a world estranged from it. In the Cross, the blood of the sinless One, shed for sinners, and by the hands of sinners, had at once judged, and condemned, and atoned for sin, and, while forgiving it, had made it supremely hateful. Through it, Paul saw the one only spring and source of justification and spiritual restoration, opened for all. Divine love had, moreover, provided that the Holy One, by His resurrection, after having died on the Cross, should be able to realise, what He had done for the race by His having become, henceforth, the Adam of a new, redeemed, and purified humanity, to which He should be the life-giving spirit, as the first Adam had been the source of our physical and sinful life.[3] The one only demand and condition of enjoying this blessedness is true living practical faith in Christ, just as a similar faith had been the condition

[1] Rom. viii. 3, 4.   [2] Acts i. 6.   [3] 1 Cor. xv. 45.

of Abraham's securing the promises granted to him, as father of the future Israel. Faith, lovingly trusting and making its own the love of God, as shown in the life and death of Christ, also, in Paul's theology, quickens the soul to grateful proof of its sincerity, by creating an earnest desire to please Him. It is, says he, the source, within us, at once of an assurance of our " standing in the grace of God,"[1] and also of our growing in a spiritual life, which no longer offers to God a slavish, outward, or formal, or selfish legalism, like the Jewish, but a childlike, joyful, and loving obedience to His commands. But, if the Law, in its eternal moral aspect, was, henceforth, the one supreme rule for all Christians, as it now had become for him,[2] it had lost all value as regarded its merely outward, threatening, detail of formal commands, which are the letter, not the spirit ; the husk, not the kernel ; so far as they had been held to involve the relations between God and man. The Jew and the Jewish Christian might continue to observe them as the custom of his nation, but for the Christian, as such, they had no longer any binding obligation, because no longer of any " justifying " power.[3]

Such are the fundamental principles of the Christianity of Paul, as they formed themselves in his mind during his long meditations in his Arabian retirement. The Baptist had withdrawn to the wilderness to ponder the high questions of the kingdom of God, and our Lord had buried Himself, for a time, after His baptism, in the loneliness of the mountains, to gird His spirit, in solitude, for the high commission on which He had entered, and it was equally necessary that Paul should equip himself for his

---

[1] 1 Cor. xᵛ. 1 ; 2 Cor. i. 24.   [2] Rom. iii. 31 ; viii. 4 ; xiii. 10.
[3] Gal. ii. 21 ; iii. 1–29 ; Rom. x. 4.

great life-work, by a similar isolation from all outward distractions. But it would be a great error to fancy that he created his theology simply from his own reflections, without drawing the material of his reasonings from the life and teachings of our Lord. It is evident that, as to him, beyond most of us, Christ was "all in all." Hence, he must have valued His words supremely, and, indeed, he shows continually in his Epistles, that he was intimately conversant with them.[1] He may have added to his knowledge of the life and sayings of Jesus in his intercourse with Peter, James, and other Apostles, and with Christians generally, but he had, no doubt, long before, gathered much as a keen listener and observer,—eager, in his hostility to the faith, to catch all he could learn respecting it, from any available source. Yet, while all he had learned was, till now, only, as it were, the confused raw material from which great results might afterwards follow, the spark of life first fell into his soul when Christ showed Himself over the Damascus road, lighting up the darkness in his mind, and illuminating the multitudinous memories of Himself and His words, hitherto dormant in it, so that the historical facts and those of his internal experience concurred in setting the seal of truth on the Gospel he embraced. The sky, we are told, is filled, even by night, with the luminous ether which makes the day, but it only becomes Light when the rising sun has quickened its slumbering waves into brightness. It was thus with Paul. To him, in the truest sense, Christ was the dayspring from on high.

Strengthened and confirmed in the faith so myste-

---

[1] **Rom.** i. 3; xv. 3; 1 Cor. vii. 10, 25; ix. 14; xi. 23–25; xv. 1–7; 2 Cor. v. 20; viii. 9; Gal. iv. 4; Phil. ii. 5–8.

riously roused by the direct illumination of the heavenly glory, and fortified, since his conversion, by continued revelations of the truth as his knowledge increased, and his spiritual communion with his Master grew more and more intimate, he felt himself able, after a time,—we do not know how long,—to return to Damascus, that he might renew, on the intended scene of his attack on Christianity, the vigorous recantation of his past hostility to it, and a no less vigorous exposure of the false grounds on which his fellow-Jews assailed it; grounds which he, himself, had once thought unchallengeable, but now saw to be based on a misconception, and consequent perversion of the sacred oracles. Saturated with the learning of the rabbis, he was a formidable foe, for he knew all the subtleties and refinements by which they read their theology into the Law and the Prophets, while he could flash a new light on each page of the Old Testament, by which, to the wonder of his hearers, it seemed to testify, long ages before, " of the sufferings of the Christ, and the glory that should follow." He had, we may suppose, taken any opportunities that offered while he was in " Arabia," to " preach Christ," for the spirit that cries out, " Woe be to me if I preach not the Gospel," [1] cannot be imagined to have been silent altogether in a region full of synagogues, as that apparently was to which he betook himself. But it was in Damascus, especially, that he, unconsciously, prepared himself most fully for his future work. Nor can it well be fancied, that his reasoning in the synagogues had no results, in winning over at least some to accept Christ as the Messiah. Growing in the knowledge of his subject, as we are told, he " increased the more in strength,"

[1] 1 Cor. ix. 16.

"proving" (from the Old Testament) "that Jesus was, indeed, the Christ," so ably, that the Jews could not confute his arguments, and were "confounded" at hearing their Scriptures turned into a library of Christian evidence, proving that the Messiah was not to be, as they had always been taught, a great political leader, but that it "behoved Him to suffer as Jesus had done, and enter into His glory, not on earth, but in the heavens, when made perfect by this very suffering."[1] They were infuriated, and Paul had to experience, in the city where he had planned sore persecution for "The Way," his own first persecution as its advocate.

Damascus, at that time, had been given to Aretas, King of Petra, by Caligula, during the interval between the retirement of Vitellius from the proconsulate of Syria, and the appointment of his successor, Petronius; a temporary honour frequently granted in those times. The Arab prince had begun his reign in A.D. 7, when Jesus was still a boy, and had been friendly with Herod Antipas till "the Fox" divorced his daughter to marry Herodias, but this affront had been avenged by an invasion in which Antipas was utterly routed. An expedition to punish Aretas for having disturbed "the Roman peace," without permission, had, as we have seen, been stopped by the death of Tiberius, in 37, and his successor, Caligula, had now, further, slighted Antipas, by handing over Damascus, temporarily, to his keeping. That there are coins of the city of the reigns of Augustus and Tiberius, but neither of that of Caligula nor of Claudius—37–41 and 41–54 — marks an interruption of Roman direct government of the district, and strengthens the explana-

[1] Luke xxiv. 26; Heb. ii. 10.

tion I have given, as the right one, of the presence of
Aretas, as ruler, during the residence of Paul in the
Syrian capital.   The Arab governor, however, having
been won over, we are told, by the Jews, sought to arrest

The escape of Paul from Damascus.   (The present wall, however, is not at all
so high as this illustration seems to imply.)

him; so keen had the hostility to him become.   The
gates were watched, and escape seemed impossible.   But
in Eastern cities, houses are often built over the walls,
so that some of their windows are outside them, as
I saw in Damascus itself, and through one of these

Paul was let down in a basket, and thus got safely away.[1]

Now, at last, three years after his conversion, the new apostle ventured to return to Jerusalem; the frenzy of the nation about the orders of Caligula to have his statue set up in the Temple, absorbing public interest so completely, as to leave no heart, either in the officials or the populace, to interfere even with such an apostate from the old faith as he had shown himself. That he had not sooner betaken himself to the scenes of the life and death of his Master, and especially to Jerusalem, the seat of the first Christian Church,—the home of the Apostles who had been with Christ through His public life, and had been witnesses of His death and resurrection,—and the spot where he could meet the relations and the mother of our Lord,—had, no doubt, in part, risen from his determination to put it beyond the power of any one, to speak of him as merely a disciple of even the highest among men. Feeling that God had revealed His Son in him, he was confident that he would receive continuous spiritual enlightenment on all the great truths of his new faith, without any merely human interposition. Was he of whom Christ had been the teacher, directly, by His appearance to him, now to become a mere pupil of man? That would be to complete in the flesh, what had been begun in the Spirit. What, moreover, could any one tell him, except incidents and recollections from the earthly life of his Lord, while he was honoured by intimate communion with the glorified Christ, seated in the heavens, at the right hand of God, and was thus fully on a footing with the original Apostles? Of all the details of Christ's

[1] 2 Cor. xii. 33.

earthly life, only His death, and resurrection, and entry
on His glory, had special significance to Paul, and the
comparatively infrequent references to the evangelical
history in his Epistles, is quite in keeping with his

House on the town wall at Damascus.

declaration: "Even though we have known Christ after
the flesh, yet now know we Him so no more." [1]   His claim
to be an apostle rested, in his mind, solely, on his having
seen Christ. So deep was his realisation of this, that, in

[1] 2 Cor. v. 16.

his defence of the doctrine of the resurrection of the dead, he winds up his list of witnesses to that of Christ, by a solemn statement, that the Saviour had appeared, last of all, to him also.[1] He had been " known fully " by his Lord; he had been " laid hold of by Him;" he had been turned by Him into " a new creature;" Christ had " been revealed in him;" he had to do with Him, not with His servants, however eminent, and, therefore, when thus drawn, as it were, to the side of Christ, " imme- diately " after being thus chosen out by the crucified One Himself, " he conferred not with flesh and blood; neither did he go up to Jerusalem, to them who were Apostles before him, but went away into Arabia; returning," after a time, not to Jerusalem, but " to Damascus."

What must have been his thoughts when, now, after three years, he passed, once more, along the track towards the Holy City ? The gardens round Damascus, though very miserable according to our standard, have, in all ages, been wonders in the eyes of Orientals, accustomed to the yellow barrenness of the desert, but to Paul they would have no charm. The tree at whose root he had thought to lay his axe, had become to him the very tree of life. Wonderful to say, he was now " a chosen vessel " of the Nazarene, destined to " bear the " once abhorred " name, before the Gentiles, and kings, and the children of Israel."[2] He could glory, now, only in the Cross of Christ, " through which," to use his own words, " the world had been crucified to him, and he to the world."[3] From the moment of the " heavenly vision," a complete revolution had been wrought in his whole being.

[1] 1 Cor. ix. 1 ; xv. 8.   [2] Acts ix. 15.   [3] Gal. vi. 14.

Henceforth, he felt constrained by the infinite goodness shown him, in the revelation of the glorified Christ, to live no more to himself, but to Him who had loved him, and given Himself for him.   The fierce strife between his fears and hopes, in his former agony to work out his own salvation, by minute fidelity to the Pharisaic law was over   He was no longer tortured by the cry in his soul after peace with God: every fibre of his heart vibrated as if with chords and harmonious sounds from a higher world.   " I thank God," he cries, " through Jesus Christ, my Lord, there is now no condemnation to them that are in Christ Jesus.   If God be for us, who is against us ?   He that spared not His own Son, but delivered Him up for us all, how shall He not, also, with Him, freely give us all things ?   Who shall lay anything to the charge of God's elect ?   It is God that justifies; who is he that shall condemn ?   It is Christ that died, yea, rather, that was raised from the dead, who is at the right hand of God, who also makes intercession for us.   Who shall separate us from the love of Christ ?   Shall tribulation, or anguish, or persecution, or famine, or nakedness, or peril, or sword ?   Nay, in all these things we are more than conquerors, through Him that loved us.   For I am persuaded, that neither death nor life, nor angels, nor principalities, nor things present, nor things to come, nor powers, nor height, nor depth, nor any other thing created, shall be able to separate us from the love of God, which is in Christ Jesus our Lord." [1]

Such thoughts must have filled the whole nature of Paul in a measure of which ordinary Christians can have no idea, for we find, in his letters that he cannot write

[1] Rom. vii. 25 ; viii. 1, and 31 ff.

even a paragraph, without breaking out into passionate adoration of Christ and some expression of his sense of boundless obligation to Him. As he slowly passed on ; perhaps, this time, by the track that leads, south of Lebanon, to the venerable Jacob's bridge over the Jordan, below Lake Merom, he would often, we may suppose, think bitterly of his past opposition to the Master he now so fervently loved. But, as we look over his whole life, from the calm distance of later ages, it is hard to imagine that had his career been different he would have been equally fitted for the great work which that Master assigned him, by express commission, through Ananias, at Damascus.[1] Every step of his past history, from his birth to his lowly acceptance of Jesus as the Messiah, had led him towards that consummation. His being born at Tarsus, gave him a wide sympathy with other races, which he could not have learned in Judæa, and prepared him for being the apostle of the great city communities of the heathen world; his being the child of fervent " Hebrews of the Hebrews," planted the germ of a zealous religiousness in his heart, and of a glowing love for his race as the people of God; his long study in the schools of the rabbis, qualified him, pre-eminently, to meet the difficulties of his brethren, in accepting the Gospel of the crucified One, and gave him a familiarity with the ancient Scriptures which put all their treasures at the service of the new faith; his early labours in spreading Judaism among his neighbours in Cilicia, trained him to missionary work, and sustained the earnestness of his nature; and even his passionate violence against Christianity urged him, in later years, to a still greater zeal

[1] Acts ix. 15 ff.

for the Gospel, as the only atonement he could make, and
filled him with a tender humility, patient towards others
and diffident of himself. Had he been born in Judæa,
and been one of the disciples of Jesus, hearing and seeing
His words and deeds, with all the narrow influences of
Palestine limiting his ideas, he would, in all probability,
like the other Apostles, have become only a missionary
to his countrymen, coloured, to the end, by ineradicable
Jewish prejudices, and a zealot for the Jewish Law,
which, by his lineage and education, was the object of
his hereditary idolatry.   But, looking on Christianity, as
he did, for years, from outside, with the keen eyes of its
enemy, he saw, clearly, that Jesus utterly rejected the
husk of traditional and formal amplifications, and laid
stress only on the kernel of pure religious life which it
taught, thus approving the rejection of the merely ceremonial and external in Judaism and all other religions,
so far as they were regarded essentials, and introducing
the grand conception of the true religion being that only
of the life of God in the soul.   There was no reason why
Paul should hide this from himself, or be silent respecting it; on the contrary, it was natural that he should
put it clearly before his mind, to justify his hostility to
Christ.   But this very fact would, assuredly, give him a
fuller insight into the scope of Christianity, in its full
sweep, than the other Apostles could possess, and raise
him to a much higher and freer position than theirs.
The wrong he had done Christ became, thus, the cause
of a more intense love to Him, as his mind opened
to more just views.   When he saw its wickedness,
his fierce persecution of the Church would make him
hate all his past life, and tear himself free with strong

revulsion of feeling, from the Judaism he had hitherto
cherished. In the fullest sense, he was a new crea-
tule. Compromise was impossible, and the zealot for the
Law, unconsciously to himself, had been already transformed—to use Christ's words, into "a chosen vessel,
to bear His name before the heathen." [1] In this abrupt
transition his many-sided culture and versatility was of
peculiar value, enabling him at once to defend and maintain his new and freer conceptions of Christianity with
consummate skill, and to show commanding power in
spreading a really spiritual religion over the world. He,
himself, indeed, realised, at times, that the good hand of
God had "separated him" for Himself "from his mother's
womb," and, at the right moment, in His wise purpose, had
"called him, by His grace, by revealing His Son in him,
that he might preach Him among the heathen." [2] The
example of his parents, and the traditions of his ances-
try, had, from the first, impressed his nature deeply, and
having inherited their sincere conscientiousness and fervent
Judaism, he had striven with enthusiastic, self-denying
zeal, to carry out, in its minutest details, that "righteousness of the Law," which alone, as he believed, made him
pleasing to God. But Jewish religionism, which was
then his little world, was a survival of twilight ages;
its modes of thought were perverted; its conceptions
elementary; its conclusions, resting on them, only worthy
of the half light in which they had been formed. Yet he
neither knew nor felt that the "light that was in him was
darkness;" or that he took human fancies for revelations
from above; though agonisingly conscious that his search
for peace of heart had not brought him to it. But this

[1] Acts ix. 15.   [2] Gal. i. 15, 16.

was, after all, a part of his Divine training, as a designed apostle. It needed but little, to make him "light, in the Lord." The ether-waves of heavenly truth lay slumbering round him, as day sleeps round us, through the night, and, at the vision of Christ, the heavenly Sun, near the gates of Damascus, they kindled, forthwith, into spiritual day.

The special object of Paul's turning towards Jerusalem, when forced to leave Damascus, was, he tells us, "that he might make the acquaintance of Peter," [1]—the chief man in the Jerusalem Church, then the centre of Christianity,—who, from that very position, and his relations to Christ, exercised great influence among the scattered Christian communities everywhere. The new apostle had laboured independently at Damascus so long, that it would not now compromise his claim, of holding his apostolic commission as the older Apostles held theirs, directly from Christ; nor could it be said that he was the disciple of either Peter or any of the Twelve; a point on which he was at all times very sensitive. " I received my ministry from the Lord Jesus," says he, to the elders of the Church at Ephesus.[2]   He was "an apostle," he told the Galatians, "not from men, neither through man, but through Jesus Christ, and God the Father." [3]   " He had been intrusted with the message he preached," he says elsewhere, " according to the commandment of God our Saviour." [4]   " I received it neither from man, nor was I taught it, but it came to me through revelation of Jesus Christ," says he, once more, to the Galatians.[5]

But it was desirable, that, in view of his future work

[1] Gal. i. 18.   [2] Acts xx. 24.   [3] Gal. i. 1.
[4] Titus i. 3.   [5] Gal. i. 12.

II.   K

among the heathen populations of the empire, to which
he had been set apart by his Master, he should establish
loving relations with the heads of the Mother Church,
and the Apostles at large; the representatives, with himself, of the risen Saviour. As an apostle, he had taken,
we may be sure, no letters of introduction from the
Christians in Damascus, if, indeed, his sudden flight
from that city had allowed his getting them. It was
his to give, not to accept such letters. Doubtless, he
assumed that the rumour of his conversion, and of his
three years' labours for Christ, had reached the Holy
City, and would secure him a welcome. But though it
was so long since he had left it, the terror of his name
still survived; for how many of the brethren must there
have been, whom he had caused to be flogged, or beaten
with sticks, or thrown into the dungeons of the priests'
jail; how many of those dear to them had he even persecuted "unto the death," [1] and how many families had
he forced to save their lives from his violence, by flight
from their homes and friends! It is not surprising, therefore, that, when he made attempts to connect himself
with the community which had suffered so fearfully at
his hands, its members were all afraid of him, and could
not believe that he was really a Christian; suspecting
him, rather, of being a spy, seeking their fellowship to
betray them.[2] Fortunately, there was one among them
who believed in him—the Levite Joseph, afterwards, from
his signal ability as a speaker, known among the Christians as Barnabas—in Aramaic, "the son of exhortation," or, as we should say, "the eminent preacher"—a
man famous in the little community, for having sold a

[1] Acts xxii. 4.   [2] Acts ix. 26.

field which he owned, and handed over the price he received for it, to the Apostles, for the benefit of the poor. He was, originally, by descent if not by birth, from the island of Cyprus, and thus, like Paul, a Hellenist, and may have met the new apostle previously, at Damascus. Seeing his trouble, this friend in need volunteered to introduce him to the chief men, and told the story so forcibly, of his having seen Christ, and of having been graciously addressed by Him, while on his journey, for the high priest, three years before, and of his subsequent baptism and his devotion ever since, as had been evidenced by his preaching boldly in the sacred name at Damascus,—that Peter received him as his guest; entertaining him while he remained at Jerusalem, which was only for fifteen days. Of the other "pillars" of the Church, however, he saw only one—James, the brother of Christ,[1] and left without putting himself in any way forward, either in the city or neighbourhood, so that, years after, he was "still unknown by face to the churches of Judæa."[2] May this have risen from his views being too advanced, as yet, for Peter and James? His ideas respecting the Law, his opinion about the conversion of the heathen without requiring them to become Jews, and the largeness of his mind generally, may have raised distrust as to his "soundness," and made them dread the result of his taking any public share in the Church-life of brethren so narrow and prejudiced as the Jewish-Christians of the capital. It is, at least, striking to find Peter,[3] immediately after this interview, acting, for the first time, in the case of the centurion at

---

[1] Acts iv. 36, 37 ; xiii. 1, 9, 27 ; Gal. i. 18, 19.
[2] Gal. i. 22.   [3] Acts ix. 31 ; xi. 18.

Cæsarea, in the spirit of Paul, though, indeed, we are told, that he and John had, previously, gone down to Samaria and preached to the townspeople there, and in many Samaritan villages—a wonderful stretch of liberality for a Jew. Yet they may have done so without abandoning the demand, that converts should accept the Law in the Jewish sense; Peter clearly thinking this essential, till freed from his hereditary conceptions, by the vision at Joppa.[1] But had his intercourse with Paul not given the mind of Peter its first impulse towards a larger view of the spirit of Christianity, finding, as he did, that it had the advocacy of a man so acute as Paul? He might reflect, moreover, that this noble liberalism had already marked his prolonged labours at Damascus, giving occasion, very possibly, beyond anything else, to the hostility of the Jews towards him. In any case, one with such views could not possibly have been a disciple of the Apostles, for with his deeper insight into the genius of Christianity than Peter, or any of the leaders of the Church, he must have been Peter's teacher rather than his scholar. As things were, it was clear that Paul could do nothing at Jerusalem. Alike as too liberal, and as associated with hateful memories, it was better for him to work elsewhere. His one hope of usefulness in the city was among the Hellenists. to whose synagogues, therefore, he betook himself, "speaking and disputing" in them, against the current Messianic ideas, but the only result was, that they plotted to seize and murder him, as they had done St. Stephen.[2]

In this strait, he himself tells us,[3] he betook himself to God, in the Temple, to seek counsel by prayer. His

[1] Acts viii. 14, 25; x. 9–16. [2] Acts ix. 29. [3] Acts xxii. 18 ff.

whole nature, we may readily conceive, was intensely
excited. His first persecution as a Christian, which had
driven him from Damascus, his narrow escape, his return
along the road so memorable to him, his agitation as to
his future, since the Church at Jerusalem so painfully
shunned him, and, above all, his spiritual exaltation of
frame and feeling, from habitual contemplation of the
transcendent experiences of the past three years, had
combined to lift him, in a measure, above ordinary mental
conditions. While he was praying in the Temple, therefore, he tells us, " he fell into a trance," and had a vision
of Christ, " seeing Him and hearing Him say, Make haste,
and get thee quickly out of Jerusalem : because they will
not receive *of thee* testimony respecting Me." In meek
reply, Paul adds that he said, " Lord, they themselves
know that I imprisoned and beat in every synagogue
them that believed on Thee : and when the blood of
Stephen Thy witness was shed, I also was standing by,
and consenting, and keeping the garments of them that
slew him." But Christ only repeated His command,
saying, " Depart : for I will send thee forth, far hence,
unto the Gentiles." [1] It is curious to find that in one of
his Epistles,[2] Paul, without any break, connects with his
account of his narrow escape from death at Damascus,
a touching allusion to " visions and revelations of the
Lord," of which he specifies, however, only one, granted
him fourteen years before ; a period carrying us, perhaps,
back to this very time. In that " trance," if we may call
it so, he says, he was caught up, whether in the body, or
out of the body, he did not know, to even the third
heaven — to Paradise, and heard unspeakable words

---

[1] Acts xxii. 18–21.   [2] 1 Cor. xi. 32–xii. 6.

which it is not lawful for a man to utter. This
wondrous incident happened to him, he tells us, when
he was already "in Christ," so that it cannot refer to the
vision on the Damascus road, for he was then a Jew.
To mention it in a passage telling of his danger when
fleeing from the Syrian capital, certainly connects it
with that time, and it may have been, just then, on his
reaching Jerusalem that this appearance of Christ was
granted to him, while he was at his Temple-devotions,
and he was again honoured by words from the Divine
lips, repeating the command previously given in Damascus, and, now, finally deciding his future life. In his
love for his nation he would fain have won them to the
Cross, and their rejection of his ministry was an agony
beyond words. But not to them; to the great heathen
world, said the Master, was he to go forth. From this
time, Palestine was to know him no more, except when
he occasionally visited it; the lands of the West were
to be the scene of his labours, his sufferings, and his
triumphs. Was not this vision, so momentous in its results, that in which he received the superlative revelations
of which he speaks so fully in his letter to the Corinthians ? What occasion can we conceive more fitting for
the renewal of those relations with His chosen servant,
amidst the upper splendours, which the risen Christ had,
before, granted him on the highway to Damascus ? He
would soon need all the consolation and support of even
such supreme assurances of the favour of his Lord, and of
his having followed no cunningly devised fables in making
known "the power and coming of the Lord Jesus Christ."
His loyalty to Him would involve sufferings which he
might without irreverence compare to those of the

Saviour Himself, but he could bear them calmly, now
that he had twice been an eye-witness of His Majesty.[1]

It is of course impossible, with our ignorance of the
higher laws of our complex nature, and, still more, of
the inter-relations with the spiritual world of which
it is susceptible, to understand phenomena so exceptional as an " ecstasy," to use the Greek word translated
in our version " a trance," in which Paul saw and heard
the words of the glorified Christ. The same expression is
used of the wonder of the friends round the daughter of
Jairus, when " she rose up and walked," after " they had
laughed Jesus to scorn, knowing that she was dead ; "[2]
of the wonder of the women, at the vision of the angel, in
the empty tomb of Christ ;[3] of the wonder of the crowd
at the healing of the paralytic,[4] and of that of those who
saw the healing of the lame beggar in the Temple, by
Peter.[5] That apostle, moreover, is said to have been in
an ecstasy, or trance, when he saw the vision on the
house-roof at Joppa, and Paul[6] similarly describes his
condition, when the vision was granted him. while praying in the Temple.[7] It, thus, means " the being out of
one's ordinary mind," whether from wonder or terror, but,
especially, a state in which the soul is unconscious of
things around, and is, for the time, raised, as it were, out
of itself, by visions of things distant or outside the usual
sphere of the senses. But all this is no explanation.
We can, at best, only turn to any imperfect parallel
which later times offers, the most striking of which is,
perhaps, the well accredited case of Mr. Grimshaw,

[1] 2 Peter i. 16 ; Col. i. 24. [2] Mark v. 42 ; Luke viii. 53.
[3] Mark xvi. 8. [4] Luke v. 26. [5] Acts iii. 10.
[6] Acts x. 10, 11. [7] Acts xxii. 17.

Rector of Haworth, afterwards the home of the Brontés.
The narrative, printed by John Newton, as given by a
trustworthy servant of Mr. Grimshaw, is as follows:—
" That she was called up that morning (September 2, 1744)
at five o'clock, but found her master was risen before her,
and was retired into a private room for prayer. After
remaining there some time, he went to a house in
Haworth, where he was engaged awhile in religious
exercises with some of his people. He then returned
home and retired for prayer, again, and from thence
went to the church. She believes he had not eaten anything that morning. While reading the second lesson he
fell down, but was soon helped and led out of the church.
He continued to talk as he went, and desired them not to
disperse, for he hoped he would soon return to them, and
he had something extraordinary to say to them. They
led him to the clerk's house, where he lay seemingly in-
sensible. She, with others, was employed in rubbing his
limbs, which were exceedingly cold, with warm cloths.
After some time he came to himself, and seemed to be in
a great rapture. The first words he spoke were, ' I have
had a glorious vision from the third heaven.' But she
does not remember that he made any mention of what he
had seen. In the afternoon he performed service in the
church, which began at two o'clock, and preached and
spoke so long to the people, that it was seven o'clock in
the evening before he returned home." The truthful-
ness and integrity of Mr. Grimshaw are vouched for by
Newton in the strongest terms, and he thoughtfully adds:
—" Perhaps there is a faculty in the human constitution,
adapted to an intercourse with the intellectual (that is
spiritual) world, as our natural senses are to the objects

which at present surround us, but which faculty is dormant while we are in health and distinctly awake, unless
when God is pleased, in some extraordinary cases, to call
it into exercise."[1]   A more striking parallel to the New
Testament narratives of such "trances" may perhaps,
however, be found in the case of Balaam,[2] who speaks of
himself as "the man whose outer eyes are closed while
his inner sight is opened; the man who hears the words
of God, who sees the vision of the Almighty, (when) fallen
(down in a trance—prostrate—and overpowered by the
Divine afflatus) but having his eyes open."[3]   Nearer than
this we cannot hope to come, in any attempts to understand what Paul tells us of his amazing experience, though
it may be well to turn to the notices scattered through
Scripture, of the phenomena of higher spiritual impulses
vouchsafed in different cases.[4]   The characteristics of
"vision" or "the inspiration of the Almighty" may have
varied in some details of communication or outward expression, but much must have been alike, whether they came
in dreams, or trances, or in other unknown modes.

In so fanatical and excitable a population as that of
Jerusalem, one who had deserted his hereditary faith, and
joined another, thought to be in deadly opposition to it,
must, at any time, have been in the greatest danger.   It
was as if an ulema of great reputed sanctity, at Mecca,
having left for a time, to convert the infidel, had returned,
himself a convert, to preach the abhorred faith which he
had laboured to destroy.   The life of such a giaour would
not be worth an hour's purchase!   But the danger at

[1] Newton's Life of Grimshaw, pp. 36, 46.
[2] Numb. xxiv. 3, 4.   [3] Dillmann.
[4] 1 Sam. xix. 24 ; Ezek. i. 28 ; Dan. viii. 18 ; x. 15–18 ; Rev. i. 10, 17.

Jerusalem was intensified, at the moment, by the wild excitement then swaying all minds in ever recurring paroxysms, respecting the attempt of Caligula to get his statue set up for worship in the Temple. Rumours spread, ever and anon, that the abomination was actually on its way by sea from Rome, and vast crowds streamed from every part of the country to wait, for weeks together, before the governor, or Agrippa, at Acre, Tiberias, or Antipatris, while such commotion made all minds so inflammable, that any one held to be an apostate, as Paul was, could not hope to find pity, if he could be seized. The little band of Christians to whom his presence in Jerusalem was known, hurried him off, therefore, to Cæsarea, the one considerable port of Palestine, but, apparently from finding no vessel ready, by which he could sail, despatched him, thence, by land, through Syria, to Tarsus, whither he had resolved to betake himself.[1] There we lose all trace of him for several years, but who can doubt that he was eagerly employed, in this retirement, in devoted labours as a Christian missionary ?

[1] Gal. i. 21.

CHAPTER VIII

IN CILICIA

C. A.D. 39–48; PAUL'S AGE, c. 29–38

PÁUL'S stay at Damascus, his fortnight's visit to Jerusalem, when he lived with Peter, and possibly the possession of early drafts of the Gospel history, written by some
who had been with Christ as apostles or disciples, had
supplemented his general knowledge of Christ's life and
work.   When, therefore, we find him in his Epistles
passing lightly over its historical details; proving the
Messiahship of Jesus rather from the Old Testament
than from His life, and laying stress on the supreme
significance of His death, rather than relating the facts
of His public labours, it does not imply a want of knowledge of these, but marks his special modes of thought.
When he saw occasion he could so "openly," or vividly,
"set forth Jesus crucified, before the very eyes" of the
Galatians, that there was no need that they should turn
to any other source of information.[1]   He speaks of the
descent of Christ from David, and of His baptism.[2]   His
poverty was well known to him,[3] and he delighted to
dwell on His gentle mildness, His self-forgetting humbly-

[1] Gal. iii. 1 ; i. 6.
[2] Rom. i. 3 ; ix. 5 ; Col. ii. 11 ; Rom. vi. 3, 4 ; 1 Cor. xii. 13 ; Gal. iii. 27.
[3] Phil. ii. 5–8.

ministering love.[1] The story of the Last Supper was
minutely familiar to him.[2] He speaks of the rulers
having crucified Christ; of His betrayal; of the reproaches
at the Cross; of our Lord's weakness as He hung on it,
and of the superscription set over Him by Pilate.[3] His
narrative of the appearances of Christ after the Resurrection, discloses instances omitted even from the Gospels,
and it is noteworthy that he expressly states that he had
received, of course from the Apostles Peter and James, or
from some one in their circle, not only the details of these
appearances, but the particulars of the death, burial, and
resurrection.[4] He seems even to have preserved for us
sayings of our Lord which would otherwise have been lost;
as, for instance, that delightful one, "It is more blessed
to give than to receive,"[5] and a striking intimation respecting the coming of Christ.[6] Other indications of
his thorough acquaintance with the story and words of his
Master abound, as may be seen from the references at
the foot of this page.[7]

But, notwithstanding this full knowledge of the evangelical history, Paul never forgets that he has to proclaim
"the Son of God revealed in him," and this so occupies
his thoughts that he only incidentally notices external

---

[1] 2 Cor. v. 14 ff.; Gal. ii. 20; Phil. i. 8.   [2] 1 Cor. xi. 23-26.
[3] 1 Cor. ii. 8; xi. 23; xv. 3; Rom. xv. 3; 2 Cor. xiii. 4; Col. ii. 14.
[4] 1 Cor. xv. 3-8.   [5] Acts xx. 35.   [6] 1 Thess. iv. 15-18.
[7] 1 Cor. ix. 14; 1 Thess. ii. 6, compared with Luke x. 7; 1 Cor. vii. 10,
compared with Matt. v. 32; Rom. xiv. 4, compared with Matt. vii. 1;
Rom. ii. 19, compared with Matt. xv. 14; 1 Cor. x. 27, compared with
Luke x. 8; Matt. xv. 11; 1 Cor. xiii. 2, compared with Matt. xvii. 20;
2 Cor. i. 17, compared with Matt. v. 37; 2 Cor. xi. 2 ff., compared with
Matt. ix. 15; xxv. 1-12; 1 Thess. iv. 14, compared with Matt. xxiv. 30;
1 Thess. iv. 16, compared with Matt. xxiv. 31; 1 Thess. iv. 17, compared
with Matt. xxiv. 30; 1 Thess. v. 1, compared with Matt. xxiv. 43, &c.

details, dwelling, habitually, on the spiritual features of Christianity, as disclosed either by revelations made to him directly, or, from what he has learned from his fellow-Christians; the two sources being so interblended that it is impossible, at times, to know to which to ascribe them.

The character of his preaching, while at Tarsus and in Cilicia, may best be conceived from a remembrance of his training, and a careful study of the Epistles. His spiritual struggles while still a Pharisee, now calmed, for ever, by the Gospel of the Cross, left much of his early tutelage which in no degree contradicted his new faith. The death of the Messiah on "the tree" had, indeed, been the solution, to Paul, of the difficulties he had felt in the Pharisaic doctrine of Justification before God, so that he could hold that as firmly after as before his conversion. Only in so far as the death of Jesus—the Messiah—affected the Pharisaic ways of thinking did he need to give up any part of them. In fact he adhered, to a large extent, to his Jewish theology to the end of his life, for to the last he speaks of himself as a Pharisee.[1] The only change demanded was to settle, how the great facts he now accepted, of the death and resurrection of the Christ, stood in reference to the Jewish teaching; the body of Rabbinical theology on nearly all other points being accepted without alteration, as indisputable, by him as by them. The fundamental principle of all religion in their system was that man must be righteous, or "justified," before God, to secure His favour. This, Paul tenaciously maintained, as he did also the Pharisaic deduction from it, that God could only save men when they had fully satisfied all His demands. But while,

[1] 2 Cor. xi. 22; Phil. iii. 5; Acts xxiii. 6.

before his conversion, he held, with his teachers, that man could be just before God by the fulfilling of the Law, he believed, now, that he could be justified only by the propitiatory death of the Messiah. As a Jew, he had expected to win a place in the approaching kingdom of God, as his due, since, " touching the righteousness which is in the Law, he would be found blameless." As a Christian, he proclaimed that " by the works of the Law shall no flesh be accounted righteous in God's sight," [1] but only " through faith in Jesus Christ." [2] The keystone of his theology, therefore, was the contradiction between righteousness which is the free gift of God, through faith—or, as he expresses it, at times,—" by God's grace, through the redemption that is in Christ Jesus," [3] and righteousness by the observance of the commands of the Law. His idea of what was implied in " fulfilling the Law," was, in fact, radically different, as a Christian, from what it had been while he remained a Jew. It extended beyond the painful keeping of all the ritual injunctions of Judaism, beyond circumcision, washings, purifications, mortifications, and acts of public and private devotion, and embraced all religious and moral duties, in their widest sense, including purity of the heart, unselfish love of all mankind, and, as the atmosphere of the soul, a perfect morality. When he speaks of the Law of Moses as able to " justify," if perfectly obeyed, he includes its moral as well as ritual demands, but since no one could claim to have obeyed it in this sweeping definition;—the best of us having to own that he has not acted up to the perfect ideal of its moral requirements, it was hopeless to look to it for the " righteousness " which alone would save.

[1] Rom. iii. 20. [2] Gal. ii. 16. [3] Rom. iii. 24 ; v. *passim.*

From this fundamental principle of his faith, Paul
builds up his disclosure of "the way of salvation." Man,
by nature, is "flesh"—that is, taken from the earth, and
superior to it only by the living breath of God in his
nostrils. Subject to disease and death, by sin, "the
flesh" is at once the symbol, and almost the source, of
our fallen moral condition. But our nature has also
"spirit," that is, a soul, though what it is we can only
judge from its being immortal, and capable of restoration
to the sinlessness which God demands, yet not in this
life. He even speaks of "spiritual bodies," illustrating
their relations to our present nature, by the springing of
the new grain, from the seed we sow.[1] The soul is quickened into Christian life by the Spirit of God, so as to become "a new creature," and thus "born again," those who
hereafter receive the "spiritual body," will pass "from
glory to glory," advancing constantly to a more complete
resemblance to "the glory of God," that is, to the splendour round about Him, till they become like the glorious
spiritual body of the risen and glorified Christ.[2] To
the Jew, until very shortly before Christ, and to the
Sadducees, to the last, the "soul" had been the living
principle in the blood, which, therefore, was prohibited
from use, in animals killed for food. The original conception of it, as only the life given to all creatures by
the quickening breath of God, was thus retained. But
with Paul, it is an immortal, invisible principle, surrounded, here, by impurity, death, and sin, but ordained,
if saved through Christ, to a higher destiny, in a world of
light, blessedness, purity, and perfect holiness. "In my
flesh," says Paul, "dwelleth sin." "I am sold under sin"

[1] 1 Cor. xv. 44.   [2] Phil. iii. 21 ; Col. iii. 4.

—that is, I am its slave.[1] The flesh is thus the seat of all evil; the enemy of all good. But, opposed to it, in the " new man," is the Law of the Spirit, to which all that is good in him is due. Paul had not thought thus when a Pharisaic Jew, hoping for salvation by his own works, but the sight of the Cross had opened his eyes, and, by revealing the spirituality of the Law, had left only a profound sense of his unworthiness.

Man, as descended from Adam, was clearly unable to conquer the " flesh," so as to stand righteous before God, by His standard of holiness. This could only be brought about through the Messiah. Before his conversion, Paul had believed that this Representative of Jehovah would come, as soon as Israel was righteous. He now held, that the Messiah had come, to make man righteous. As descended from the Adam of Eden, mankind could not gain that new creation which the Spirit of God imparted, for, by him, had come death, in the widest sense. The Messiah must, therefore, come as a new spiritual Adam, in whose likeness men might be endowed with a nobler life, governed by new laws.[2] Only by such a renovation of our nature, could we be freed from slavery to the " flesh." Christ had existed from eternity, and through Him God had made the worlds. " Being in the form of God, He counted it not a prize to be grasped, to be on an equality with God."[3] He is thus infinitely above all imperfections of the " flesh," and, also, above all distinctions of race or nation. As, moreover, only by Him, and in His image, the new humanity is created, He is the Second Adam. In the fulness of time, laying aside the glory which He

[1] Rom. vii. 14, 17.   [2] 2 Cor. v. 17 ; 1 Cor. xv. 45, 47.

[3] Phil. ii. 6 ; Col. i. 15–17 ; 1 Cor. viii. 6.

had with the Father, before the world was, "He took on
Himself the form of a servant, being made in the likeness
of men; and being found in fashion as a man, He humbled
Himself, becoming obedient even to death; yea, the death
of the Cross.   Wherefore, also, God highly exalted Him,
and gave Him the name which is above every name;
that in the name of Jesus every knee should bow, of
things in heaven, and things on earth, and things under
the earth and that every tongue should confess that Jesus
Christ is Lord, to the glory of God the Father."[1]   His
death was a divinely appointed offering for sin; that sin
past and future might not go unpunished.   "Bearing our
sins, in His own body, on the tree," He endured the penalty
due for them, and thus redeemed man, who had fallen
away from the Law.   He is our "Passover, sacrificed for
us," to save us from wrath, as the Paschal lamb saved
Israel.[2]   Faith in His atoning death, witnessed by a
godly life, secures man all that the Redeemer represents;
victory over the flesh, and, also, over the curse pronounced
on it—death here and hereafter.   The righteousness of
God being vindicated, by the propitiation offered by His
"own Son;" the way is opened for the gift of the Spirit,
to build up the new life of the believer, and lead him on,
"from glory to glory."   The death of the body is to be
followed by the resurrection of all the dead, who will be
judged by the glorified Messiah, and then will come the
final entrance of "the saints" into possession of their
"inheritance," "purchased" for them by the sacrificial
death of Christ, and, thus, the "kingdom of God," or "of
heaven"—the equivalent of the Messianic kingdom of the
Jew, will be established.

[1] Phil. ii. 7–11.   [2] 1 Cor. v. 7; 2 Cor. v. 21; Rom. iii. 25; Gal. iii. 13.

The correspondences, and also the differences, between the Jewish idea of this kingdom of the Messiah, held, no doubt by Paul, in common with all his race, till his opinions were revolutionised by the incident on the Damascus road, are curious and interesting, as showing the points on which he would need specially to combat the prejudices of his fellow-Jews, on this subject, in his teaching. The great national Pharisee party talked, like the Christians, of "this age" and of the "coming age."[1] These two great periods were separated by the day of judgment, which, in the theology of both, was to take place "in the last time," or "in the end of days." The curiosity of the disciples to learn "when these things would be?"[2] was only an expression of that desire to know the future, which is natural to man. But it was especially keen in our Lord's day, impelling the rabbis to all modes of calculation, to satisfy it; for they were the old-world counterparts of those, among ourselves, who pry into the secrets of Providence by elaborate studies of the Book of Daniel, or the mysterious hints of "Revelation." But speculations as to the time of the final catastrophe, led on to anticipations of its details, and it was, hence, taught, that the approach of the great consummation would be heralded by fearful portents. The Temple would be desecrated, and hitherto unequalled calamities would smite the nations; forecasts in striking correspondence with the teaching of our Lord Himself, and, also, of Paul.[3] Swords would appear in the sky at midnight, and blood trickle from the

---

[1] *Aiōn*, "age," "world," Luke xvi. 8; xviii. 30; xx. 34, 35; Rom. xii. 2; 1 Cor. i. 20; ii. 8; 2 Cor. iv. 4; Gal. i. 4; Heb. ix. 26; "last days," Jas. v. 3; 2 Tim. iii. 1; 2 Pet. iii. 3, &c., &c.

[2] Mark xiii. 4; Acts i. 6.

[3] Matt. xxiv. *passim*; 2 Thess. iv. ff.

rocks. The whole course of nature would, in fact, be deranged. An appalling outbreak of idolatry and wickedness, would, moreover, remind men of the days before the flood.[1] The Messiah was to be of the race of David, but He was simply to be a great king. endowed with high powers by God, for the glory of Israel. The heathen rulers, it was affirmed, would gather against the chosen people, to wage war on them, but would be utterly destroyed by the sword of the Messiah, or, rather, by a sword going out of His mouth, just as in Revelation.[2] He would then reign, as a righteous king, over Israel, holding all the heathen nations in subjection; setting up His throne in Jerusalem, and reigning from it, as His great capital, over all peoples, for ever. This was the Jewish " kingdom of God," to enter on the felicities of which was the deepest longing of every Israelite. It was to be in this world, but sin and the devil would be destroyed. The scattered tribes would return ; Jerusalem would be rebuilt with surpassing glory ; the earth would be fruitful as Eden ; wild beasts become tame, and men live peacefully through centuries. After a cycle like this, the final judgment would, at last, take place. Till then, the souls of the dead would dwell under the earth, or in some region of the west. The fallen angels, meanwhile, lay bound under the earth.[3] At the day of judgment, however, they would be thrown into a fiery abyss. Good men would inherit glory, but the wicked would be turned into hell. The change in Paul's views, from this narrowly Jewish conception, when he became a Christian, must have made it

---

- Luke xvii. 22–36 ; 1 Pet. iii. 20.
[2] Rev. xix. 15, 21 ; 2 Thess. ii. 8.
[3] Rev. ix. 14 ; xx. 2 ; xii. 9 ; 2 Pet. ii. 4 ; Jude 5, 6.

very difficult to secure a patient hearing from his proud
and bigoted fellow-Jews, for Christ's kingdom, which he
preached, was only a spiritual one, and the heathen were
to be admitted to it on the same footing as others, while
the Crucified One was to reign, not on earth, but at the
right hand of the majesty in the heavens, till He had put
all His enemies, including death, under His feet.[1] This
would take place at Christ's coming from the heavens,
but this coming was expected, no one knew how soon.
The Thessalonians, in fact, looked for it at any moment,
and were sorely troubled lest those of their friends who
had died, should lose their place, as it were, when Christ
appeared, and be more or less thrown into the shade by
those who might still be alive. Paul comforts them in
regard to this, though he speaks of Christ coming while
he and others were still living.[2] This advent would break
on men unexpectedly, as a thief comes in the night. But
the Thessalonians, being forewarned, might watch, and not
let it overtake them unawares. Yet, whether it would find
this one alive, or, that one, dead, was uncertain. In his
second Epistle, written, like the first, in A.D. 54, he regrets
that his words have disturbed their minds, and tones them
down, by intimating that certain things must happen before
the day of the Lord, recalling to their memories that he
had spoken in this way when he was at Thessalonica.
The impression they had received, however, was, that the
eventful hour was close at hand.—Two years later, in his
first letter to the Corinthians, he writes—" Judge nothing
before the time, until the Lord come."—" We shall not
all sleep (that is, die), but we shall all be changed—at
the last trump," and he ends the Epistle by the word

[1] 1 Cor. xv. 25, 26.   [2] 1 Thess. iv. 15–17 ; v. 10, 23.

Maranatha, which was the Aramaic **for** "the Lord cometh!" Still two years later, in 58, he rouses the Roman believers by the trumpet sound—"The night is far spent, and the day is at hand," and comforts them by the assurance that "The God of peace shall bruise Satan under their feet shortly," an expression explained by his language to the Thessalonians—that "The Lord Jesus would slay the Wicked (or Lawless) one . . . by the manifestation of His coming." Four years later, he writes to the Philippians, in A.D. 62, that " the good work begun in them will be perfected until the day of Jesus Christ;" and that he and they were, alike, "waiting for a Saviour, the Lord Jesus Christ, coming," and towards the end of the Epistle, he exhorts them to forbearance, by reminding them that "The Lord is at hand." In the same year, he tells the Colossians, in words which must be understood by his language in other Epistles, that "When Christ shall be manifested, then ye, also, shall, with him, be manifested in glory." Finally, in his letter to Titus, written in the year 64,— the year before his martyrdom—he reminds him that "We are looking for the blessed hope, and appearing of the glory of our great God and Saviour, Jesus Christ." [1] Thus, Paul preached, no doubt, from first to last, at Tarsus and round it, to his old fellow-townsmen and neighbours, in their synagogues, or wherever he was permitted. But in proclaiming the possibly immediate coming of Christ, he only repeated the expectation of the Apostles and of the general body of Christians. "The coming of the Lord is at hand," says St. James;

[1] 2 Thess. iii. 4; 1 Cor. iv. 5; xv. 51; xvi. 22; Rom. xiii. 11, 12; xvi. 20; Phil. i. 6; iii. 20; iv. 5; Col. iii. 4; Titus ii. 13.

" the Judge standeth before the doors." [1]   " Exhort one
another the more, as ye see the day approaching," says
the author of the Epistle to the Hebrews.[2]   " The end
of all things is at hand," says St. Peter.[3]   Similarly,
" Revelation" opens by announcing, " Behold, He cometh
with clouds, and every eye shall see Him, and they also
who pierced Him "—so that His accusers and executioners
would be still alive when He returned.[4]   At its close,
moreover, Christ Himself is introduced as saying, " Behold, I come quickly," and that " the time is at hand; " [5]
repeating, in the last verse of all—" Surely, I come
quickly."   Moreover, Jesus Himself tells us that the
then living generation would not pass away till all that
He had just foretold should be accomplished, including
His return from the other world, in overpowering majesty.
" Then shall appear the sign of the Son of Man in heaven :
and then shall all the tribes of the earth mourn, and they
shall see the Son of Man coming in the clouds of heaven
with power and great glory.   And He shall send forth
His angels with a great sound of a trumpet, and they
shall gather together His elect from the four winds—that
is, from all quarters of the earth—from one end of heaven
to another.   Verily I say unto you, This generation shall
not pass away, till all these things be accomplished.
Heaven and earth shall pass away, but My words shall
not pass away; " [6] a passage from which Paul evidently
draws his picture of the near future, in his letter to the
Thessalonians.[7]   We all know the effect of a wide announcement that the Advent is near, for it has once and

---

[1] Jas. v. 8, 9.   [2] Heb. x. 25.   [3] 1 Pet. iv. 7 ; 2 Pet. iii. 8, 9.
[4] Rev i. 7.   [5] Rev. xxii. 10, 12.
[6] Matt. xxiv. 30, 31, 34, 35.   [7] 1 Thess. iv. 13–18.

again, in every century, led to great excitement in all
classes. We can fancy, then, the power it would have,
in an age so much more easily stirred by religious
portents, than our colder times; how it would startle
the unhappy slaves and poor of the first age, who were
the bulk of the audiences of the Apostles, and not a
few who, though in a better position, felt the awful
burden of a hopeless life, such as heathenism offered.
For to all these it would seem indeed from the heavens,
since, to all who accepted Jesus as the Saviour, whether
they were Jews or heathen, free or slaves, barbarians, or
cultured, the rolling thunders, and the trump of God that
announced His approach would be the proclamation of
eternal bliss; when they would be caught up to meet the
Lord in the air, and so be for ever with Him! If the
Jew hesitated, unwilling to relinquish his dream of a
world-wide Jewish empire, and a triumphant "kingdom
of God," upon earth, when he would be able to revenge
himself on the Gentile, for all that his race had suffered;
to the millions like sheep without a shepherd, in the wide
world outside Judaism, it must often have seemed, in
very deed, a voice from the heavens, bringing a Divine
message of hope and gladness to the hitherto despairing,
dignifying even the most sunken by its overtures of
heavenly love and a blissful future life, and lighting
up even the cell of the slave by its declaration, that,
he also was a son of the Great Father and an object
of His tender and beneficent regard.

It is of course impossible to give more than a very imperfect sketch of even the great characteristics of Paul's
preaching, as shown in his written remains, but the few
outlines I have offered, will help us to realise his mode

of address, among those to whom he had, now, once more, turned.

We are so accustomed to think of Paul as the apostle of the "Gentiles" that we fancy him as giving his special care to them rather than to his own race. But this is a misconception; for throughout his whole career, his mission, to use his own words, was to preach "the Gospel" as "the power of God unto salvation to every one that believes; to the Jew first, but also to the Greek,"[1] or, as Christ expressed the same idea, he was to "begin at Jerusalem."[2] When, therefore, he left Palestine for Cilicia, he would, assuredly, address himself, primarily, to the Jews, in their synagogues, and, doubtless, also, from house to house, as he had opportunity;[3] turning to the Gentiles, or heathen, only when no longer able to get a hearing from his own people.[4] At the same time, the seeds of future trouble with his narrow-minded race must have been early sown, by his frank avowal that Jehovah was not the God of the Jews only, but also of the Gentiles.[5] Had he sought the conversion of the heathen chiefly, he might well have stayed at Antioch, or in Cilicia. There was no need to go off to Cyprus, or to climb the steep passes of the Taurus range, to reach the interior of Asia Minor. Leaving the teeming Gentile population of Cilicia and Tarsus, however, we find him sailing away to the densely Jewish Cyprus. In Asia Minor, he makes his missionary centres in the cities where there were Jewish communities, and on reaching Europe, he merely passes through the Greek Neapolis, to push his way to the less considerable mining town of Philippi, because it was strong in Jews. The

---

[1] Rom. i. 17.　　　[2] Luke xxiv. 47.　　　[3] Acts xx. 20.
[4] Acts xiii. 46 ; xviii. 6 ; xxviii. 28.　　　[5] Rom. iii. 29.

great object of his labours was, thus, first, to carry the message of the propitiation through the Messiah, Jesus, to the scattered settlements of his nation, and only in a secondary degree to evangelise the heathen.

Realising this, the wandering life of the apostle reveals its inspiring motive. The return of Jesus was near. The saying, everywhere heard in the Christian assemblies and homes, was equally true to Paul: "Yet a very little while; He that cometh, will come, and will not tarry." [1] As the Jews of Palestine rejected the salvation offered them, it was the more imperative to carry the message to the "Dispersion," in all Gentile lands, though he fully recognised that both Jew and Gentile were free to accept it, on equal terms; holding, strongly, that "there is no distinction between Jew and Greek; the same Lord being Lord of all, and rich to all that call upon Him; whosoever calls upon His name being assuredly saved." [2] Many religiously inclined heathen were, already, in the habit of associating with the Jews of their locality, from sympathy with their monotheism and moral teaching, though not joining themselves formally to Judaism by circumcision, and among these he could hope to win converts, while still devoting his first thoughts to his own countrymen. It was only after the failure of his efforts with the Jews, that he rose to the full realisation of the commission given him by Christ Himself, on the way to Damascus, "as a chosen vessel to Him, to bear His name before the Gentiles, and kings, and the children of Israel." [3] But this Divine command had, from that hour, made missionary work his absorbing passion; the words of his glorified Lord impressing it on him, that he had been " separated "

[1] Heb. x. 37, R.V.   [2] Rom. x. 12, 13.   [3] Acts ix. 15.

—that is, marked out from among mankind—by God, from his birth, and "called" at the due time by His grace, with the express purpose, in both the "separating" and the "calling," "of revealing His Son in him, that he might preach Him among the Gentiles." [1] Henceforth, he could say: "I press on, if so be that I may lay hold of that prize for which I too have, (myself), been laid hold of by Christ Jesus," (which was that I should) "know Him, and the power of His resurrection, and share in His sufferings; (living, like Him, a martyr's life, and, like Him, dying a martyr's death);—if, by any means, I may attain unto the resurrection of the dead. This one thing (therefore) I do; forgetting the things behind, and stretching forward to the things that are before, I press on toward the goal, to the prize of the call given to me from heaven, by God, in Christ Jesus." [2] His absorbing desire, henceforward, was, in accordance with this, that, when Jesus appeared again, he might be able to present to Him a noble band of Christian communities; his "joy" and "crown of honour," that Christ might thus be "glorified in His saints." The churches were the "virgin bride" of His Lord, and he would fain lead many to Him, as the Heavenly Bridegroom, on that day of His espousals.[3] Yet he claimed no merit for this enthusiasm. It was the irresistible impulse of the Divine Voice, ever echoing in his soul. "If I preach the Gospel," says he, "I have nothing to glory of; for necessity is laid upon me; for woe is unto me, if I preach not the Gospel!"[4] The profound conviction that

---

[1] Gal. i. 15, 16.   [2] Phil. iii. 10–14.
[3] 2 Cor. xi. 2; 1 Thess. ii. 19; 2 Thess. i. 7; Phil. ii. 16; Col. i. 28.
[4] 1 Cor. ix. 16.

he had been "called to be an apostle by the will of
God," [1] that his missionary life was ordained by God from
before his birth, that he had not, of his own motive
only, chosen the self-sacrificing career he led, but was
carrying out by it the Divine counsels, that he was no
more his own, but the "slave" of Christ, bought with
His most precious blood, and, as such, a "steward" to
whom, as his life-long care, the interests of his Master
were intrusted, that he was the captive of His grace, led
about, by God, in his Master's "triumph," over all the
earth—the profound conviction of all this, left him no
desire or boast beyond the being able to say, "To me to
live is Christ." [2]

Nor were Paul's endowments for his great life-work
less striking than his devotion to it. He had been
specially qualified by God, for the task assigned him.
His peculiar power, he rightly tells us, was to "lay foundations, as a wise master builder, for others to build
upon." [3] He was emphatically fitted to be a pioneer,
opening the way, and making the first clearances in the
wilds, where the sound of the axe had not before been
heard. He possessed, indeed, all the qualifications demanded in one who had to break down the first opposition
to Christianity. Among these may be reckoned, his gift
of powerful speech, though we find him quoting a strange
slander of his opponents, that "His letters are weighty
and strong; but his bodily presence is weak, and his
speech of no account." [4] Nor was this, in a certain sense,
without some truth. Often ailing, and always weak; often
hindered from the full use of his gifts, by bodily troubles,

[1] 1 Cor. i. 1, &c.   [2] Rom. i. 1, &c. ; 1 Cor. iv. 1, 2 ; 2 Cor. ii. 14.
[3] 1 Cor. iii. 10.   [4] 2 Cor. x. 11.

or by spiritual or mental influences, he repeatedly laments his trying difficulties.[1] Yet he could say, "The weapons of our warfare are not of the flesh, but mighty before God, to the casting down of strongholds; casting down imaginations, and every high thing that is exalted against the knowledge of God, and bringing every thought into captivity to the obedience of Christ; and being ready to punish all the disobedient, when your obedience is complete."[2] Can we, indeed, conceive of the composer of the Praise of Heavenly Love, or of the peroration on the Triumph over Death, in the letter to the Corinthians, or of the Vindication of Christian Hope, in his letter to the Romans, as less than a magnificent orator![3] How must the spoken outbursts of such an eloquence have melted or roused the hearers, when first poured forth in some address, on the impulse of the moment, in tones trembling with the loftiest rapture, or the most pathetic sensibility! He did not indeed, trick out his words with the tinsel of artificial rhetoric, in the euphuistic fashion of the day, but his passionate, adoring love of Christ, and the grand enthusiasm for humanity which that love transferred, from the Master, to his own bosom, needed no "words which man's wisdom teaches," to adorn his appeals, but kindled his whole being with its sacred fire, when Christ, or the salvation He had won, was his theme.[4]

This often resistless eloquence which "made manifest the secrets of the heart," so that the hearer not infrequently, with Eastern emotion, would "fall down on his face (in the assembly) and worship God, declaring that He was among them indeed,"[5] was doubtless heightened

---

[1] Gal. iv. 13; 1 Cor. ii. 3. [2] 2 Cor. x. 4–6.
[3] 1 Cor. xiii., xv.; Rom. viii. [4] 1 Cor. ii. 13. [5] 1 Cor. xiv. 25.

in its power, by the contrast it offered to the outward
characteristics of the speaker. He frankly admits the
humility which his opponents deprecated,[1] and tells us
how they sneered at him, as bearing himself without
spirit when with them, and commanding no deference
when he addressed them.[2] They insinuated that he was
insincere, using flattering words to please his hearers,[3]
that he was wanting in due self-respect; if, indeed, his
"abasing himself" was not a cloak for personal ends, and
even went so far as to maintain that he was designedly
deceitful and fickle, so that men could not say whether
he meant yes or no when he spoke.[4] Yet, on the other
hand, all his letters show that, from the mass of his
converts, he constantly received proofs of the deepest
love and admiration; the chief lament of even disturbed
churches being that he did not come to them as often as
they would have liked; longing as they did for his visits so
much that he himself could speak of them as "favours."[5]

The apparent weakness, and underlying charms, which
thus reveal themselves in the personality of the Apostle,
must be kept in mind in any attempt to realise the story
of his life. Like every able man he knew his power,
though at heart so humble. His "weapons," he felt,
were "mighty before God" to the "casting down" of all
opposition,[6] and his letters, throughout, show a spiritual
power working with intense energy, and inflexible tenacity towards its special ends. To attain these, he employs
in turn, reasons, proofs, entreaties, threats, warnings,
adjurations, and invective, and makes his way into the
heart and understanding of his readers by a thousand

---

[1] 2 Cor. x. 1.   [2] 2 Cor. x. 10.   [3] Gal. i. 10 ; 1 Thess. ii. 4.
[4] 2 Cor. xi. 7 ; xii. 16; i. 12–18.   [5] 2 Cor. i. 15.   [6] 2 Cor. x. 4 ff.

arguments, which still leave the impression that he has
by no means said all he thought, or expressed fully
his own depth of conviction. But in all this, there is
nothing egoistic. We feel that he is only the mouthpiece of a Divine impulse; only the "vessel" for its
conveyance, in words, to mankind. As his zeal for the
Law in his early years, stimulated him, despite his gentle
temperament, to fiery energy as a persecutor, so, as a
Christian, he could say, "I live, yet not I, but Christ
lives in me." [1] Such absorption in the aim to which he
had given himself, harmonises well with the depreciation
of his physical characteristics by his opponents. From
the middle of the next century a remembrance of his
personal appearance was current, which pictured him
as short and almost insignificant in figure, so that the
people of Lystra, on the other side of Taurus, had taken for
granted, at once, that his finer-looking companion Barnabas was Jupiter, while Paul must be the small eloquent
messenger of the gods, Mercury. But he was not only
of poor physique; his health was very indifferent. In all
his Epistles he bewails the bodily weakness that oppresses
him, the sicknesses by which he has been tried, hindering
his free use of his powers. "I was with you," he writes
to the Corinthians, "in weakness, and in fear, and in
much trembling," [2] "and an infirmity of the flesh" bore
him down, when he was among the Galatians. [3] Such
depression, indeed, weighed on him all through life, that
he could write, "In this earthly house of our bodily
frame we groan, longing to be clothed upon with our
habitation which is of heaven. For, indeed, we that are
in this bodily frame do groan, being burdened." [4] His

[1] Gal. ii. 20.   [2] 1 Cor. ii. 3.   [3] Gal. iv. 13.   [4] 2 Cor. v. 2–4

body is only a poor "clay vessel,"[1] so feeble that the
labour of earning his simple living by his hands, is so
great a trial that he thinks more of it than of all his
other sufferings.[2]

What special ailment it may have been, which thus so
wearily tried Paul, is not clear. A passage in one of his
Epistles seems to throw light on it, but the language is so
vague and figurative, that it, in reality, makes the matter
very little less difficult. "By reason of the exceeding
greatness of the revelations" vouchsafed him, he tells us,
"in order that I should not be exalted overmuch, there
was given to me a thorn in the flesh, a messenger of
Satan, to buffet me."[3] To Satan, in the New Testament,
is ascribed the infliction of all evils, ghostly and bodily,
which befall us, so that this expression defines nothing.[4]
Whatever it was, he compares it to suffering the continuous blows of a man's fist, beating and bruising him,
as one might in a continued attack of an overmastering
adversary. Some have fancied he refers to stings of
conscience for his former persecution of the churches;
others think of his being tried by blasphemous sugges-
tions; others, of the worry of his opponents; others, of
the distractions of his apostolic work. But none of these
account for the physical troubles of which he so often
speaks. It is, in my opinion, far more reasonable to
regard the "thorn" as some form of bodily suffering,
which was chronic, and terribly distressing. Epilepsy,
among other diseases, has been suggested, but we really
know, only, that the apostle was afflicted with some
painful malady, which he ascribed to the malevolence of

[1] 2 Cor. iv. 7.   [2] 1 Cor. ix. 15; 1 Thess. ii. 6, 9.   [3] 2 Cor. xii. 7.
[4] Matt. iv. 10; Mark iv. 15; Luke xiii. 16; xxii. 3; 1 Cor. vii. 5, &c.

Satan, just as Luther ascribed to the arch enemy the physical agonies he suffered in Schmalkald. All we can discover. farther, is that its paroxysms, as already noticed, were accompanied by such distressing pain as could only be compared to the achings of one beaten all over by a boxer.

With a frame so weak and ailing; a nervous system so stimulated into morbid sensitiveness; and a highly emotional temperament, Paul, nevertheless, presented mental and moral qualities which soon made any physical considerations forgotten. Whether in speech or writing, his keen and subtle intellect, able to follow out an argument to its farthest logical conclusions, was at once apparent, for no rabbi could defend an opinion he upheld, or assail one he disputed, with more varied resources of quick wit, light irony, minute analysis, accumulated learning of the Jewish kind, or easy skill in statement of his case. But along with this equipment of high intellectual ability, men saw, continually, the workings of the most delicate moral sensibility; a conscience true to his convictions as the climbing flower to the sun, or the north star to the pole; a courage which cheerfully followed duty through whatever dangers it might lead him; a religious enthusiasm which irradiated his whole nature and kindled that of others; and a passionate delight in loving, which became sublime, as it laboured to express itself towards the Father of all in the heavens, or Jesus Christ, His Son, the Saviour. Nor was this overflowing tenderness limited to the Divine; love filled his soul towards all mankind. The strangely mingled influences of such a temperament, at once so affectionate and so agitated by physical conditions, shows itself throughout. At one moment he writes in eager heat; the next, he is all gentleness.[1]   Impulsive, he at times expresses himself,—as he presently thinks,—too strongly, and hastens to make amends for it, by a loving self-negation of which colder natures are not capable. Easily excited, made ill by contradiction, his feelings show themselves by language proportionately strong. " You did not despise or spit me out," says he to the Galatians.[2] He is, he tells us, " made the filth and offscourings of all things "[3] by his opponents. " I count all things but dung," says he, " that I may gain Christ."[4]   When he feels he has been over-warm, he presently wishes he were with the Galatians, that " he might change his voice,"[5] and he soothes the Corinthians, after an outburst of strong feeling, by telling them, that " out of much affliction and anguish of heart he had written to them, with many tears."[6]   If, for a moment, he see or suspect wrong, his loving nature, ever looking out for what he can praise as worthy, presently discovers some compensating good.

We have thus, in the apostle, a personality at once emotional and profound; easily roused to warmth, but magnificently honest.   He is, in fact, like only himself. If he show the heat of Jewish blood, and its passionate zeal, he is wholly free from the common Jewish stamp of narrowness or rancour.   While, as a whole, " peace that passed understanding guarded his heart and thoughts, in Christ Jesus,"[7] his active mind knew no rest, and inevitably secured him prominence in any movement he joined.   Men saw in him one whose intellect, to use Hall's expression respecting Dr. Johnson, shone keenly on the angles of a thought, while his power of speech

---

[1] Gal. iv. 12.   [2] Gal. iv. 14.   [3] 1 Cor. iv. 13.   [4] Phil iii. 8.
[5] Gal. iv. 20.   [6] 2 Cor. ii. 4.   [7] Phil. iv. 7.

II.   M

set his ideas in the clearest light, and his wondrous energy was equal to any demand, for the carrying out of whatever he had at heart. Hence, we find him accepted as the leader in the Jerusalem persecution, though then so young, and trusted with a weighty commission by even so formal a body as the Jewish high court. That he should have become the foremost figure in the story of the Apostolic Church, was, therefore, only the natural result of his varied and singular gifts. The whole man was an apostle. His perfect faith in his convictions opened the way for their undoubting acceptance by others; for the influence on the multitude, of a strong mind, possessed by an overmastering idea, is always great. But he had, besides, a restless hunger for new conquests, an instinctive knowledge of men, and a capacity of adapting himself to all, which made him at home, as a Jew, in a Jewish home, and as a Greek, in the household of a Greek; dexterous to avoid wounding the prejudices of the weak-minded, and liberal, where breadth of view was possible; qualities needed, before all others, in laying the "foundations" of a new faith.[1] He emphatically became, in innocent ways, "all things to all men."[2] "I have made myself servant to all," says he, "that I might gain the more."[3] Hence, he was friendly with the slaves of Chloe's household, visiting them, no doubt, in their hovels,[4] and he must have made his way to the cellars of thieves at Ephesus, for he admitted some poor reclaimed creatures of that class into the church there;[5] but he is none the less at home with well-to-do burgesses,[6] and bears himself with dignity in the presence of a king.[7]

[1] 1 Cor. ix. 20.   [2] 1 Cor. x. 33.   [3] 1 Cor. ix. 19.
[4] 1 Cor. i. 11.   [5] Eph. iv. 28.   [6] Rom. xvi. 21 ff.
[7] Acts xxvi. 27.

As in all his after life, so, no doubt, in his first labours in Tarsus and Cilicia, he would, we may be sure, be ever eager to press on to a fresh field, after laying the ground work of a Christian community in any given locality; for he had the ideal of the missionary spirit. The villages and towns of the great foot-hills of the Taurus, and the rolling plains below them, stretching, in varying breadth, from Syria to Pamphylia,—the widest and most extended tract of comparatively open country, south of the Taurus range—would offer admirable training places for his wide labours in future years, while they stimulated the passion for ever-extending enterprise. To settle down permanently, in any one spot, was impossible with Paul. The name of Christ must be carried from land to land. Race after race must bow before it. The only limit to his toils in proclaiming it, through region after region, was that of physical endurance. Year by year, the impulse to conquer fresh territory for his Lord grew stronger. We shall soon see him climbing the snowy steeps of Taurus, to reach the central tableland, with its great trade routes, its numerous cities, and its wild and half-barbarous rural districts. Ere long, he reaches the distant western bounds of Asia, and looks, over the Ægean, to the dim shores of still heathen Europe. A dream by night determines his visiting Macedonia. Athens hears from him of Jesus and the Resurrection. He goes on to Corinth, from which vessels are constantly leaving for Italy, and he presently writes to Rome, "how unceasingly he prays, if, by any means, now, at length, he may be prospered by the will of God to visit" it.[1] He longs to preach the Gospel in remote Spain.[2] As Xavier was wont to cry, "Farther

---

[1] Rom. i. 9.   [2] Rom. xv. 24.

east, farthe1 east!" Paul heard voices summoning him,
hour by hour, to press farther to the great West.   The
words of the prophet—"How beautiful are the feet of
them that bring glad tidings of good things,"[1] were
the animating music of his soul, ever cheering him and
quickening his steps.   He glories in each advance in his
self-imposed course.   " From Jerusalem, and round about
even to Illyricum," he rejoices to think, " he has fully
preached the Gospel of Christ."[2]   He "glories" in the
thought, that he had been the first to preach Christ in
Corinth.[3]   He boasts that the triumphal chariot on
which his Lord bears him about, as His willing captive,
along the highways and through the cities of the world,
has everywhere left behind it "a sweet savour of
his knowledge," like the smoke of incense.[4]   To win
souls was the passion of his life, for besides adding
to the number of the redeemed, he thus increased
the multitude of the glorified, who should exalt the
triumph of Christ when He came back to earth, no
longer the despised man of Calvary, but in the glory of
God, amidst the clouds of heaven, and attended by the ten
thousands of its angels.   Filled with this sublime ambition, he was indifferent to all things else.   " I think
God," he writes to the Corinthians, " has set forth us,
the Apostles, as men doomed to death : for we are made
a spectacle to the world, and to angels, and to men.   We
are fools for Christ's sake,—we are weak—we have dishonour.   Even to this present hour we both hunger, and
thirst, and are naked, and are buffeted, and have no
certain dwelling-place.   We toil, working with our own

[1] Isa. lii. 7 ; Rom. x. 18.   [2] Rom. xv. 19.
[3] 2 Cor. x. 13.   [4] 2 Cor. ii. 14.

hands: being reviled, we bless; being persecuted, we
endure; being defamed, we entreat; we are made as the
filth of the world, the offscouring of all things, even until
now." [1] Yet, eager as he was to conquer new territory,
his tenacity in holding all he won was no less marked.
Churches, once gathered, were watched by him with
ceaseless care, and wonderful skill in dealing with their
special characteristics. He could be "gentle among them,
as when a nursing mother cherishes her own children," [2]
but though, by his nature, he delighted in "love and
meekness," he could come to an offending community
with a rod.[3] He knew how to lead men,—now, by
quickening their self-respect, now, by scornfully dashing
aside their unworthy pretensions, whether intellectual
or moral. He rejoiced to fan the smoking flax, but he
ruthlessly cast down the "high imaginations" of self-
righteousness or vanity. Great as an organiser, he was
equally so as a ruler.

The secret of this power lay, no doubt, in the tender
relations he established with the individual members of
the various infant communities. "Ye are witnesses," he
writes to the Thessalonians, "how I dealt with each one
of you, as a father with his own children, exhorting and
encouraging you," [4] and he could appeal to the elders of the
Ephesian Church, as witnesses to his bearing during the
three years of his sojourn among them—how he had spent
them in "serving the Lord with all lowliness of mind, and
with tears," and how, in spite of the plots of the Jews,
which threatened his death at any moment, "he shrank not
from declaring to them anything that was for their good,

---

[1] 1 Cor. iv. 10–13.   [2] 1 Thess. ii. 7.
[3] 1 Cor. iv. 21.   [4] 1 Thess. ii. 11.

and teaching them both publicly, and from house to
house."[1] What the toiling from house to house involved,
is conceivable, if we think what a town missionary's labours
would be in the narrow and lofty streets of modern
Naples, or what they are in the equally narrow and
high "lands" of the old wynds of Glasgow or Edinburgh.
There were, doubtless, multitudes of fine buildings, and
not a few fine streets, in the cities of Italy and of the
provinces, in Paul's day; thanks to the impulse given
to such improvements by Augustus; but this did not affect
the poor quarters, in which "the base," "the despised,"
"the offscourings,"[2] who, almost wholly, constituted the
Apostolic Churches, had their wretched homes.   Even
under Tiberius the complaint was loud in Rome, that
the houses were so high and the streets so narrow, that
there was neither protection from fire, nor a possibility
of getting out of the way of a mob.   We may see this,
indeed, from the narrow lanes that served for streets in
Pompeii, with their yard-broad side walks, and space,
between, for only one vehicle.   The houses in Rome
were not, indeed, so high as in some parts of modern
cities, as for instance of Genoa, Paris, Manchester, or
Edinburgh, and their height no doubt varied in different
towns of the empire, but, even in Rome, they were often
three storeys and a half, and the humble poor whom Paul
had to visit, nestled, according to Juvenal, like doves,
under the roof.   Houses for renting out, moreover, were
allowed to be higher, so that Martial could speak of a
poor creature having to mount two hundred steps to his
garret.[3] There was no lighting of the streets by night,
and they were made still more dangerous, from thieves

[1] Acts xx. 20, 21.   [2] 1 Cor. i. 28.   [3] Juv. iii. 199 ; Mart. vii. 20.

or robbers finding lurking places behind countless booths and projections before the houses, as in some east-end London streets now, at least on costers' days, and even in the Strand and in Fleet Street some generations ago,[1] or as in the streets of Damascus or Cairo. The population lived in the streets by day, and carried on most of their occupations in the open air, as in the East still, or in the rudest of open wooden stalls, often taking up the whole breadth of the pavement, so that even prætors were forced to walk in the mud of the carriage-way. Indeed, the fronts of the houses, storey above storey, as in Damascus, had projections of every shape, to increase the narrow space within; for a chamber, in antiquity, as we see in Pompeii, was, as a rule, so small, that it would take four to make a modern room. The condition of the slaves and lowest classes, with whom, especially, Paul had to do, was wretched in the extreme. After climbing the two hundred steps to his attic, it was so low that the miserable tenant had to bend to enter. His hearth was often cold, even in winter; a crock with its handle broken, a sleeping-mat, a little straw, and an empty bedstead, the only furniture; a short tunic the only protection from the cold, by day or night; sour wine, like vinegar, and black bread, the ordinary food. Among the classes a step above these, vegetables were the main diet, cabbage, beans, lentils, onions, garlic, turnips, and peas; a sheep's head boiled with leeks being a rare high-festival. Each term-day saw numbers turned out of their homes for rent, with the few trifles left after the landlord had satisfied his claims: a broken bedstead, perhaps, or a table wanting a leg, and the like. On the bridges, at

[1] Fortunes of Nigel, i. 43.

street corners, in the market-place, or in front of the
temples, stood crowds of beggars, seeking to excite pity
by their doleful looks, their rags or nakedness, their sores
or physical defects, and keeping up a constant clamour
for alms, in a wailing sing-song. In the cold, rainy, or
frosty nights of winter, the only refuge of these poor
creatures was, perhaps, an open arch; their dog their
only companion; their whole possessions a stick, a cover-
let, or mat, and a wallet; death, in some lonely corner,
their only deliverance from the burden of life.[1]

Such were the people, among whom Paul tells us he
went "from house to house." A few whom he could
visit were, no doubt, better off, but he himself paints his
converts as mainly from the very humblest ranks. The appearance of such a man as the apostle, in scenes of such
repelling wretchedness,—with no airs of condescension,
but as a brother, respecting the manhood of the lowliest
as essentially identical with that of the loftiest, recognising, in the most despised, a son of the Eternal Father, as
much as if he wore the imperial purple, and lighting up
the gloom of his miserable shelter, by the announcement of
a message of love from the heavens, which, if met with a
corresponding love, showing itself in a worthy life, would,
erelong, raise him far above the fear of the lash, or the
pangs of hunger, and even above the state and glory of the
haughtiest of his oppressors,—would bring a joy like that
of the return of day after the darkness of a more than
Arctic night. For to the lowliest as to the highest, Paul
told how, as in Adam all died, so, also, in Christ all shall
be made alive, since, having been raised from the dead,
that great Redeemer had become the first-fruits of them

[1] See Friedlaender's "Rom's Sittengesch," i. 381.

that are asleep, thus triumphing over death and the grave, and throwing open the gates of a blissful immortality to all believers, whether slaves or freemen, rich or poor, Greek or Roman, barbarian or Scythian, without distinction of rank or race.' It was this, indeed, which gave Christianity its supreme attraction to that age; for the proclamation of a world beyond the present, redressing the inequalities and wrongs of this life, broke over the earth like a trumpet-peal from the Infinite, startling mankind from the despair in which the mysteries of life had sunk them, and fixing its gaze on the hitherto impenetrable heavens, from which, it now seemed, they might momentarily look for the appearance of the Judge of the living and the dead, of whose near approach that trumpet-voice had been the herald.

Recalling, once more, how great an effect the preaching of the nearness of "the second advent" has, even now; what must have been its effect on the miserable throngs of domestic slaves of antiquity, or on the mass of human wretchedness that, in those days, filled the alleys and wynds of cities like Rome, or on the naked and hungry crowds of field-hands and wandering shepherds, whose lives were less regarded than those of the beasts among which they were passed? For, even apart from the light shed over their darkness, by the prospect of a bright hereafter, there was the mighty support of a recognition, by the Eternal Father, of the essential equality of all men, and the announcement that the only distinctions He acknowledged were those of greater or less moral worth. We need look no further for an explanation of the rapid spread of Christianity.

Working amidst such materials, it was important that

no suspicion of a sordid motive for his eagerness to win
converts, should be possible, for even the gain of his daily
bread, on the humblest scale, might seem, to people so
abjectly poor as many whom he addressed, quite object
enough for the wandering preacher - life he followed.
Indeed, they saw. day by day, roving sectaries, begging
from street to street, like the Roman Catholic friars, and
living well, compared to themselves, on the contributions
given to the mendicants, as associated with this or that
divinity.   He was, therefore, careful to maintain himself
by his own manual labour, at the craft he had learned.
Nor was this cautiousness unnecessary, for we find him defending himself even to the Corinthians, in their wealthy
city, from insinuations of cunning self-interest in this
matter.   "Did I commit a sin," he asks, "in abasing
myself that ye might be exalted, because I preached to
you the Gospel of God for nought?   I robbed other
churches, taking wages of them, that I might minister
unto you; and when I was present with you, and was in
want, I was not a burden on any man; for the brethren,
when they came from Macedonia, supplied the measure
of my needs; and in everything I kept myself from being
burdensome to you, and so will I keep myself.   As the
truth of Christ is in me, no man shall stop me of this
glorying, in the regions of Achaia." [1]   "Ye remember,
brethren," he writes to the Thessalonian converts,
gathered in another very wealthy city, "our labour and
travail: "how, working night and day, that we might not
burden any of you, we preached to you the Gospel of
God." [2]   How poor must have been the remuneration
and how great the toil, when he had to slave wearily

[1] 2 Cor. xi. 7–10 ; see also xii. 13.   [2] 1 Thess. ii. 9.

both night and day, at his tent-making, in every interval
of his higher work, to earn his modest support, and how
naturally was it a grief to him, to have his energies,
which he would fain have expended on his apostolic
labours, wasted so largely in providing daily bread. Yet
there was the satisfaction that his working, thus, with
his hands, made the poor feel no hesitation in coming
to him, as, practically, one of themselves. It made him,
moreover, perfectly independent, so " that he could use
to the full, his right to the Gospel." [1] Nor must we
forget that mechanical work of any kind was held in
contempt in the great Gentile world, in Paul's day.
Slaves constituted the only " working classes;" to all
others, however poor, to support themselves by their
own hands or industry, was regarded as degrading, just
as, in Scott's novel, the cattle-lifter Rob Roy took it as
an insult that a son of his should be offered a business
position, or as the poor whites in the Southern States
relegate handicrafts to " niggers," as fit only for them, or
as the Irish largely despise " business," in any shape, as
beneath them, preferring poverty which they fancy genteel,
to any commercial occupation. Wherever Paul went, there
were vast numbers of pauper " clients," who hung on the
skirts of patricians, giving them their votes, when needed,
in exchange for a contemptuous dole, for which they
scrambled daily in the ante-chambers of the great house;
living, in fact, like " the tail " of Fergus McIvor, in
" Waverley," in idle, semi-starvation, relieved by occasional robbery, rather than soil their dignity by " trade "
in any form, or even by tilling the ground or working a
garden. Against this despicable mockery of real manhood

[1] 1 Cor. ix. 18.

the apostle made his example a lesson. "For yourselves," he writes to the Thessalonians, "know how ye ought to imitate us: for we behaved not ourselves disorderly among you; neither did we eat bread for nought at any man's hand, but in labour and travail, working night and day, that we might not burden any of you: not because we have not the right, but to make ourselves an example unto you, that ye should imitate us. For even when we were with you, this we commanded you, If any will **not** **work**, neither let him eat."[1]

[1] **2 Thess.** iii. **7–10.**

CHAPTER IX

IN ANTIOCH

A.D. 48–49; PAUL'S AGE, c. 38–39

PAUL had been at work first in Syria,—especially, no doubt, in Antioch,—and then in Tarsus and Cilicia, from the year 39—when the excitement roused by the mad attempt of Caligula, to get his statue set up in the Temple, was growing daily more intense,—till the year 48; the seventh year of the Emperor Claudius, son of Drusus, who succeeded the murdered Caligula, on the 24th of January, 41. Thus while that Emperor was enjoying himself at Lyons, from which he returned, in August 40, to Rome, to celebrate a triumph for his mock German and British campaigns, Egypt and Syria were in the wildest despair for their synagogues and Temple. Far away in Cilicia, these commotions were felt only by slow-spreading reports, which broke on so distant a land like the last undulations of a remote storm, on quiet shores, leaving the apostle free to push forward his great missionary work. So successful did this, in the end, become, that news of his labours were carried back to Judæa, where he was still personally unknown; brethren from Cilicia telling those of Palestine, when visiting the motherland for religion or business, that he who had once persecuted Christians, now preached the faith of which he had formerly made havoc; tidings

189

for which, says Paul, " they glorified God in me."[1] He
had, indeed, gathered churches in Cilicia,[2] which consisted, in part, at least, of former heathen, won, largely, we
may suppose, from the " devout " among the non-Jewish
population, who frequented Jewish worship. It is noteworthy, moreover, that these " first-fruits of the Gentiles "
had been received by him into Christian brotherhood,
without being required to conform to Judaism; a startling innovation which he had also introduced into the
churches in Antioch and Syria.

The flight of the Hellenist brethren from Jerusalem, to
escape the persecution which began with the death of
Stephen, had brought some of them as far as Antioch,
and, there, they had spread the new faith, not only in that
great city, but, far and near, through Syria. To have
secured a footing in the capital of the west of Asia, was
a great matter for the future of Christianity, for Jerusalem was soon to fall, and a new centre of the faith being
needed, none could have been more suitable than Antioch,
a Greek community in the main, which had liberalised,
in a measure, the various races found in it, and, in the
converts it yielded to Christ, supplied a counterpoise to
the narrow bigotry of the Palestinian Jew, who still clung,
even after embracing Christianity, to the Judaism of his
fathers. Phœnicia, Cyprus, and Syria speedily showed
larger or smaller Christian communities; at first, of strictly
Jewish Christians only, but, ere long, through the teaching of some Hellenists, who, though resident in Jerusalem,
were men of the island of Cyprus, and of Cyrene—the
district of North Africa west of Egypt—a great number
of " Greeks "—that is, Greek-speaking people; mostly, no

[1] Gal. i. 24.   [2] Acts xv. 23, 41.

doubt, heathen, "believed and turned to the Lord." [1] The
news of this spread of the faith having reached Jerusalem, excited great interest, and led to the Church
sending the Levite Joseph,—called by them, as a name of
honour, Barnabas,—a Cyprus man, to Antioch, to show
their sympathy, and also, no doubt, to learn, whether all
was being done in the right way. The result, however,
was so encouraging, that Joseph presently felt the need
of help, and naturally turned to Paul, to whom he had
been the first friend in the Jerusalem Church, and who
was, himself, well known, already, in Antioch and Syria,
by his missionary labours there, before he went on to
Cilicia. Setting out, therefore, in search of him, he found
him at Tarsus, and persuaded him to return with him to
Antioch, apparently in the year 48.

Paul came back, to find a great change in affairs,
in Palestine. Since his accession, Claudius had made
Agrippa king of all Palestine. The Jewish adventurer
was then at Rome, and had been in attendance on Caligula
at the time of his patron's murder, managing, however, to
escape the daggers many would have wished to plunge
in his own body ; his favour with the Emperor, and the
worthlessness of his character, having made him bitterly
hated at Rome. Claudius, whom his mother wittily called
" the outline of a man, which had not been filled up," was
in mortal terror when dragged forward by the prætorians
who had just killed Caligula, and hailed as Emperor ;
dreading a violent death at their hands, presently, for
it was quite a question if the Senate would ratify the
selection. To secure needed delay, Agrippa had instantly gone to the senate-house, and occupied the time, in

[1] Acts xi. 21.

connection with the claims of Claudius, till the cry of the
soldiery having been caught up by the rabble, such popular
acclaim had made it unsafe for the senators, to hesitate
any longer in accepting him as Emperor.   The new ruler
thus owed everything to him, and he eagerly showed that
he felt this, by profuse favours, as Agrippa had intended he
should.   A brass tablet was put up in the Capitol by the
Senate, at the Emperor's command, proclaiming the high
services he had rendered the State, and an imperial edict
announced them to all the world.[1]   Moreover, he received
the territory of Abilene, between Hermon and Damascus,
while his eldest brother was presented with the principality of Chalcis, in the north of Syria.   Agrippa, not long
before a fugitive bankrupt, arrested for debt in Palestine,
and able to leave it only by the services of a money-lender,
bought at a great price, on the faith that his Roman friends
would see to repayment, was thus, now, lord of a territory
more splendid than any Jewish king, David and Herod
not excepted, had ever held under his sceptre.   He was
even treated, in the ratification of the appointment, as if
he were an independent prince, entering on his hereditary
dominion.   He was, also, raised to consular rank, and with
his brother, the Prince of Chalcis, made a prætor, that he
might be able to appear in the Senate and return thanks
in Greek.   Privileges to the Jews, of whom Agrippa
shrewdly made himself the patron, as, himself, a Jew,
speedily followed.   Those of Alexandria saw their griev-
ances redressed, and a rescript was sent through the
Empire, conferring special favours on the Diaspora, or
Jews of the Dispersion, including liberty of worship, and
trial by their own courts, as granted of old by the "divine
Augustus."

[1] *Bell.* ii. 11, 5; *Ant.* xix. 5, 1.

The first act of the miraculously fortunate scapegrace, on returning to Judæa, marked the policy on which he henceforth conducted his government. The golden chain given him by Caligula, on his being set free from prison, at the death of Tiberius, was piously hung up over the Temple treasury, " as a memorial of his former misfortunes and of his present elevation ; to teach how God could raise up those that were cast down." [1]

At the same time, he presented a thank-offering, " for he would not neglect any prescription of the Law," and paid the amount required to discharge the vows of a large number of Nazarites. The golden age had returned for the Pharisee, or national party ; his reward being that he gained craftily, what he sought; their praise as a zealous Jew. " Of his own accord," says Josephus, " he lived much in Jerusalem, and punctually observed the traditions of the fathers. His life was faultlessly pure," in the legal sense, " and no day passed without his presenting an offering." [2] The Talmud, moreover, proclaims how he carried the first-fruits to the Temple, like a simple Israelite, taking his basket of them on his shoulder, and bearing it to the fore-courts. [3] Nor was his external homage to Judaism confined to Judæa. A band of heathen youths having, for a freak, set up an image of the Emperor in the synagogue of Dora, a Phœnician town on the coast, he procured a command from the legate in Syria strongly forbidding such outrages, and ordering the punishment of the offenders. [4] On marrying his daughter Drusilla, moreover, to King Antiochus of Commagene, he required that, as the bridegroom of a Jewess, he should be circumcised, [5] and on his refusal,

---

[1] *Ant.* xix. 6, 1.   [2] *Ant.* xix. 7, 3.   [3] *Mischna Bikkuram* ii. 1.
[4] *Ant.* xix. 6, 3.   [5] *Ant.* xx. 7, 1.

II.   N

broke off the marriage. Such "piety" secured him the fervent loyalty of a race led by the Pharisees. A signal illustration of this was given at the Feast of Tabernacles in A.D. 41. He had revived the old custom of reading the Book of Deuteronomy, in public, at this festival, and condescended to come to the reader's stand, and, himself, read the whole aloud. Ere long, however, he stopped, bursting into tears, as if quite overcome, when he reached the words, "Thou mayest not set a stranger over thee, who is not thy brother."[1] His partly Edomite blood made him dread incurring the hatred his grand-father, Herod the Great, had borne, on account of this detested blot on his origin, and he took this clever way of escaping it. Moved by his well-acted grief, the mul-titude forthwith cried out, "Don't weep, Agrippa, thou art our brother! Thou art our brother!"[2] To play the part of a perfervid Jew was a cheap penalty for such a political victory! Could a more perfect prototype of Reinecke Fuchs be imagined than Herod Agrippa—the still wilier brother-in-law of "The Fox" of Tiberias— Herod Antipas!

Yet his popularity was not based entirely on this flat-tery of the Pharisee party. He showed himself grateful to his old friends, and capable of a wise clemency even to some who spoke to his disadvantage. He began, moreover, a new wall round Jerusalem, which would have made it well-nigh impregnable, adding thus to his popularity, though Rome prevented him from completing his purpose. Still more, to flatter the Jewish craving for at least nominal independence, he summoned a gathering of vassal-princes of Rome, to meet him at Tiberias, but

[1] Deut. xvii. 15.   [2] M. Sota, vii. 8.

the viceroy of Syria came with them, and ordered them instantly to go home again. Agrippa had, however, shown his people what he seemed to wish, though unable to go further.

But there was a darker side to his servility to the dominant Jewish party. The hatred of the Christians, which had been overridden for a time by the national crisis, under Caligula, once more broke out, now that a Pharisee king sat on the throne of Jerusalem. This gave the opportunity for a further step in popular favour "Because it pleased the Jews, he put forth his hands to afflict" the obscure Christian community, taking measures to do so during the Passover week of the year 44, when Paul and Barnabas were busy at Antioch, and when the vast gathering of pilgrims at Jerusalem, would proclaim the royal zeal for the Law over the whole Jewish world. Arresting and beheading James, the brother of John, he unconsciously fulfilled the words of Jesus, that this early and loved disciple should drink of his Lord's cup;[1] but the catastrophe is brightened by an old tradition that the apostle's accuser was converted by the martyr's words and bearing, and was beheaded with him. Finding this crime won him popular credit, Agrippa next flew at still higher game, seizing Peter, who, though, like James, a Christian, was also a zealous Jew; throwing him into prison, and ordering that he should be guarded by four watchers at a time, renewed each six hours; the prisoner being chained by the two wrists to two of them. Under such circumstances the fate of Peter would have been hopeless, if left to human help, and, indeed, his escape was due to a miracle wrought on his behalf.[2]

[1] Matt. xx. 23.   [2] Acts xii. 1-19.

The success of this policy of zealous Judaism was complete, as far as regarded the all-powerful Pharisee party. They had bitterly hated the Herods in the past, but Agrippa won them over to abiding loyalty to his dynasty. How could they, indeed, refuse homage to the king who wore the phylactery on his brow and arm, made broad the hem of his garment, and, above all, surrounded himself with the most famous rabbis, and devoutly sought their counsel! What an unrivalled Katerfelto of political mountebanks!

Among the Hebrew jurisconsults thus associated with him was the illustrious Gamaliel, grandson of Hillel, now president of the Sanhedrim, under Agrippa. The crafty make-believe having restored to that court its ancient privilege of using the Law as the national code, and having otherwise increased the authority of its chairman, Gamaliel became, in fact, its real, as well as nominal head; sending out the mandates, rescripts, citations, &c., to all the Jewish communities, at home and abroad, hitherto sent by the Sanhedrim; for the Jews everywhere, acknowledged the authority of the high court and its president, as we see in the missives to the synagogue elders at Damascus, intrusted to Paul. It is curious, by the way, to see of what some of its ukases treated. One runs thus: "To our brethren, the dispersed in Babylon, Media, Greece (Ionia), and to all the rest of the Dispersion of Israel, greeting. We announce to you, that since the lambs of this year are still feeble, and the doves are not full fledged, spring being late, it pleases me and my colleagues to lengthen this year by thirty days." Availing himself of the liberality of Gamaliel, the shrewd Agrippa soon removed the difficulties which created tension between

the Jews and idolaters. It was ordered that the Gentile
poor should no longer be prevented from gleaning in
Jewish fields, and heathen were to be greeted, even when
they were going to their temples, on their feast-days,
instead of being insulted by looks of hatred; while their
poor and sick, in towns of mixed population, were to be
treated kindly, and share in alms and attention.[1] Moreover, to please the Pharisees, the reign of their hated
rivals, the Sadducees, in the highest places of the priesthood, was interrupted; Theophilus, the son of Hannas,
being displaced from the high priesthood, in favour of a
member of a family connected with the Herods, Simon
Kanthera. To remove another trouble, he coined money
without any likeness of Caligula or Claudius on it, as
his original mintage had had, that his subjects might
not be defiled by touching an image. When in Jerusalem, he even submitted to restrict himself to Jewish
cookery, though he made amends when elsewhere. It is
possible that, now he was fifty, Agrippa might wish to
atone for his shameful past and be a better man, but
such thoughts could only be momentary, for his general
life showed that all his punctiliousness about the Law was
only a comedy played for effect and popularity. When
at Cæsarea he became at once the same profligate he had
been in Rome, surrounding himself with his old circle, as
far as he could. Even his daughters, brought up at Rome
amidst the abominations of the court, had so bad a name,
that, at their father's death, the mob carried off their
busts and set them up over houses of ill fame. He
had, himself, so little outgrown his old nature, that he
still hankered after the time when he and his imperial

[1] Grætz, iii. 374.

companions delighted in seeing men fight with the twice-sharpened "Drusian" swords. Not only did he build a theatre and a circus, for the heathen, at Berytus; at the opening of the latter, he ordered a fight of 1400 gladiators, whom he hypocritically declared criminals; requiring them to continue the combat till all were killed.[1] Josephus is mean enough to tell us that he did this to please the spectators, and that the gladiators were all malefactors; the pious king thus only meting out to them their due punishment, while, graciously humouring the populace by a sight of war in a time of peace![2]

But his end was near. In the summer following close on the beheading of James, when he had reigned three years, Paul would hear, in Antioch, how Divine justice overtook him. A dispute with Tyre and Sidon had led to his prohibiting them from exporting grain, an unendurable edict for great trading cities. Anxious to mollify him, they had, therefore, through his high chamberlain Blastus, secured an audience, while the king was celebrating heathen games at Cæsarea, in honour of the Emperor Claudius, as decreed by the Senate for the Empire at large, to signalise the pretended triumphs of the poor mock emperor, over Britain. A vast multitude assembled to see the festival and games, and before these, the king, in all the pride of high state, appeared, in robes inwrought with silver threads. The time chosen was daybreak, so that the kindling sun, shining on this grand mantle, lighted it into dazzling splendour. Presently, some of the flatterers always at hand beside a king, raised the cry, echoing a reminiscence of the days of Caligula, "Deign to be gracious to us, thou Divine one!

---

[1] Grætz, iii. 375.   [2] *Ant.* xix. 7, 5.

therto we have honoured thee as a man; henceforth we own thee more than mortal!" Instead of rebuking such lying servility, the worthless creature drank in this hollow adulation with high pleasure. When a prisoner under Tiberius, an owl had once lighted on the wall over his head, and as everything in those days was regarded as an omen, this was interpreted by a German on the spot, as a messenger of death sent to warn Agrippa; its next appearance marking that his hour had come. Looking up, says Josephus, while the cries of the fawning multitude were yet in his ears, behold, there sat the owl, on a rope over his head! Next moment, a great pain racked his bowels. Conscience-stricken, as a Jew, at his blasphemous folly, the poor wretch felt that the wrath of God had struck him down, and the cry rose from him, in his agony, "See, your god must now give up life, and hastens into the arms of corruption!" In the Acts, we are told that he "was eaten of worms."[1] Round his palace at Cæsarea, where he lay five days in sore distress before he died, vast numbers of Jews in sackcloth and ashes, lay prostrate, shrieking, and imploring the Holy One to spare the king's life. But it was otherwise among the heathen population and the Samaritans. As soon as it was certain that he was dead, disgraceful riots broke out among both. The head men held feasts, with their heads wreathed with flowers and fragrant with anointing oil, and toasted Charon for ferrying the Jew king across the Styx, from which there was no return! The scandals of his private life were raked up, and the mob stormed the palace, and bore off the busts of his daughters, for the dishonour already named. At Shechem, all this was repeated, even

[1] *Ant.* xix. 8, 2; Acts xii. 23.

the troops there, joining in the tumults; so universal was
the abhorrence, outside the Jews, of the hypocrisy of the
old profligate.   It is sufficient proof of his worthlessness,
that, with a revenue of about £450,000 a year, raised in
part by the most cruel extortion, from his outlying

ANTIOCH.

territories,—for he was careful not to oppress the Jews,—
he died, as he had lived, in debt.

The apparent design of Agrippa to be independent,
was, for the time, fatal to the prospects of his son.   The
country was once more put under Roman procurators, and

the future Agrippa the Second, relegated to private life.
Antioch, where Paul and Barnabas were labouring in
these months, was not only the capital of Syria, and even
of the eastern half of the Roman Empire, till the founding
of Constantinople, but the third, or at least the fourth
city of the Roman world; coming only behind Rome,
Alexandria, and, perhaps, Seleucia, on the Tigris, in importance.   Yet it was one of the youngest places in
Syria, and owed its existence to public policy; not to
its commercial position.   It had been created by the
Macedonian conquerors, as a central military stronghold,
from which, by keeping in touch with the Mediterranean,
they could effectively guard a dominion which, at first,
embraced Asia Minor, Western Asia, and Egypt.   Since
its foundation, in B.C. 301,—at the command of Seleucus,
a lieutenant of Alexander the Great, or at that of his
son Antiochus,—it had grown into a group of four towns,
enclosed within common walls, though each had others
of its own.   After the conquest of Greece by the Romans,
Antiochus the Great had given free citizenship to all
Greeks, to induce as many as possible to emigrate to
Antioch.   Special privileges had also been given to the
Jews, so that it became the centre of the Dispersion; a
fact which tended not a little to its development and
growth.   When Syria became, in B.C. 64, a Roman province, Antioch still retained its dignity as the capital.
The mint for the East, and the great arsenals, and
foundries of military weapons and material, gave it additional importance, but its port, Seleucia, was badly suited
for commerce, and the city was a failure as a great
commercial centre, although vast sums were spent, for
centuries, on docks, and on canals to bring goods to it.

It was, hence, more a place for expenditure than for gain. In all antiquity there was no city, where the mere enjoyment of life was so much the chief pursuit and passion of the inhabitants. Everything contributed to thoughtlessness and pleasure. Lying picturesquely in a rich plain between the Orontes, which flowed westwards towards the sea, just outside the northern walls, and the lofty mountain, Silpius, on the south, everything combined to delight the eye, and minister to the pride of the citizens. Silpius rose nobly with slopes and heights glorious with trees and verdure amid a wide expanse of equal luxuriance, far and near; streams tinkled through the streets; public gardens invited idlers; a great four-sided triumphal archway linked the four quarters of the city where they met; a magnificent palace on a crescent-shaped island of great size, made by a division, at the spot, of the broad Orontes, adorned the north side of the walls; a splendid theatre and an amphitheatre rose on the slopes of Silpius, on which, also, was the massive citadel; a grand basilica for the courts and public offices near by, and a large forum, embellished the plain below; while a gorgeous senate-house; a museum; splendid aqueducts; a temple to Jupiter "magnificent with gold;" and public baths for all, worthy of Rome, were only part of the local glories. A splendid street, with double lines of columns on each side, ran across the city, on a perfect level, for four miles, from east to west, and another, built by Herod the Great, paved with marble, and lined with rows of pillars, stretched out for two miles and a half. Everywhere, moreover, the finest works of Grecian art showed the love of splendour, and the sense of beauty that marked the Greek origin of the city. In all the good houses there was a continuous water

supply, as now in Damascus—a supreme boast in the
sultry East,—and one could walk through street after

The Jupiter of Pheidias at Olympia.   It was 60 feet high, and equal in bulk to
that of 1000 men.

street protected from the rain or heat, by covered arcades,
while, at night, every street was lighted up; a luxury

enjoyed by no other city of antiquity, so far as we know.
Nor were the charms of Antioch, itself, enough for its
voluptuous population. In Daphne, five miles off, it had
a huge aggregate of delights; the whole way to it being,
moreover, lined with splendid villas and gardens.   At
Daphne the citizens and the countless visitors found all
possible dissipations, amidst famous laurel groves from
which it took its name, and under its equally famous old
cypresses. Brooks flowed, and fountains sparkled, on every
side, and the cathedral-like temple of Apollo boasted a
colossal statue of the god, in marble, and a still grander
one of Jupiter, in ivory and gold, towering aloft in its halls.
The festivals of these divinities were attended by crowds
like those which came to the Passover at Jerusalem, but
they were the scenes of unimaginable impurity; which,
indeed, reigned all the year in this headquarters of sensuality. A few words of Marcus Aurelius tell its foul story
—" I have given to Avidius Cassius the Syrian legions de-
bauched by luxury and the morals of Daphne." To restore
their tone Cassius dismissed or punished every soldier who
was seen in this sink of vileness. Yet Daphne only holds
up the mirror to antiquity as a whole.

In such a community literature found small favour. It
was a place of amusement and dissipation only, or mainly.
Musical displays, the ballet, fights of wild beasts and of
gladiators, were the supreme delight. The applause or
hisses of the Antioch crowd decided the fame or failure of
a dancer through the whole Empire. Jockeys, and other
heroes of the circus or the theatre, came mostly from Syria.
It gave Rome its dancers, conjurers, clowns and tumblers.
So besotted, indeed, were the Antioch public in their devotion to amusement that according to a probable tradition,

the saddest catastrophe which in those ages befell the city,
— its capture by Sapor, King of Persia, in the year 260,—
was effected by surprise while the theatre was crowded.
The Persians climbed the farther side of Silpius, and pouring down their arrows on the thousands filling the huge
open structure on the slopes below, made Antioch their
own before any one suspected their approach. Immorality
abounded in all ancient cities, but in none so dreadfully
as in Antioch. Rome traced its foulest depths of wickedness to her. The Orontes, said Juvenal, had overflowed
into the Tiber. Even the religions of Syria imported to
Italy abominations previously unknown. Endless bands of
Syrian harlots sailed to it, along with a perpetual stream
of other ministers of vice and folly of every kind. How,
indeed, could it be otherwise, when the Syrian gods had in
every temple great establishments of courtesans, formally
selected and enrolled as a chief source of its income?
One gift only, of a special kind, could be claimed by
Antioch as peculiarly its own—skill in mocking jibes and
smart nicknames. The player or dancer of the theatre
was not beneath its shafts, nor the Emperor above them.
They had a passion for an irritating or injurious use of
their tongues, nor could they be cured of this, even by
penalties imposed on the city by the dignitaries whom,
generation after generation, they turned into ridicule.
Was it one of the derisive sallies of this mocking spirit
that led to " believers " being first called " Christians " at
Antioch?

Boasting, in the days of Paul, a population of 500,000,
this once great community is represented, now, by about
6000 inhabitants of a poor and squalid town, made up
largely of dreary heaps of ruins, and unsightly, patched,

and dilapidated houses, rising among mounds of rubbish and garbage.   The Orontes still wheels its eddies of milky water, as of old, through it, but its chief use, now, is to turn huge mill-waterwheels, one of which, close to the town, is about a hundred feet across.   The walls, which once zigzagged, almost perpendicularly, from the river to the very top of Silpius, thick with towers and bastions; some, sixty feet high, are now no longer what they were when Paul looked up to them, but still show great fragments, here and there.   When perfect, they enclosed a space of seven miles, leaping from rock to rock, even on the mountain top, as portions remaining, show; cresting huge precipices, and, in one place, stretching across a savage ravine, bridged by mighty substructions built up from the gulf below.   At Daphne, not a vestige of temple or shrine now remains, but nature retains its perfect loveliness.   The luxuriant laurels and cypresses, once covering a circle of ten miles, still flourish as of old, and, as at Cæsarea Philippi, countless brooks, descending from the hills around, make the whole region delightful.   Nor is Seleucia, the port of ancient Antioch, more fortunate. Canals long silted up; piers and moles still magnificent in their ruin, and even still, in some spots, imperishably perfect; galleries and tunnels cut for aqueducts and overflow channels, through the limestone rocks, mark its ancient greatness and its present utter decay and disappearance; its once splendid harbour, offering, now, only a broad level of pestilential morass.

In this region, and especially in Antioch itself, Paul and Barnabas spent A.D. 44; the year in which Agrippa died.   Never could there have been a more perfect ideal of Bunyan's "town, Vanity, at which there is a fair kept all the year long, called Vanity Fair," than here, with its motley population of Greeks, Syrians and Jews, and a representation of well-nigh every nationality of East and West, attracted by the shrewd liberality which conferred citizenship on every new-comer who settled in the gay city. Jews, especially, as I have said, streamed to Antioch; the founder of the town having granted them unrestrained liberty of worship, and the wants and vices of the inhabitants assuring them of plentiful gains. Such a generous policy, however, reacted favourably on both the heathen and Hebrew, softening prejudices on both sides, too bitter elsewhere. The frozen exclusiveness of the Jewish character gave way, more than in any other place; a half friendly intercourse with the "Gentile" prevailing, in its stead; though the Jews, still held fast to the religion of their fathers, and even attracted many of their Greek and Syrian fellow-citizens to adopt it, more or less fully.

The "good seed of the kingdom" had, as we have seen, been early sown on this favourable soil, for one of the seven "ministers to the poor" in the Jerusalem church was Nicolas, a proselyte from Antioch. A frightful earthquake which visited the city on the 23rd March of the year 37, had, moreover, prepared the way for a still wider diffusion of the new faith; waking terror in the light-minded and superstitious multitude, and disposing them to listen thoughtfully, to the proclamation of the speedy descent from heaven of the Messiah, Jesus, and to embrace the purer life, which, alone, would save them from His wrath. Hellenist Christians, driven from Jerusalem by the murder of Stephen—men from Cyprus and Cyrene,— and Paul himself, had come, preaching "Jesus and the resurrection," and a surprising success had followed their labours; numerous conversions resulting, and a vigorous Christian community speedily rising in this heathen centre. Six or seven years later, Paul and Barnabas returned to help the local band of missionaries, of whom the names of three, recognised as teachers and "prophets" by their brethren, have reached us—Simeon, known among the heathen population, by the name of Niger,—which was common among the Romans, as its counterpart, "Black," is, among ourselves,—Lucius, from Cyrene, possibly a kinsman of Paul [1] but not the evangelist Luke, and Manaen, or Menahem, who is called "the foster-brother" of Herod Antipas, the tetrarch; which may either mean that he was the child of the nurse of Herod, or that he had been brought up with Herod, as his companion. In any case, he must have been connected, one way or other, with the court of Herod the Great, the father of Antipas, who succeeded to the tetrarchy of Galilee on his father's death, soon after Christ's birth. Manaen, must, therefore, have been an old man when he embraced Christianity. and his adhesion to it must have been additionally noteworthy, from his strange early history. That he should have been an officer in the Antioch church is, moreover, a pleasant indication that, even thus soon, Christianity was making its way into the higher classes. A year passed quickly in common labour; Paul and Barnabas, working with these local brethren; displaying in their teaching a noble spirit of liberality, which put in the foreground the fundamental principle of the new faith that Jew and Gentile should find in it a common brotherhood.

For this end they ignored the hindrances which had, at

[1] Rom. xvi. 21.

first, kept Jewish disciples, in some things, apart from those of heathen birth, bringing both sections to unite freely in daily meals, contrary to Jewish prejudice or fear of defilement. Stimulated by this wise policy, the growth of the Church amongst the Gentile population increased so rapidly, as to awaken a desire to send the Gospel to other Gentile communities at a distance, especially where a large Jewish local element enabled ground to be easily broken in the synagogues, and the surrounding heathen populations thus reached, as they had been at Antioch.

Meanwhile the quiet life of the Church there was varied by arrivals from that of Jerusalem. "Prophets," that is, men who delivered religious exhortations under strong inspiration—the prediction of future events being only one feature of their office—came down, we are told, from the mother church to Antioch,—we may suppose, to help the great work. Among these, one Agabus had the special gift of foreknowledge, and, by this, was able to announce that there would be a famine through the Empire, demanding, as a proof of the love borne the very poor community at Jerusalem, that the comparatively rich church at Antioch should send money to them, to buy food. A voluntary contribution was forthwith made, which, it was resolved, should be sent by the hands of Barnabas and Paul, to the elders in Jerusalem. Barnabas must, however, have gone alone, after all, for Paul himself tells us that, after his first brief stay at the Holy City, on his return from Damascus he did not revisit it for fourteen years;[1] if, indeed, that period is not rather to be counted from the date of his conversion. That the famine did take place, is established by the testimony of Josephus and Eusebius, who

[1] Gal. ii. 1.

record that such a plague smote the earth in the year 44, when Claudius was Emperor.[1] This however was only a passing incident in the Church-life of Antioch. Interest in the wide spread of Christianity grew daily stronger. Hitherto missionary work had been confined to the free action of individuals, but it was now, for the first time, proposed that it should be made the business of the Church, as an organisation, to undertake and promote it. Paul had shown, by his manifold gifts among them, both then and during his earlier visit, that he was pre-eminently fitted to carry the truth to far-off lands, and the effective power of addressing men that marked Barnabas, as well as his sweet spirit, pointed him out as a most fitting companion. He had indeed been the first friend of Paul among the Jerusalem Christians, and had gone after him to Cilicia and brought him to Antioch. Our Lord had sent out Apostles two by two; Paul must, even on this ground, have a fellow-labourer, but it is noteworthy that the name of Barnabas still stood first in the minds of the Church; that of Paul coming after his. A solemn fast was held and earnest prayers were made before God, for guidance in this momentous matter, and, then, "the prophets and teachers" laid their hands on them, and sent them on their way, with many a warm commendation to the Master, above. With them, as their attendant, went Paul's nephew, John Mark, who was in Antioch at the time—his relationship to Paul specially fitting him to accompany his uncle on such a journey.[2]

---

[1] *Ant.* xx. 6 ; v. 2 ; Eusebius, Church Hist., ii. 11.
[2] Acts xiii. 1–3, 5.

CHAPTER X

THE FIRST MISSIONARY JOURNEY

LATE IN A.D. 48, OR IN SPRING OF A.D. 49—JULY A.D. 51 ; PAUL'S AGE, c. 38–41

In the time of St. Paul, Judæa was still the centre of Judaism, but an emigration, enforced or voluntary, had, for generations, reduced to a very small proportion the importance of the Father-land, compared with that of the Greater Judæa, represented by the diffusion of the race over all parts of the then known world. In almost every country there were Jewish communities, larger or smaller, linked, on the one hand, by profound affection, to Palestine, and, on the other, standing in lively inter-course with the non-Jewish races, and thus, at once, exerting a deep influence on the heathen culture around them, and themselves so influenced by it as to bring about a development of Judaism in its theological aspects.

Assyria and Babylon had, in past ages, carried off great numbers of Jews to the East, where, as a rule, they had ultimately made their permanent home. Their pros-perity, and the narrow limits of Judæa, had induced multitudes, in later times, to seek abroad, advantages impossible to secure at home; just as the Greek had wan-dered from his petty and mountainous native country, to seek a home in Ionia, Western Asia, Egypt, Sicily and the other islands of the Mediterranean, Italy, and southern France. The Macedonian conquest of Asia, by bringing Judæa into contact with Greek-speaking races, had intensified this tendency to seek richer and larger countries than their own. The inducements held out to those who might settle in the countless Greek cities, founded in their new conquests by the Greeks, was another powerful impulse to Jewish diffusion, and large numbers were, moreover, deported by the Syro-Greek kings, to Asia Minor and elsewhere, as prisoners of war, in the wild times which led to the Maccabæan rising. Then, after a time, came Pompey, who led off large numbers, to grace his triumph at Rome. But trade and profit were the great factors in this immense emigration, which can only be compared, in modern days, with the migrations of British and European races to distant lands. Countries near Judæa were naturally most attractive; the troubles rising so frequently in it, from its position involving it in all the commotions so frequent between Syria and Egypt, no doubt stimulating the readiness to wander to more quiet homes. Alexandria became almost as much a Jewish as a Greek city; no fewer than a million of Jews being found in Egypt as a whole. Antioch, as we have seen, was another favourite spot with them; both it and Alexandria, like the newly founded Greek cities generally, offering them weighty local privileges. Next to Syria and Egypt, Asia Minor seemed to have special charms, particularly the towns on the Ionian coast, though they also flocked to all the more important ports and commercial centres bordering the Mediterranean. Already, 140 years before Christ, the Jewish Sibylline verses boasted that every land and sea

was full of Jews.[1] About the same time, the Roman
Senate directed a rescript requiring protection of the
Jews, to many kings; no fewer than twenty-four being
mentioned in Maccabees,[2] including, Parthia on the East,
and Egypt, and, among lands afterwards visited by Paul,
Syria, Pamphylia, Lycia, and Cyprus, with Cyrene, and the
other chief countries and islands of the Mediterranean.
Josephus could, therefore, fearlessly remind his fellow-
countrymen, when dissuading them from rising against
Rome, that "there is no people in the world who have
not some of you among them; "[3] a statement borne out
by the list of countries given in Acts, from which
pilgrims had come to Jerusalem to attend Pentecost.[4]
So dense was the Jewish population, in fact, in the
Syrian towns, that we read of ten or even eighteen
thousand being massacred at Damascus in the great
war.[5] King Agrippa, in a letter to Caligula, in behalf
of his race, after recounting their numbers in Egypt,
Syria, Phœnicia, and Cœle-Syria, dwells on their multitudes in Asia Minor. They abound, he tells the Emperor,
"in Pamphylia, Cilicia, in almost every part of proconsular Asia even to Bithynia, and in the farthest corner
of Pontus; "[6] while the presence of numerous inscriptions
in the Crimea, even to our time, shows that they had
crossed the Black Sea. They swarmed, indeed, in every
town of Greek Asia Minor,[7] as we see in the whole
narrative of Paul's life. In Cyrene, the region west of

---

[1] *Orac. Sibyll.* iii. 271.
[2] 1 Macc. xv. 16–24.
[3] *Bell. Jud.* ii. 16, 4.
[4] Acts ii. 9–11.
[5] *Bell. Jud.* ii. 20, 2 ; vii. 8, 7.
[6] Philo, *Legat. ad Caium*, sec. 36 ; *Mang.* ii. 587.
[7] Philo, *Legat. ad Caium*, sec. 33 ; *Mang.* ii. 582.

Egypt, now Tripoli,—they were countless, and, like their brethren of Alexandria, much given to tumults and discontent; the great Jewish insurrection of the time of Trajan having its strongest seat in Cyrenaica, where the Jews massacred more than 200,000 of their non-Jewish fellow-citizens, with every circumstance of fanatical madness. The number of Jews in Greece is shown from the Epistles; synagogues being found by Paul in Thessalonica, Borœa, Athens, and Corinth. Agrippa's letter confirms this, in a wider list which includes "Thessaly, Bœotia, Macedonia, Ætolia, Attica, Argos, Corinth, and all the fairest parts of the Peloponnesus." "And not only," the king adds, "is the continent full of Jews, but all the chief islands, Eubœa, Cyprus and Crete." In Cyprus, indeed, they were so numerous, that in the great rising under Trajan, they followed the example of their brethren of Cyrenaica, by murdering no fewer than 240,000 non-Jewish inhabitants of the island, adding to this achievement the sacking and destruction of Salamis, the capital. It is easy to understand, from such a state of things, how "men of Cyprus and Cyrene are so often mentioned in Scripture."[1] Of the Jews in Rome I shall speak hereafter. With those of Asia, east of Syria, the story of Paul has no relations. They were quite as numerous, however, on the Euphrates and beyond it, as in the west. In Mesopotamia, Media, and Babylonia, the descendants of the Ten Tribes, and of the captives from Judah, formed great communities, increased by subsequent voluntary or forced additions, so that the Jewish population of these provinces, in the Roman times, were to be counted not

[1] 2 Macc. ii. 23; Matt. xxvii. 32; Mark xv. 21; Luke xxiii. 26; Acts ii. 10; vi. 9; xi. 30; xiii. 1.

by thousands but by millions. Beyond these regions, in
Parthia, and as far as the hope of trade enticed them,
they were to be met everywhere. The only comparison
offered in modern times is that of the spread of the Irish,
who form a vast community in the United States, and in
every province of the British Empire—keeping, in many
ways, apart from the general population, alike in religion
and politics; an alien and isolated confederacy, under
their own leaders, for their own ends. Like them, the
Jews in the Roman Empire, indifferent or hostile to the
ideas of the community which gave them shelter, were
always conspiring, always loyal only to their own aims;
following the orders of the Pharisaic leaders at Jerusalem.
They were, in fact, everywhere, an empire within the
Empire, not submitting, like other citizens, to the local
and general laws, but largely self-governed, by permission
wrung by turbulence or intrigue, from the State. The
fanatical expectation of a Jewish world-empire—with
Jerusalem for its capital—destined to crush that of Rome,
animated them to a restless propaganda, which, as the
Gospels tell us "compassed sea and land to make one
proselyte;"[1] the idea being that every convert was one
recruit more for the Jewish armies, when the appearance
of the Messiah should give the signal for such universal
insurrection, as broke out in the reign of Trajan, and
afterwards in that of Hadrian. In their eagerness to
gain soldiers for this holy war, they even relaxed their
exclusiveness so that "half proselytes" were allowed,
who, though not required to be circumcised, were admitted
to the Jewish communion. The abominations of heathenism, moreover, contrasted with the simple monotheism,

[1] Matt. xxiii. 15.

and the high morality of Judaism, everywhere attracted
large numbers of the more serious of the non-Jewish races,
to a faith so much above their own ; the attraction, however, in very many cases, extending only to a friendly
sympathy, like that of the centurions of Capernaum and
Cæsarea, who acknowledged the Jewish God and worshipped Him, but went no farther.

Throughout this vast Greater Judæa, which embraced all
lands, neither the local influences which maintained bitter
exclusiveness, and an inflexible benumbed theology, among
the Jews of Palestine,—nor those of other lands, which
modified national feeling, and transformed the religious
philosophy of the millions living in contact with Greek-
speaking races, made any breach in the essential unity
of all Israelites.   In spite of the fierce sectarian hatreds
that divided them even in Judæa, and led, in the end,
to open war between the rival sectaries; in spite of the
innovations of Alexandrian theology, which sought to
bridge the gulf between Judaism and Greek philosophy;
in spite of the introduction of foreign races into the
hitherto narrow Hebrew faith ; in spite even of the
crumbling away of the old landmarks of a bigoted
orthodoxy, under the influence of intrusive Hellenism, all
Israel remained united in a grand sense, as one and in-
divisible, by the universally honoured central attraction
of the Temple, of which the only analogies in our time
are, perhaps, the Vatican of the Roman Church, or the
Kaaba of Mecca.   The Holy City remained the citadel;
the Temple, the Palladium, of universal Judaism, whether
it lived under Rome or under Parthia, whether it spoke
Aramaic or Greek, or, even, whether it believed in the
Jehovah of Palestine or the Lord God of Alexandria.

That the Eternal, their patron and protector, had granted
the spiritual head of their faith, a local "temporal power,"
was as undoubted by the Jew as it is now by the ultra-
Romanist; the petty size of Judæa, which he regarded
as the fief of his Church, troubling him as little, as the
wider or narrower sweep of Papal territory in any age,
disturbed the conviction of Romanists. Every member of
the Jewish communion had to send, yearly, to Jerusalem
a didrachmon, that is, half a shekel, as Temple tax, which
was regularly laid up in the treasury, as the national
revenue. Every one was pledged to go at least once
in his lifetime, to sacrifice personally, at the place which,
alone, in the world, was well pleasing to Jehovah.
Theology remained the passion of the Babylonian and
Alexandrian rabbi, alike. The uniquely tenacious national
sentiment which had expressed itself in the returning
exiles from the Euphrates, knew no decay in those they
left behind, and beat with equal strength in the breasts
of every subsequent community of Hebrews, wherever it
found itself, over the whole earth. Judaism was the Freemasonry of the ancient world. To all other men, the Jew
remained a mere neighbour, but every Jew saw a brother in
each member of his race. Aliens from the commonwealth
of Israel, the great nations of mankind, in all their ranks,
were to the Jew, no better than the Pariah or the Sudra is
to the Brahmin, or the "infidel" to the scowling dervish.

Yet the universal presence of the Jew through the
Gentile world, whatever its other aspects, had been of
unspeakable advantage for the spread of Christianity, by
spreading the idea of the One Living God, in opposition
to the polytheism everywhere prevailing, and by the
teaching of a high morality. The synagogue, moreover,

offered an open door, at least at first, for the preaching
of the new faith. It was in fact, from it, that Christianity
went forth to the heathen, when the Jew rejected the
message brought him, but it was only because the Gentile
mind had been unconsciously prepared by Judaism, for
listening to the Apostles, that they found the hearing
vouchsafed them in heathen communities. The Jew had
cast up in the desert a highway for the Messiah-Jesus.
Jews and Jewish-minded heathen, made ready the soil of
the world for St. Paul and his fellow-labourers.

Having been designated for missionary work outside
Syria, Paul and Barnabas, with their attendant John
Mark, Paul's nephew, lost no time in carrying out the
wishes of the church at Antioch, under whose auspices
they had been thus commissioned. It was only about
sixteen miles to Seleucia, the port of Antioch, by road,
but more than forty by the course of the swift-flowing
Orontes, which doubles hither and thither on the left or
south side of the track, but could hardly, in any case,
have been used by the missionaries, as the river was
barely navigable even for very small craft, as far as to
Antioch. The road is a lovely one, passing through wild
ravines—wild now, but, then dotted with country-houses,
often of great magnificence. Many streamlets hurry
down from the Pierian Hills, which form a glorious landscape along the north of the track, to join the Orontes;
their bridges long since gone, so that one needs to ford
them now. The highest point of the journey reached,
the Mediterranean bursts into sight, with the plain of
Seleucia and the Orontes winding through it, as it
stretches out, in charming richness of verdure, to the
sea-shore. A magnificent city lay before Paul, on the

slopes of Pieria, a few miles north of the river mouth, to which, however, it was joined by continuous suburbs, terminating in a great port, the plan of which can still be distinctly traced, with its walls, basins, quays, flood-gates, and defences.   The entrance from the inner to the outer harbour, is marked by two magnificent piers of vast stones, clamped together with iron, of which the southern-most, 120 yards long, is still in admirable preservation, and could not be surpassed for solidity or finish by any modern work.   From one of these moles, Paul and his companions stepped on board the vessel which was to take them to Salamis, the capital, or, rather the chief city, of Cyprus; a voyage of about 130 miles, in a straight line, to the south-west.   The plain, in those days picturesque with every detail of wealth and high culture, round splen-did villas, is now dotted with cottages and some better houses, embosomed in gardens of pomegranates and other fruit-trees.   Innumerable tombs remain in the upper scarps of the hill-part of the city, on the north, and the wreck of many sarcophagi, besides some whole ones, mostly empty, lie exposed here and there.   Remains of two of the city gates, of an amphitheatre, and of the old fortifications, recall the scene round the apostle, as he approached. In the low ground before the city, are great walls, now enclosing a marsh, once the inner harbour, to which a canal, several hundred yards long, but now choked up, led from the sea.   On the north side of the harbour is a series of galleries and tunnels, said to be 1200 yards long, cut through the solid limestone rock, which supplied Seleucia with water, and also provided an escape for floods coming down the ravines behind.

From the deck of the vessel which bore them away, the

missionaries, if they cared to look at it, had a wondrously beautiful view before them. On the north, stretched away a mountainous coast; lofty hills, sweeping to the east, framed-in the landscape behind, on both sides of the river, while, to the south, the mighty limestone cone of Mount Casius rose nearly six thousand feet out of the ocean waters, a few miles off. On the town hill, moreover, the castellated citadel, standing out against the sky, was before them, while temples and splendid public buildings, everywhere showed themselves above the maze of streets, parks, squares, warehouses, and mansions. But Paul never alludes to natural beauties; his concentrated engrossment in the great object of his life apparently making him indifferent to everything else; if, indeed, he had any touch of the poet in his nature, which seems doubtful. His strength, abundant as it was, lay in another direction.

Cyprus, as you approach it from the sea, looks very mountainous, but the centre of the island, from east to west, forms a wide plain, from which rises a comparatively low chain of rather barren hills, skirting the coast on the north, while a much higher range covers the southern half of the island; climbing to nearly 8000 feet in height at what used to be called "Mount Olympus," the summit of which, with that of one or two other mountains, is covered with snow for some time in most winters. The most charming valleys run among these hills, rich in all kinds of growth, as may be judged from the exports of the island as a whole, including, even now, wine, grain, cotton, tobacco, timber, fruit, and much else. But the metal which takes its name—copper—from Cyprus, through the Latin Cyprium, was, with precious stones, the greatest source of wealth in Roman days, though gold and silver were also obtained. The presence of ruins, everywhere, shows the density of the population in these times, but it was of an Eastern type in its religion, and consequently very immoral and corrupt. Phœnician nature-worship, in fact, with obscene rites from the wild Phrygian faith, prevailed; the Syrian Astarte under another name being the goddess of the island, worshipped in the form of a rude conical stone.[1] Sensuality held a carnival round the year. Lust was deified, and received universal homage. The exuberance of nature; the warmth of the summer climate, the strength of the Cyprian wine, the deliciousness of mere existence, in a place so lovely and so exciting to every sense, made Cyprus another Daphne. I know few landscapes more perfect than some of those in the island, amidst which to pass a dreamy life of abandonment to the lower pleasures, if one be so degraded as to make them his delight.

Salamis, to which the missioners now came, was at the east end of the island, near the wretched modern town of Famagusta. It lay on low ground, at the extremity of the great central plain, a little south of the Pediæus, the only true river in Cyprus. A good harbour attracted commerce, which, in its turn, brought great numbers of Jews, universally present, then as now, wherever money was to be made. That they had several synagogues, while many towns had only one, shows, at once the size of the city as a whole, and the largeness of the Semitic element. The frightful massacre of the general population in the rising under Trajan[2] implies, moreover, that Jews were no less numerous through the island at large. That so clement an emperor should have utterly destroyed Salamis,

---

[1] Tac., *Hist.* ii. 3.   [2] See p. 214.

as Trajan then did, tells, also, its own story of the local numbers and character of the insurrectionary multitude.

The Apostles had, in Christ's lifetime, been strictly travelling preachers, passing from town to town, and hamlet to hamlet, with the news of the kingdom of God, set up by Christ. The course taken by Paul was quite different. The apostle, on coming to any place, settled down in it for a longer or shorter period, maintaining himself by his handicraft as a tent-maker; in fact, as a mechanic. He had left Antioch, no doubt accompanied by loving brethren, who had gone on foot, or ridden on asses, alongside of him, past the rich hill slopes, covered with myrtles, arbutus, laurel, and evergreen oak, and dotted with villages, which made the road from Antioch. so charming. Then, after many tender farewells, with loving embraces and prayers broken by tears, as they knelt together on the strand, he and his companions had gone finally on board, and sailed out of the harbour from which, year by year, in strange contrast to the present mission, a crowd of degraded beings of all kinds, the creations of the moral corruption of Syria and the East, set out to pollute even Rome, already so vile. The lofty Mount Casius, from which, three centuries later, the last smoke of a pagan sacrifice was to ascend; the snowy peaks of Taurus; the masses of nearer mountains, and the glories of the great Syrian port faded from sight. On landing at Salamis, however, Paul would find himself, still, among his own people, and even be able to make his temporary home in the bosom of some Christian household. But while for the moment accepting hospitality, his independent spirit would forthwith seek work of some kind, by which he could avoid living at their cost. There has

always been an Arab-like Freemasonry among Jews,—
retained, no doubt from the days of the tent life of their
ancestors,—which opens a home, in all lands, to the passing brother Jew, and would think it a reproach, to let him
go to an inn.   Even now, wherever there is an organised
Jewry, the Israelite on his travels, passes from ghetto to
ghetto, carrying letters of commendation, which secure
him a home in some Jewish family.   On his appearance
in the synagogue on the Sabbath, he is at once noticed
and invited to tell whom he is, whence he comes, who is,
or was, his father, and what Jewish news he brings from
the community he has just left.   It would be exactly thus
with Paul, as long as he continued in communion with
the synagogue, and such would, consequently, be his reception in Salamis.   These local Jewries were admirable
centres, for the propagation of new religious ideas.   Every
one knew the other ; each unceasingly kept his eye on
his neighbour.   Jews did not then mix themselves up with
the politics of their chance Gentile home, and, indeed, even
now, do so only to advance Jewish interests.   Keeping
apart from public affairs, as a rule, their religion absorbed
their thoughts.   Any doubt thrown on the minutest
detail of their distinctive practices or hereditary opinions,
set the whole community on fire.   Forthwith, all feuds
and schisms previously distracting them for the time,
disappeared in the common excitement at the proposed
innovation.

The synagogues were naturally founded in the cities
and towns along the great lines of commercial intercourse,
and at its centres.   In those days, however, they had no
distinction of architecture, but were ordinary houses,
known as synagogues to the Jews only, or those in

sympathy with them. It was the custom in the Sabbath
devotions, when the officials saw any one presumably able
to speak effectively, from earnestness or apparent rabbinical knowledge, to invite him to say a few words to the
congregation. Our Lord had been thus called up in the
synagogue at Nazareth,[1] and the apostle took advantage
of the usage, to lay before the audience the new Christian
teaching. At first, he, as a rule, met only with eager
questioning, but, in the end, this, too often, degenerated
into heated opposition, before which further discussion
was useless; if, indeed, even violence could be escaped.

The close inter-relations of emigrant Jews with their
old homes, and with their race as a whole, must have
secured Paul a welcome in Cyprus, from some households
connected by blood, or otherwise, with members of the
now large Christian community of Antioch. Barnabas,
moreover, was among his own people, and various Cypri-
otes were among the churches even of Judæa.[2] How long
the little band stayed at Salamis is not said, but we do not
hear of any Christian church being formed. After a time,
therefore, they left it, and went on to the West, preaching,
no doubt, in the synagogues of the cities to which they
came, till they had passed from one end of the island to
the other; arriving, finally, at New Paphos, a town seven
or eight miles east of the old town of the same name,
famous as the chief seat of the worship of Venus. Cyprus
was a senatorial province, and hence received a new proconsul yearly; the dignity at this time, being held by
Sergius Paulus, who, at the moment of Paul's visit, had
his official residence in New Paphos. It is a striking
rebuke to the ultra-criticism which disparages every state-

[1] Luke iv. 16.   [2] Acts xi. 19, 20; xxi. 16.

ment in the Acts, to find Pliny the elder speaking, twenty years later, of a Roman savant of the same name with the proconsul, as an authority on the physical characteristics of the island.[1] His palace was at New Paphos, at the eastern extremity of Cyprus, the point which could soonest receive news from Rome. It was at Old Paphos, however, that the Paphian goddess had her much sought oracles, which even Titus, the conqueror of Jerusalem, did not hesitate to consult at a critical time,[2] and her sanctuary there was the centre of Venus worship, not only in Cyprus but for the whole earth. Hither she had come when she rose out of the sea, and hither, as Aphrodite, she attracted a multitude to her shrine, day by day, from every land. The foundations of her immense temple are yet visible, but in Paul's day, it was in its glory; illustrating the foulness of the old religions by the multitudes of prostitutes formally connected with its establishment; the wages of their calling being a main source of the ecclesiastical revenue. Bands of catamites, moreover, also belonging to the temple—the debased male prostitutes of antiquity—paraded the city, and round the country, far and near, with their wild music, and disgusting orgies. Nor need it be wondered that the practice of the black arts in all their varieties, throve on the superstition and vice of such a community. But even the huge Venus temple did not give outlet enough for the prevailing moral corruption. No fewer than three grand temples, of which the plan is still traceable, were so many additional centres from which lewdness and religious imposition of every kind, spread their deadly influences.

Among the crowd of wandering adventurers, at the

---

[1] Pliny, *Index of Authors*, before Books ii. and xviii.   [2] Tac., *Hist.* v. 3

time in New Paphos, was a Jew called Bar Jesus, meaning, "the son of Joshua," who, for greater effect, had assumed the Arabic name of Elymas, "the Magian," or "powerful one,"—that is, in spells, divinations, insight into the future, and all other weird accomplishments and quackeries; the first century equivalent, in fact, of the modern Cagliostro, with his "elixir of perpetual youth"—and affectation of being a physician, alchemist, Freemason, necromancer, or, in short, anything that audacity could suggest, by which to dupe the world and make money. He is described as a "sorcerer and false prophet," such as then abounded, who, by sleight-of-hand jugglery, spells, pretended knowledge of magical books, and, perhaps, the wonders of animal magnetism, gained great influence, not only over the ignorant, but even over the educated classes. If the name he took be any sign, he was probably from Arabia, which was, in antiquity, famous for its "wisdom." At New Paphos, he had won great popularity, as Simon, "the Magus," had done, in Samaria, till, at length, the proconsul, "a man of understanding," unsatisfied, like many others of his class, with paganism, had sent for him, to see what his pretensions were worth. The clear head of the Roman, however, had, more or less, seen through him, and he, therefore, now summoned the Christian missionaries to the palace, to find whether they could tell him anything more satisfactory. It was life or death to Elymas to prevent their gaining influence over the great man, for, with the patronage of the proconsul, that of the public would disappear. Attending, probably by invitation, when Paul and Barnabas were admitted to the palace, he used all his arts to keep his footing, as the Egyptian magicians had done in their contest with Moses, before Pharaoh, till, at last, Paul, indignant at his pertinacity in opposing "the right ways of the Lord"—steadily gazing at him, denounced him as "full of all guile and all villany, a son of the devil, the father of lies, and an enemy of all righteousness," adding that, to mark what God thought of him, he should, forthwith, be blind for a time. Presently, we are told, "there fell on him a mist and a darkness; and he went about, seeking some to lead him by the hand." Such a proof of Divine support to the apostle was, as might have been expected, a convincing evidence to the governor, of the truth of the new faith, and led to his instant acceptance of it, as "the teaching of the Lord."

From this time, the Hebrew name "Saul," hitherto that of the apostle, disappears, and he becomes Paul: perhaps as an honourable memento of this conversion of so high a dignitary; possibly, as the name henceforth assumed by him, now that he was distinctly identified with work among "the Gentiles;" to whom a Roman name would be more acceptable than a Jewish one. Indeed such concessions to Gentile life were generally recognised by his race, who were accustomed to have two names, one that of their infancy; the other a Greek or Roman one. From this time, moreover, Paul takes the foremost place in the missionary narrative; Barnabas passing into a wholly secondary importance. Paphos was the starting-point in his career as the Apostle of the Gentiles.

How long the Christian missionaries remained in Cyprus is not told, but, now, they resolved to leave it for wider fields. Henceforward, the island was given over to Barnabas, as his sphere,—a natural arrangement, as Barnabas was a Cypriote,—and Paul never returned to it. Nor does he ever speak of any churches as founded by him in it; as if the tour had not been marked by any large results.

Asia Minor, to which the apostle was presently to sail, lay only about thirty miles north of the nearest point of Cyprus, though the voyage from Paphos to Attalia, where Paul was to land, was not less in a straight line, than 170 miles. Washed by three seas, the Black, the Archipelago, or Ægean, and the Mediterranean,—this great peninsula, one of the richest of lands, under good government, was the home, in Paul's day, of the survivors of many nationalities. The Thracian element predominated in the larger half of Bithynia; Phrygia, Lydia, Cilicia, and Cappadocia, were marked by large remains of early races whose very speech is still a riddle. But all these elements had, more or less, faded, before the advance of Greek civilisation, so that, in the first century, only three nationalities appear prominent, the Greek, the Celtic,—which had seized wide regions, during the troubled times of the Syrian successors of Alexander,—and the Roman. It is, as a whole, a land of mountains, the one large tract without them being the central tableland of Lycaonia, now known as the plains of the Axylon, which are reached, from the south, only by ascending the lofty and rough passes of the great Taurus range. This vast chain stretches along the whole of the peninsula, in huge summits, many covered, atop, with snow, till late in spring; the time when I was at their foot; their rough sides clothed with forests; streams and rivers rushing down through the wildest confusion of gorge and glen and precipice; while the labyrinth of Alp above and beyond Alp is threaded only by rude tracks, impracticable except to native horses, hereditarily surefooted and enduring. Asia Minor, in the

most vivid sense, may, indeed, be called a land of the
mountain and the flood, as Paul often had to realise. The
boundaries of the different provinces were very undefined,
from the imperfect Romanising of a great part of the
peninsula, but, in the apostolic age, according to Professor
Ramsay, the greatest living authority on the subject,[1] they
were as follows.   On the west, the province of "Asia,"
—which then included Mysia, on its north—extended over
the whole country, for nearly 200 miles from north to
south, and for about 300 from west to east in its northern
half; contracting to about 150 in its southern.   Lycia
was the roughly semicircular bend of the land, immediately south of this huge province; a tract of about 100
miles, east and west, by about 60, north and south.   Next,—
also on the south coast,—lay Pamphylia,—a strip bending
round the bay of the same name for about 120 miles, with
a breadth of about 20 miles at each end, and of about 40
in its centre.   From the east edge of this, a great wedge,
about 100 miles across on the south, ran for about 150
miles, north, where, at last, it was little more than 30
miles broad; a surviving part of the old kingdom of the
Græco-Syrian kings.   Then, finishing the southern coast-
line, came Cilicia, the province of Paul; about 140 miles,
east and west, and varying from about 60 at its west
end, to a breadth twice as great, in the other two-thirds.
North of Cilicia, the immense province of Cappadocia
extended, at its broadest, more than 250 miles east and
west, and not far from 200 north and south; a province
belonging to a vassal king, reaching, beyond it, to the Black
Sea.   Along the shores of that sea stretched the province
of Pontus, with a coast-line of nearly 400 miles, but a

[1] Map to the Church in the Roman Empire.

depth varying from 100 miles to hardly 20. West of
Pontus, along the shores of the Euxine, Bithynia completed
the belt of outer provinces, joining Mysia, and sharing,
with it, the shores of the present Sea of Marmora. This
enumeration, it may be noticed, leaves unmentioned a
vast interior territory, extending from the narrow bounds
of Pamphylia, on the south coast, to within a very little
of the Euxine, and filling up the wide region between
" Asia " and Cappadocia ; a province by far the largest in
the peninsula. This was the Galatia of Paul's day, comprising, it may almost be said, the whole centre part of
Asia Minor, from sea to sea. " The churches of Galatia,"
therefore, must have been very far apart, if they were
scattered over this immense tract, as a whole.

The new field of missionary enterprise was, thus, a very
wide theatre for every form of activity, through successive
generations. In round numbers, about 800 miles from
east to west, and 400 from north to south, it contained
about 300,000 square miles, or nearly six times the area
of all England. The rich fringe of coast bordering the
Ægean, had early attracted an extensive Greek immigra-
tion, and had thus gradually Hellenised what, in Paul's
day, formed the great province of " Asia ; " planting towns,
step by step, over its length and breadth, till it boasted of
having no fewer than five hundred. Greek civilisation was
thus, ultimately, supreme in the wide territory originally
held by the Mysians, Lydians, and Carians, so that Ionia
became virtually a part of "Greater Greece." The slow
advance of this transformation, however, throws light on
the difficulties in the way of permeating the country,
as a whole, with settled and peaceful institutions. The
multitude of harbours, and the beauty and fertility of

the border of lowland, on the edge of the province, and the facilities for settlement offered by the lower parts of the river-courses, filled these spots with a busy population, long before colonists ventured to make their way into the lofty and often comparatively poor interior; where, moreover, they were face to face with powerful native princes, and suffered by their isolation from their brethren in the coast cities. After the great deeds of Alexander, however, the Greeks became more ambitious, and ventured to assail the native kings, founding cities which became centres of Greek influence, and setting up Greek dynasties, under which civilisation steadily spread. The Romans came on the scene only in the second century before Christ, but did little to annex the country till a century later. Syria and Cilicia became Roman provinces only under Pompey, about sixty years before our era. Galatia fell into Roman hands only in B.C. 25; Cappadocia, in A.D. 17, and the confederated cities of Lydia were only incorporated into the Roman system under Claudius, in A.D. 43, though the Imperial City had, in each case, but in a more or less vague way, been virtually paramount at a much earlier time. " Asia " became Roman by the "will" of Attalus the Third, of Pergamos, who died B.C. 133. The great territory of Bithynia and Pontus was not Roman till about sixty years before Christ, and Crete fell to the Republic, only after Pompey's war with the pirates, in B.C. 66. It is not surprising, therefore, to learn that, even under the earlier emperors, half-robber chiefs could still carve out principalities for themselves, in the Phrygian mountains on the north, or that the legions had to be sent into the mountains of Western Cilicia so late as the very day of Paul, in A.D. 36, and again, in A.D. 52, to reduce turbulent clans, and put an end, if possible, to their wild marauding. For they were, in truth, only fierce highland raiders by land, and remorseless pirates by sea; their pathless mountains enabling them to come down and harry the cities on the rich coast plain, and also offering every facility for launching their pirate galleys from the innumerable creeks, where the mountains extended to the sea. Galatia,—as we have seen, an immense tract of country,—retained native rulers, as vassals of Rome, till they were set aside, finally, by Augustus, who died in A.D. 14, its population, even then, being a mixture of Greek, Celtic, and Phrygian races. Paul's experience of "perils of robbers" may be thus vividly realised; for, in a country, great districts of which were still as little settled, as the Scotch Highlands were before 1745, or as Southern Italy, with its hordes of brigands, has been in our own day, a traveller's life, in many localities, must have hung on a frail thread.

The religions of Asia Minor were as varied as her population. Under the Romans, the great festival of the year, through the land at large, was that of the Emperor. Augustus had allowed the senates of "Asia" and Bithynia, in the year B.C. 25, to erect temples to him as a god, and this set the fashion for all the future. What the Passover was to the Jews, or the Olympic games to the Greeks, the high festival of the worship of the Emperor became to Asia Minor. It was celebrated with grand processions, in which the high priest entered the city in purple robes, with a garland on his head, boys before him swinging smoking censers amidst immense display by all classes, and, erelong, it was treason to refuse to burn incense on the altar, set beside the statue of the divine

Cæsar of the day. Pergamos was famous for the miraculous cures wrought by her local Esculapius, the god of
health, and every other part had its own deities and rites,
often half savage, and more than half Oriental in their
wild excitement and measureless obscenity.

On the far greater part of the country, Rome, gradually
imposed the order and respect for law which secured public
security, so that, on the great highroads, men moved from
place to place without fear. The Pax Romana reigned
over all the accessible portions of the land, as the Pax
Britannica does in India now. But, as I have said, in
the savage mountain regions, and in the barren and waste
districts of the deep interior; especially on the borders
of Mysia and Bithynia, and in the mountain valleys of
Pisidia and Isauria, the clans were still as lawless plun-
derers, as some of the wild hill tribes of India have been
till almost to-day.

Under the strong hand of Rome, with her fixed laws
and regular legal system, and her municipal institutions,
St. Paul would find the country, as a whole, in a state of
prosperity in striking contrast to its appearance at present.
I have looked up long-drawn valleys in Asia Minor, rich
with every form of verdure, and beautiful beyond thought,
in their sweeping landscapes, but now, like a thousand
others as charming, utterly depopulated; a few fierce
mountaineers, armed, each, with a whole arsenal of weapons,
living in the hills, out of reach of police, the only samples
of humanity one met. Yet, in Paul's day, these very
vales of Paradise were the homes of a flourishing population; the hill-slopes and the rich valleys waved with all
forms of rural wealth; busy towns cheered every landscape, and well-made roads gave easy means of communi-

cation between all parts. A writer of a century later than the apostle, quoted by Mommsen, from whom I have gathered the materials for this sketch,[1] tells us of the district round Smyrna, "No province can show so many towns as ours, and none like our finest. Everything helps them; the lovely country, the delicious climate, the manifold productions of the soil, the position in the centre of the Empire, a circle of contented peoples around, the good order, the rarity of crime, the kindly treatment of slaves, the thoughtfulness and goodwill of the rulers." The partially ill-watered interior of Phrygia, Lycaonia, Galatia, and Cappadocia, fit, for the most part, only for pasture, might be sparsely inhabited, but the coast lands of the peninsula generally, were not far behind the province of Asia, for dense and prosperous communities. A picture of a small country town near the Lycian coast, yet remains, to aid our realising the communities round the apostle in his wanderings through these regions. Its name was Sidyma, and it had been built under Claudius, just about the time when Paul was in these parts. It lay at the foot of a hill, in a lovely and fertile valley, amidst bracing Alpine air, and the glory of southern vegetation; embosomed in wooded mountains and slopes, rich in myrtles and many kinds of fragrant shrubs and plants. In its market-place are still to be seen the ruins of a four-chambered temple, and a stately colonnade, built in his native place, by a physician who had made money in his profession. Statues of the Emperor, and of famous citizens of the mother-city, close by, which this new one supplanted, adorned the market; and there were in the town, besides, a temple to its guardian divinities, Artemis

[1] *Römische Gesch.* v. 327.

and Apollo, baths and gymnasia for all kinds of athletic
exercises, while, outside the gates, a row of stone funereal
monuments, striking and costly, lined the main road, which
sank steeply down, towards the coast. But places like
this little hill-town, were repeated in countless numbers,
over the whole land, though the last traces of most of
them have long since vanished. Not that they were so
many Edens. The immorality of heathenism threw in
abundant shadow, and bad municipal government and
exacting imperial officialism, added to the failings of
ordinary human nature, helped to make it still deeper.
The finances were managed badly; local ambition too
often striving at what was beyond its means, so that what
was most needed, was neglected for mere show. The
poorer townsmen drew on the public chest, or on the
pockets of their richer neighbours, for the oil used in the
baths, for public feasts, and amusements. The fine houses
had their throngs of " clients," with their servile flatteries,
their intrigues for larger doles, and their bitter factions.
The most deadly rivalry existed between town and town,
as in the Italy of the Middle Ages, and even between this
set and that, or between one single family and its neighbour. There was no common public spirit; no manly
energy for common ends; no civic valour to maintain
personal or public rights.

Yet Asia Minor, especially the western part of it, was
one of the richest States of the whole Empire. The
frightful misgovernment by the Republic, the calamities
of the Mithridatic wars, the plunder by wild marauders
by sea and land, till put down by Pompey, and, finally,
the awful catastrophe of the four years of civil war, had,
for the time, brought ruin over all. But when Augustus

died, in the year A.D. 14, these wounds had healed, and
the land enjoyed the highest prosperity, for the next three
hundred years; Asia Minor yielding more than almost
any other province to the imperial revenue.   Roads,
which were sorely needed, were pushed from one military
station to another, and in every way, wealth made the
land, as a whole, as pleasant for its huge population, as it
is now the reverse, for the sparse communities that still
make it their home.

This prosperity rested on the varied sources, of pasture,
agriculture, industry, and trade.   The fertile coast came
first, in the products of the soil, but Paul would see, in
many places, the steep sides of the hills cultivated as
diligently, as they are now in Sicily, or on the banks of
the Rhine.   The vast pastures of the interior, with their
numberless flocks of sheep and goats, made Lesser Asia
the headquarters of the wool and weaving industries;
Galatia, for example, supplying an endless amount of
Angora wool, while the Phrygian Laodicea was famous
for its cloth and stuffs.   The tumult in Ephesus, at the
injury to the local silver- and gold-smiths, caused by
Paul's preaching, which spoiled the demand for their
little images of Diana, shows how busy these crafts were
there.

The towns were divided into trades' quarters; wool-
weavers, shoemakers, and many others, having their own
district, as in Oriental cities now.   A large factory population, like that of our Lancashire towns, was to be found
in some parts.   Galatian slave-dealers, with their coffles
of men and women, would often meet the apostle, as he
walked, or rode his ass, on his journeys.   Roman traders
were in such numbers, in many towns, that their guild

shared with the citizens in municipal affairs; which speaks of an eager export and import rivalry, and a large seafaring activity, to and from Italy, and other parts. Teachers went, in large numbers, from Asia Minor to Italy and all other Latin speaking countries, and so did large numbers of physicians; often returning, in old age, to spend their competence in their own country. Nor were literary men wanting in this emigration; the West offering advantages comparable to those London now holds out to authors. Indeed, it is wonderful how many names of famous literary men of these times, are those of poets, rhetoricians, or philosophers, from Asia Minor.

Such was the land towards which Paul now bent his course.

CHAPTER XI

HAVING ended his work at Paphos, Paul, who, from this time, apparently from his prominent part in the incident of Elymas and the proconsul, is always named first in the narrative of the Acts, " set sail " for the continent, choosing for the next scene of his labours, the portion of Asia Minor lying north from Cyprus, and landing at Attalia, after a voyage of about a hundred and seventy miles in a straight line, though the wind and currents may have made it considerably longer. The lowland district known as Pamphylia, where Attalia was the port of Perga, the capital, was, as elsewhere in the peninsula, a comparatively narrow strip, from which, as from the whole of the coast of Asia Minor, rise vast mountains, many of the summits of which were more or less white with snow when I saw them late in the spring. Nothing could be more wild, or more forbidding as a route of travel. Deep, dark ravines, without roads, rushing torrents, without bridges, densely wooded tracts to be passed through, rough paths, with great walls of rock on one side and dizzy precipitous abysses, a few feet off, on the other— often the only track, and, with all this, the terror at every step, of an attack from some of the robber mountain clans—were in the time of the apostle, as they still are, the characteristics of these savage parts.

The coast towns of Pamphylia were originally Greek settlements, dating from a distant past, and by their isolation had preserved their national traits, with inevitable local peculiarities, developing them, in the end, into an almost independent nationality, with a national speech and writing much as in Lycia, close by. The coast had been held by Egyptians, Græco-Syrians, the kings of Pergamos,—from one of whom, Attalia, his creation, took its name,—and in then recent times, by the Romans, its masters when Paul came to it. The tribes in the wild mountains, however, had practically maintained their independence ; their fierce lawlessness making them a terror to the civilisation on the sea-edge, to which they were continually coming down on plundering forays. On the east, where the mountains reached the sea, piracy took the place of marauding by land ; but all through the lofty, inaccessible highlands of the whole region, whether called Pisidia, Isauria, or Western Cilicia, there was a constant petty warfare of savagery against all richer or more civilised than itself.

Few places even in Asia Minor are more picturesque or interesting than Adalia—the modern representative of the "Attalia" of the apostle. It stands at the head of the gulf to which, on English charts at least, it gives its name. The scenery in the neighbourhood is remarkably fine. Less than ten miles off, to westward, rises the rugged summit of Mount Climax; while a *sierra* of remarkable peaks stretches away to the south till it is lost in the turn of the Lycian coast at Cape Khelidonia. The city is built on the steep, but not very lofty, heights that

embrace the small and almost exactly semicircular inden-
tation which forms the port. To the west lies a rocky
and barren plateau, which is succeeded by a great stretch
of low-lying plain, running up to the spurs of Climax,
and edged by the sea, with a narrow strip of steep and
pebbly beach. Eastward of the town there is a beautiful
tract of fertile and highly cultivated land, abounding in
streams, and terminating, seaward, in a range of bluffs
from 50 feet to 100 feet high, over the edge of which
an extraordinary number of cascades foam down into the
sea ; no fewer than seven occurring within the space of a
few hundred yards. All are beautiful, and all have their
beauty heightened, in the warm months, by the delicious
sense of coolness they impart.

The neighbourhood is as interesting historically as it
is attractive and picturesque. Round the base of Climax
Alexander waded breast-high for a whole day, while his
army was threading the passes inland. Sidé, where the
great Macedonian halted, is only some thirty miles off.
The Eurymedon, off which Cimon, with the Athenian
fleet, gained his great victory over that of the Persians,
and on the banks of which his crews triumphed again
over the Persian army, is within a few hours' sail. The
ruins of Perge, the Perga of St. Paul, are within an
easy ride. The site of Aspendus is not far off. Laara,
the modern successor of Attalia, is not more than half-
a-dozen miles away along the coast. Xenophon, and
Alexander, Roman proconsuls and emperors, Frank
crusaders and Barbarian conquerors have marched by.
The Venetian seamen of the Middle Ages have left in-
delible traces of their occupation in the battlemented
wall that still surrounds the city. Since the foundation

of the town by Attalus II., King of Pergamos, from whom it took its name, Attalia, seems to have specially illustrated the policy of the successive lords of these parts, in the fortifying their coast cities. Fragments of the massive moles that once sheltered the ancient port are still visible; and on them, as on a secure foundation, later occupiers have raised ponderous masonry which once presented a formidable front to hostile comers over the sea. It is now ruinous and threatening to fall, but its castellated form and prominent site still make its appearance imposing. A lofty wall, battlemented at the top, and flanked with rectangular towers, protected the city on its sea face in the Venetian days. A similar one encloses it on the land side; and remains of other walls here and there among the houses, indicate the frequent enlargement of the area thought worth defending. The lower courses of masonry, in most of the walls, are composed of neatly squared stones of large size, which show that they date from an ancient period. A beautiful circular building, a sort of tomb of Cœcilia Metella of reduced dimensions, is built into the wall just at the edge of the eastern bluff; at the junction of the sea and land defences. Facing a suburb containing many handsome houses and some large cafés, and standing in smiling gardens, is a handsome gateway of the Emperor Hadrian's time, showing three arches, and a cornice supported in front and rear by graceful Corinthian columns, only two or three, however, being now in place. On each side of this gateway there is a square flanking tower, built of bevelled stones of considerable dimensions, which proclaim the antiquity of this part of the defences.

II.   Q

Attalia, now Adalia, is a busy place, in spite of the unsuitability of its port for modern ships. Some of the best wheat in Asia Minor is grown in the fertile fields near it, and is exported to less favoured countries. Maize is largely cultivated; and the woollen manufactures of Konieh, the ancient Iconium, Marash, and Karamania generally—principally rugs, carpets, waist-sashes, and saddle-bags—find their way to the outside world through Adalia. A bazaar of great extent stretches along the land wall, on the heights outside the city. The wooden booths are filled with cheap English and German cottons, striped calicoes from Aleppo, Broussa silks, Damascus embroidery, variegated saddle-bags from Konieh, and leather-work of many kinds. Excepting gaudy cotton prints, European goods are few. Earthenware vessels of ancient pattern and elegant shapes, are stacked in heaps at certain points. In some places, vines are trailed across the narrow roadway, and afford a welcome shelter from the scorching sun. The scene during the forenoon is very animated. All the booths are open, and the pathways are thronged. Strings of donkeys carry jars of water slung in wooden frames, or huge panniers filled with grapes, or snow from the mountains. Sturdy Karamanian peasants, in turbans and flowing garments, ride in on wiry little horses to make their purchases. There is an incessant tinkling from the stalls of the sherbet-sellers, and shouts nearly as incessant from the riders and donkey-drivers, to warn foot-passengers out of their way. To enable them to cope with such purchasers as may turn up among their English visitors, the Spanish Jews, to whom many of the booths in the bazaar belong, have added to their

curious dialect of Spanish mixed with Italian a few
English words, and the voluble Greek has invented a
mongrel patchwork of language equally surprising.

As far as waterfalls and running streams tend to alle-
viate the discomforts of a hot season, Adalia is happy
in the possession of abundant palliatives of the ardours
of the Pamphylian summer. Two conspicuous cascades
tumble headlong down the steep rocks, within the city
itself, and clear and sparkling water runs through an
open channel, down the middle of many of its tortuous
streets.   The trees that surround it and grow within
its walls, and the spacious gardens and shrubberies that
lie outside, show by the freshness of their verdure, even
when it is hottest, that they have no lack of copious
irrigation.

It is pleasant to escape from the sweltering thorough-
fares of the town and ramble about the verdant country
east of the city. The rippling of its many streams and
the grateful shade of its abundant trees go some way
towards making one forget the heat, which glows fiercely
in the afternoons.   As the sun declines, parties from the
Christian quarters of the city come out to the cooler spots
among the gardens.   The men loll about on the grass and
smoke.   The girls and younger women play a sort of
rudimentary cricket, on the lawn-like patches of grass.
The dress of the Christian ladies suits sports of the kind.
On the head is worn, indoors as well as out, a maroon-
coloured fez, richly embroidered with gold, on the crown.
A thin cotton vest covers—or, more correctly, exposes—
the upper part of the person, while the lower is clad in a
garment which may be described as the "divided skirt"
carried to its logical conclusion.   The feet are inserted in

shoes with sharply curving toes. Stockings are rarely
worn by the gentler sex, but when used, they are thickly
embroidered in bright colours. It has doubtless been a
never-failing pleasure to the inhabitants in all ages to
stroll about the shady paths, watching from the elevation
of the eastern bluffs, the busy operations of the ships
below, and must have been a characteristic of the place
in Paul's day as much as it is in our own.

Adalia has a population of about 30,000, of whom 20 000
are Turks and Mohammedans with many mosques, and
10,000 Greeks with seven churches. There are about 100
Armenians and 150 Jews in the town; besides one or two
Englishmen as occasional residents, and a few Frenchmen
($Γαυλοι$) and Italians. In the Christian quarter there
are many fine houses; some of them quite new. The
older houses are built of masonry below and wood above.
The upper storeys, where they look upon the street, seem
to consist almost entirely of dark-timbered oriels jutting
out over the narrow way. In the Turkish quarter these
are jealously latticed; the streets there resembling many
at Constantinople. Sets of families inhabit the larger
Christian dwellings; and a glance through the open door-
way discovers a group of many generations. The design
of the houses is evidently ancient. Inside the door is a
wide vestibule paved with pebbles in a neat pattern. This
joins a court, the wooden columns of which support the
cross-beams of the upper floor, and behind, there is a
garden. In the hot season the members of the family
spend much time in lounging on wide settles of unpainted
wood, covered with gaily hued Karamanian carpets or
rugs from Alifarandim.

This sketch of the modern Turkish town, cannot, of

course, be taken as reproducing the city, on one of the
wharves of which Paul and his companions landed, but the
features of the general locality are, necessarily, the same,
and life must always have been much what it is now, in
these unchanging regions.   Whether the voyage was
without incident, or the reverse, is not told, but it was
quite long enough to have let loose on the galley that
bore them, especially if they sailed in the autumn or
spring, one of the three "shipwrecks" which Paul tells us
befell him, though nothing is known of them; since that
of the great corn-ship, at Malta, happened much later than
when he speaks of these three.[1]

The rolling plain behind Attalia is only about twenty
miles broad at its widest; but across this flow three short
rivers, one of them—up which, perhaps, Paul sailed—
navigable, in his day, seven miles, to the city of Perga.
Marked for ages only by mounds of ruin, while Attalia
has still about thirty thousand inhabitants, Perga was
then a famous city, boasting a temple of Diana, "very
ancient and very holy," to whose gilded splendours there
was a yearly pilgrimage of vast numbers, like that of the
Jews to the Passover.

Paul and his "company" seem, however, to have only
passed through Perga; but their brief visit was marked
by an incident that seems to have long pained the sensitive
mind of the apostle.   From some cause, John Mark, Paul's
nephew, on whose company the loving-hearted man had
no doubt counted, if only as keeping a relative's friendly
face near him in his apparently frequent bad health,
declined to go farther.   It is often assumed that his
courage failed him, when he found Paul resolved to leave

[1] 2 Cor. xi. 25.

the peaceful lowlands, and cross the wild and savage mountains, to the interior tableland. But it is not necessary to imagine so invidious a ground for the young "deacon's" action. They may have reached the coast in the summer, and the heat in Asia Minor is then terrible. Mark had been ready to come to Pamphylia, but when something caused Paul to determine on penetrating the upper country, where everything would be quite new, and dangers of all kinds must be faced, he may have felt that the alteration of plan set him free; though it certainly was not very chivalrous, to hesitate in encountering risks which his uncle felt necessary to be run. Is it unreasonable to connect Paul's change of route with the peculiarities of the climate? Its relaxing and enervating effects are known to every one who has visited it. On the coast plain, fever is never absent; the moistness and rank fertility of the soil creating permanent malaria, which is especially dangerous to strangers. The huge masses of Taurus, rising from 5000 to 9000 feet high, close behind, shut out the cooling north wind, and doom the lowlands to an atmosphere which steams like an oven; and while so hot, is also heavy with moisture.[1] Worn by his long foot-journeys in Cyprus, and by the excitement of his work, Paul may very probably, have been struck down by the malarial fever, from which the only escape would be, to leave the lowlands and make for the lofty interior, at any cost of exertion or even of danger; for it was disastrous, if not even fatal, to attempt to brave it on the plains. We see, indeed, at this time, in Pamphylia, an annual migration like that by which all who can do so, hurry up, in summer, from the deep-lying shore of the Lake of

[1] See Ramsay's Church under the Empire, 63, &c.

Galilee, notorious in all ages for its malarial fevers, to the
hills round or beyond Safed; or from Damascus, which lies
low, on its river, to the mountains near at hand on the
north. It seems a corroboration of this idea, that Paul
tells the Galatians, whom he visited on this journey, that
his preaching the Gospel to them "for the first time," was
"because of an infirmity of the flesh," language explained
if illness had forced him to cross the mountain rampart of
Pamphylia, and thus enabled him to appear among them,
but which may allude, on the other hand, to a new indispo-
sition while passing through Galatia. For, indeed, he does
not appear to have intended to stay among the Galatians
when he reached them, but to have utilised a forced deten-
tion by illness, to preach, as he best could amidst such
weakness, and win them for his Master. He could never
forget how lovingly they received him and how sympathetically they listened to him, when he was so little able
to appear before them.[1] Nor does it appear improbable
that he alludes to this attack when he speaks to the
Corinthians of "a thorn (or stake) in the flesh having
been given him, a messenger of Satan to buffet him (as a
prize-fighter might), that he should not be exalted too
much by the exceeding greatness of the revelations granted
him."[2] Bishop Lightfoot's words in referring this allusion
to an incident in the first journey reads, in fact, as if he
had intended to describe just such a visitation of the local
fever, when he calls it, "A return of his old malady, 'the
thorn in the flesh,' the 'messenger of Satan sent to buffet
him;' some sharp and violent attack it would appear, which
humiliated him and prostrated his physical strength."[3]
Only in part recovered from its languor and depressing

[1] Gal. iv. 13.   [2] 2 Cor. xii. 7.   [3] Lightfoot's Galatians, c. iv. 13–15.

weakness, he would, indeed, be ill able, as he says, to preach with any vigour to the Galatians, during his forced rest, when at last he reached them.

Everything thus points to the "ambassadors of God, on behalf of Christ,"[1] having reached Perga about June or later. I have assumed that they landed at Attalia, but Perga itself was accessible, by the now silted-up mouth of the small river Cestrus, on which it lay about eight miles inland, and it is possible that the vessel which bore them from Paphos, was shallow enough in its draught, to go direct to the wharf at Perga itself. How they got north to Antioch is a more difficult question, for there was only a poor track, not a regularly made road, direct from Perga, north. This, we may assume they took, and now began that stern experience which Paul so touchingly recounts to the Corinthian Christians. "Are they " (his detractors at Corinth) "ministers of Christ? I more. In labours more abundantly, in prisons more abundantly, in stripes above measure, in deaths oft. Of the Jews" (at their synagogue courts) "five times received I forty stripes save one. Thrice was I scourged with rods " (by the Roman authorities—a punishment so dreadful that its victims often died under it), "once was I stoned, thrice have I suffered shipwreck " (a statement that shows how many sea journeys of the apostle are unknown to us, and how imperfect is the narrative of the Acts), "a night and a day have I been in the deep " (clinging to a drifting piece of wreck, amidst the waves, till I was rescued); "in journeyings often, in perils of rivers, in perils of robbers, in perils from my countrymen, in perils from the Gentiles, in perils in the city, in perils in the wilderness, in perils

[1] 2 Cor. v. 20.

in the sea, in perils among false brethren; in labour and travail, in watchings often, in hunger and thirst, in fastings often, in cold and nakedness."

For about ten miles, the path led up the valley of the Cestrus, climbing from height to height, even thus early; the river foaming down on their right, close by. Often there would be hardly any road at all, but a rough, unmade, camel or donkey track; for the want of roads, except from one Roman military station to another, was almost as great in Asia Minor in those days, as it is to-day, though the Roman roads there were, supplied lines of travel for commerce, in the interior; especially along the great route of military garrisons, from the coast to the Euphrates. But, in the mountains, everything was left as nature created it. If any bridges ever crossed the many torrents, they would often be traditions of the past. Boulders, landslides, huge gulfs washed out in the track, by winter floods sweeping down from the heights, a precipitous descent here, an almost perpendicular ascent there, between rocks, through forests, across swamps; a hundred fordings of ice-cold, arrow-swift torrents, in the course of the long climb of day after day, to the tableland beyond the mountains, would be the continually changing experience. The scenery, of course, was grand; peak rising beyond peak, in mighty vastness, on every side, many of them flashing in the upper heavens with the splendours of stainless snows; their sides, below, covered with unbroken forest, while the rich glories of laurel, myrtle, arbutus, and all the varied luxuriance of the south, clothed the nearer slopes and the wide valleys. Such a route passed through the very homes of the robber mountaineers, still unsubdued, even after campaigns of regular troops against them. Shelter by night would be often wanting, but if a caravanserai now and then offered harbourage, its charms might be like those of one in the mountains near Tarsus, at this time. The floor was of mud; the stone walls at least four feet thick, plastered with mud, and the grimy roof, blackened by almost ages of smoke. Horses or asses, if there were any, shared the one chamber with the traveller. Every one had to bring his own bed and bedding, but nothing could be allowed to touch the floor, under penalty of attracting countless abominations, alive and dead. Those who had no beds, needed to lie on the ground, as, very probably, the apostle did, and who can conceive their wretchedness? The door had neither key, lock, nor latch, but a bar of iron was found and put up against it, as a man had lately been robbed while he slept. The road between Jerusalem and Jericho, where the wayfarer was stripped by robbers, and beaten so that he was left half-dead, was, however, a more close parallel to the road over Taurus in the apostle's day, than any mere furtive spoiling.

Crossing the Cestrus ten miles from Perga, the two missionaries had a steep rough journey before them of over thirty miles to Adada. Then, followed another stretch of forty miles, to Neapolis, where they reached, at last, the military road from Antioch,—south and east,—to Lystra; made to enable the troops to march, at their will, from their military centre at Antioch, into the Pisidian and Isaurian mountains, to keep the wild hill tribes in some measure of subjection. Perhaps, however, they kept on their way without turning aside to Neapolis, and joined the good road a few miles nearer Antioch, which lay only about ten miles farther on; the whole distance

from Perga in a straight line being about ninety miles.
But such miles! The perils of rivers and of robbers they
involved, is shown by some still existing inscriptions,
which refer to the Pisidian highlands, not far from the
road traversed by Paul. One is a dedication and thank-
offering to Jupiter and all the gods, and to the river
Eurus, after being saved from drowning in it, doubtless
when it was swollen by a sudden flood, for there is no
local river dangerous to any one, except after heavy rains.
The next, is an epitaph over a son slain by robbers.
There are also references, very often, to the armed police,
of various names, who were needed in so unruly a district,
few soldiers being stationed in it, and in one inscription
mention is made of a "stationarius," part of whose duty
it was, to aid in the capture of escaped slaves, often the
most dangerous of brigands.[1]

Adada, strange to say, appears to have preserved in its
present name, Kara Baulo, that of Paul, Baulo being the
exact modern pronunciation. A church dedicated to him
as having been there, was, in all probability, the origin of
this pleasant reminiscence. Numerous cases, indeed, are
still found, in Asia Minor, of corruptions of the names
of Christian saints, once honoured as the local ghostly
patrons of the community, being retained as the Turkish
names of the towns of to-day.[2] Adada is, however, now,
only a lonely expanse of ruins, imposing from its extent,
with several small temples still comparatively perfect; the
stones not having been carried off for building, as, among
other instances, in the case of Cairo, which has absorbed
the ancient remains all round it, or Joppa, which has

[1] Ramsay, 23, 24.
[2] Ramsay's Hist. Geog. of Asia Minor, 227 *n.*

plundered Cæsarea, or Rome, which made a quarry for its palaces of the magnificent Colosseum.

Antioch of Pisidia, when regarded from its topographical relations to the old division of the country, or of Galatia, when the extension of that province under the Romans, for military and political ends absorbed Pisidia in its wide bounds,—was at the height of its prosperity when Paul came to it; the completion of the conquest and organisation of Southern Galatia, for the carrying out of which it was the centre, being then in vigorous progress. Standing on sloping ground, on the edge of some low hills, it rose high above the plain, and being surrounded with massive walls, formed a strong fortress. It lay on the southern base of the lofty range of Sultan Dagh, which towered four thousand feet above it, immediately behind, bending, thence, in a wide angle, like the letter V, to the southwest and south-east, till, in both directions, it merged into the huge chain of Taurus. Below Neapolis, Paul had skirted the north-west corner of the great Lake Karalis, dotted with islands over its thirty miles of extent, north and south. But the citizens of Antioch looked with haughty contempt on the regions to the south, between them and Pamphylia, as the "barbarian" mountain country of Pisidia; a rude tract denounced by them as destitute of Greek culture, and ignorant of Greek games or arts, and still largely savage. Antioch, on the contrary, was essentially Greek, and besides the culture this implied, could boast of having been made by Augustus, a colony, with Italian rights, and honoured by being allowed to append Cæsarea to its name; a dignity stamped thenceforth on all its coins. It had a great temple to the god Men, the Phrygian deity of the months, regarded by the

Romans as their Luna, the moon, but these hard masters had stripped this sanctuary of its former wealth in slaves and lands.[1] Ruins of the city wall still remain, and twenty arches of an aqueduct, built of large uncemented stones. Traces of a theatre, a temple of Bacchus, and of what may have been the temple of Men, are yet seen, while masses of grand marble cornices, and several fluted columns, lie here and there; one more sample of the de-population of this magnificent country by the barbarous Turk and his congeners.

As a military colony, Antioch would in Paul's time be more Roman in its speech and feelings, than usual, in these parts, but there were,—besides a large Greek-speak-ing population,—a good many native Pisidians, using their own language, and a settlement of Jews, who, though only numerous enough to have one synagogue, were very influential. They had even made many pro-selytes from their heathen fellow-citizens, including a number of formerly heathen ladies, "of honourable estate." Indeed, they did this everywhere; as we see in the cases of Berœa and Thessalonica, in the Acts; while Josephus tells us, that the Damascenes had, at a later time, to be cautious in their plot to assassinate the local Jews, "through fear of their women, all of whom, except a few, were attached to the Jewish worship."[2]

Paul and Barnabas would, no doubt, find ready shelter in some Hebrew family in the Jewish quarter on their arrival, meeting many of their people in their narrow streets, and before the Sabbath, becoming almost members of the local Jewry; for, as I have said, Jews were every-where Freemasons of a kind. The synagogues of all ages

---

[1] Pauly. Real Ency. i. 537.   [2] Jos., *Bell. Jud.* ii. 20, 2.

have been very much alike. An open chamber, with or
without a latticed gallery for women; its absence being
supplied by a latticed or curtained space at the back
corner; an enclosed desk of wood, in the middle, from
which the reader could recite the due portions of the Law
and the Prophets, in full sight of the congregation; the
sacred recess, or ark, behind this, at the side nearest
Jerusalem; a niche in the wall directing every one, in
prayer, exactly towards the Temple on the far-off holy
hill; mats on the floor for the worshippers,—" seats "
of any kind, in our sense, being unknown, in those days;
the first row, nearest the ark, set apart for the rabbis
who might be present, and for the " elders," who formed
the " rulers " of the congregation, alike in worship and in
secular affairs. The synagogue, it is to be remembered,
was the fountain of law for Jewish life as a whole,
under the liberal concessions of Rome; its rulers, as the
magistrates over their people, deciding their litigation and
inflicting punishment, by scourging and otherwise, on
offenders.

Hither, duly arrayed in their square tallith or scarf,
with its four tassels at the corners, after having bound
their phylacteries on their left arm and brow, the two
missionaries betook themselves, turbans on head, to be
retained during the service. Sitting down on mats at the
back,—after joining in the prayers, and listening to the
lessons read at the desk from the Law and the Prophets,—
which preceded what we should call the sermon,—the
" rulers," who had already learned all about Paul and his
companion, " sent to them " requesting that one of them
would address them. " Brethren," ran the message, " if
you have any word of exhortation to the people, say on."

Thus called upon, Paul forthwith rose from his mat, and stretching out his hand as was his manner,[1] began the first missionary address that has come down to us. It ran as follows, the text being a little amplified, to make it more clear to modern ideas.

" Men of Israel and ye Gentile proselytes of the gate, who worship Jehovah, though still uncircumcised, hearken. The God of our fathers chose them, as a people, from amidst all other races of men, and made Israel numerous and powerful while they lived in Egypt, and then led them forth from it with uplifted arm, ready to protect and defend them, and for forty years bore them about in the wilderness, and cared for them, as a nurse carries about and cares for a child. And when they had destroyed the chief nations of Canaan, he gave them the land thus conquered. Four hundred and fifty years passed, including the time of the Judges, and then came Samuel the prophet, who anointed Saul to be king over them. But, he being dead, God raised up David to be their king.— ' *a man,*' he declared, ' *after His own heart,*' [2] since, as king he would carry out the Divine will, withou departing from it to seek his personal desires, as Saul had done."

Paul had, in these sentences, prepared the minds of his hearers very skilfully for the introduction of Christ, the true Messiah, of whom David was regarded as the type and forerunner. The period assigned by him for the interval between the Exodus and Solomon differs from that given in the Book of Kings,[3] but it agrees with that followed by Josephus; so that it would seem as if both he and Paul had used some mode of reckoning common in that age, and then accepted as the correct one ; though it was

[1] Acts xxvi. 1.
[2] Ps. lxxxix. 20, comp. with 1 Sam. xiii. 14. From the LXX.: not verbatim, but seemingly from memory.
[3] 1 Kings vi. 1.

of no moment, for Paul's object, to decide the exact chronology. He now presses on to the ma'n purpose of his speech,—the announcement of the Messiah, as having appeared in Jesus, a son of David, whom John the Baptist had heralded.

"Of the descendants of this David, God, as He had promised, has brought to Israel a Messiah, Jesus, whom I now preach to you; John having before His appearing prepared the way for Him,[1] by proclaiming to all Israel the need of baptism as a pledge of change of heart. Nor is there any question of John himself being the Messiah; for when his course was well nigh closed, he emphatically repudiated the idea that he was more than His forerunner, and thought himself so much beneath Him in dignity, that the slave's task of loosening His sandals was too great an honour to crave.

"Yes, Jesus was indeed the Messiah. Nevertheless He has been put to death by the people of Jerusalem and their rulers, because they did not know His supreme worth, or the predictions of the Prophets, that the Messiah should suffer and die; though they might well have been wiser, since the Prophets, who speak of Him, are read in the synagogue every Sabbath day. But, in truth, there was no ground for His being brought before Pilate; and yet His death was demanded. Yes, and He was laid in the tomb, and all thought that they would hear no more of Him. But God raised Him from the dead; thus showing that He accepted Him as the Messiah, and designed that all men should honour Him. Those who had companied with Him, moreover, were witnesses of His having been seen again and again, after His resurrection, in many places, from Galilee to Jerusalem.

"And now, while these proclaim Him in Palestine, we do so here. We bring you the good tidings that God has com-pletely fulfilled the promise of a Messiah, given to our fathers, by raising up Jesus from the grave, which was a fulfilment of

[1] Mal. iii. 1, quoted in Matt. xi. 10—after the Hebrew.

the words in the Second Psalm, '*Thou art my Son, this day have I begotten thee.*'[1] And, farther, as proof that He raised Him from the dead, now no more to return to corruption, God has also said, '*I will give you the holy and sure blessings of David,*'[2] and elsewhere, '*Thou wilt not give thy Holy One to see corruption.*'[3] These words could not apply to David himself, for he did see corruption; but they do apply to Jesus, who, though He was buried, yet saw no corruption. But if Jesus be thus the Messiah, He must be the Hope of Israel; for God has been pleased to promise forgiveness of sins to all who believe on His name, and this I announce to you.

"Nor is this forgiveness only partial; it includes all your sins. Even where the Law provides no way of escape, the forgiveness provided in Jesus opens a new and perfect deliverance; for every man who believes in Him is forgiven all his sins, whatever they may have been. And as all men are guilty before God, and there is no other salvation than that now offered through Christ, beware of rejecting it, lest that befall you which has been spoken by the prophets: '*Behold, ye despisers, and wonder and perish; for I work a work in your days, a work which ye shall in no wise believe, if one declare it unto you.*'"[4]

This quotation is from the Greek version, which was that in use among the Jews outside Palestine, and is a striking illustration of the way in which the sacred writers apply to a spiritual aim, words which, in their original purpose, had a different meaning; for these lines were spoken by the prophet, in the first instance, of a threatened invasion of the Jewish territory by the Chaldeans.

This address over, the congregation was, as usual, dismissed by the chief ruler, as representing the priestly office,

[1] Ps. ii. 7 (LXX.).   [2] Isa. iv. 3 (LXX.).
[3] Ps. xvi. 10 (LXX.).   [4] Hab. i. 5 (LXX.).

pronouncing the beautiful benediction of the old wilderness time, used, ever since, in the Tabernacle, Temple, and Synagogue, to this day: "The Lord bless thee, and keep thee: The Lord make His face shine upon thee, and be gracious unto thee: The Lord lift up His countenance upon thee, and give thee peace."[1] Service thus ended, Paul and Barnabas found themselves the centre of eager interest, the congregation as it broke up, crowding round them, begging that Paul would speak again to them, next Sabbath, on his great subject; many, both of the Jews and of the proselytes, even following them along the narrow street, inquiring about the strange story, of the Messiah having actually come. Nothing could be more gratifying to the missionaries, who fondly responded to every question, and at last bade them adieu, with an earnest exhortation that they should "continue in the grace of God," which was manifestly working in them; this anxiety about the words they had heard, being in the belief of Paul, evidently from above.

In such a closely connected guild-like community as that of the Jew quarter, the interval before next Sabbath would spread the discussion of the new teaching through every household; Paul and Barnabas aiding it by visits to many of the Hebrew families, and also to some homes of the proselytes, besides attending the services in the synagogue on the Monday and Thursday. A great excitement among even the outside population was the result, so that when Saturday, the Jewish Sabbath, came, the synagogue was crowded; large numbers of thoughtful heathen coming, as well as every Jew who could attend; so that, apparently, the very street was full. But that

[1] Numb. vi. 24-26.

heathen should, in such crowds, show their interest in
the new preaching, about the Messiah having already
come, roused the jealousy of the rabidly narrow-minded
Jews, who claimed Him as coming only for them, the
race of Abraham, and in no sense for heathen, who, not
knowing the Law, were under God's curse and predestined to damnation.[1] Furious at the idea of any but
themselves being addressed about a matter which they
regarded as exclusively a Jewish doctrine, dear to their
hearts, as, in their opinion, the means designed, by Jehovah,
for overthrowing the heathen, in the great and terrible
day of the Lord, and for raising again the fallen tent of
David to universal monarchy, they turned bitterly against
Paul as he spoke, contradicting everything he said. They
even broke out into contemptuous railing and blasphemous
words against Jesus; such, no doubt, as had been heard at
Calvary; scoffs at a crucified Messiah, and ridicule at one
who could not save Himself, being set forth as the Saviour
of the world! Every one acquainted with Orientals can
picture the scene; the wild fury, the tempest of voices;
the fierce gesticulations; the storm of curses. The missionaries, now regarded as traitors to Israel, had no chance
of further hearing. Indeed, they might think it fortunate,
if they escaped with life and limb. But they bent to
the storm with a few dignified words, delivered, we may
imagine, with their loudest voice, to make them heard
above the uproar: " It was necessary that the word of
God should first be spoken to you, but, seeing that ye
thrust it from you, and judge yourselves unworthy of
eternal life; lo, we turn to the heathen. For so the Lord
commanded us, saying, ' I have set thee for a light of the

[1] John vii. 49.

Gentiles, that thou shouldest be for salvation unto the uttermost part of the earth.' " [1] No words could be more stinging
to a mob who looked on themselves as already having a
Divine grant of eternal life, as Jews, and as having fortified
that title by the exact fulfilment of the Law. That they
should see the heathen rejoicing at the declaration of
Paul, offering to them, on an equal footing with Israel,
that message of grace which they spurned, and promising
them, also, a place in the kingdom of the Messiah, kindled
a rage that knew no bounds. Nor did the provocation
die away, for the missionaries stayed in the city, preaching
to the heathen, who eagerly listened, till " the word of
the Lord was spread abroad throughout all the region,"
and quite a number of converts, hitherto heathen, had
been won. The Jews could not brook this, but stirred
up a persecution, through their proselytes from among
the wives and daughters of many leading men of Antioch,
who got their fathers or husbands to raise an agitation
against Paul and Barnabas, and obtained their being driven
out of the city.[2] That their expulsion should have been
brought about thus, was possible from the fact, that in the
cities of Asia Minor, women then enjoyed honours and
influence, remarkable in any age. Under the Roman
Empire, we find, in these, women who were magistrates,
presidents of games, and holding other public honours:
the custom influencing even the Jews, so much, that, in
Smyrna, we find a woman made the ruler of a synagogue.[3]
References to this stormy conflict, which was continued
against the Christian society gathered by Paul, even after

---

[1] Isa. xlix. 6, quoted with a slight variation, from the Sept. See Isa.
xlii. 6 ; Luke ii. 32.
[2] Acts xiii. 50.   [3] See authorities quoted in Ramsay, 68.

he had left, occur in his letter to the Galatians, written, among others, to the Church in Galatian Antioch, and to the congregations at Iconium, Derbe, Lystra and elsewhere. " Did ye suffer so many things in vain ? " he asks. " As Ishmael, Hagar's son, mocked Isaac, the son of the free woman, Sarah, so do the Jews still persecute us, the true sons of Abraham, the true children of the promise." And when some Galatian Christians had been won over to submit to circumcision, and were urging others to follow their example, and gain, like them, a favourable relation to the synagogue, he tells them it is " only that they may not be persecuted for the cross of Christ." [1]

How long the stay made at Antioch may have been, is not said, but it must have extended over some months, to have secured the wide spread of the new teaching, of which we read. Cheering success, therefore, had repaid Paul and Barnabas for climbing the terrible passes of the Taurus, with fierce class of robbers and cut-throats in their labyrinths of almost inaccessible gorges and glens ; where, as in a Roman Caucasus, they still dared the imperial troops. Now, however, driven out by the ever increasing hostility of the Jews, the missioners had to seek new fields. There were settlements of their own race, farther on, in this Southern Galatia, and though repelled at Antioch, the obligation under which they believed themselves laid, to preach Jesus, as the Messiah, first to Israel ; [2]—the command of Christ Himself being held conclusively to require this,[3]—determined them to make for any other towns where the presence of their brethren would enable them to do so. The region on

---

[1] Gal. iii. 4 ; iv. 28, 29 ; vi. 12.
[2] Rom. i. 16 ; Acts iii. 26 ; xiii. 26, 46 ; Rom. ii. 9.   [3] Luke xxiv. 47

the south-east of Antioch, to which they resolved to turn,
was much more provincial than that which they were
leaving; Greek civilisation having, of course, made greater
progress in and round the head city of Galatia, than in
its remoter parts. The population amidst which they
would now find themselves was a mixed one, of Phrygians,
Gauls, Greeks, Jews, and Roman traders and officials. The
first of these were the strictly native race; a people of
quiet and peaceful disposition, given to agriculture and
the growth of the vine; so little warlike, in fact, that
their Persian conquerors treated them with contempt, and
that their name gradually became almost equivalent to
"slave," like the word "negro" in America. They had
come, originally, from farther east, and brought with them
a religion closely resembling the Syrian nature-worship,
with its grossness, and wild, excited, and often cruel rites.
In the third century before Christ, however, a branch of
the Celtic or Gaulish tribes, who after flooding Europe,
had turned again to the east, and, passing by Italy,—which
they had invaded nearly a century before, sacking Rome
itself, and seizing permanently on the glorious valley of
the Po,—attempted to conquer Greece. Being driven
back at Delphi, however, they had, then, crossed the
Hellespont, and ravaged a large part of Asia Minor;
finally, after being checked by Attalus of Pergamos,
settling in the territory, formerly Phrygian, but, henceforth, known as Galatia, under kings and chiefs of their
own, about 230 years before Christ. Fifty years later,
the Roman arms had reached them, and from B.C. 189 had
acquired a more or less effective suzerainty over them,
till, at last, their country was incorporated into the Roman
dominions in B.C. 25.

The Druidism of these fierce invaders, with its terrible human sacrifices, and its slavish submission to the priest, gradually, in a climate so enervating, and so different from the colder regions from which they had come, yielded, with the advancing deterioration of the old warlike ferocity of the race, to the influence of the local rites, till they, virtually, in this respect, became Phrygians. "Given, beyond measure, to religion," as Cæsar characterises the Gauls as a race, the fine temples, the wild ritual, appealing in its robes, music, and display, to the love of the sensuous in the Celtic nature; the grossness of the worship, moreover, moving their lower passions, and, withal, the priesthood, as a profession, offering a source of spiritual power and easy maintenance, they accepted the Phrygian goddess Cybele as their deity.

Her worship was essentially the same as that of Adonis and Astarte of Syria, Cybele being the personification of the generative powers of Nature, and Attis, the representative of Adonis, the youthful spring Sun-god, slain by the winter, but returning with the opening of the following year. Yet the poetical myths about the gods were so many and so confusing, that Attis was regarded by the Romans as identical with the moon. In any case, like Adonis, he was killed, and his body, on a fixed day, was sought by the maidens of the temples, and brought to the sanctuary, on a bier, amidst loud wailing when affected to have been found. Then, on another day, as in the case of Adonis, he came to life, by the power of Cybele. Locally, he was a beautiful shepherd whom Cybele passionately loved, but it would be idle to recount all the versions of the legends, which vary widely. The worship, however, was intensely hateful, whatever the

interpretation of its symbolism. For a week together, at
the opening of spring, each day brought fresh abominations. Emasculated priests marched in procession, amid
horn-blowing, the clash of cymbals, and the roll of drums,
filling the air with wild laments for the dead god, or
equally wild uproar at his resurrection. Dressed in complete armour, they whirled in madly furious dances like
those of modern dervishes, exciting themselves and all
round to the utmost, till men ran to the altar and seizing
the specially formed knife laid on it for the purpose,
mutilated themselves in honour of the goddess, as in the
orgies at the Syrian worship of Astarte. The whole worship was in fact a saturnalia of obscenity, dashed in with
frantic self-sacrifice, under the excitement of maddening
uproar. Their character may, indeed, be realised from
"Corybantes"—the name for the priests of Cybele—being
applied to persons carried away by frenzy or furious, uncontrollable raving.

In the words of Paul, the Galatians were enslaved by
the elements of the world—the rigid observance of days,
and months, and seasons, and years, to which, indeed, he
tells them, they were returning, when they forsook the
simplicity of the Gospel he taught, for the bondage of
Judaism.[1] Nor is he without a keen reference to the
worship they had once followed, when, hinting at the
emasculation of the priests of Cybele, he tells them that
he "would that they who unsettled them about circumcision were to go a step farther, and openly identify
themselves with Cybele-worship by mutilating themselves
completely, so that they might no more trouble the converts."[2]

[1] Gal. iv. 10.   [2] Gal. v. 13.

Notwithstanding, however, the gradual assimilation of the Galatians, in the course of centuries, to the modes of life and thought of the Greeks and Phrygians around them, the tenacity of national character showed itself as strongly among them, in the days of Paul, as in earlier times. The traits that distinguish one race from another are, indeed, ineradicable, for even the language of a people may perish, while the varied peculiarities of temperament and endowments which marked their remotest forefathers, remain as prominent as ever. The Cornish, the Welsh, and the old French Gauls of Brittany have well-nigh disappeared, but the Cornishman, the Welshman, and the Frenchman are still true to their respective hereditary types. So with the Irish. Indebted to the English and Scotch for their passing from the rudeness of tribal life, to that of a common nationality; living for ages under British laws, and knowing, as a rule, no language but that of England, they are, in the south and west, where the Celt has made his special home, as distinct from their Teutonic fellow-countrymen, to-day, as they were in the days of Strongbow, more than seven hundred years ago. The same historical law was illustrated in the Galatians. Their language, indeed, survived long after the apostolic times, for Jerome tells us, as one who had been at both places, that the speech of the Gauls of Asia Minor was practically identical, at the close of the fourth century,[1] at Treves on the Moselle, and in Paul's Galatia.[2]

The characteristics of the Celt of all ages or countries, wherever he is found, marked the race in Asia Minor, as we see from many details of Paul's epistle. Tamed down from his ancient barbarism, though still far from

[1] Jerome died A.D. 420.   [2] Hieron. *in Epist. ad Gal. lib.* 2, *præf.*

subdued to all that was implied in Greek civilisation, the
Celts were the same in Galatia as Cæsar had painted them in
Gaul. The love of strong drink and wild excesses, natural
to them in any country, according to the universal verdict
of antiquity, but stimulated by their living in the land of
the Asiatic Bacchus, and amidst the orgies of Cybele worship, is recalled by Paul's warning them against "drunkenness and revellings."[1] That he twice speaks in his epistle,
of the magic arts which fascinated them, whether expressed in wizard mutterings, invocations, spells, unholy
rites, or idolatrous amulets, identifies them, in another
aspect, with this ever superstitious race.[2] Nor did the
apostle fail to detect the rank sensuality which was the
greatest danger to his converts. This inborn vice of the
effeminate Phrygians, had so thoroughly infected the Gaul,
that he had to be specially warned against it, as "warring"
against the "Spirit." Indeed, the Galatian provinces, in
after times, went over to Islam, and utterly abandoned
Christianity, because they could not bear the restraints
of monogamy. How various the forms in which impurity
enslaved the Galatian, as it does, still, the population of
Asia Minor, may be seen in the long list of sins against
which Paul calls on them to guard.[3] Their avarice, which
was almost proverbial in antiquity, is denounced in his
allusion to their meanness in almsgiving, as a "mockery
of God."[4] Their hot passionate blood, which not seldom
led to murder, in its outbursts of mad fury, and constantly
showed itself in fierce and rancorous disputes and quarrels,
creating feuds and factions, and leading to never-closing
strife; their self-assertion, in fact, which blazed into flame

[1] Gal. v. 21. [2] Gal. iii. 1; v. 20.
[3] Gal. v. 19-21. [4] Gal. vi. 6, 7.

with or without occasion, are condemned in the apostle's
protest against their "strife and vain glory," in airing
which they grew so excited, as literally, one might say,
to " bite and devour each other." [1] They were not without charming qualities. Impulsive as children, they could
not be too kind and loving while the humour lasted.
To Paul, in his weakness from recent illness, they were
romantically demonstrative. In spite of the meanness of
his presence, he found not only that they did not reject
or despise him, for his "infirmity of the flesh," though it
might well have tempted them to do so, but "received
him as an angel of God, even as Christ Jesus," and tended
him so fondly that it seemed as if, "had it been possible,
they would have plucked out their eyes, and given them
to him." [2] Yet this excess of kindly feeling very soon
passed away, proving only superficial and evanescent—
the mere quick springing, and as quick drying up, of
what had no deepness of earth; leading even Paul, so
accustomed to men, to "marvel that they were so soon
changing." [3] The transition from fervour to indifference
was, indeed, only a sign of their proverbial fickleness. No
reliance could be put on their professions. Bright, prompt,
emotional, imaginative, amiable exceedingly, when they
chose, they illustrated what Bishop Wordsworth tells us
was said of a modern Celt, Mr. Gladstone, by his father—
that " he had plenty of ability and only wanted stability."
There was no counting on the Galatian. He was as un-
stable as Reuben. There was no solidity of nature in
him. Here to-day, and yonder to-morrow, he was the
plaything of every passing interest or excitement, and
hence, too often, treacherous and false, except to his

[1] Gal. v. 15, 20, 21 ; vi. 3.   [2] Gal. iv. 13–15.   [3] Gal. i. 6.

immediate family. So marked, in fact, was his prone-
ness to betray confidence, that Cæsar learned to count on
it; feeling sure that, in case of any plot, he was sure to
find informers ready to sell their brethren, a feature still
characterising the Celtic Irish. Such were the people,
still largely true to the genius of their race, though widely
intermarried with the peaceful, industrious, superstitious,
half-civilised, Phrygians, amidst whom Paul and Barnabas
were now to find themselves.

CHAPTER XII

A.D. 49–51 ; AGE OF PAUL, c. 39–41

THE missioners had been some months at Antioch, if we
may judge from the wide spread of the new faith in the
district round it,[1] but, at last, the intrigues of the synagogue had broken out into such bitter hostility, that they
"shook off the dust of their feet" against their persecutors, to express their scorn for them; as if the very dust
of their town were a defilement; and began their journey
towards Iconium, now Konieh, a city about eighty miles
to the south-east, by the road they would have to travel.
Whether they went on foot or had the luxury of asses,
the ordinary mode of riding, we do not know; but we
can in some measure picture to ourselves the features of
their journey, from similar experiences. Paul is described,
in concurring traditions, as below average height, and bent
forward from ill-health; his hair sparse; his beard and
whiskers, which encircled his whole face, abundant, and all,
alike, grizzled,—making his pale complexion still paler;
his strongly prominent nose arched over by eyebrows
which joined above his blue-grey eyes. Whether this
sketch be right or not, he himself, as we have seen, felt
that his appearance gave opponents a handle for contrasting

[1] Acts xiii. 49.

his insignificant bodily presence with the authority and vigour of his letters.[1] Habitual attacks of one malady or another, moreover, still more enfeebling his weak frame, often compelled him, sorely against his will, to intermit his labours for a time.[2] He was, in fact, at this moment, struggling on under "an infirmity of the flesh." At Corinth he had to lament "weakness, and fear, and much trembling."[3] In his second letter also, to that city, he speaks of his "weakness"[4] and of "a thorn in the flesh," sent, as he believed, by Satan, in his ill-will against the kingdom of God.[5] Against the faintness of the body, thus "buffeted" by successive blows, as if of a pugilist, only his iron will enabled him to contend. But with all these difficulties in his way, his grand qualities of heart and head made him the greatest of all missionaries. His body might be weak, but it was supported by an energy and tenacity of purpose, which wrung from it exertions, wonderful even had he been a strong man, and bore him triumphantly through them; as we see in the recital of the perils of all kinds he had encountered and overcome.[6] Absolutely devoted to his Master, his courage was invincible. Noble in his liberality of mind, he could make himself at home with men of all opinions and classes, while his magnificent unselfishness, the sensitive independence which kept him from burdening any one, his tender and lively sense of honour, and above all his woman-like affectionateness, which bore all his converts in his heart, and cared for them with a father's guardianship and a mother's devotion, combined to form a character, which, through all the centuries, shines with a light

[1] 2 Cor. x. 10.   [2] Gal. iv. 13.   [3] 1 Cor. ii. 3.

[4] 2 Cor. xi. 30.   [5] 2 Cor. xii. 7, 9.   [6] 2 Cor. xi. 23.

peculiarly its own.[1] Heightening all this, was the glowing zeal of his absolute unwavering convictions, for he
only can persuade others who is, himself, felt to be sincere. But external advantages were not wanting in his
full equipment for his work. Brought up from childhood
among Greek-speaking races, he was intimately familiar
with their conversational language, and thus free to mix
with them. No care of a family hampered him, and
finally, if he chose to exercise it, he had a protection
from illegal violence, wherever he might wander, in his
possession of the Roman citizenship.

The route taken by Paul and Barnabas from Antioch
to Iconium brought them, after six hours' travel, south,
by the military road made under Augustus, as one of a
number connecting the Roman colonies of veterans, which
guarded the wild Pisidian frontier, to Neapolis, then growing into a prosperous town. The next stage was Misthia
near the north-east corner of the great lake Karalis. A
little beyond this, however, they turned east, from the
Roman road, and went on, by a very easy track, through
the town of Vasada, to Iconium, which was reckoned
twenty-seven hours from Antioch. This was the route
for all kinds of goods and produce, and resting-places for
travellers were provided on it. Camels, or, perhaps, wag-
gons, loaded with timber, wood, oil, gum, and resin, hides,

---

[1] One is reminded of Shakspere's words—

> " He was a man, take him for all in all,
> I shall not look upon his like again."
>
> —*Hamlet*, Act I. sc. ii.

or those of Byron—

> " Sighing that nature formed but one such man,
> And broke the die—in moulding Sheridan."
>
> —*Monody on Sheridan*, line 22.

sheep and goats' wool, with much else, and constant flocks
and herds, passing to and from the markets and pastures,
would enliven the way, which, fortunately for the travellers, was unusually free from hills.   Very curiously, a
legend has come down to us, connecting Paul with this
road.   A certain Onesiphorus, it is said, living at Iconium,
had heard that Paul was coming from Antioch, and kindly
set out to meet him, and invite him to accept hospitality.
Watching all who passed, he at last recognised him,
giving the description of his person which I have already
quoted.[1]

The region of Lycaonia, to which the missionaries had
now come, extended from the northern side of the great
mountain chain of Taurus, for the most part in vast
steppes, to the far-off mountains of Cappadocia, in the
north; a largely uninviting country, the soil being so
impregnated to a considerable depth with particles of
salt, over wide districts, that this is the chief mineral
product; the earth being dug up and the salt washed out,
for sale.   The landscapes are, hence, mainly pastoral,
large flocks of sheep,—many of them of the fat-tailed
variety which one sees in Greece and the East,—roaming
over it; the salt of the scanty herbage being liked by
them, as it is by the strings of camels which are continually moving along the tracks.   In Paul's day, moreover,
herds of wild asses, as we learn from Strabo, wandered in
these lonely parts.   The springs are largely salt, so that
there is a want of good drinking water, which a traveller
tells us he found sold in one place at a higher price than
milk.   The streams from the southern mountains, instead

---

[1] *Acts of Paul and Thekla,* which seems to date from the latter part of
the second century.

of uniting into rivers, form lakes, and, between Derbe
and Iconium, vast marshes. Lying out of the way, and
being a land comparatively waterless, Lycaonia had retained much of its primitive simplicity, and the people
still, largely, spoke their native language; remaining, in
many ways, so rude, that a refined Roman thought himself among savages when in their smaller towns. Yet
they were rather warlike in their tastes and famous as
archers.[1]

Iconium, thanks to a stream flowing by, is embedded
in great gardens and orchards, amidst which the water is
distributed. It lies at the west end of immense plains,
with mountains rising, six miles off, on the west, while
others swell up ten or twelve miles away, on the north
and south; the two snowy peaks of the Hassan Dagh
being visible a hundred miles off, nearly east. Few
memorials of the old Greek or Roman city are to be seen,
except inscriptions and carved stones, built into modern
walls. The city was the capital of the Seljukian Turks
in the twelfth century, and still boasts of walls between
two and three miles round, pierced by no fewer than
eighty gates; the walls built, mainly, of the stones of the
ancient city. The population is about thirty thousand.
Till shortly before Paul's visit Iconium was an inconsider-
able place, but it had been made a "colony" about that
date, by Claudius, and its name changed, in his honour,
to Claudia, or Claudiconium. This transformed it into
a military settlement of discharged soldiers, on whom,
thenceforward, devolved the duty of specially guarding
the region from the wild tribes of the southern mountains; a plan followed, in our own times, with the greatest

[1] Pauly, art. Lycaonia.

success, in Cape Colony, by Sir George Grey, who settled numbers of the disbanded Foreign Legion enlisted for the Crimean war, on farms, along the borders of Caffreland, on condition of their preventing the Caffre inroads, which had previously brought on a succession of colonial wars. Though in Lycaonia, Iconium prided itself on its originally Phrygian nationality, which is curiously illustrated in a quotation by Ramsay [1] from the record of a trial of a Christian at Rome, in A.D. 163. Asked by the judge who his parents were, he replied, "My earthly parents are dead; and I have come hither (as a slave), torn away from Iconium of Phrygia." When, therefore, in Acts,[2] we find Iconium omitted from the "cities of Lycaonia," the omission shows a local knowledge hardly possible in one who had not actually lived in the city, and learned the way of thinking in this matter, which was peculiar to it, and contrary to the usage of the country outside. The minute accuracy of the Acts, and its historical basis, as derived from immediate intimacy with the apostle whose story it tells, is thus vindicated, to the discomfiture of destructive critics. Iconium had been a part of Phrygia, under the Persian rule, but, at a later time, it was known to the world at large as the chief city of Lycaonia, long before the visit of Paul, though the citizens still spoke among themselves of their being Phrygian. Greek civilisation had been slow in making its way into the country districts of Asia Minor, but as the Roman arms spread, it advanced with them; every one who could, learning Greek, adopting Greek manners, and probably Greek dress; assuming Greek names, and giving them to their children and their gods. Between these "progressists," or

[1] Ramsay, 39.   [2] Acts xiv. 6.

"sycophants," and the sturdy upholders of the native **lan-**
guage and ways, the bitterness was extreme. But this
desire to adopt everything Greek must have been specially
characteristic of the capital, for it would be fancied to
mark the citizens as people of superior refinement compared with the stolid unprogressive rustic population. In
Paul's time, therefore, where the term "Iconians" would
have been out of place, they would no longer wish to be
addressed as Phrygians, which had come to be equivalent to "slaves," but, rather, as "Galatians," or "Greeks,"
which is the expression used by Paul, as a skilful orator,[1]
when he does not confine himself to the simple word
"gentlemen." It was through this diffusion of Greek
thought and language, that the new faith was able to
make such rapid progress, but it was long before the rural
districts became Christian.[2] Indeed it was the spread of
Christianity which, in the end, effaced the native languages
and made Greek universal in Asia Minor.

In Iconium, the missionaries, as at Antioch, found, at
first, a hearty welcome from their Jewish countrymen,
who were numerous in the town, as everywhere else, but
here also opposition soon rose, when the more bigoted
in the synagogue saw that the new doctrine won over
many of their brethren, and also of the devout Greeks
associated with them in worship, though going only so far
as to recognise Jehovah and discard idolatry. Paul had
no intention of founding heathen churches when he set
out, though he was more than willing to receive Gentiles
through the gate of the synagogue; but the violence of the
Jewish leaders at Antioch, had forced him to take the
momentous innovation of establishing congregations **of**

---

[1] Gal. iii. 28.   [2] Ramsay, 42–45.

heathen converts, without further reference to Judaism.
Similar causes led to the same course at Iconium. He
and Barnabas had either to preach to the "Gentiles" or
abandon their mission, and hence they turned to those
willing to hear them, and continued to work "a long
time" among them. The zealots for Judaism, however,
determined not to be beaten, persistently agitated the city
against them, till it was at last divided into two hostile
camps, one holding with the Jews; the other with the
Apostles. Meanwhile, "signs and wonders" wrought by
the missionaries, and, still more, their announcement of the
near end of the existing state of things, and the coming of
Jesus from heaven, to judge mankind, living and dead, disturbed and alarmed the heathen citizens: while the cry
of "The Law in danger" roused the Jews, and the calum-
nies which described the new teachers as disturbers of
the peace, moved the officials,—exciting a general determination to drive them away. There can be no doubt,
indeed, from his language in the Epistles, that the synagogue addresses of Paul must have frequently seemed
dangerously bold, to fanatical Jews. For example, in the
Romans, he says "The Law works wrath;" it entered, that
"the offence might abound;" and "it wrought in himself
all manner of concupiscence," while, in the Galatians, he
affirms that "it could not give life."[1] In the Second
Epistle to the Corinthians, he speaks of Moses as having
intentionally concealed from Israel the temporary character of the Law.[2] In Galatians, moreover, he compares
the Law to Sinai, barren and blasted, and also to the
slave Hagar, whose children were slaves.[3] Such criti-

[1] Rom. iv. 15; v. 20; vii. 8; Gal. iii. 21.   [2] 2 Cor. iv. 13.
[3] Gal. iv. 24, 25.

cisms of the holy words,—so audacious, so unfavourable,
so nearly sarcastic,—addressed to men who honoured
every jot and tittle of them as Divine, not on earth only,
and even believed that in the seventh heavens, schools of
celestial rabbis and all the angels pored over them with
wondering awe;—words in every letter of which God was
believed to dwell, making the recess in which they were
kept in each synagogue, a very Holy of Holies—demanded,
in the opinion of the fanatical Jew, the stoning of Paul,
as a blasphemer, as justly, as the words of St. Stephen,
announcing the approaching end of the Temple worship,
had seemed to Paul himself, to call for the stoning of
the first martyr. The rulers and congregation of the
synagogue at Iconium were furious against the fancied
blasphemies of the new-comer, and were eager for his
death, as their due punishment. The city was a self-
governing one, and it was only necessary to win over
the archons, or town rulers, to their side, to secure their
desire, and this they at last effected; the heathen citizens, and the party representing traditional Judaism, with
the authorities of both, uniting in a riotous attack on the
Apostles, to ill-treat them, or even to carry out the Jewish
Law against them, by stoning them to death. But the intended victims were fortunate enough to hear of their
danger, and fled, not from Roman officials—for Iconium
was not the residence of the Roman governor, but from
the municipal authorities, to Lystra, which, like Iconium,
was self-governing, and, thus, outside the local authority
of any other place, so that, there, they would, for the time
at least, be safe.

We are indebted to Professor Ramsay[1] for the first

[1] Ramsay, 47.

exact description of the site of Lystra, which I venture to give from his admirable book. "This 'city of refuge' for the Apostles, lay six hours south-south-west from Iconium, the road to it leading, for at least a mile, through fine gardens, and then across the plain, which ascends imperceptibly for the next fourteen miles, to a range of low hills, which, after attaining a height of about 500 feet, sinks slowly away to the east, till the plain once more begins, ten miles farther on. On the farther side of the hills, you reach a mile-broad valley, down the middle of which flows a stream, and on the southern side of this, about a mile from the hills, stands a village—Khatyn Serai, 'The Lady's mansion,' so called, no doubt, from its having been the country-seat of some Seljukian sultana; this spot lying over 400 feet higher than her lord's capital, Iconium." [1]

On a hill in the centre of the valley, a mile north of the modern village, a large inscribed pedestal was found by Professor Sterret, in 1885, evidently in its original position, with an inscription recording the honour paid by the "colony," Lystra, to its founder, Augustus. Since then, moreover, some coins have been found, showing that Lystra was really a colony, so that no doubt exists any longer, either of the true site of the town, or of its being one of the network of military settlements, established to secure the peace of these previously unsettled parts. The hill on which Lystra stood rises from about 100 to 150 feet above the plain, with steep sides, little remaining to mark a town having been on it, though a ruined church of no great antiquity stands below the hill, with a fountain once called "holy," gushing out beside it, from under

---

[1] Iconium is 3350 feet above the sea; K. Serai, 3777 (Ramsay, 48).

a low arch; the Turkish corruption of the Greek word for
"holy" still marking it as once sacred, in the opinion of
the Christians of the town. The standing of the city in
Paul's day, as a place of note since it had become a colony,
is curiously shown by an inscription found at Galatian
Antioch, on a pedestal which once supported a statue of
Concord:—

"To the very brilliant colony of Antioch, her sister,
the very brilliant colony of Lystra, did honour, by presenting the statue of Concord." [1]

The missionaries must have been greatly moved by the
repetition in Iconium of the persecution they had encountered at Antioch. But they had done good work, the
results of which were abiding. Some of the converts,
indeed, unable to endure the persistent enmity of the
synagogue, sought peace by accepting Judaism, though
they were Gentiles,[2] but the Church, as a whole, remained
so faithful, in spite of what they had to suffer, that it is
more frequently mentioned than any other Galatian congregation,[3] and that men still remembered, generations
after, how Paul had been there; as is shown in the Acts
of Paul and Thekla.[4] If, however, the apostle hoped to
escape trouble at Lystra, he was doomed to a speedy dis-
appointment. There was no synagogue in the town, so
that he had to address the heathen population wherever
he could, as a modern missionary takes advantage of any
opportunity of gathering a group round him; commonly
in the open air. He could not speak to such Gentile
audiences as he would have done to Jews, but we may
conjecture, from similar cases in his journeys, that he

[1] Ramsay, 50.   [2] Gal. vi. 1
[3] Acts xiii. 51 ; xiv. 1, 19, 21 ; xvi. 2 ; 2 Tim. iii. 11.   [4] See p. 272

would expose the folly of idols, and disclose the great doctrine of the unity of God, His constant providence, and our duty to worship Him alone. He would, moreover, be sure to introduce the news of the salvation offered through Jesus Christ, His resurrection, and the certainty of His speedy return in glory, to judge the world; for the coming of the Saviour Judge, no one knew how soon, was the central burden of apostolic theology.

During one of these public preachings, a man lame from his birth was so deeply affected, that Paul's attention was drawn to him; the sight of a hearer touched by the truth instantly making him the object of special interest. His earnestness was evident, and to him who has spiritual sympathy, it is always possible to give help towards an increase of it. Paul saw that to remove his deformity would win his heart for ever to Christ, through whom, alone, he would thus be made whole, and that the healing of his body, would also kindle Divine life in his soul. Fastening his eyes on him, therefore, to secure his attention, he called out loudly to the poor heathen, "Stand upright, on thy feet." The crowd of ignorant Lycaonians round, provincials who knew nothing of Western culture, but spoke, still, the rude dialect of their race, as the peasant of the west of Ireland may still speak Irish, looked on with wonder. Paul had used Greek, which, though not the tongue of the common people, was understood, as English is in a Welsh-speaking district, and had been quite intelligible to the miserable object of charity before them. The next moment, the hitherto helpless man was on his feet, leaping for joy, with Oriental excitabi'lity, and walking hither and thither, in the delight of his new power. "The gods have come down to us in

the likeness of men!" shouted the crowd, in Lycaonian.
A poetical tradition ran, in that very region, that Baucis
and Philemon, a humble country pair, had entertained
Jupiter and Mercury, in the likeness of men, in their
lowly home, when these gods were on a visit to earth.
Ovid had sung the legend in exquisite verse, two generations before,[1] for the lovely story had spread far and wide.
Was it possible that the two immortals had come back
again ? If so, they must not, as on their first visit, find
a want of due homage, nor must it be left to some humble
soul, full of piety, to secure the favour of heaven.   Barnabas, the finer man in appearance, must be the Father
of the gods and of man, and Paul, the chief speaker, could
be no other than the eloquent Mercury, the interpreter of
the celestials. The city was in a tumult. At the temple
of Jupiter, perhaps beside the inscribed pedestal still rising
on the town hill, the priests soon heard of the wonder. A
sacrifice must be offered to the Divine visitors ! Oxen were
at hand, duly examined for fitness, and garlands, to twine
round their horns, hung up in the temple. Forthwith,
therefore, the proposed victims, with the garlands, were
brought out by the inferior priests, to the altar, which
stood just within the gates of the temple grounds, or, perhaps, of the town ; for an inscription still preserved at
Claudiopolis in Isauria speaks of a temple of " Jupiter
before the town "—and in a few minutes more, the
sacrifice would have been bleeding on it.

Word had, however, been brought to the Apostles,
probably by some townsman already won to Christ, of
what was going on. Idolatry was intensely abhorrent to
any Jew, but that they, of all men, should be the object

[1] Ovid, *Metamorph.* viii. 621-726. Ovid was born, B.C. 43, died A.D. 18.

of it, was beyond measure hateful. "Rending their clothes" for indignant grief; that is, tearing their outer garment at the breast, perhaps to the waist, in Oriental fashion, they rushed out to the town gate, and pressing through the crowd outside it, reached the clear space in which stood the priest and his assistants, with the garland-crowned ox, about to be slaughtered in their honour. Everything, we may fancy, was hushed, at the presence of the supposed divinities, and the next instant the voice of Paul, the fancied orator of the gods, was heard.

"Sirs," cried he, in his loudest voice—"why do ye these things? We are only men, of the same nature and mould as yourselves, and have come here, as men, to bring you the good news we preach, that they may move you to turn from the worship of the empty unreal divinities ye suppose us to be,— divinities which are only the fancies of the brain,—to worship the true and only God—the one God alone existing; that one God, who, I repeat, is the only God there really is,—instead of these statues, and the shadows they represent, which are no more than names: the God who has shown Himself the one Living God, by His having made the heavens, and the earth, and the sea, and all that is in them. He made them all,—not the idol gods of your fancies, which do not even exist. In past ages He has left the nations to walk in their own ways, not guiding them by any special revelation ; though, indeed, He did not leave Himself without self-disclosures and proofs of His goodness and power, since He has always been gracious to them ; as, for example, He has been to you ; giving you, from heaven, the rains needed for your thirsty pastures, and for fruitful seasons in your fields and vineyards, and thus filling your hearts with gladness, for the food and joys which He only, though you did not know it, had sent you !"

It is hard to break at once the spell of hereditary ideas

especially in religion, and it takes time to cool down from such an excitement as that which surged round the Apostles, so that it was only with the greatest difficulty, after all his dissuasions, that they were able to prevent the multitude from offering sacrifice to them.

But nothing is so fickle as the caprice of the mob—"the gusty plebs."[1] The sport of every excitement, it passes from one extreme to the other as each fresh impulse moves it; or, to use a figure,—it is a pipe on which craft may play what stop it pleases. Theological hatred is the fiercest of human passions, and blazed with furnace fury, amidst the tolerance of antiquity, in the breast of every Jew. A frozen conservatism denounced anything like a new thought in the domain of the rabbi, as a sin against the Church, to be visited with death. Centuries before Christianity, it had persecuted to the death every one who dared to think in advance of it, either in morals or religion. "They killed the prophets and stoned those sent to them from God," said Christ Himself,[2] and the author of the Epistle to the Hebrews repeats the ghastly indictment, with horrible details of their genius for cruelty towards every one, in succession, who was an honour to their race.[3] Paul had roused this demoniacal fanaticism at Antioch and Iconium, by his daring Broad Churchism in the interpretation of the Law, by his glances of sympathy towards the heathen, but especially by finally breaking away altogether from the synagogue, and actually broaching the revolutionary idea that God cared for the Gentiles as much as for the Jews, and that they might be saved, through faith in Jesus of Nazareth, without becoming

---

[1] "Ventosæ plebis suffragia," Hor. *Ep.* i. 19, 37.
[2] Matt. xxiii. 37.   [3] Heb. xi. 35–38.

Jews at all. Nothing would do but the extirpation of such deadly heresy, which threatened to turn the Jewish world, at least, upside down, and to extend to the abhorred uncircumcised, citizenship in the kingdom of God, hitherto the patrimony of the sons of Jacob. We know how it maddened their Palestine brethren to hear Jesus say that "many would come from the Gentile lands of the east and west, and sit down with Abraham, and Isaac, and Jacob, in the kingdom of heaven, but the sons of the kingdom, the Jews, to whom exclusively, as the sons of Abraham, the proud title to it had seemed a legal birthright and inheritance, would be cast forth into the outer darkness;"[1] an expressive figure taken from the contrast between the light and festivity in some royal hall and the pitchy darkness of the utterly unlighted streets outside. The author of Second Esdras, which dates from before the fall of Jerusalem, embodied the unutterable spiritual pride of all Jews of the century, when he reminded God that He had called Israel "His people, His first-born, His only-begotten, His fervent lover, among whom, alone, of all nations, His name was to be found,—and His chosen race." The audience of Paul, in the synagogues of Antioch and Iconium, firmly believed all this, and no less firmly his cry, "O Lord, Thou madest the world for our sakes and as to the other nations, Thou hast said that they are nothing, but are like spittle; and hast compared them to a drop that falleth from a cask." The wine in the cask was Israel, the rest of mankind only the filthy oozings from it! And had not the prophets declared that the Jew would reign from sea to sea, and from the river to the ends of the earth? and that God would dwell in Zion

[1] Matt. viii. 12 ; Luke xiii. 28, 29 ; Matt. xxi. 43–45.

for ever, and that all nations would come to the Temple,
from which the Law, and the word, of Jehovah, should go
forth; and were not all the nations to serve the Jewish
Messiah-King, and all kings fall down before Him?[1]   To
hunt to the death such traitorous apostates as the preachers
of the crucified Nazarene Messiah, with their flouting of
the Law, and their insults to the hope of Israel, was
demanded, at once by loyalty to God and by patriotism.
Furious zealots had set off, therefore, from Antioch to
Iconium, and with infinite Oriental duplicity, had worked
on numbers of the heathen population there, till, as we
have seen, they raised a wild tumult, intending to stone
the Apostles as blasphemers; a plot which failed, only by
timely warning having enabled their proposed victims to
escape to Lystra.   But, hither, also, the Antioch Jews,
recruited by volunteers from Iconium, speedily followed,
and set to work to stir up the rabble against the men they
had so recently sought to worship.   Probably they painted
the new teaching as contrary to Roman law, and thus
certain to rouse the imperial authorities against them,
for allowing it.   The priests and Pharisees at Jerusalem
had inflamed excitement against Christ, by predicting
national ruin at the hands of their heathen masters, if
they let Him escape death, and here, at Lystra, their representatives would, we may suppose, alarm the citizens
by clamouring that if the missionaries were tolerated, the
Romans would come and take away their privileges—as
a colony, for example—and possibly even move the whole
community elsewhere, and give Lystra to others![2]   A
mob never thinks.   Noisy orators and plotters can always

---

[1] Isa. ii. 2–4; xxvii. 13; Micah iv. 1–3; Ps. lxxii. 8–11; 2 Esdras iii,
34; vi. 56, 57.   [2] John xi. 48.

play on their fears or wishes. This time, the Jew zealots whose estimate of their heathen neighbours we know, from their spokesman in Esdras, were only too successful. A riot was created, and before the Apostles were aware of their danger, Paul, the special object of Jewish hatred, as the preacher of the new heresy, and the leader of the mission, was knocked down in the public street by a shower of stones hurled at him by the now infuriated crowd, under the leading of the Jews. At Jerusalem, Stephen had been dragged outside the town-gate before such violence was shown him;—to keep the Holy City from defilement by his martyrdom within it,—but a heathen town was incapable of more pollution than in any case clung to it. And now it seemed as if Judaism would sate its fury on the offender. Stone followed stone, from strong arms, till the apostle lay unconscious, and so battered and bleeding, that his enemies, fancying him dead, pulled him outside the town gate, and left him, contemptuously, amidst the dust-heaps and rubbish lying around. As yet they had not attacked his converts, and it speaks volumes for both him and them that they did not leave him even in this extremity, but gathered to where he lay, as soon as the mob dispersed, with the intention no doubt of securing the body that most sacred rite in all antiquity, honourable burial. Paul had only been stunned, however, and gradually regained consciousness while they still were by, managing, after a time, even to rise, and with their help, to make his way back to his temporary home The next day, moreover, we are told, he was able to set out with Barnabas for the town of Derbe, between thirty and forty miles off, on the south-west, among the foot-hills of Taurus. But the memory of this scene was

ineffaceable.   It was one of the many " perils from his own
countrymen and from the heathen; " one of his being " in
deaths oft," which sank deepest into his mind.   " Once,"
says he, " I was stoned."   Henceforth, in the remembrance of his sufferings, he regarded himself as " always
bearing about in the body the putting to death of Jesus,"
and could tell the Galatians, in whose province he had
thus suffered, " Let no man trouble me, for I bear in my
body the marks of the Lord Jesus; " the marks of the
stones showered on him at Lystra, and of the scourgings
with great whips or thick rods, lacerating the flesh to the
bone, which he had endured no fewer than eight times.[1]

A long bare slope, with bushes and loose stones scattered over it, and a few ruined buildings of comparatively modern date, lead up to a broad low mound which
crowns it, and under this, in all probability, lie the remains
of the Derbe of Paul.   It was the frontier city of the
Roman province, towards the south-east, and, as such,
was honoured by a connection with the name of Claudius,
as Claudio-Derbe.   The Apostles had started from the
Syrian Antioch when navigation opened, about April, and,
after perhaps two months' labour in Cyprus, had landed
in Asia Minor somewhere about June.   Attacked, apparently, by some illness, probably malarial fever, Paul had
been forced to make for the uplands of the interior, to
shake it off, and may have reached Antioch, after a hard
climb of eight days at the least, about the beginning of
August.   How long he stayed in the Pisidian capital is
not stated, but as we are not told that he was there " a long
time," as is said of his stay in Iconium, we may suppose
he was in it somewhere about six months.   The journey

[1] 2 Cor. xi. 23–28 ; iv. 10 ; Gal. vi. 17.

to Iconium, which would take three or four days, may thus have been made about November, the whole of the subsequent winter being spent there. The flight to Lystra may have marked the spring or summer of A.D. 50, and, there, in the hills of Isauria, the Apostles would have abundant work among such as understood Greek, though they would perhaps be few in number, for it was a rough uncultivated district. Professor Ramsay has an ingenious conjecture that the opposition they too soon met, may have risen from the coming of Jew middlemen, from Antioch and Iconium, to buy up the ripening harvest, as traders still do in many parts of the East, but I should rather fancy that the deadly bitterness at the new teaching had, of itself, urged some fanatics to hunt the missionaries from place to place. Yet it may be too much to think of Jews acting from bigotry alone, without some dream of profit as well, so that it was probably from travelling dealers of one kind or other that troubles rose. The journey to Derbe, and the work in and round it, would bring the winter months, when the great mountain chain of Taurus would be made impassable by snowdrifts. The Apostles could not go farther east without entering territory not Roman. Their only possible course was to retrace their steps, if they wished to return home, which now seemed desirable. Besides, it was of the utmost moment, that they should revisit the scenes of their past labours and successes, and though they had been driven out from Antioch and Lystra, as well as, virtually, from Iconium, they had not been permanently banished; the local magistrates not having power to do so. They could, therefore, return, now that a little time had elapsed since the tumults raised against them, especially if, as seems to have been the case, the term of office of the magistrates who had actively or by connivance proceeded against them, had expired.

"Many disciples" had joined the new faith in Derbe, and thus another church of former heathen had been formed. But, now, it was desirable to consolidate the results of the mission, and this the Apostles resolved to do, however perilous it might seem, by retracing their steps over the ground by which they had advanced. They had little indeed to fear at Lystra, for the authorities there had compromised themselves with the Roman law, by inflicting or sanctioning, an illegal punishment on Paul, a Roman citizen. Nor was it remarkable that a Jew should have this honour, for already, in this century, a great number of Hebrews in Asia Minor possessed it,[1] and there were many thousand Roman citizens of various nationalities in the province.[2] There was, therefore, no excuse for the illegality of the magistrates of Lystra. The election of new magistrates at Iconium and Antioch, further protected them in these cities, and thus they would be able to pass the winter months in their former scenes of labour, without interference from the authorities, though it is not probable that they attempted to preach or otherwise provoke public notice. The neighbourhood of Derbe had seen an expedition against some of the hill tribes round, so recently as the year 37—fifteen years before Paul's visit[3] —so that he had been in wild regions, and he must have been glad to find himself, once more, among the converts of large settled communities.

---

[1] Jos. *Ant.* xiv. 10, 13, 14, 16, 17, 19.   [2] Schürer ii. 538.
[3] Tac. *Ant.* vi. 41.

It was of vital importance to organise the congregations that had been gathered, so that they might maintain
their corporate life, and develop on healthy lines, under
recognised institutions, and in the use of rules of worship
and Church government sanctioned by the Apostles. The
Greek Bible was used in the synagogues,[1] and the Epistle
to the Galatians shows that the Old Testament, of course
in Greek, was familiar to the converts, and formed the
central foundation of their Christian edification. But
it is hardly probable that they would be without some
written "Gospel," as well, for the wondrous story of
the Messiah-King, Jesus, would be too precious not to
have been engrossed in a permanent form, when so
easily learned from the lips of the Apostles. The only
ecclesiastical organisation familiar to Paul and Barnabas
was the synagogue, but it was dear to their heart from
hereditary associations, and as having been frequented
by their Master. It was therefore continued under the
new faith, making the transition easy for their Jewish
brethren, from the usages of Judaism, and thus we find
its constitution that of the first apostolic churches.
Elders, or, to use the equivalent Greek word, presbyters,
forming the exact counterpart of the "rulers of the
synagogue," were chosen by the votes of the whole congregation, given apparently by their holding up the hand,[2]
and when thus elected were set formally apart to their
office by the Apostles. Each congregation had a number
of these, as we see in the case of that of Ephesus,[3] and
that of Philippi,[4] where they are called *episcopoi* or "overseers;" another equivalent for "rulers" or "presbyters,'

[1] Schürer ii. 544.
[2] χαιροτονήσαντες.
[3] Acts xx. 17.
[4] Phil. i. 1.

that is, "elders;" presbyter being a Greek translation
of the Hebrew title, and *episcopoi*, the usual Greek term
for those intrusted with any oversight or superintend-
ence, of large or small positions.[1] "The *episcopi* and
the *presbyteri*," says St. Jerome, "were the same among
the early Christians; the one word referring to rank,
the other, to age."[2] In the Church at Philippi we
find deacons, and may suppose that there were similar
helpers, or "ministers" in the Galatian congregations,
though they are not mentioned. Such assistants were
the counterparts of similar inferior functionaries in the
synagogue; the chazans, or "messengers,"—discharging
all subordinate duties for the rulers and congregation.[3]
They, also, we may assume, were chosen by vote; even
the "brother" sent by the Corinthian church, to travel
with Paul, in connection with the contribution to the
poor of Jerusalem, being "appointed"—that is, in the
Greek, "chosen by vote"—by the congregation, to do
so.[4] Yet it would be a great mistake to imagine, that
because the election of its officers rested with the
congregations, their nomination for election, was unre-
strictedly left to them. Such an arrangement would,
at any time, invite rivalries, disputes, and divisions,
while, in such assemblies as the earliest "churches,"
there would, at least in the case of those gathered from
the "Gentiles," be very little security for the right persons being selected. Where the voters were of such a
class that Paul could describe them, to themselves, as
"foolish," "weak," "base," "despised," "beneath notice,"
or, in other words, the very humblest,—the class,
in fact, known among ourselves, of late, as the "sub-

---

[1] פֹּל = πρεσβυτερος = elder.   [2] *Hier. Ep.* 82 *ad Oceanum.*
[3] Buxtorff, Lex. 1177.   [4] 2 Cor. viii. 19.

merged tenth" of the community, and that not only in circumstances or position, but even in morals, and necessarily in corresponding ignorance,—it would have been contrary to every dictate of prudence to leave them without guidance. The fitting persons for office would, therefore, we may assume, be indicated by the Apostles, or by the rulers whom they had accepted and set apart. That a missionary among the Indians of America, or the Matabele of Africa, should leave the organisation of his converts into an orderly "church," to the unassisted nomination and votes of the natives, would be hardly more conceivable than that Apostles should "ordain" all arrangements in the first churches, and take steps that "all things should be done decently and in order," and yet hand over uncontrolled and absolute authority to the aggregate of communities which they describe in such unflattering terms.[1] Still, when we remember that the Ten Thousand of Xenophon elected even their own officers, and that the Greeks were so madly democratic that they ruined their country by ultra-individualism, it would be rash to conjecture the details of the system laid down by even Apostles, though there must have been some restrictions.

The election of elders, however, was only an incident in the stay of the missionaries in each city. Unless the converts remained faithful, all else would be worthless. Supreme attention was, therefore, given to the confirming them in their faith in Christ, by earnest exhortation, setting forth, doubtless, the mighty inducements there were to fidelity, even though, as was certain, Christians must pass through the fires of many tribulations. They might well bear up under these, however, since they secured,

[1] 1 Cor. i. 27, 28; iv. 17–21; vii. 17; xi. 34; xiv. 40; 2 Cor. ii. 28; Tit. i. 5.

hereafter, an entrance into the glorious kingdom of the Messiah, to be set up at the coming of the Lord, which was so near; "the Judge," in the words of St. James, "standing," already, "before the doors!"[1] When, at last, the time of leaving had arrived, there was, we are told, a final service, for which all prepared by fasting, a custom immemorial in the East, and possible in such warm climates while injurious in others, and as beautiful when voluntary and sincere as it is worthless when formally prescribed and mechanical. Thus sacredly drawn apart from the world, for the time, they were "commended" by the Apostles, in prayer, "to the Lord on whom they had believed,"[2] and thus the mission closed.

The passes of the mountains would not be open before the middle of May, but about that time Paul and Barnabas bade their last farewells to the brethren at the Pisidian Antioch, and made their way down to Perga, where they seem to have stayed some weeks, preaching "the Word," as they had been unable to do so when there before. Then, perhaps in July, they went to Attalia, and sailed out of its small harbour, round which the streets now rise, one above the other, like the seats of a theatre, with a fringe of square towers surmounting the flat top of the hills,—and then coasted the land eastward, often in full view of the vast mountains, beyond which they had gathered to Christ, the first fruits of the Gentiles of Asia Minor, won with so much suffering, and yet worth it all, as the earnest of the conversion of the great heathen world to the faith of the Cross. They were making for Antioch of Syria, from which they had been sent out, and there they may have arrived about July 51, after a journey lasting about two years and a half.

<hr>

[1] Jas. v. 9.   [2] Acts xiv. 23.

CHAPTER XIII

JUDÆA AFTER THE DEATH OF AGRIPPA I.—THE EPISTLE OF JAMES

A.D. 44–52 ; PAUL'S AGE, c. 34–42

INDICATIONS of a design on the part of Agrippa to push steadily forwards in a scheme of local independence of Rome had naturally made the imperial advisers—now glorified " freedmen," the first remove above slaves—hesitate in raising his son to his father's throne. The younger Agrippa was, therefore, set aside, on the pretext of his being only seventeen years old, though Claudius had sworn to his father that he should have the succession.[1] He was kept, moreover, still in Rome, the Emperor showing his friendly feeling to him, however, by the doubtful favour of consigning him, under his personal oversight, to the study of Græco-Roman culture, in the palace. But the daily sight of the weakness of Claudius, his subjection to the rule of women and slaves, and constant familiarity with every form of dissipation in the imperial circle, undermined any hereditary virtues the lad may have had, and formed a character worthy of one trained in the school of Messalina; so wanting did he ultimately prove in all moral qualities.[2] It was not till A.D. 48 that he got a footing in Palestine; the little Lebanon

[1] Jos. *Ant.* xix. 5, 1.
[2] Jos. *Vita*, 65 ; *Con. Apion*, i. 9 ; *Ant.* xix. 9, 1 ; xx. 9, 4.
294

principality of Chalcis being then given him, on the death of his uncle, Herod, previously its ruler.

The first procurator of Judæa after the death of Agrippa I., was Cuspius Fadus, who entered on his office in A.D. 44; the year of Agrippa's death. Willing to act justly, the new ruler, nevertheless, showed an irritating want of sympathy with Jewish ideas, by proposing that the high priestly robes, which had been given into the hands of the Jewish authorities a few years before, should be restored to Roman keeping. Fortunately for the public peace, Fadus, and the Proconsul of Syria, Cassius Longinus, who had come to Jerusalem on hearing of the agitation caused by this order, were wise enough to allow a Jewish embassy to be sent to Rome, to get the imperial decision on this delicate question, and, there, the younger Agrippa, always shrewdly alive to the prudence of pleasing his race, in view of future personal possibilities, was able to induce Claudius to leave the robes in Jewish hands. But a more serious trouble soon broke out, which shows the state of things amidst which the infant Christian movement had to make its way. The never abating ferment in the popular mind, respecting the eagerly expected Messiah, had brought forward a new pretended prophet, called Theudas, who attracted a multitude of followers, with whom he marched out to the Jordan, giving forth that he would prove his claim to lead them, by dividing the river, and opening a path for them through its dry bed, as Joshua had done, ages before. Shown, by this miracle, to have been sent from God, and thus the Messiah, he would then lead them victoriously against the Romans. A division of cavalry, however, sent against him by Fadus, forthwith ended his enterprise.

Falling on him unexpectedly, many of his adherents were hewn down or taken prisoners, and he, himself, being captured, and put to death, his head was cut off and carried to Jerusalem. A difficulty has been found in a Theudas being mentioned by Gamaliel, the great Sanhedrim rabbi, in his speech, made years before Fadus appeared, and by this disturber being put, in that speech, even before Judas the Gaulonite,[1] who rose before the census in A.D. 6–7, but the scrupulous exactness of " Acts," proved by Ramsay as to even the smallest local details, makes it hard to believe that any error could have crept in here. It would be useless to go into details of the discussions that have darkened this subject, a very satisfactory solution of the matter being suggested by Wieseler, who thinks the reference by Gamaliel is to a similar false prophet mentioned by Josephus, as appearing just before the death of Herod, his name being given in the Aramaic form of Matthias, which is claimed to be the equivalent of Theudas, being derived from Theodoros, the Greek rendering of Matthias.[2]

Fadus was succeeded by Tiberius Alexander, as procurator, it is not known exactly when; his reign lasting till A.D. 48. He was an apostate Jew, the son of one of the most distinguished Hebrew families of Alexandria, and thus the bigoted population of Zion had the spectacle of a heathen Jew ruling on the throne of David; a sight hardly fitted to abate their horror of their Roman masters. It is not to be wondered at, therefore, that he encountered another Messianic rising; this time led by two sons of the famous zealot Judas the Galilæan. But it ended, of course, badly for the patriots, both of the leaders being

[1] Acts v. 34 ff.   [2] Wieseler, Synopse, &c., 103 ff.

taken and crucified. That the atmosphere was electric in
these years is evident.   To add to the popular excitement,
a great famine, which had already begun under Fadus,
became terrible in its severity; the same famine mentioned in the Acts, as falling on Judæa, somewhere about
the time of Agrippa's death, in the reign of Claudius.[1]
In a general sense, indeed, the reign of Claudius, as The
Acts tells us, was marked by very widespread dearths;
for, apart from that in Palestine, Rome suffered in this
way in the beginning of the reign, Greece in the eighth or
ninth year, and Rome, again, in the eleventh year.[2]

The chronic excitement against the subjection of "the
heritage of Jehovah" to the abhorred Gentile, had broken
out, from time to time, for more than a generation past,
in wild and hopeless revolt, culminating in the delirious
rising under Theudas, in the days of Fadus, in the mutterings of revolt under Tiberius, and in the rising of the
sons of Judas the Gaulonite, true representatives of the
Maccabean zeal for the Law, of Mattathias and his illustrious family, but all that had been hitherto seen, was
as nothing to what followed, in the procuratorship of
Cumanus, who held office from A.D. 48 to 52, while Paul
and Barnabas were in Antioch, or away in Asia Minor,
and James, the brother of Christ, was acting, with the
other Apostles, as seemed best in such troubled times, for
the interests of the new faith, in Jerusalem and Judæa.
The Holy City was, indeed, the most fitting centre from
which the "Apostles of the circumcision" could extend
their influence; the gathering to it of vast numbers of
Jews to the various feasts, enabling them to win converts,
who, on their return to their distant homes, might spread

---

[1] Acts xi. 28, 29; Jos. *Ant.* xx. 2, 6; 5, 2.   [2] Schürer i. 171

among their brethren around them the story of the
Messiah, Jesus. That no little success was attained in
this direction is seen in the " Epistle of James," written,
apparently in these years, to Jewish-Christian communities outside Palestine, among " the twelve tribes of the
Dispersion," or, rather, to these communities, regarded by
St. James as the true Israel, to whom, as believers in the
message of God through Christ, belonged the promises
given to their fathers. As yet, in fact, no sharp division
had taken place, between a religion rooted in Judaism,
and, still, among the leaders in Jerusalem, strictly honouring it, and the Jewish world, which was invited to adopt
the new faith. The era of alienation and bitter opposition
came later.

The first outbreak with which Cumanus had to contend
rose from the thoughtless act of a soldier, in the force
stationed, as usual, in the Temple courts at the Passover,
to keep the multitudes from raising any tumults. The
offender having been silly enough to make some offensive
gesture of contempt at the crowd, this was enough to
raise to fury the tens of thousands then thronging the
great Temple-close and the city. Rushing in wild rage
to the procurator's palace, they howled for vengeance on
the poor legionary, and when Cumanus himself, coming
out, tried to appease them, so lost all control of themselves, as to hurl great volleys of insults at the would-be
pacificator. Irritated at last beyond endurance, he finally
ordered the soldiery to disperse them, which they did
with such a heartiness of ill-will to a race so hated,
that, if we may believe Josephus, no fewer than 20,000
men were trampled under foot and killed, in the attempt
to get away from their weapons, through the narrow

streets.[1] No spark could be too small, in such a community, to light the most terrible conflagration, and, hence, it was not long before there was another. A servant of the government having been attacked and robbed on the public road, not far from Jerusalem, the hamlets round were given up to plunder, but, unfortunately, among the booty, a soldier came upon a roll of the Law, and in his abhorrence and contempt, thoughtlessly tore it to pieces, with ridicule and coarse words. Instantly, all Jewry was in flames of excitement, and, as the cherished habit was, streamed off, in thousands, to Cæsarea, to demand the punishment of one guilty of such blasphemy and outrage. Had Cumanus hesitated, a national revolt would presently have followed, so the poor soldier had to die, to calm the storm.[2]

But these troubles were less serious, and less bloody, than a third incident, which cost Cumanus, not his life indeed, but his office. Some Galilæan Jews, on their way to the feast at Jerusalem, had been attacked and murdered, as they passed through Samaria, by the people of a Samaritan village. Revenge was instantly demanded by the Jews, but Cumanus, who had been bribed by the Samaritans, whom, moreover, the Romans liked as much as they detested the Jews, failed to take measures against the offenders. Thereupon, the Jews determined to take the law into their own hands, and avenge their fellows in their own way. A great band, therefore, led by two fierce zealots, Eleasar and Alexander, marched into Samaria, and massacred every one they could,—old men, women, and children, utterly desolating village after village, till

---

[1] *Ant.* xx. 5, 3 ; *Bell. Jud.* ii. 12, 1.
[2] *Ant.* xx. 5, 4 ; *Bell. Jud.* ii. 12, 2.

stopped by troops sent from Cumanus, who killed many
of the invading horde, and took others off as prisoners.
Before long, an embassy from the Samaritans came before
the Proconsul of Syria, Ummidius Quadratus, and made a
formal complaint, respecting this bloody foray of the Jews
upon their people.   But, at the same time, a deputation
from the Jews appeared before Quadratus, not only accusing the Samaritans, but charging Cumanus with having
been bribed by them, to neglect his duty.   On this, the
Proconsul came to Samaria, and instituted a strict inquiry
into the whole matter.   All the rioters captured by Cumanus were crucified; five, who, in addition, had actually
been parties to the fight against the Roman soldiers, were
beheaded, but the chief men of both Jews and Samaritans,
and also Cumanus, were sent off to Rome, to answer for
themselves there.   Luckily for the Jews, Agrippa was in
the imperial city, and, with lively expectations of favours
to come, as usual took the side of his people, influencing
the weak-minded Claudius so effectively, that the Jews
were acquitted, the Samaritans put to death, and Cumanus
not only deposed but banished.[1]

It was apparently amidst the manifold distractions of
the stormy rule of Cumanus, that the first of the Epistles,
that of St. James, was written, the absence from it of
any reference to the leading doctrine of St. Paul, that
"man is justified by faith apart from the works of the
Law," [2] showing that it is earlier than the publication of

---

[1] Jos. *Ant.* xx. 6, 1–3; Jos. ii. 12, 3–7.   Tacitus (*Annal.* xii. 54)
speaks of Cumanus as only procurator of Galilee, and of Felix as being, at
the same time, procurator of Samaria and Judæa.   But Josephus says
that Felix was appointed only after the fall of Cumanus, and he was more
likely to know the facts than Tacitus.

[2] Rom. iii. 28.

the Epistles of the Apostle of the Gentiles. At a later time, this doctrine had so deeply moved the Christian communities, that it seems impossible James should have laid it down, without qualification, that " by works a man is justified, and not only by faith,"[1] had he written after Paul's formula had been generally spread among the churches, so as to be known universally which it was, very early. The whole tone of the Epistle, indeed, breathes an atmosphere of old Hebrew piety, which had adoringly accepted the crucified One as " the Desire of Israel," the promised King-Messiah of the ancient prophets, but clung none the less fondly, to the faith of the race, and to the Temple whose consecration to His worship had been accepted by Jehovah. For James, as tradition tells us, was, to the end, a specially strict Jew. " He has been called ' The Just,' " says Hegesippus,[2] " from the time of our Lord to our own days.—He was holy from his mother's womb, and drank neither wine nor strong drink, and ate no animal food. A razor never came on his head, and he did not anoint himself with oil, or use the bath. He alone might go into the holy place, for he wore no woollen clothes, but only linen. And he was constantly found alone in the Temple, praying for the forgiveness of Israel, so that his knees became dry and hard like the knees of a camel, from his thus constantly pleading for his people. For such exceeding righteousness, he was called ' The Just,' and ' Oblias,' which means, in Greek, ' the bulwark of the people,' and ' righteousness.' " He had not believed in Jesus as the Messiah at a very late period in our Lord's life,[3] but appears in close relations with the

---

[1] Jas. ii. 24.   [2] Eus. Hist. ii. 23; Routh's Rel. Sacr. 208, Oxf. 1846.
[3] John vii. 5.

Apostles for the first time, after the Ascension; the Resurrection of Jesus, and His subsequent appearance to him, having, apparently, won him to Christianity.[1] Erelong, we find him, as might be expected, so much esteemed in the Church at Jerusalem, that he seemed to be the head of it, not, however, as a "bishop," distinct from the "elders," of whom he was one, for he was never an apostle, and was marked out, therefore, not by any special official rank, but by the nobleness of his personality.[2] In his Epistle everything marks his reverence for Jewish ways and feelings, yet not so as to make the observance of the "Law" a necessary means of acceptance before God, in addition to "faith," but as the divinely-given rule of life, by which the true Israel, that is, in his conception of it, those Jews who had become followers of Christ, should guide their course in the free obedience of faith. Thus, while he remained to the end a Jew, he did not make the mistake of regarding Christianity only as a transfiguration of Judaism, but regarded it as the appointed means through which the blessing, promised to mankind by God, should be extended to the heathen without their needing to be brought under the Mosaic Law. Yet the position of James towards Judaism, was different from that of Paul, for while the latter regarded himself as "dead to the Law, through the body of Christ,"[3] and therefore held himself free to be, to the Jew a Jew, and to those that were "without law, as without law," though he was always "under law to Christ," James considered it a holy duty, in a Christian, to keep that Law which God had given to His people through Moses. Hence we find his Epistle addressed to Jewish Christians;[4] their place of meeting called by him

[1] 1 Cor. xv. 5.   [2] Acts xv. 23, 24.   [3] Rom. vii. 4; Gal. ii. 19.   [4] Jas. ii. 2

a synagogue; monotheism specially noticed, in accordance with Jewish feelings;[1] swearing by the usual Jewish oaths forbidden;[2] anointing with oil for medical purposes, as was practised by the Jews mentioned; while the moral errors reproved are all of a kind which point to specially Jewish failings.

The Epistle, which illustrates the life of the Church, in the years preceding Paul's return from his first missionary journey, reads as follows, the text being slightly amplified, where necessary, to make the meaning more clear.

EPISTLE OF JAMES.

I. 1. James, a servant of God and of the Lord Jesus Christ, to the twelve tribes of the Dispersion,[3] greeting. 2. Consider it so much cause for joy, when you are assailed by trials and temptations in many forms; trials from without, because you are Christians; temptations from within; 3. Knowing, as ye do, that such putting of your faith to the test brings about its purifying and strengthening, and, through this, enduring constancy. 4. And see that you let the effect of this patient steadfastness be a perfect one, that it may accomplish fully, its end, and secure that it be complete in all its parts, that is, in all the graces of the Christian life; wanting in nothing. 5. As to such possible shortcomings; if any of you be wanting in the wisdom which will guide safely amidst trials and temptations, let him ask it from God, from whom alone true wisdom comes, and he will obtain it, for God giveth all graces to every one, without regard of person, and without thinking of anything but free bounty, and never upbraids him to whom he grants his gifts, for needing to ask them. Yes, what he asks shall be given; whether

---

[1] Jas. ii. 19.   [2] Jas. v. 12. See Matt. v. 33–36.
[3] Jewish Christian communities, though not in contrast to heathen Christians, who came later.

wisdom, as in this case, or any other worthy petition.
6. But, to secure an answer, he must offer "*the prayer of faith,*"[1] that is, with perfect trust in the power and love of God, as able and ready to grant the request : for he that doubts is like a sea-billow, driven before the wind, and heaved hither and thither. 7. Therefore, do not let the doubter suppose that he will receive anything from God ; 8. He, as a man of two minds, turned now to God, now away from him, being changeful and fickle in all his ways. God gives heavenly wisdom to him only who is turned with his whole heart to Him, and has no divided affections. 9. But as regards this world, let the brother of low degree amidst all his trials, glory in his high estate as heir of the promises in Christ : and the rich brother, in that he is made low, for, when stripped of his wealth, he will be humble, and thus secure real wealth, with the poor, hereafter ; being no longer harsh to his poor brother, as when he was well-to-do :[2] because for his pride of wealth he will be judged by God, and made to pass away like the flower of the grass. 11. For the sun rises with the glowing wind, and withers up the grass ; and its flower falls and its beauty perishes. So, the rich man, overtaken by the judgment of God, in the midst of his schemes and ambitions, suddenly perishes, as the flower is laid low by the burning sun, in the midst of its pride. 12. But blessed is the man who does not give way, under the trials and temptations he may have to suffer : for when, having been tried as by fire, he shall be found purified gold, he shall receive the crown of life, which the Lord has promised to them that love him. 13. As to him who does not resist and overcome temptations, let no man say when he is tempted, as an excuse for his falling, "I am tempted of God ; " for God is high above all temptation to evil, and He Himself tempts no man. 14. But each man is tempted when drawn away by his own lust, and allured. 15. Then, when lust has conceived, it bears sin ; and the sin, when it comes to its full

---

[1] Chap. v. 15.   [2] Chaps. ii. 6, 7 ; v. 1-6.

growth, brings forth death.   16. Do not be deceived, my
beloved brethren.   17. No; temptation cannot come from
God, but every good gift and every morally perfect gift
and bounty is from above, coming down from the Father of
Lights, with whom there cannot be, as in the heavenly bodies,
any variation, or shadow cast by turning.   18. So far from
tempting us, of His own will God gave us the new birth as
Christians, by the word of truth, that is, the Gospel. in order
that we should be a kind of firstfruits of His creatures.   19.
You know it is so, beloved brethren.   Let every man, therefore, be swift to hear, slow to speak, slow to wrath : 20. For
the wrath of man worketh not the righteousness of God.   21.
Wherefore, putting away all filthiness and all the wickedness
flooding up round you, receive with meekness the word im-
planted by God in you, which is able to save your souls.   22.
But the " word " must be so heard as to colour your lives.
Be ye, therefore, doers of it, and not merely hearers, deceiving
your own selves.   23. For if any one is only a hearer of the
word, and not also a doer of it, he is like a man looking at
his natural face in a mirror ; 24. For he looks at himself and
goes away, and forthwith forgets what he was like.   25. But
he who makes his study the perfect law, that is, the Gospel, in
its working by love, and making obedience voluntary and
delightful, not by fear, like the Law of Moses, and continues
in it, being not a mere hearer who forgets, but a doer of the
work it enjoins, this man will be blessed in his working.   26.
If any one think that he is serving God while he is for ever
talking rather than working, and is thus deceiving his heart,
that man's service is worthless.   27. True service of God
made pure and undefiled by the " Word " dwelling in the
soul, and acknowledged as such before our God and Father,
is this ; to visit the fatherless and widows in their affliction,
and to keep one's self unspotted in his intercourse with men,
alike in his soul and in his acts.

II. 1. But how different from this the spirit of some !
My brethren, for such you are, do you hold what you can
II.   U

call the faith of our Lord Jesus Christ, the Lord of glory, if you show respect and make distinctions between persons according to their worldly position? 2. For if there come into your synagogue a man with a gold ring, splendidly dressed, and also a poor man, in sordid clothes; 3. And ye have respect to him who wears the fine clothes, and say, " *Sit thou here, in this nice place*," and say to the poor man, " *Stand thou there*," or, " *Sit* on the floor *at my feet;* " 4. Are you not divided in your mind, as to the truth that, in Christ, rich and poor are one, and that outward appearance is nothing, and are you not making yourselves judges, with evil thoughts? 5. Hear me, beloved brethren; did not God choose the poor, as to this world, to be rich in faith, and heirs of the kingdom which he promised to those who love him? 6. But ye have, by acting thus, dishonoured the poor man. Can you not sympathise with the poor, for do not the rich opponents of the faith oppress you, yourselves, and drag you before the Jewish and heathen judgment seats? 7. Do they not blaspheme the goodly name which was called over you at baptism? 8. If, then, ye fulfil the royal, that is, the supreme, law, according to the Scripture, " *Thou shalt love thy neighbour as thyself*," you do well: 9. But if you have respect of persons, you commit sin, being convicted under that law, as transgressors. 10. For he who keeps the whole law, and yet fails in one point, has become guilty of all. 11. For he who said, " *Do not commit adultery*,"—said also, " *Do not kill*." Though then, you do not commit adultery, yet if you kill some one, you have become a transgressor of the law. The transgression of one command shows a moral defect which makes the fulfilment of the other commands impossible. 12. Speak and act as men who will be judged by the law of love, that is of liberty, obedience being the spontaneous tribute of the loving heart. 13. For judgment is pitiless to him who has shown no mercy, but mercy bears with it the joyful confidence that it will triumph over the threatenings of judgment.

14. It is faith that saves us,[1] but faith proved by works. What, then, doth it profit, my brethren, if a man say he has faith, but have not works? Can that faith save him? **15.** If a brother or a sister be naked, and in want of daily food, and one of you say to them, *"Go in peace, may you be warmed with clothing, and fed"*—and yet you do not give them what the body needs; what good is it? **17.** Thus, therefore, if it have not works, faith is in itself, dead. **18.** But some man will say, that he has faith, and I have works:—and what right have I to lay more stress on works than the speaker has to lay such special stress on faith? Show me thy faith apart from thy works, and I will show thee my faith by my works. Have you really faith? Then, if it be real, it must show itself, but that is impossible without works. As to me, who have works, they are a proof that I have faith, for without faith I could not do the works. **19.** Do you fancy that barren faith will save you? You are an orthodox Jew; you believe that God is one, only; in this you do well, so far, but the devils—the heathen gods—also believe this, and tremble before their future judge. **20.** But would you have further proof, O foolish man, that faith without works is dead? **21.** You and I are Jews, and was not Abraham our father justified by works, seeing that God justified him because he offered up Isaac, his son, upon the altar? **22.** His faith was thus, not dead, but active. You see that faith co-operated with his works, and that by his works his faith was made perfect by its bearing the sorest test; and the Scripture[2] was fulfilled which says: *"And Abraham believed God, and it was reckoned to him for righteousness;"* and he was called The Friend of God. **24.** You see, thus, that man is justified, that is, declared righteous before God, by works, and not by faith only. **25.** The same truth is shown in the case of Rahab the harlot. Was not she, also, justified by works, her life being spared by Joshua, from the destruction denounced against Jericho, because she received the spies, and sent them out

[1] Chap. i. 18, 21.   [2] Gen. xv. 6; xxii. 16.

another way? 26. For, as the body without the spirit, is dead, so faith without works is also dead.

III. 1. Alas! instead of works, you abound in words!—not being slow to speak, or bridling your tongues, as I have exhorted you,[1] but aspiring to be leaders. Be not many of you teachers, my brethren; bethinking yourselves that we, teachers, shall receive a heavier judgment, having more for which to answer. 2. For all of us fail in many things. If there be any one who never speaks amiss, he is a perfect man, able to bridle the whole body. 3. For it is with us as with horses: the bridling of our mouths controls the whole man, just as if we put bridles into the mouths of horses, that they may obey us, we turn about their whole body. 4. The tongue may be small, but look at the ships. Though they are so large, and are driven by rough winds, yet they are turned about by a very small rudder, at the will of the steersman! 5. So the tongue is a small part of the body, yet plumes itself on being able to do great things! See how much wood may be kindled by how little fire! 6. So, the tongue is a fire. It is the world of iniquity among our members, that defiles the whole body, and sets on fire the whole course of life as it circles, wheel like, from birth, on, and it, itself, is set on fire of hell! 7. For every kind of beasts and birds, of reptiles and creeping things, and things in the sea, is tamed, and has been tamed, by mankind. 8. But the tongue can no man tame; it is a restless evil; it is full of deadly poison. 9. We bless the Lord and Father with it, and with it we curse men, who are made after the likeness of God: 10. Out of the same mouth come blessing and cursing. My brethren, these things ought not so to be. 11. Does the fountain send out, from the same mouth, sweet water and bitter? 12. Can a fig, my brethren, yield olives, or a vine, figs? Neither can salt water yield sweet.

13. Who is wise and intelligently thoughtful among you? let him, by a good life, show his works, marked by the gentleness of true heavenly wisdom. 14. But if ye have bitter

---

[1] Chap. i. 19, 26.

jealousy and faction in your heart, glory not **as possessing this wisdom**, and lie not, **in doing so**, against the truth.   **15.** This wisdom, **of jealousy and faction**, is not a wisdom that comes down from above, but is earthly, born of our lower nature, devilish.   **16.** For where jealousy and faction are, there is anarchy and everything vile.   17. But the wisdom that is, **really**, from above, is first pure, then peaceable, gentle, **not stubborn but** easily persuaded, full of mercy and good fruits, without changeableness, and without hypocrisy.   18. And the **seed which yields** the fruit of righteousness, **that is, of godliness**, is sown in peace, **not in jealousy and confusion**, by those who make peace.

IV. 1. But whence spring **these** fightings and strifes among **you, of which I have spoken?** Do they not rise from your sinful pleasures that stir your whole nature to war **against right ? 2.** Ye lust **for worldly aims**, but possession does not follow : you are filled with murderous hate and bitter faction, yet cannot secure **that for which you hate and strive : your fightings and strivings bring you no nearer your end ; and this** not getting **what you seek is** because you do not pray for it.   **3. Or** if some do ask, and **yet** do not receive, **it is** because you ask unworthily, that you may have wherewithal to spend on your **sinful** pleasures.   **4. As the prophets called your fathers, for their unfaithfulness to Jehovah,**[1] so, I call you, ye Christian assemblies,—Adulteresses ! Do ye not know that to feel friendly with the world **around you, the kingdom of evil among men, divorced from communion with God**, is **to show** enmity against God ? Whosoever, therefore, chooses to be a friend of this **present, evil** world, **sunk in heathen vice and wickedness**, is the enemy of God.   **5.** Do you think that the words of Scripture, which say this, are untrue.   Is it not true that God even jealously longs (to save) the spirit He made to dwell in us ; **6.** And, further, gives increase of favour **to him who yields himself up to him ; to impress which on you**

[1] Ezek. xxiii. 4 ff., &c.

the Scripture says, " *God resisteth the proud, but giveth grace to the humble*"?[1]   7. Submit yourselves, then, ye proud, to God, but resist the devil, and he will flee from you.   8. Draw nigh to God, and He will draw nigh to you.   Cleanse your hands, ye sinners, by keeping them from sinful, and giving them only to good uses, and purify your hearts, ye double-minded, who are half for God, half for sin,—by henceforth resisting unholy desires and cultivating holy thoughts. 9. Show the sincerity of your repentance; be deeply sorry for your sins, and mourn, and weep; let your laughter be turned to mourning, and your joy to shame.   10. Humble yourselves in the sight of the Lord, and He shall exalt you. 11. Do not speak one against another, brethren.   He who speaks against a brother, or judges his brother, speaks against the law of Christian love—the law of your Christian life, and condemns that law : but if thou condemnest the law, thou art not a doer of the law, but a judge.   12. One, only, is the lawgiver and judge, namely, he who can save or destroy: but who art thou that judgest thy neighbour?   13. Go to now; bethink yourselves,—ye that say, "To-day or to-morrow we will go to this or that town, and spend a year there, and push trade, and make gain :"   14. Whereas ye know not what shall be on the morrow.   What is your life?   For ye are a vapour, that appeareth for a little time, and then vanishes away. 15. You speak thus, instead of saying, "If the Lord will, we shall both live, and do this or that."   16. But, now, ye glory in your vain boastings about worldly success ; all such boasting is sinful.   17. He, then, who knows to do what is right, and fails to do it ; that neglect, to him, is sin.

V. 1. Go to, now, ye rich men, weep and howl for your miseries that are coming upon you.   2. Your riches are corrupted, and your garments are moth-eaten.   3. Your gold and your silver are rusted ; and the rust shall be a witness against you, and shall eat your flesh like fire.   Ye have

[1] Ps. cxxxviii. 6 ; Prov. iii. 34 ; xxiii., &c.

stored up treasure in the last days, **knowing that the end is near. 4.** Behold, the hire of your labourers who reaped your fields, which is kept back by you fraudulently, cries out : and the cries of the harvesters have entered into the ears of the Lord of Sabaoth. **5.** You have lived in the lap of pleasure and prodigality on the earth ; you have satiated your heart's desires, in this, to you a day of slaughter, **judgment being at hand ; up to the very breaking forth of which, you have lived like the beasts that eat till they are killed. 6.** You have condemned, you have killed the righteous man **when his integrity hindered your schemes ;** and he suffered meekly ; not resisting **your violence, by violence ; the judgment being nigh !**

7. Be patient, therefore, brethren, until the coming of the Lord. Behold, the husbandman waits for the precious fruit of the earth, and has long patience for it, till it receive the autumn and the spring rains. **8.** Be ye also **equally** patient ; stablish your hearts ; for the coming of the Lord is at hand ! Mutter not one against another, that ye be not judged : behold, the Judge stands before the door ! **10.** Take, brethren, the prophets who spoke in the name of the Lord, for an example of suffering wrong, and of patience **under it. 11.** Behold, we call them blessed who endured **patiently.** Ye have heard of the patience of Job, and have seen **by** the end given **by** the Lord, that the Lord is very pitiful and **of** tender mercy.

12. But above all things, my brethren, swear not, neither by the heaven, nor by the earth, nor by any other oath : but let your Yea be a simple Yea, and your Nay, **a simple Nay ;** that you may not fall under judgment.

13. Is any one of you suffering ? let him pray. Is any one in good heart ? let him sing songs of praise. **14.** Is any one among you sick ? let him call **to himself the presiding elders of the congregation to which he belongs ;** and let them pray over him, anointing him with oil in the name of the Lord : **15.** And the prayer of faith shall save him that is sick, **from his**

sickness, and the Lord will raise him up ; and if he have committed sins, they shall be forgiven him,—his strong faith, that
healed him, carrying healing to the soul as well. 16. Confess,
therefore, your sins, one to another, and pray for one another,
that ye may be healed—the sickness sent as punishment of
some sin, being removed, when the sin, by contrition, is forgiven. The prayer of a righteous man is mighty in its power.
17. Elijah, for example, was just such a man as ourselves, and
he cried to God in prayer, of course earnestly, that it might
not rain : and it rained not on the earth for three years and
six months. 18. And he prayed again ; and the heaven gave
rain, and the earth brought forth her fruit.

19. My brethren, if any among you let himself be led astray
from the truth, and one turn him back again to it, let him who
does so know, that he who turns a sinner from the error of
his way,—his going astray from the right road, the truth,—will
save a soul from death,—towards which he was advancing—
and will cover a multitude of sins in him who is thus saved.

The contrast between this earliest epistle, written by a
Jewish Christian, and the Epistles of Paul, lies on the surface. Substantially identical in the fundamental position,
that a loving faith, shown by its fruits, is the one condition of acceptance with God, through Jesus Christ, the
one document is as simple and elementary in its theology,
as the others are scientific and elaborate. " James " is,
above all things, practical; " Paul " is as practical, in
effect, but the intellectual side of Christianity, as was
natural in a rabbi like the apostle of the heathen, is
much more prominent. Nothing could be more striking
than the development of the language of " James," into
the close reasoning and abstruse " system," of the Epistle
to the Romans, and, more or less, of all the Epistles of
Paul, " wherein," to use the words of Second Peter, " are

some things hard to be understood, which the ignorant and unsteadfast wrest, as they do also the other Scriptures, to their own destruction."[1]

Meanwhile, amidst the anxiety of James and the Apostles, for the spread of Christianity among their countrymen, at home and abroad, Judaism was, for the time, making even more striking conquests. No less a triumph marked those years, than the conversion of the royal house of Adiabene, a kingdom lying on the east side of the Upper Euphrates, where it filled up the triangle between that river and the river Lycus, with its apex at what had once been the site of Nineveh, and its base in the towering mountains of modern Kurdistan. In the time of Claudius, the reigning king of this far-off region was one Izates, who, with his mother Helena, embraced Judaism; his brother Monobazus, and his other relations, following their example at a later period.[2] As a result, these royal personages connected themselves in many ways with Jerusalem; Izates even sending five of his sons to it for their education. Helena, herself, further, made a pilgrimage to it, and spent large sums in feeding the poor, during the famine of which we read in the Acts.[3] She was, indeed, so pleased with the Holy City, that she made it a home for at least fourteen, some say, for twenty-eight years, living as a Nazarite, in the strictest observance of the Law, and building a palace in it for herself, as did also Monobazus, who succeeded his brother on the throne of Adiabene. That they enriched the Temple with costly gifts was a matter of course. Nor did their loyalty to the Jewish faith end at their death, for Helena caused a grand tomb to be excavated in the horizontal

---

[1] 2 Pet. iii. 16.   [2] Jos. *Ant.* xx. 2–4.   [3] Acts xi. 28.

limestone ridge, north of Jerusalem, and was buried there,
with Izates. She had returned home before her death,
but her body was brought to Jerusalem for burial. Her
resting-place, now empty, is identified with what are
called the Tombs of the Kings; a very grand sepulchre,
containing a great many places for bodies, and various
outer courts, and chambers within, piercing the rock over
a breadth of more than twenty-eight yards, and a depth
of more than eighteen; Izates having had no fewer than
twenty-four sons. Beautiful sarcophagi once added to
the sad splendour, but few traces of them now remain.
The different chambers had, also, once, stone doors, close
fitting, but these have vanished. There is still, however,
outside, a rolling-stone, in grooves, for shutting up the
external entrance. All this magnificence dates from the
years of James and the Apostles, who must often have
talked of the architectural wonders of this great mauso-
leum, as they grew under their eyes. Indeed, they could
hardly have seen anything in Jerusalem, to compare with
the carved front of the great tomb, with its broad mould-
ings, and wreaths of fruit and foliage, beautiful still, after
more than eighteen hundred years. Even the sunken
court before the tomb, cut down into the rock, would be
a wonder to them, for it measures no less than thirty
yards long, and twenty-seven yards broad.[1] Such a
flattery of Jewish pride as the gaining a royal family to
their faith, must have added no little to the difficulties of
the Galilæans, in winning converts to the lowly Messiah
of Nazareth. To the Jewish mind, it would, doubtless,
seem a beginning of that glorious day when " kings would
be the nursing fathers, and queens the nursing mothers of

[1] Bædeker's Palestine, 236.

Zion; when they would bow down to her with their face toward the earth, and lick up the dust of her feet." [1] Nor was the incident a passing one, for connections of the family fought on the Jewish side, against the Romans, in the great war.

In the year 48, while Paul and Barnabas were just setting out on their great missionary journey, the Jews in Rome had so irritated the authorities by their illegal magic arts, their feuds with the populace, and their Messianic plots and restless intrigues, that Claudius had banished them from the city. The race was indeed a constant thorn in the side of the Empire from these causes, and from its self-assumed isolation, alike in customs, feelings, social life, and political aims, and its virtual antagonism to everything not Jewish. Agrippa, the younger, had, in the same year, been made King of Chalcis, and through this, had been, for some time, near Palestine, when James was sending out his encyclical to the Jewish Christian congregations of the East and West. Agrippa was now, also, "president of the Temple," "superintendent of the Temple treasury," and had the nomination of the high priest; privileges inherited with his new dignity. Cumanus had, moreover, been deposed just about the time when Paul was coming to Jerusalem from Antioch, to consult with the Mother Church, respecting the relation of the heathen converts to the Mosaic Law; his place having been taken by Felix, a freedman, [2] whose advent to power was very soon marked by the murder of the former high priest Jonathan, who had tried to induce the new ruler, to do some act of justice which was against his personal designs. Such a man,

---

[1] Isa. xlix. 23.   [2] A.D. 52–60.

ruling a proud race as he only could who had himself been a slave, and this immediately in succession to the troubled procuratorship of Cumanus, with its legacy of exasperations and its brooding hopes of revenge: at a time, above all, when the fanatical pride of the Jew, and his wild dream, of world-empire under the Messiah had been excited beyond all previous bounds, by his triumph over Caligula in the attempt to pollute the Temple, and by the conversion of the royal house of Adiabene to the faith of Israel—made peace between Rome and Jerusalem hopeless. As regarded Christianity, moreover, it must, as I have said, have in great measure stopped its spread in the Holy City and Judæa at large, where it did not lead to active opposition. The confusion of the times, the hopes, fears, plots, and perils, filling the air must have virtually paralysed any new movement. Jewish national life had already glided into the broken water of its later years, dashing ever more swiftly from rock to rock as it now irredeemably hurried towards its final leap into the abyss.

CHAPTER XIV

"MUST CHRISTIANS BE JEWS AS WELL?"

WINTER OF A.D. 51–52 ; PAUL'S AGE, c. 41–42

THE religions of antiquity were, in all cases, intensely ritualistic. A sacrifice, or a private function, must, alike, be carried out in exact accordance with prescribed rules, if it were to have a claim on the gods, but when everything had been done as required, they were put under an obligation to answer favourably, which they were bound to honour. Yet, in the sphere of ordinary life, nearly all races of men were free. They could eat and drink as they pleased, mix with their fellow-men, perform the common offices of daily existence, or of social intercourse, without interference from the priest. Among the Jews, however, as among their ancient fellow-countrymen in Mesopotamia,—the Accadians, or as among the ancient Egyptians, with whom they had lived for centuries before the Exodus, not only every detail of religion, but every minute particular of ordinary life, was the subject of religious prescriptions, believed to be Divine, and therefore, to be obeyed, on peril of offending, and even insulting, the Higher Powers. The Jew must bear on his person the mark of a holy observance, must perform endless cleansings of a more or less formal nature, must repeat, at prescribed times, each day, so many prescribed prayers, must eat and drink only prescribed supports and refreshments, prepared in prescribed modes, must submit from his cradle to his grave to "customs' and "traditions" of sacredly binding authority, at every step of his daily life, and must perform prescribed pilgrimages, from any adopted country, however distant, to the national shrine at Jerusalem, to satisfy what he conceived the demands of Jehovah.   Among the Western races, Paul had to discuss questions of doctrine, such as the Resurrection and immortality, or the grounds of a soul's justification before God, and had to denounce gross sins, and novel and equivocal innovations, " of which he had to say, We have no such custom, neither the Churches of God." [1]   In Palestine, and among the Jews everywhere, the burning question of the age, was the position of the uncircumcised converts to Christianity, towards circumcision.   Could they be saved without becoming, at least to this length, Jews, or even without, further, observing the whole Jewish Ceremonial Law ; or would they be accepted by God though they lived without recognition of either ?

Paul had always, in his preaching, wherever he went, turned to his own race first, at once in fulfilment of the command of Christ, to "begin at Jerusalem," and because they offered, in some measure, a prepared soil for a religion based on sacred writings which they practically worshipped, and were intently looking for the appearance of the Messiah.   But when driven out of the synagogues by them, amidst blasphemy and violence, he had turned to the heathen, among whom he had found a ready hearing instead of fierce hostility.   He had been large and liberal in his practice, however, bearing himself to the Jew as a

[1] 1 Cor. xi. 16.

Jew, even while dispensing with Jewish obligations in the
case of Gentiles.[1]   But the unbending pride of his race,
scandalised at his declaration that their fetish, the Law,
was imperfect and insufficient, and finding no room in
their idea of the Messiah, for His death on the cross, made
access to it, with the Gospel, more and more difficult,
while, on the other hand, the heathen systems were only
pale survivals of a faith which was a tradition of the
past.   Splendid temples, no doubt, rose in holy cities, but
only immemorial usage honoured them with sacrifices and
incense.   The gods were no longer realities, with any
class but the peasant.   The multitude, for ever estranged
from the faith of their fathers, lived without thought.
Bright minds scourged with bitter ridicule all that their
forefathers had revered; deeper natures, in which the
religious sense was not wholly extinct, sought peace of
heart in the schools of philosophy, or in the numerous
secret guilds of the day, or in the fantastic and mystic
worship of Eastern gods, then in favour throughout the
Empire.   Especially, however, was Judaism an increasing
subject of interest in the upper circles of society, to the
bitter regret of not a few, who, in bewailing the final decay
of the old religion, were grieved, above all things, at the
constantly growing success of Jewish proselytism.[2]   But
to the sympathisers with Judaism from among the heathen,
standing as they virtually did, in the fore-court of Christianity, by this partial conversion, that nobler faith offered
many special attractions, while it did not burden them
with the intolerable infliction of the Jewish Ceremonial

---

[1] 1 Cor. ix. 19.

[2] Cic. *pro Flacco.* xxviii. ; Juvenal, xiv. 100 ff.; Tac. Hist. v. 4, 5 ;
Pliny, *Ep.* x. 97 ; Dio. Cass. lii. 36.

Law. From among these, therefore, Paul won many
believers. Not a few heathen, moreover, who had no
connection with Judaism, found, even on a superficial
consideration of Christianity, that it opened to them,
thirsting as they did, for the high and eternal, a fountain of life such as neither philosophy, nor Oriental
mysticism could offer. Thus, to a large extent, the seed
of Christianity scattered among the heathen proved to
have fallen on good soil.

Paul's experience at Antioch before starting on his
mission, must have helped to bring about the new attitude towards the Law, which he soon took. The congregation in this great Syrian capital, had been founded
by some of the Greek speaking, or Hellenist brethren, who
had fled from Jerusalem on the martyrdom of Stephen,
and was thus in about the fourteenth or fifteenth year of
its prosperous growth. At first, no doubt, mainly Jewish,
it had nevertheless always been much more liberal in its
bearing towards the mixed Gentile population round, than
if its founders had been Jews of Palestine. Ere long,
large numbers of proselytes had joined it, who had
not become, in the full sense, Jews, but the actually
Jewish brethren, none the less, associated freely with
them, silently ignoring the letter of the Law [1] by joining
them in the love-feasts, although it was forbidden a Jew
to recline at table with the uncircumcised, and though
the bread contributed by these brethren to the common
meal was, according to the rabbis, more defiling than
unclean flesh.

How soon Paul came to regard strict conformity to
"the Law" as unnecessary to Christians, is not indicated,

[1] Gal. ii. 14.

but his experience at Antioch must have led him far
towards wide and liberal views. When, however, he
found, on his missionary tour, that the Jews fiercely rejected the Gospel, and were his bitter persecutors from
city to city, he faltered in his hereditary assumption that
as they had been the elect people of the Old Dispensation,
they were the elect heirs of the New Covenant, to the
exclusion of other races, except on condition of their
becoming Jews. In this state of mind it was easy to
come to the conclusion, that the heathen were "called,"
as such, to share in the offers of the Gospel, and could
enter the new kingdom of the Messiah Jesus, as full
members of it, directly from heathenism. He must have
realised already that the supremacy of the Law was
destroyed by the death of Christ, and that this cardinal
fact must have the weightiest bearing on Christian practice. If the Law was not needed for salvation, why
burden the lives of heathen converts with the multitudinous rules and observances of Judaism, which kept
back so many weak and earnest minds, by requiring
them to bear a load which Christ Himself had declared
to be intolerable?[1]

The clear mind and brave heart of the apostle, thus
moved, he ere long took the final step, and repudiated,
finally and for ever, the contention of the Judaisers, that
the heathen needed to become Jews in becoming Christians. The momentous seriousness of this position is seen
at once, when we recollect how intimately the Law was
interwoven with the whole being of a Jew, and how even
its most trifling detail, was regarded as an eternally
binding Divine command. What an unheard of and

[1] Matt. xxiii. 4; Luke xi. 46; Acts xv. 10; Gal. vi. 13.

II.   X

inexpiable offence in the eyes not only of Jews, but
even of strict Jewish-Christians, to declare that Law as
obsolete and not binding, which Moses had received on
Mount Sinai from the very hand of God! There had,
indeed, been isolated gleams of a similar attitude towards
Moses, in earlier ages, and Paul could appeal to the action
of revered precursors in defence of his bold innovation,
based on the intuition of a living faith. He could point
to King Hezekiah, who destroyed an old national object
of reverence, the brazen serpent, consecrated by Moses as
an emblem of God's saving might; to Isaiah, who declared
that a weighty portion of the demands of the Law, the
sacrifices, were of no worth in themselves; and, above all,
to his Master,—recognised as Messiah even by the Jewish-
Christians,—who, without scruple, broke the Jewish Sabbath laws, and justified His disciples for following His
example. The walls of Jewish legalism were thus breached
already in more places than one, but it was the lot of Paul
to lay them utterly in ruins.[1] Such a complete repudiation
of " the traditions of the elders" as he proclaimed, was
revolutionary to the last degree. Henceforth, no heathen
convert needed to be circumcised, every difference between clean and unclean foods was abolished, the Jewish
Sabbath and the new moons were declared to belong to
the past; Christianity, in fact, was made wholly independent of Judaism.

Such was the theological attitude of Paul when he returned from Asia Minor to Antioch. A great assembly
of the church, that is, of the congregation, was, ere
long, summoned, to hear the report of their missionary
experiences from him and Barnabas, and at this, the new

[1] 2 Kings xviii. 4 ; Isa. i. 13 ff. ; Mark ii. 18, 25.

teaching was for the first time set forth; "the door of faith," as distinguished from that of faith and law, having, it was joyfully announced, been opened to the heathen.

In the free air of Antioch these radical innovations appear to have been accepted without question, as amply justified by the success vouchsafed by God, in connection with them, among the heathen population of Asia Minor. It was not for man to dispute changes to which God had so evidently set the seal of His approval. News of what was being done in the free church of Antioch were not long, however, in reaching Jerusalem, and there, as was natural, such advanced liberalism embittered the stern Palestine Jewish-Christians, rather than convinced them. The strong expressions of Paul, in reference to the Law and the great lawgiver, kindled a corresponding zeal for both, in the strict Jews of the Mother Church, who were scandalised by what they heard of the doings in the far north. Hitherto, the calm of its morning hours had hallowed the cradle of the infant faith, but heated debates now rose, in which the Christian life could not flourish. Among the Apostles themselves, one had belonged to the ultra-Jewish party—the left wing, as it were, of Judaism —its irreconcilables — and, besides Simon, many other "zealots" must have brought into the new faith their fanatical intolerance of any compromise with Gentile laxness towards the Law. The triumph over Caligula in his attempt against the honour of the Temple must also have, if possible, intensified the religious pride of the victorious Pharisees from among whom these were gathered, and have made them still more besotted in their theological pedantry, notwithstanding their acceptance of Jesus as the Messiah; for man is a creature of contradictions. To such owl-eyed dogmatists, the light that had glorified the new Christianity of Paul, and the liberality of the Jewish brethren at Antioch, had been suffered too long, and must at once be shut out again. The more yielding section of the Jerusalem assembly—the Hellenists—had been scattered, years before, and were now in the minority. While, therefore, the Antioch brethren were rejoicing in Paul's proclamation of a " door of faith " being opened to the heathen, without their being required to submit to the Law, some of the " zealots " in the Jerusalem congregation took it upon them, to go to Antioch, to arrest the spreading heresy. It was intolerable to them that the proud belief they had imbibed with their mother's milk, that the Jew had a monopoly of the favour of God, and that only his race and Gentiles who fully accepted Judaism could be saved, should be challenged and put aside by Paul, as had been the case in his Galatian mission. " The uncircumcised " had, in all ages of their history, been the contemptuous by-name for all the non-Jewish world,[1] so that even Isaiah had spoken of them and of the unclean as the same, and Ezekiel had painted it as a nameless horror to lie, even in Sheol, beside them [2]—and were Jews to give their hand to such despised Pariahs, as brethren ? Paul was actually preaching that men became Christians through the " new birth," independently of the Law, and that it was indifferent whether they were Jews or Greeks, since, in Christ all, alike, became new creatures ! Nay, he even spoke as if it were hurtful to be a Jew. All that, as one, had been gain to him before God, he declared he counted loss for Christ, and even of his Hebrew birth, and blameless

[1] Judg. xiv. 3 ; xv. 18 ; 1 Sam. xiv. 6 ; xvii. 26, 30.
[2] Isa. lii. 1 ; Ezek. xxxii. 19, 21, 24, 25, 26, 29, 32.

legal righteousness,[1] he openly said, he "counted them
but filth." Were they to forget their dignity, and treat
defilement as nothing? Paul had gone so far as to
suggest whether the Law had a claim on any Christian, or
was even compatible with Christianity. It was only, he
said, our humble conductor or lowly first schoolmaster,
to bring us to Christ our true teacher; like the slave who
went with a boy to school, to see him there safely.[2] It
was a horror to them to be told that, so far from being able
to save us, or of any use in our salvation, the office of the
Law was to convict us as guilty, and thus reveal the sin
from which Christ was the one means of deliverance. Did
not Moses expressly say that "if a man do" the commands of the Law "he shall live in them?"[3] And how
did Paul get over this in his new preaching? Did he not
venture to affirm that Moses had put a veil on his face,
that the children of Israel should not look steadfastly on
the end of that "glory," which was passing away; thus
implying that the great lawgiver had, purposely, veiled
from their knowledge, the temporary character of his
Law?[4] No wonder Paul himself admitted that such an
insinuation was "great boldness!"

Hurrying off, therefore, to Antioch, the champions of
frozen conservatism, mingling in the assembly of the local
Christians, and using the synagogue privilege of rising
and speaking, declared that all Paul had said about the
conditions of salvation was wrong, and that unless they
were circumcised after the custom of Moses, which was the
usual formula for obeying the whole Law, they could not

---

[1] Phil. iii. 4–10.   [2] Gal. iii. 3, 24.
[3] Lev. xviii. 5; Deut. viii. 3; Ezek. xx. 11, 13, 21; Rom. x. 5; Gal
iii. 12.   [4] 2 Cor. iii. 12.

be saved.[1] The point thus raised was of the greatest
moment, for on its solution depended, whether Christianity
was to be another merely ritual system, of washings,
purifyings, division of clean and unclean foods, persons,
and things, or whether it was to be the assertion of the
grand doctrine of Christ, that God's new kingdom " is not
eating and drinking, but righteousness, and peace, and joy
in the Holy Ghost :" [2] whether, in short, the heart was
what God wanted, with a worship in spirit and truth ; not
in fasts and forms.[3] The controversy grew fierce, and
was like to rend the young Church in pieces. To Paul,
the matter was vital. If the Judaisers won the day, " he
had run, and was running, in vain." [4] " He would not give
way, no not for an hour, that the truth of the Gospel "
might be preserved to the churches.[5] So keenly did he
feel the danger, that, even years after, he could see in
the disturbers only " false brethren secretly brought in,
who came in secretly, to spy out the liberty the Antioch
and Galatian brethren had in Christ Jesus ; " [6] " that they
might make slaves of them." [7] He was moved to the
very depths of his nature, at attacks which threatened to
destroy his newly established congregations, and to weld on
them again the chains of the Law, just broken. We may
picture to ourselves the wild excitement of " the dissen-
sion and questioning " in the Christian Church at Antioch,
from the passion kindled against our Lord in the synagogue
at Nazareth, when the congregation " filled with wrath,
rose up, and cast Him out," not from the building only,
but from the village, and even attempted to throw Him
headlong over a cliff,[8]—or from the tempest of voices that

[1] Acts xv. 1.   [2] Rom. xiv. 17.   [3] Jas. iv. 24.   [4] Gal. ii. 2.
[5] Gal. ii. 5.   [6] Gal. ii. 4.   [7] Gal. ii. 4.   [8] Luke iv. 28.

assailed St. Stephen in his disputes with the Hellenists.[1]
It was clear that nothing could be done on the Orentes,
to settle the matter definitely, for the churches at large,
outside Palestine; though Paul's standing, and the remembrance of his mighty labours in the past, might,
possibly, conjure away the threatening storm from Antioch
itself. But what would be gained by this, when the same
strife was sure to burn up in church after church, without his being able to help them by his presence? What
would be gained, if the claims of a development of
Christianity, free from the Law, and independent of
Moses, were tenaciously denied, and those who disputed
them covered themselves with the authority of the elder
Apostles, the more easily to ensnare the simple? Ever
eager to go to the bottom of any matter, he resolved to
carry the war into the citadel of his enemies, and wring
from them, in Jerusalem itself, a recognition of his free
Gospel. The agitation of mind this sore trouble caused
him, had indeed, so affected his whole nature, that he tells
us he had a vision in connection with it,[2] which decided
him. His purpose, made known to the brethren, was
heartily approved, and it was determined to support him
and Barnabas by a deputation from themselves; Paul, for
his part, taking Titus, a young Greek, that is, a heathen
convert won in Asia Minor, and received as a Christian
brother, without being circumcised. His presence would
be a protest against the Judaisers, and a sign impossible
to overlook, that they could not hope to press him back
from the position he had taken.

Fourteen years had passed since Paul had visited the
Holy City, his journey to which, apparently on foot, with

Acts vi. 9.   [2] Gal. ii. 2.

Ba·nabas and his other companions, was cheered by meetings with the brethren, at each stage, southwards, through Phœnicia and Samaria; the coast road being followed, in all probability, to Ptolemais, whence the short route would stretch across Esdraelon, through Samaria. " The conversion of the heathen " was, naturally, the one great theme of discourse, and, as told by the two missionaries, "caused great joy to all the brethren ; " an earnest of victory in the coming discussion, which must have encouraged the hearts of both. From the account left us by Paul himself, in his letter to the Galatians,[1] he took the wise precaution of first securing the support of the apostolic leaders of the Church, "laying before them who were of repute, privately, the Gospel which he preached among the heathen Gentiles." The "pillars" with whom he thus held weighty communion, were, he tells us, James, Peter, and John, the order of their mention pointing, we may presume, to their respective rank in the Jerusalem congregation. On his first visit, after his conversion, he had made himself acquainted with Peter only, who must thus, we may suppose, at that time, have held the dignity now transferred to James; perhaps in part, as the brother of our Lord. Peter's fiery impulsive nature, open-hearted for everything generous or worthy, had won him a place in the inner circle of Christ's disciples, and, indeed, the foremost position among them. He was, however, by no means the man of rocklike firmness which his name would indicate, but rather inclined to undue variableness and to the fear of man ; as his denial of Christ had already shown, and as was to be shown, still more clearly, in a future case. It may, therefore, have happened that, when the opposition between heathen and Jewish

[1] Gal. ii.

Christianity began to be more defined, and the stricter party got the upper hand, the firmer character of James brought him finally to the front. I have already described him, as he is painted by tradition; a man of the highest worth; devoted to the usages of the old faith, and honouring them so scrupulously, as to win respect even from the bigoted outside Pharisaic population.[1] The third "pillar" was the beloved disciple,—a man originally, at least, little inclined by temperament to such liberality as that of Paul, as seen in the rebuke of his narrow-mindedness and want of charity, by Jesus Himself.[2] Years, indeed, softened his character, but he remained to the end so very much a Jew, that even in the Apocalypse, written towards the evening of his life,—for I believe he was its author,—he anticipates in glowing terms the speedy coming of Christ, to set up a great world-kingdom, with a new Jerusalem of inconceivable magnificence, which had come down from heaven, as its capital, in accordance with the belief of his race.[3]

It was to these fathers of the faith, that Paul now detailed his views respecting the Gentiles, and his ideas as to their relation to the Church, and the grounds of their acceptance before God, apart from submission to Judaism. The presence of Titus brought the whole matter in dispute at Antioch, at once into the foreground. It was evidently assumed that the hated rite had been only put off, at his conversion, and that he would now make up for the delay, and submit to it. But Paul would not hear of this. With the firmest decision he refused any compromise. "I gave place," he tells us, "in the way of subjection, no, not an hour." Such immovableness,

---

[1] See p. 301.   [2] Mark ix. 38; Luke ix. 50–55.
[3] Rev. xxi. 2; ii. 24–26.

he adds, sprang from his recognition of the crucial importance of the dispute, on which hung, whether "the truth of
the Gospel should continue with the Gentile converts."[1]
His unyielding attitude inevitably drew out at once,
attack and defence.   We have no record of Paul's arguments, but from the treatment of the question in the
Epistles, we may conclude that both parties appealed to
the Old Testament in proof of their opposite views.   The
apostle could quote many passages, which looked beyond
the conceptions of Jewish exposition, as where Isaiah says,
"I will also give thee for a light to the Gentiles, that
thou mayest be My salvation to the ends of the earth,"[2]
and he might claim that this found its fulfilment in his
preaching.   But far more powerful than these texts,
which the Jewish-Christian "pillars" could always meet
with some counter-text, would be the fact, that the two
missionaries could point to rich fruits of their apostolic
labours.   A whole list of prosperous churches, which
Paul had founded and organised, were a speaking proof
that even where it was not rooted in the soil of Jewish
legality, the new faith not only retained all its inherent
powers, but nobly developed them.   Could the Galilæan
followers of Him who had shown a charity embracing all
mankind, shut their eyes to this evidence of His having
owned and blessed the preaching of His two servants
before them ?   They might, indeed, have wished that these
new churches had been associated with Judaism, but they
could not deny that the transition from heathenism to
Christianity, even without the converts becoming Jews,
was a distinct step in advance.   Here, however, the ways
of the two parties diverged.   A surrender of opinions held

[1] Gal. ii. 5.   [2] Isa. xlix. 6.

from birth, was not to be expected, but, from the old
point of view, it was a great concession, to realise the
hopelessness of any attempt to change the mind of Paul,
and not to demand that he should incorporate Jewish-
Christian elements in his announcement of the Gospel.
And to this they agreed. It is pleasant to think that,
though they could not come to an inner unity of feeling,
the two parties found a peaceful solution of their differences, which preserved them in mutual harmony. Paul,
himself, relates, that they gave him and Barnabas "the
right hands of fellowship," recognising Paul as "intrusted
(by God) with the Gospel of the uncircumcision, as Peter
had been with the Gospel of the circumcision;" the same
grace being bestowed on the labours of the one, among
the heathen, as on those of the other, among the Jews.
The right hand of fellowship was the sign of Christian
confidence, and essential agreement, and now pledged
the old Apostles, that they should limit their labours to
their own people, while Paul was to announce the Gospel
to the heathen races. In all the discussion, however,
Paul is careful to tell us, the heads of the Mother Church
"imparted nothing to him," either in instruction, or in
claiming to give him authority as an apostle; a dignity
which he always regarded as bestowed on him by Christ, at
his conversion. But he had now obtained a formal apostolic
recognition of his own apostleship to the heathen; one
condition only being annexed, that he should not forget the
numerous poor of the Jerusalem Church; a duty near his
own heart, and faithfully remembered by him, all his life.

To this narrative by the apostle himself, Acts adds
what we must regard as supplementary particulars.[1] The

[1] Acts xv. 4 ff.

way had thus been prepared, by private interviews with
the leaders of the Church, for bringing the whole matter
before the brethren at large, as was desirable; that
the destructive agitation which was distracting every
one, might be abated, and future disturbance of mixed
churches at a distance, such as Antioch, by self-appointed
emissaries from Jerusalem, might be stopped. A gathering of the collective brethren in the city was, therefore,
arranged, and on the fixed evening, "the whole church"[1]
accordingly assembled; that they could thus come together
in one chamber, showing that, by flight from the old persecutions, or by removals, or return to distant homes, the
number of Christians actually in Jerusalem was not very
large. The first object of the meeting proved to be, that
a cordial welcome, and public official reception, might be
given to the missionaries. Having duly taken their places,
in the midst of the Apostles and elders; for the churches,
as will be remembered, were as yet modelled on the
synagogues, Paul and Barnabas, no doubt after the service
had been opened by prayer, followed probably by the
chanting of a psalm, "rehearsed all that God had done
with them" in their arduous travels in Cyprus, Asia
Minor, and Syria. The story might well have silenced all
cavil, but if the great majority were at one with the leading
men, in according the speakers their hearty sympathy and
brotherly greeting, dull bigotry could not change its nature.
Some brethren who, though Christians, were not only still
Jews in their feelings, but even clung to the Pharisees,
the most intensely Judaistic part of the nation, stood
up, objecting to what they had heard, and claiming that it
was needful, for their salvation, to require the heathen to

[1] Ver. 22.

become Jews in the fullest sense, and to keep the Law of
Moses, as the rabbis expounded it. Forthwith there was
a hot, and we may be sure, an angry storm of question
and attempted reply; confusion growing at least so wild,
that Peter rose to calm it down. Always ready of speech,
he now reminded the assembly, how, in the early days of
the Church, God had sent him to Cornelius at Joppa, that
he, a heathen, should hear from his lips the Gospel, and
believe; and how, knowing the heart as He did, God had
borne clear witness to Cornelius and those who believed
with him,—all heathen—that He received their profession of faith, by giving them the Holy Ghost as freely as
He had given it to Jews, making no distinction between
them and Gentiles, but cleansing the hearts of both alike,
by faith. Why should they demand new declarations of
His will in this matter, from God? It was no better than
putting Him to the test, after He had shown them His
pleasure; as if they would not believe Him unless He
repeated His announcement; one declaration not being
held sufficient. Why should they, moreover, tempt Him
to wrath against them, by seeking, contrary to His expressed will, to put the yoke of the Law on the necks of
the heathen converts, when neither they nor their fathers
were able to bear it? As for us, said he, Apostles and
elders, we believe that there is only one door into the
kingdom, through the grace of the Lord Jesus Christ, and
that we Jews, and these heathen converts, must be saved
in the same way, and on the same footing.

Having spoken thus, Peter sat down. The addresses
of Paul and Barnabas had been sadly disturbed before,
but, now, silence was obtained, while they finished their
rehearsal of the signs and wonders God had wrought

among the heathen, by them; thus corroborating the testimony to the Father's acceptance of believing Gentiles, as he had formerly done at Joppa.

James now rose, with his long-flowing Nazarite locks and beard, the strictest of Jews in his observance of the Law, but none the less firmly a disciple of Christ, his brother, and, like Him, full of generous charity. As head of the community, and venerable alike from his birth and his exact and holy life, his words fell with the greatest weight on the audience. "Symeon," he told them, had reminded them of what had happened at Joppa; which showed how God visited the heathen, to take out of them a people for His name. Then, in keeping with his supreme homage to the Old Testament, he quoted, from the Greek Bible, a passage of the prophet Amos,[1] clearly, in his opinion, anticipating the admission of the Gentiles into the kingdom of God, without any hint of their needing, first, to become Jews. "I, therefore," he added, in conclusion, " give it as my judgment," without dictating to others, " that we should not trouble those Gentiles who are turning to God " with the yoke of the Law, " but that we write to them that they abstain from the pollutions caused by the use of flesh offered to idols,[2] and from fornication, and from the flesh of creatures caught in snares, so that the blood has not been allowed to escape,—and, indeed, from blood in any way." That he urged even these limitations, rose, he told them, from the fact, that Jews were settled everywhere among the heathen; and, to lessen the shock of the abrogation of the Law, as no longer binding on heathen brethren, it was indispensable that their feelings be spared, on the points he had named, which were cardinal prin-

[1] Amos ix. 11, &c.   [2] Ver. 29.

ciples with all Jews. The Christians still attended the
synagogue more or less closely, and there, as also in their
own assembly, had "Moses" read to them continually.
It would, at once, rouse all Jews who were not yet Christians, against the faith, and kindle hopeless strife in all
Jewish-Christians, against their Gentile brethren, and
wreck the churches everywhere,[1] if less were required.

It was then proposed that a formal document, embodying the ideas of James, should be written out and sent
to Antioch, and the resolution having been put to the
assembly, it was adopted unanimously, by the Apostles,
the elders, and the brotherhood at large. Men were,
further, nominated to accompany Paul and Barnabas on
their return to Antioch; one, Judas Barsabbas, of whom,
otherwise, we know nothing, and Silas, or Silvanus, the
future companion of Paul; both of those thus honoured
being, we are told, "chief men among the brethren."
They were to carry with them the letter from the Jerusalem Church, while they were also to make known the
high esteem in which the two missionaries stood with the
mother congregation, as "men that have hazarded their
lives for the name of our Lord Jesus Christ."

This meeting of the Christians of Jerusalem, at which
the Apostles were present, from their being members of
the local church and in the city at the time, has often
been spoken of as "the first Christian council;" but a
council is an assembly of deputies, or representatives,
from a number of churches, and never a meeting of only
one congregation. It is a gross anachronism, therefore,
to apply the name to this assembly, for councils are of a
much later date.

[1] Lev. xvii. 13, 14 ; Deut. xii. 16, 23.

The effect of the letter from Jerusalem was all that could be wished, though, unfortunately, the peace it brought was only temporary, for religious controversies are the most irreligious of any. The "multitude" at Antioch, we are told, was duly summoned, and the letter delivered, filling all with joy at the consolation it brought. What became of a document so all-important is a curious question. To have produced it, when assailed, in his future journeys, by the same Judaising troublers, would surely have silenced them at once, and would naturally have given the same consolation to the distracted churches of Galatia and other parts, as it had given to that of Antioch. Yet we nowhere find the least allusion to it in the letters of Paul,—several of them filled with a defence of the liberal views which it covers with apostolic sanction—against the most embittered hostility and personal attacks. To have produced such a missive, signed by the Apostles themselves, should, assuredly, have ended the controversy and shamed his opponents, but he never refers even to its existence. It is not enough to suppose that his strong feeling of independence as an apostle dictated this withholding such support to his position, for he had communicated the document to the Church at Antioch and to those in the cities of Asia Minor, through which they passed.[1] May it have been, that the Judaistic attitude assumed very soon in the Jerusalem Church and its apostolic leaders, virtually neutralised the agreement with Paul, and deprived their letter of any moral weight when the controversy broke out fiercely once more, making the document of no value in view of their personal sentiments?

[1] Acts xv. 30 ; xvi. 4.

CHAPTER XV

PETER AT ANTIOCH

PAUL'S return to Antioch had been cheered by the consciousness that he "was not running, and had not run
in vain," yet the hopes of future harmony that for the
moment cheered him, were soon overclouded. Peace
had hardly been sealed before the hated strife broke out
afresh, far more bitterly than ever, absorbing, henceforth,
the best energies of his remaining years, and prolonging
the fatal division in the Church even after his death.

It must have been clear to him, indeed, on reflection,
that the action of the Jerusalem Church and of the
Apostles, had left the central question, in reality, unde-
cided. It remained doubtful whether it had been settled
that the heathen converts should be circumcised, or
whether they should retain their freedom till Christ,
whose return they all eagerly expected, from day to day,
should, Himself, definitely give His judgment on the
matter. On one point only, all were agreed, that, if Paul
could win heathen to Christ, no difficulty would be raised
against his doing so. As to the other Apostles, they
would, as hitherto, confine themselves to the circumcision.
This division of sphere is, indeed, constantly recognised
by Paul. He was "an apostle of Gentiles; a minister of

Christ Jesus" to them,[1] but this did not exclude the hope, on the part of the Judaisers, and possibly of James, who was so zealous for the Law, that hereafter, multitudes of heathen, and perhaps even Paul's converts, might be won to Jewish Christianity. Paul only once refers to the meeting at Jerusalem, and, then, merely to show that a positive result had not been formulated at it.[2] Yet it was a noteworthy sign of the loving spirit widely prevailing for the time, that differences, even on a matter so all-important to a Jew, did not hinder the right hand of fellowship being given to the daring innovator. That Paul had been "called" by Christ was acknowledged, though nothing was formally said of his recognition as an apostle; but this admission of the "grace given to him," was enough for mutual friendliness. The appeal for kind help to the poor of the community met, therefore, a glad response from him; all the heartier that, of his own accord, he was eager to soften the hard lot of the Jerusalem brethren. Their position was, indeed, sad, for without assistance from outside, the Church was in danger of breaking up. Things had been bad enough under Cumanus. The patriotic movement against the Romans, which was daily growing stronger, had led to the first bloody conflict during his procuratorship, and, now, the freed slave Felix, with his slave instincts, had succeeded to the government. A brother of the all-powerful Pallas, he forthwith began to plunder the unhappy province, till, at length, despair found vent in hordes of banditti, and the rise of the secret societies of Sicarii or dagger-men, who, coming to the front, in the last stage of the struggle in Jerusalem, became its rulers. Famine became chronic, and emigra-

[1] Rom. xi. 13; xv. 14–16; 2 Cor. x. 13–16; Gal. ii. 7–19.   [2] Gal. ii. 3.

tion swept off all who could flee from the land. To help those left behind, lay near the loving heart of Paul. "To do good to every one, but specially to those that were of the household of faith," was his motto for all the churches, but, above all, we may feel sure, for the Mother Church which had been the cradle of the faith; a spirit which introduces the needs of the brethren, by such touching words as that "God loveth a cheerful giver," and that if we "sow sparingly, we shall also reap sparingly."

Meanwhile, the great apostle must have pondered, in all lights, the issue of the Jerusalem meeting. It was clear that from whatever point of view it was regarded, the compromise of the old Apostles was hopelessly illogical. If Paul had convinced them of the truth of his gospel, they were not free to impose a limitation on themselves, which was tantamount to a shirking of part of their apostolic duty, but must, as much as he, feel bound to preach the faith to the heathen, without requiring circumcision. If, on the other hand, they still held that the Mosaic Law was permanently binding, they could not rightly admit that, alongside Jewish Christianity, there should be, with their sanction and approval, a heathen Christianity wholly independent of that Law. It would be a virtual contradiction of the claim, that entrance into the new kingdom could be secured only by its strict observance. Nevertheless, the "pillar" Apostles, when they bade adieu to Paul, remained, as before, "Apostles of the circumcision," and had no desire to work outside Judaism. They had, originally, been sent to the lost sheep of the house of Israel, and they remembered the words of Christ, "Ye shall not have gone through the

cities of Israel, till the Son of man be come." [1] It throws
an ominous light on the situation, moreover, that Paul
never speaks of any formal recognition of his apostolate,
when, in defending himself, he narrates the proceedings
at Jerusalem. So far from his full apostleship having
been accepted as officially recognised, the dispute respecting it began to come prominently forward again, very soon,
and the renewed controversy about the claims of the Law
led to authority being pitted against authority—that of
the Jerusalem Apostles being urged in their support, while
that of Paul, as their equal, was ridiculed. Nor was the
freedom of heathen converts from the Law more definitely
secured, than the acknowledgment of the independent
apostolicity of Paul. On the contrary, the discussion
at Jerusalem had for its result, that the zealots for the
Law everywhere dogged his footsteps, proclaiming the
Divine necessity of Judaism, among all the churches he
had gathered out of the heathen, and denouncing their
Christianity as fatally imperfect till they had accepted
Mosaism in its fullest sense.

The treaty of peace, if we may so speak, was thus, at best,
only a temporary truce, soon to be broken by the fanatical
majority of the Jerusalem Church ; a compromise like that
of the Peace of Augsburg, between Romanists and Pro-
testants, which really settled nothing, solving no difficulties, but only deferring their solution ; a mere patching
up of disputes, which would certainly be followed by a
struggle fiercer than that which had been momentarily
lulled.

Nor was the mortal antipathy to the New Liberalism
long in flaming out again more fiercely than ever, to blaze

[1] Matt. x. 23.

henceforth, inextinguishably, for a generation. It is notice-
able that none of the Apostles are said to have supported
Paul and Barnabas in their resolute opposition to the
proposed circumcision of Titus, though they are not said
to have sided against them. But they clearly remained
in heart devoted to their old opinions, else they would
hardly have separated themselves so entirely from Paul's
ideas, as is implied in their definitely confining themselves
to mission work among Jews only; leaving the outside,
uncircumcised nations to Paul and his fellow-workers.
This formal designation to evangelical labour appears to
have led to the leaders who were at Jerusalem, James excepted, setting out, soon after the departure of Paul and
Barnabas to Syria, on a mission tour through what one
might call the home districts; comprising the various
towns and villages of Palestine, where there were Christian communities or where preaching was hopeful — Lydda,
Joppa, Cæsarea, Sidon, Tyre, and perhaps Samaria, among
others; though we do not read of churches in Galilee, the
old birth-land of the faith. Peter and the "brethren
of the Lord" are named as thus occupying themselves;
their efficiency being aided by their taking with them
their wives, who could help them as Christian sisters;[1]
the Apostles generally, it would seem, adopting this custom. They lived, moreover, at the cost of the churches;[2]
in striking contrast to the practice of Paul, who had only
"brethren" as his companions and helpers on his tours,
and supported himself by his own manual labour, as did
those also who were with him. Mark, who had left Paul,
perhaps shrinking from his liberal innovations towards
the Gentiles, appears to have accompanied Peter habitually;

[1] 1 Cor. ix. 5.   [2] 1 Cor. ix. 4-6.

becoming like a son to him;[1] his attendance being perhaps at once necessary and grateful, if we are to suppose the old Galilæan fisherman unable to speak or write
in Greek, as was very probably the case.[2]

Coming to Antioch, either in the course of his missionary journey, or as seems more probable, by invitation
from the open-hearted "apostle of the heathen," Peter
had an opportunity of seeing for himself the work of a
Pauline church, and enjoying intercourse with its members.
The result, for a time, was highly satisfactory, for the
impulsive warmth of the apostle's nature found no difficulty in his joining heartily in the liberal usages that
prevailed. He not only consorted freely with the converted heathen, but, going far beyond this, took part in
the "love-feasts," or "Agapæ," in which they and the
local Jewish-Christians ate together, and virtually identified himself with the once heathen brethren by so completely assuming their Syrian ways, that Paul could say
he "lived as the Gentiles lived, and not like the Jews."[3]
It thus seemed as if the ultra-Jewish party in Antioch
was finally discredited. But this fond dream did not last
long. Peter had only repeated the hasty warmth which
had once before ventured on an element on which it
could not bear itself up, and had cried out, presently,
"Save, else I perish!" But he and the brethren who
had come with Paul, were not the only visitors who made
their way from Jerusalem to Antioch.

James of Jerusalem, who as the brother of Christ had
risen to a position of immense authority in the Church,
had apparently more or less shrunk back, as Peter was

---

[1] 1 Pet. v. 13.   [2] Eus. Hist. ii. 15, 16 ; iii. 39 ; vi. 14, 25.
[3] Gal. ii. 14.

too soon to do, from his momentary non-Jewish liberality

ST. PETER AND ST. PAUL (ON GLASS, VATICAN LIBRARY, DE ROSSI).

The lower portion represents the Lamb standing on Mount Sion (Rev. xiv. 1), from which, as from Eden, four streams issue, symbolising the Four Gospels, to unite in the mystical Jordan, the emblem of the waters of Baptism. On each side of the Lamb are the faithful—Jews and Gentiles—coming from the two cities Jerusalem (Jerusale) and Bethlehem (Becle).

The upper portion represents Christ (Dominus) on the Mountain of Glory, at the foot of which the Jordan flows in seven streams. He is giving commission to St. Peter, who bears the cross, the symbol of martyrdom, and to St. Paul. Behind each apostle rises the palm tree, the symbol, at once, of the fruitfulness of their labours, and of their triumphal welcome above, while the phœnix stands on the top, behind St. Paul; the symbol of immortality. Stars on the right and left hand of Christ (Rev. i. 16) represent the churches. Clusters of dates hang from each palm. A crown lies at the feet of St. Paul, and a palm branch is before his right hand, soon to be grasped by him, while the circles, on each side of the palm tree behind him, may be star-emblems of the churches planted by him, or, possibly, of his Epistles.

shown in the local conference with Paul and Barnabas.

He had stood aloof from Christ till after the Resurrection, when the appearance of the Crucified One to him, decided his thenceforth joining the disciples.[1] In the Jerusalem Church, when once more gathered after the martyrdom of Stephen, his relationship to Jesus, and also his commanding personality, though only a simple elder,[2] had raised him to a position which outshone that of any of the Apostles, especially as time wore on, and separated them more or less from the Holy City, which he never left. Like Peter he had fancied a sound compromise possible between the old and new preaching of his party and that of Paul. But when Peter had understood this in a more generous sense than the strict Jewish-Christians of the Mother Church, James, as one with them, and indeed their representative and mouthpiece, sent down delegates from himself to Antioch, to stop this irregularity, and these very soon forced weak-minded Peter back into his old Judaism. At the convention, James had treated the Mosaic laws of food as not essential to salvation, and therefore not to be laid on the heathen converts, but he none the less regarded them as permanently binding on born Jews, like Peter; though Christians. He could not, in fact, admit that Israel had the right to set aside any of the divinely given "customs" of the nation. Far more than Peter, he was, thus, the representative of the most intolerant section of Jewish Christianity, which accepted the essentials of New Testament faith, only as an addition to Judaism; its members remaining, indeed, in all respects, Jews, though recognising Christ as the Messiah. A Christian only after Calvary, he retained to the end his intense zeal for the Law, clinging devotedly to all

---

[1] 1 Cor. xv. 7 ; Acts i. 13.   [2] Acts xxi. 18.

the ritual and rabbinical frivolities which Christ had
unsparingly ridiculed. A Nazarite from his birth, never
tasting animal food, nor wine, nor fermented liquors,
never anointing his person, as is so necessary in such a
climate, never using a bath, never letting his head be
shaved, though the heat made head-shaving universal,
and never wearing any garments of wool, whatever the
weather, but only thin linen,—he was, indeed, a Jew ex-
tremist, to whom the least concession to a brother Jew,
as regarded the Law, or any admission of the possibility
of a Gentile's salvation, as such, would seem heterodox.
The despatch of emissaries from a dignitary so superstitiously venerated; armed, as they doubtless were, with
official letters signed by him,[1] proclaimed the opening of a
more disastrous crisis in the Church than would have seemed
possible in a religion based on love and spiritual worship.
But the average human mind is a small affair, and even
among Apostles, for one Paul, who realises the spirit of
the Master's teaching, and preaches it, there are always
at least the eleven, who find their heaven in the letter.

These half-converted Pharisees, far more Jewish than
Christian; loudly declaring that they alone represented the
truth; exalting the brother of Christ, their leader—at the
expense of the Cilician intruder Paul, of whom they would
not have a good word to say; soon broke up the harmony
prevailing till James had launched them against the great
Syrian congregation. That Peter should in any non-
Jewish way associate with the non-Jewish converts was
not to be endured. The will of the Jerusalem Church,
now represented by them—the church to separate from
which was schism—required a Jew to be faithful, every-

[1] Gal. ii. 12; 2 Cor. iii. 1; v. 12; x. 12, 18; xii. 11.

where, to every detail of the traditions of the fathers, and Peter had not been so, for had not he, a Jew, sat down in the common meals of the Antioch Church with non-Jews? They demanded therefore, in the name of James, as the representative of the Christianity of the Mother Church, that Peter should be the same man in Antioch as he was in the Holy City, and not repudiate in the one what he upheld in the other. But having sanctioned the Syrian innovation, the apostle could not draw back without at once injuring the local church, breaking faith with Paul, and exposing himself to the remarks of both parties. Nor had he any such clear convictions as might have enabled him to play the man. Rome—the Rome of these first days—had spoken, and he dared not disobey. To do so would be to break with "the Church." The strong will of James was too alarming to his impulsive nature to make independence possible, and he therefore surrendered unconditionally; "separating himself" from all social relations with the non-Jew converts, "for fear of the circumcision." The Gentile part of the church had thought him one of the "pillars" of Christianity, but found he was, in this case, only a reed shaken in the wind. The Jewish-Christian brethren, moreover, had their old scruples kindled into new life, and followed Peter in withdrawing from communion with the heathen-Christian brotherhood; no longer even joining them in the social love feast, or otherwise. The Judaisers, in fact, by winning over Peter, succeeded in making the Jewish brethren believe, once more, that the Law was binding on all Christians, and even waked the same old belief in Barnabas, who, perhaps bethinking himself of his belonging to the tribe of Levi, went over to the reaction, though he had so lately con-

tended, at the side of Paul, in Jerusalem, for evangelical
freedom; and had travelled with him on his great missionary journey, in which he had necessarily been a party
to the teaching which he now treated as error.   Perhaps
Paul, in frankly repudiating the authority of the Law, in
Antioch, had gone a step farther than Barnabas could
follow.   In any case, the results of the counter-revolution
were disastrous.   That heathen and Jewish converts could
no longer eat together was felt unendurable, yet a common
table, the Judaisers said, could only be restored, by the
heathen converts becoming, in all respects, Jews.   Against
such pretensions, the strong logical mind of Paul protested
with the utmost earnestness.   Nor did he mince his language, but, like Christ Himself, in his denunciation of
insincerity; like all sincere natures, in fact, in every age,
spoke out his opinion of the tergiversation of Peter and
Barnabas, with most unflattering directness.   Such conduct, he told them, was not " walking uprightly according
to the truth of the Gospel."   It was nothing but dissimula-
tion, that is, hypocrisy!   It both saddened and roused his
indignation, to see men who, yesterday, gave their hand
freely to a heathen brother, now drawing back from his
touch as polluting; to see those who had long eaten with
Gentiles,—dipping their hand into the same dish and thus
slighting the rules of Levitical isolation,—making, now,
scrupulous distinctions between clean and unclean, though
they had, hitherto, echoed the words of their teacher, Paul:
" To the pure all things are pure."   " The Jews," that is,
the Jewish-Christians of the church, " dissembled,"—in
other words, played the hypocrite,—" with Peter," said the
offended apostle of the heathen, " insomuch that even
Barnabas was carried away with their hypocrisy."   The

great cause of free Christianity, and, with it, of all the
potential expansiveness it embodied, for mankind at large,
had in Paul its one champion. Nor did he fail to see how
much was on the die, or how the most resolute and energetic decision and boldness were needed, to crush the threatening danger. When, therefore, Peter now came forward,
and demanded that the heathen Christians should restore
peace, by submitting to the Judaisers, and agreeing to
keep the rabbinical precepts, and also to be circumcised,
Paul stepped out before the whole congregation, and
"resisted him to the face," scourging his vacillation with
stinging words, and exposing the insincerity and indefensibleness of his conduct. "I said unto Cephas before them
all," he tells the Galatians, "If you, being a Jew—have
been living like a Gentile, and not like a Jew—as we have
seen you doing, till now,—how can you seek to compel
Gentiles to live like Jews?"

Paul, as usual, spoke with such uncompromising vigour,
that, from this time, opposition to his work became permanently active and embittered, as if he had irritated his
enemies till they had finally thrown away the scabbard,
and proclaimed irreconcilable hostility. In the Antioch
Church itself, he appears to have effected a restoration of
harmonious communion, but the extreme party of Judaisers could not so easily lay aside their passionate bigotry.
Henceforth, the churches, everywhere, were convulsed
with the excitement of a bitter and excited struggle,
between the champions of Jewish ritualism and the
defenders of spiritual religion. Nor would Paul bate a
jot of his principle. The whole future of Christianity was
involved in the dispute. The Judaisers accepted the
current rabbinical doctrine, that the Law, whether oral or

written, had been "ordained by angels," amidst the light-
nings of Sinai, "in the hands of a mediator,"—Moses,—and
assigned a moral quality to all its innumerable requirements; beginning with circumcision. It was as impossible
to get them to think of a perfect religious life, where
modes and forms and many specific rites, which they regarded as divinely appointed, were put aside, as it would
be, to-day, to get a bigoted Mahomedan to believe that he
could be religious, while repudiating the directions left by
the Prophet; or deduced from the Koran, since his day, by
the mollahs and muftis, its accredited official expounders.
Both Jew and Mahomedan held or hold, that exact obedience to ordained forms, is necessary, to give validity
to religious acts. The husk had, in fact, come to be
regarded essential. Paul's doctrine that we were saved
by faith, "without the deeds of the Law," was, to them,
equivalent to saying that, to be saved, we must sin. But,
to this, the apostle replied, trenchantly, that since faith in
Christ was all-sufficient, the idea of supplementing it by
"the righteousness of the Law" was to disparage it, as
needing to be eked out by mechanical acts; worthless in
themselves, as having no moral quality; and even hurtful,
as only a vain attempt to make a righteousness of our
own. A holy life, resting on loving faith in Christ, fulfilled, he held, all that was permanent in the Law of
Moses; bringing to the soul the "righteousness of God,"
won for us by the atoning death of His Son.

A theology so ideal, and so distinctively individual,
could not be easily introduced, among a race of hereditary legalists like his countrymen; especially, in an
age of the world when, as yet, outward form was of the
essence of worship. For we must not forget that Jesus

Christ stood absolutely alone among men of any race or
creed, in slighting washings, fastings, and rites, and that
Paul succeeded to his solitary protest on behalf of a religion of "spirit and truth." Nor must we forget how
hard it has been, in every age, to keep any number of
men to the height of a simple spiritual faith, or how
universally the materialistic has been craved, to supply,
through the senses, the realism which the grossness of
our religious faculties demands. Our own age, indeed,
even in English-speaking lands, shows, in the revival of
Mediævalism, how native to humanity is the temperament
that sees importance in ritual.

Under such circumstances, the Antioch controversy was
decisive as to the future career of Paul. From that time, he
took, fully and finally, the position to which his spirit and
character, as well as the express designation of his Master,
called him, and stepped out as the unfettered head of
heathen Christianity, with the whole fervour of his being.
He could hope for support only from disciples trained in
his school, for even Barnabas had left him; the last personal link that bound him to the Jewish-Christians. His
opponents could now assail him with less restraint and
more recklessly, when the companion of his journeys, who
had such close relations with the Jerusalem congregation,
retired from his side. Not that Barnabas fell back into
Judaism, for Paul speaks of him as still his friend, long
after their separation,[1] which, though caused originally
by a difference about Mark, must, none the less, be associated with the reproof Paul felt called upon to give him,
as well as Peter, at Antioch.[2] The worry of this miserable
controversy had, meanwhile, rekindled in Paul the desire

[1] 1 Cor. ix. 6.   [2] Gal. ii. 13.

for the relief of a new missionary expedition. There were
still men of " the circumcision," in Antioch, like Silas,—
known outside Judaism, as Silvanus ;—a " prophet" of the
church at Jerusalem,—who remained faithful to the apostle
during all the weary regretful strife, and was afterwards
chosen as his associate in the journey now projected.
He soon, moreover, won, in Galatia, the young Timothy,
whom he himself seems to have circumcised, and, ere long,
he, further, surrounded himself with a group of heathen
converts, whom he employed as preachers of the Messiah
Jesus; a phenomenon unique in those times, and hence
raising higher than ever, the distrust of the ultra-Judaisers.
But though the Apostles and Paul were, in one sense,
separated, there was no approach to schism. The recognised principle of this first generation was, that they
differed without dividing. Varying opinions might pre-
vail, and might lead to hot disputes, but the brethren
remained ready to work together ; believing that the
Master, when He came, as they believed He soon must,
would decide all. He might feel deeply moved by what
he regarded as the unworthy truckling of some, and the
airs of others, towards himself, but he never forgot the
poverty of the Jerusalem brethren, never ceased to speak
with love and esteem of Barnabas, and never, for a moment,
questioned the possession of the true Gospel by the heads
of the Mother Church, though they more or less identified
themselves with his opponents. That they, on their part,
rather discouraged than fanned, the ultra-zeal of the
Pharisaic firebrands, is clear, from the first bearing of
Peter at Antioch, and from the story of similar confusion
at a later time, at Corinth. Had there not been such a
mutual respect and essential confidence, it is inconceivable

that Paul would have visited Jerusalem twice, afterwards, as he did. Yet it is equally certain that the Jewish emigrants, in their constantly increasing spread among the foreign congregations, urged the highest claims of the Law as binding on all Christians. The sad traces of this odious agitation, indeed, met Paul in this very year, when, for the **second** time, he travelled through Galatia.

CHAPTER XVI

THE SECOND MISSIONARY JOURNEY

APRIL (?) A.D. 52—SPRING 55; PAUL'S AGE, c. 42-45

ANTIOCH must have been a far from pleasant place for Paul, after the commotion through which the Judaisers had dragged him, and, moreover, he had been, for one so unsettled, a long time in it. The restless energy of his nature had its vent only in missionary travel, which had become his passion, and he had now the letter of the Jerusalem Church, to show to the heathen Christians "in Syria and Cilicia," as it had already been handed to those at Antioch. The hostile Jews were constant in their attempts to undo his work in these regions, and thus, on many grounds, it was desirable that he should "return, and visit the brethren in every city, in which he and Barnabas had proclaimed the word of the Lord, to see how they fared." The difference with his old companion, though still unforgotten, had been more than forgiven, and he, therefore, proposed that the two should once more start together. But an unforeseen difficulty frustrated this generous design. Mark, or, as he is sometimes called, John, the cousin or nephew of Barnabas, had started with them on their former journey, but from some cause,—apparently, faintheartedness at the thought of crossing the mighty Taurus chain, and launching out on the unknown regions of the central tableland of Asia Minor,—had left them at Perga, in the unhealthy Pamphylian lowlands; where Paul, it would seem, had been already struck down by malaria, and thus, especially, needed a young man to remain with him. He was now in Antioch, and Barnabas, always gentle, wished him to be taken with them a second time. But Paul, like Christ, thought it a fatal sign when one who had put his hand to the plough looked back, and resolutely refused to take him. Barnabas, however, would not give way. The old sore of the recent Judaising was still fresh : "sharp contention" rose, and, in the end, Paul decided to start without Barnabas, since he insisted on Mark going with them. Each, therefore, chose his own field; turning each to his native province; Barnabas, who belonged to Cyprus, going thither with Mark; Paul setting out with his new companion, Silas, for Cilicia, whence he proposed to proceed to the scenes of his former labours. But the estrangement was by no means permanent, either towards Barnabas or Mark, for in the first letter of Paul to the Corinthians,[1] he speaks of Barnabas as the one man who, like himself, had kept from marrying on account of the missionary work, and had maintained himself by his own manual labour, instead of taking any support from the churches. Mark, moreover, reappears, in the kindest expressions, in Paul's letters, commending him to the hospitable graces of friends, and speaking of him as profitable to him for ministering.[2] But after the notice of him by Paul, Barnabas disappears from the New Testament, and only untrustworthy legends remain, which transfer him to Milan, Rome, and Alexandria, finally assigning him a

1 Cor. ix. 5, 6.   2 Col. iv. 10 ; 2 Tim. iv. 11.

martyr's death in his native Cyprus; where, indeed, a tomb, claiming to be his, is shown as the representative of the ancient Salamis. Of Mark we know almost as little. Many suppose he was the young man who fled at Christ's arrest, to escape capture, leaving behind his linen sleeping-cloth, in which, alone, he had hurried to Gethsemane; only the Gospel bearing his name recording the incident.[1] He seems to have been won for Christ by Peter, since that apostle calls him his son; the common phrase of "a father in Christ" for his converts.[2] In his latest epistle Paul asks, with endearing expressions, that he be sent to him as his helper, and since the apostle was a prisoner at Rome, Mark must thus have remained faithful to the last. He is said to have been the amanuensis of Peter, and, as such, according to tradition reaching back virtually to the apostolic age, "transmitted to us in writing, what had been preached by him."[3] In his later years, he is said to have laboured in Egypt, and to have founded the church at Alexandria. Peter, at an earlier time, speaks of him, moreover, as with him at "Babylon;" very possibly the city on the Euphrates, but possibly a symbolical name for Rome.

Silas or Silvanus, the new companion of Paul, had been a "prophet," or teacher, in the church at Jerusalem; whence, as we have seen, he was sent, among others, to Antioch, with the letter of the Apostles and presbyters, or elders. There, Paul came to know him, and the two substantially agreeing in ideas, he was chosen in the place of Barnabas as a fellow-traveller on the second great journey. The two, as we shall find, journeyed together through Asia Minor, and suffered imprisonment together, at

---

[1] Mark xiv. 51, 52.   [2] 1 Pet. v. 13.   [3] Eus. Hist. v. 8.

Philippi, where Paul speaks of both as being Roman citizens.[1] When Paul had to leave Berœa, Silas was left behind, with Timothy, to build up the converts, and rejoined Paul only at Corinth.[2] The letters written thence to the church at Thessalonica, were sent forth in the joint names of both, and Silas is further mentioned honourably, as a fellow-worker, by Paul, in his second letter to the church at Corinth, written, apparently, in the year 58.[3] From that time, however, he disappears from the company of the apostle, perhaps having returned to his labours among his fellow-countrymen; his name occurring in connection with Peter, whose first epistle he conveyed to the churches of Asia Minor.[4] But here the curtain falls ; all further notices of him being without any historical worth. He has been regarded by some as possibly the author of the Epistle to the Hebrews, but that he was so is a mere conjecture.

Some time about April 52, Paul and his new colleague were on their way to one after another of the churches of Syria, dear to the apostle as founded or built up by him, in his earliest labours, after his return to Jerusalem from Damascus.[5] Where these had been gathered is now as unknown, as is the locality of the churches of Galilee or those of Samaria, which are incidentally mentioned only in a single text.[6] Silas would naturally tell them of the Jerusalem meeting, and the letters from the church there, respecting the wretched controversy about Judaism, which was distracting all infant Christendom, would be read or delivered. They would then turn their faces towards

[1] Acts xvi. 37.　　　[2] Acts xvii. 10, 14 ; xviii. 5.
[3] 2 Cor. i. 19.　　　[4] 1 Pet. v. 12.
[5] Gal. i. 21.　　　[6] Acts ix. 31.

Cilicia, the home-land of Paul, reaching it by crossing the stupendous mountain chain of Amanus, either by the pass known as the Syrian Gates, or by that called the Amanus Gates, about forty miles farther north.[1] There are, in fact, three passes in the range, but each is only a narrow opening in the great sea of mountains, so difficult to cross, that Cicero thought no country could be better protected than Cilicia was, against Syria, by such natural ramparts; each pass being capable of defence by a very few men, from its narrowness. The Syrian Gates, through which the travellers may have penetrated to Asia Minor, are due north of Antioch, from which they are only twenty miles distant. The track, when it reaches the mountains, runs through dark defiles, four to five thousand feet deep, ending in a tremendous gorge, so narrow in one place, that it was barred by a gateway in the time of Xenophon; whence its name of the Syrian Gates. Once through this frightful labyrinth of peaks and precipices, the road sank towards the sea-shore, to which the mountains extended, as they do along the coast of Italy, or north of Beyrout, or at Carmel. The road by the Amanus Pass joined that through the Syrian Gates, at the river Pyramos, one of the chief streams of Asia Minor, which, after forcing its way through a glen of the Taurus range, so narrow in some parts, that, to use the words of Strabo,[2] a dog could leap across it, flows south-west, with a deep and rapid current, about a furlong broad and exceptionally muddy. Once over this, it is to be hoped by a bridge, it was only about forty miles to Tarsus, though they had to cross the Sarus, a river 300 feet wide, to reach it. In the then learned capital, attractive to Paul, alike from its

---

[1] Ainsworth's Map, London Geog. Jour., viii. 185.   [2] Strab. xii. 536.

varie**d** Gentile population, and its numerous colony of
Jews, including his father's family and the friends of his
youth, Paul would find abundant work as a missioner;
the one thing for which he cared.

Outside Turkey, it would be difficult to find meaner
streets in any part of the world, than those of Tarsus
at present; the very gate through which, perhaps, Paul
entered it, now standing isolated, in mouldering ruin.
But statues, temples, and altars then, doubtless, rose
everywhere, and grand public buildings showed that it
was the metropolis of Cilicia, while the gardens that still
stretch out round it, would be embellished by stately
mansions. Paul had spent some years, at one period or
other, in the city and neighbourhood, " preaching Christ,"
and his heart would, we may feel sure, rejoice over proofs
that he had not " run in vain," for, even within a few years
back, large numbers of lamps and figures, associated with
idolatry, have been found, in this region, not broken or
worn out, but apparently thrown deliberately away; as if
their owners, having abandoned idols, whose images the
lamps bore, and with whose service the figures had been
connected, had cast them " to the moles and to the bats;"
their characteristics, moreover, showing that they date
from the apostolic age.

But the heart of the great missionary yearned after the
little flocks he had been forced to leave, in the moral
wilderness beyond the mighty summits that looked down
on Tarsus, from a few miles distance. To reach the tableland of the interior, meant a journey of at least forty
miles of constant and often perilous and exhausting ascent;
for the foot hills of the great range come down almost to
the city. He could not cross the mountains before June;

the track being buried in snow-drifts till then, but it was probably still later when the two "ambassadors for Christ"[1] bade farewell to their friends and fellow-Christians at Tarsus, and set out, presumably on foot, on their arduous mission of love. The terrible difficulties of the pass prevented all heavy traffic from using it either way, nor was it practicable even for camels or pedestrians, except at a cost of exertion and even danger, hard for dwellers in Western lands to imagine. Wild torrents have to be crossed a hundred times; fearful descents, and as fearful ascents to be overcome; here, the track skirts a dark precipice; there, it creeps along the edge of a mighty perpendicular wall of rock. Even to look up to the fearful heights, one beyond another, inspires awe. I saw them in April, when they stood out against the sky, black with forests, to their upper peaks, which stretched away, in snowy grandeur, far up into the lofty heavens. The fact that Ibrahim Pasha had to blast a passage for his artillery, before it could be got through the one pass from Tarsus, known as the Cilician Gates,—an opening so narrow till then that loaded camels could just get through, of itself speaks volumes for the hardship such a route involved. Reaching the tableland at last, the travellers must have followed the road which skirted the north face of the mountains, with occasional ascents of outlying spurs; their destination being Derbe, which lay about a hundred and twenty miles west of the Cilician Gates.[2] Nothing is told us of the incidents of the meeting between Paul and his converts. The greetings of his new companion; the inquiries after the fondly remembered Barnabas; the story

---

[1] 2 Cor. v. 20.   [2] Ramsay's Map.

of their little history since the apostle's former visit; the
counsels, encouragements, and exhortations he gave them,
in public, and in their separate houses, must be left to our
imagination. We may be sure, however, that the great
danger of a reaction towards Judaism; threatened, even
so early, from the sleepless intrigues of local Jews, or of
Jewish-Christian zealots, whom trade journeys brought to
Derbe, would not be forgotten. It was, in fact, the pressing anxiety on Paul's mind; for if no one could be a
Christian without first submitting to become a Jew, and
adopting Jewish life in its isolating peculiarities, the new
faith could never be more than a petty sect, instead of
revealing itself as a universal religion, destined to be co-
extensive with the Roman Empire, and even with the
whole habitable world. What disaster would it bring on
his aspirations, if a Christian, by being so, could not enter
a neighbour's house for fear of defilement; if he could
not eat without ascertaining if the food was Levitically
clean and the flesh Levitically killed ; or,—if bought in the
market,—proved not to have been part of a creature of
which some portion had been offered to an idol ; whether
the fruit on the table had grown in the garden of a
heathen ; whether the vessels used for a meal had been
Levitically purified ! If a Christian learned, like the Jew,
to look on a heathen neighbour with abhorrence, from his
wanting the peculiar physical mark of an Israelite,—drawing back from him as he would from the swine's flesh
which the one loved and the other counted abomination,
—what hope could there be for the wide spread of the
Messiahship of Jesus, so dear to Paul's heart! Still more,
if converts were won over to believe, that the thousand
petty rites and traditions of the rabbis were essential to

salvation, what became of that righteousness by faith
in Christ, which Paul rightly held able to save to the
uttermost, that is, completely, all who draw nigh to God
through Him?[1] Christ speaks of the zealots of His day,—
the scribes and Pharisees,—whom He pronounces hypo-
crites,—as compassing sea and land to make one proselyte; these long-frocked recruiting-sergeants of Judaism,
devoting their lives, supremely, as has been already said,
to thus enrolling a secret militia, against the final breaking
out of the great War of Independence, under the Messiah,
when Rome would be crushed, and Jerusalem take its
place as the capital of the world. The milder sections of
Israel were contented if Gentiles adopted the morality
of the Law, without the observance of its rites, or submission to its legally initiatory humiliation, but the wilder
bigots would hear of no compromise. Thus Josephus
tells us, respecting the conversion of the royal family of
Adiabene,[2] that a Jewish trader who had won over the
ladies of the court, and Izates, the future king, to worship God, dissuaded the prince from being circumcised,
telling him he could worship God without the hateful
rite; the worship of God being of more importance than
circumcision; a liberal and noble view, which the prince's
wife, Helena, supported by the strong argument, that she
would leave him if he turned in the full sense a Jew,
since in such a case she feared for his throne and life.
Another Jew, however, from Galilee, appeared after a
time, on the scene; a bigot who held, like the Christian
Jews who came from James at Jerusalem, to Antioch,
that except a man was circumcised, he could not be saved.[3]
Coming upon Izates when he was reading the Law in

[1] Heb. vii. 25.   [2] Page 313.   [3] Acts xv. 1.

private, this rigorist forthwith told him that "it was necessary, not only to read the Law, but to observe it; that he was guilty of great impiety in acting as he did; outraging the Law, and, through it, God Himself. How long would he remain uncircumcised, when the Law made that rite its first imperative demand;" language so alarming to the prince that he submitted to the humiliation forthwith, at the risk of losing his kingdom.[1] But to be marked thus as a Jew, was to become an object of ridicule to the world at large, while, on the other hand, the Jew looked with insulting contempt on all outside his small race, because they had not this stamp of belonging to the people of God. No wonder, then, that Paul urged, with all his boundless fervour, the vital importance of contending for the liberty wherewith Christ had made His followers free, and that they should stand fast in it and not be again entangled in the bondage of the Law.[2]

From Derbe, the missionaries bent their steps to Lystra, from thirty to forty miles north-west,—avoiding the great marshes on the north,—to the plain below Derbe, and skirting the Isaurian hills,—the old Lycaonia,—then, as now, a wild and partially unsettled country of little culture. It was here that the multitude had sought to worship him and Barnabas, on his former visit; but things had quieted down so that we hear of no disturbances now.

The disciples of Jesus had gone out two by two, and Paul, in accordance with this, liked to have two companions; the one a full associate; the other, as it were, a young helper, useful for many things, and at the same time, receiving the best possible training for independent action in the future. He had set out with Barnabas and

[1] Jos, *Ant.* xx. 2, 5.   [2] Gal, v. 1.

Mark, on his former journey, and, now, he was so fortunate as to find Timothy, the dearest of all his junior companions. Among the converts won when at Lystra before, had been a household of whom we know only the grandmother Lois, the first convert, the mother Eunice, and the grandson Timothy. The lad had been t ught the Scriptures from a child, for the family had always been pious Jews, though Eunice had married a Greek. Under Paul's preaching, however, they had accepted Jesus as the Messiah, and Timothy, ever since his turning a Christian, had made himself useful, not only at Lystra, but even so far off as Iconium ; the brethren at both places speaking very favourably of him.[1] His whole soul was, thus, evidently, devoted to the Christian cause, and his aptness in its service was in keeping with his love of it; for *heart* in such matters is the fundamental guarantee of fitness. Of this early enthusiast for Christianity, we have a specially full memorial; his master's love of him delighting in personal allusions, which bring him vividly before us in the two epistles that bear his name. He must have been only a lad at this time, for twelve years later, not long before the death of Paul, the apostle tells him, in the first letter to him, not to submit to be treated slightingly on account of his youth. The duties at that time intrusted to him, show, farther, the modest position he must have held so many years before. He was to be an example to all the Christian membership, in word,—that is, in his religious instructions and tone of speech generally, whether in public, in the church assemblies, or in private intercourse,—in manner of life, in love, in faith, in purity ; and to give attention, till Paul's arrival, to the

[1] 2 Tim. i. 5 ; iii. 15 ; Acts xvi. 2.

reading of the lessons in public worship; for the Christians had adopted and continued, the Jewish custom of reading prescribed portions of the Law and the Prophets, at their services. And as the reader was in the habit of addressing the congregation,—he was also to give heedful attention to the enforcement of the doctrinal and practical deductions from them;—to make them, in fact, his care and study. To these duties he had evidently only gradually been advanced. Paul's love for him was touching. He was his "true son in the faith," his "beloved and faithful child in the Lord," his "brother and God's minister in the Gospel of Christ,"[1] and was trusted by him with the most confidential commissions.[2] He seems to have been of a very modest and almost shy nature, for Paul bespeaks for him, incidentally, such a welcome from the Corinthian brethren as may make him "without fear."[3] Yet, timid as he was, Paul sets him high above all his other fellow-workers, nor did he deceive himself in doing so; for, in all his persecutions and imprisonments, the young attendant remained true to him, when stronger natures had drawn back. No wonder that, since the child is father of the man, brethren at Derbe, Lystra, and Iconium, had foretold his future admirable career.[4] As is said of Jesus, with the young man; that, beholding him, He loved him, Paul evidently loved Timothy at first sight, but as he was the son of a Jewess, and as in these times of Judaistic contention, it was desirable to avoid such useless irritation to the legalists, as the going about with a half Jew by blood, who had not the special mark of the race on him;

---

[1] 1 Tim. i. 2 ; 1 Cor. iv. 17 ; 1 Thess. iii. 2.
[2] Rom. xvi. 21 ; Col. i. 1 ; 1 Tim. i. 18 ; 2 Tim. i. 2, and other texts.
[3] 1 Cor. xvi. 10.   [4] 1 Tim. i. 18.

wishing, perhaps, also, to please his mother and grandmother, who may have retained Jewish feeling in the
matter, the apostle induced Timothy to submit to the
Jewish rite, which he apparently himself performed on him.
The Jews were always very indignant when the child of a
Jewess, whose father was still heathen, was made, as they
thought, an apostate from the faith of his people, by being
left uncircumcised; just as the Roman Church makes a
great ado, if the children of mixed marriages are not
baptized and brought up Roman Catholics.

Some weeks would pass before the party could start, but
when all was ready, Paul and Silas, with Timothy, "went
on their way through the cities" in which Paul had
preached and gathered churches on his former journey,
"delivering them the decrees to keep, which had been
ordained by the Apostles and elders at Jerusalem."[1] This
would require them to spend some time in the country
parts where there were small churches; but the main
points must have been Iconium and Pisidian Antioch.
Henceforth, Paul always appears with two companions,
as on the former mission, for, as Silas and Timothy were
with him now, Titus and Timothy were with him in
Macedonia and Achaia, and Luke and Aristarchus accompanied him when he went to Rome. To reach Antioch,
they had to pass through Phrygian Galatia; Phrygian by
one way of speaking, Galatian by another,—the region in
which Antioch stood. North Galatia, a vast bare country
of bleak uplands, hot and dusty in summer, and buried
in snow in winter, had few attractions for them, but the
cities of Nicomedia and Nicæa, in Bithynia, were the
centres of local civilisation, wealth and administration,

[1] Acts xvi. 4.

and, hence, we may conclude, had a more or less numerous Jewish population. among whom Paul thought an opening might be found for the Gospel. A great line of travel, moreover, linked Antioch to this region, stretching north, through Dorylaion.

Paul's original intention had been to preach in the province of Asia, which extended from some distance east of Antioch, though that city was not in its limits, to the coast, on the west; including, in all, about a third part of the whole of Proconsular Asia, or, as we say, Asia Minor. The old Phrygian country, linked in the popular mind with Galatia, by its pre-Roman history, and now absorbed in the "province of Asia," lay north and west of Antioch. But, some reasons having come in the way of his itinerating in it as he had proposed, reasons very properly assumed as Divine intimations, the little band set out across the Phrygio-Galatian part of "Asia," through which they were free to pass, though they could not preach, in doing so; their idea, now, being to go into Bithynia, the border of which lay more than a hundred miles north of Antioch.

They had already travelled so far north as to be "over against" the province of Mysia, that is, apparently, so far north as to have it on their left hand; which was first possible after they had journeyed sixty or seventy miles north of Antioch; when, a second time, hindrances rose; coming, as Paul expresses it, from "The Spirit of Jesus," which "suffered them not" to enter Bithynia at all. One may suppose that a sudden fit of illness is meant, for, with Paul, everything that happened to him was always viewed as "a messenger," either from above, or from Satan. They had, therefore, to turn westward, and skirt the south edge of Mysia; a course which, at last, brought them to Troas, on the coast of the Ægæan, close to the Hellespont, and thus to Europe.

That their way should have been guided to this spot sufficiently explained the "hindrances" so trying for the time. Before them there now rose the vision of the great Western world; the world of all those races whose genius and energy had subdued the East; the world of culture and political power, to win which for Christ, must have been the cherished dream of such a mind as that of Paul. To gather churches in Asia Minor was well, but to make the religion of the Cross that of the mighty empire which dominated the earth, would be a triumph worthy the name; replacing the crown of thorns by the diadem of universal sovereignty over the spirits of all mankind.

Some time in the course of his comparatively early relations to Paul, the young helper, Timothy, whom his mother had so generously spared for attendance on the apostle, was set formally apart to the higher work of the "ministry." He had, at first, been, apparently, like the attendants on Old Testament prophets; such for example as Elisha, in his relations to Elijah; with the view of ulti- mately being advanced to the responsibilities of a Chris- tian teacher and leader; as the attendant on the prophet was, in due time, admitted to the full rank of the pro- phetic office. When this took place, in Timothy's case, is not said, but I cannot imagine, with some, that it could have happened before leaving Lystra, when he had en- joyed any of the advantages of training under the eye of Paul. It would, however, seem natural to think of this solemnity, as taking place in some congregation where Timothy was known; if only to make it the more impressive on himself and those present. The proceedings at this earliest "ordination," to the public service of Christ, reported from apostolic times, are, fortunately, in some measure, to be gathered from hints left by Paul. First of all, it would appear, the deacon-elect "confessed the good confession," of faith in Jesus as the risen and glorified Messiah, "in the sight of many witnesses;" that is, no doubt, before the public assembly of the local Christian community, met in their "synagogue."[1] Then, apparently, members of the brotherhood gave their testimony respecting him,—stating how every one had long foretold the kind of man he would prove. The imposition of hands followed, in imitation of the practice of our Lord, when, asked to "lay His hands" on little children, or, according to SS. Mark and Luke, to "touch them."[2] It was, indeed, an immemorially old and beautiful usage among the Hebrews, for Jacob had laid his hands on the heads of the sons of Joseph,[3] and Moses had laid his hand on Joshua, when he was appointed to be leader of the people.[4] Hence, the Semicha, or "laying on of hands," had, from remotest antiquity, become the recognised form of setting apart rabbis, judges, or magistrates. In the case of a rabbi, the chief of those present added the words, "I promote thee to be a rabbi; be thus promoted." From the time of Hillel, that is, from the generation before Christ, only the official holding a formal written authorisation, from the head of the Sanhedrim, could confer this "degree" on any one; two witnesses, moreover, being required, to testify in favour of the candidate. The license thus given to act as a rabbi, might, however, be a partial

---

[1] 1 Tim. vi. 12.   [2] Matt. xix. 13-15; Mark x. 13-16; Luke xviii. 15-17
[3] Gen. xlviii. 14.   [4] Numb. xxvii. 18; Deut. xxxiv. 9.

one, allowing the recipient, for example, only to judge in money causes, but not to teach respecting the permitted and the forbidden, or the reverse; or giving power to judge money matters, but not criminal; and the authority might be granted for only a fixed time. The candidate, duly admitted as a rabbi, by the laying on of the hands of a duly authorised member of the order, was not, however, allowed to take the name of rabbi while he who ordained him lived, but was known as his habair,—colleague, disciple, or attendant,—nor was he allowed to teach publicly, till thought worthy. A newly ordained rabbi, moreover, taught, sitting on the ground; or standing, if his ordainer was present.[1] This "ordination" Timothy now received; the elders of the little community and the apostle unitedly laying their hands on him.[2] The hands of Ananias had been laid on Paul, himself, at Damascus, and he had again been similarly set apart to his missionary journey, by the hands of the "prophets and teachers" of the congregation at Antioch.[3] In the early Church, every office was called a "gift,"[4] and that to which Timothy might feel himself divinely chosen, was to be indicated by his special aptitudes in his future labours. Meanwhile, he had received official sanction, as, like the young rabbi, capable of promotion hereafter, to any section of Christian activity for which he might show fitness. He had, as it were, obtained his commission; his rise to any post was now possible, though as yet he was only an ensign or lieutenant, or as we now say, a "deacon," in the Christian warfare.

[1] Buxtorff, Lex., art. *Semicha*, 1498.   [2] 1 Tim. iv. 14; 2 Tim. i. 6.
[3] Acts ix. 12; xiii. 3.
[4] Rom. xii. 6–8; 1 Cor. xii. 28–30; Eph. iv. 11, 12; 1 Pet. iv. 10, 11.

In spite of the company of Silas and of his dear young friend Timothy, Paul must have been broken and wearied, alike in mind and body, when, after walking, for weeks, from Derbe, with occasional rests where there were churches, he at last reached Troas. After leaving Iconium, where he was on the west edge of the great Lycaonian plain, the whole country through which he and his companions had passed, was more or less mountainous; huge conical isolated mountain masses rising, from point to point, even where the prospect was comparatively open; as the great " Black Mountain " had lifted its huge bulk far up into the heavens, in the landscape of Iconium. Travelling on foot, day after day, over hill passes, or through valleys often rough; with very humble food, very poor accommodation by night, and constant exposure to heat, or cold, or tempest, as might happen, was sadly exhausting. Hence Paul, a feeble man, at best, seems to have quite broken down long before the journey ended; his health, very probably, being the indication which he regarded as Providential, that he should not preach in " Asia," and should not enter Bithynia. But, in addition to all this, there was the corroding anxiety as to the permanence of his work. Whether from Celtic excitability, or, rather, as is more probable, in the regions he visited, from the Oriental natures of peoples like those of Lycaonia and Phrygio-Galatia,—instinctively fond of a ritual and ceremonial system like Judaism,—there seemed too much likelihood that the Jewish-Christian agitators, who had already disturbed the churches he had gathered, would be still more energetic and hurtful in his absence. It appears, indeed, as if a particular opponent, whom he does not name, but who must have been of some consequence and standing in the little Christian world, was a special trouble to him. Perhaps Paul did not hear whom it was, or know his name, but his words show how much he was distressed. " Ye were running well, *who* did hinder you, that ye should not obey the truth ?—A little leaven leaveneth the whole lump,—he that troubleth you shall bear his judgment, *whosoever he be.*" [1] The disturber may, very probably, have had no special bias against Paul, but may have been some Jewish-Christian, or even a Jew, who, like countless others of the race, utilised his passing through a region, to preach his faith at every stopping-place. It was thus, indeed, to a large extent, that Christianity and Judaism spread. Men travelling on petty or larger business, were very often the first-century missionaries, and this may have been one of them.

One gleam of joy, however, lighted up the hours of Paul's stay in Troas, for here he met Luke, " the beloved physician ;" [2] henceforth the most esteemed of all his "fellow-labourers," [3] and his close companion, to the very last, except at intervals of work assigned him at a distance, for the apostle writes, from his second confinement at Rome, a short time before his martyrdom; " only Luke is with me." [4] Tradition says, he was born in Antioch, of Gentile, not Jewish blood, and Paul mentions him apart from those companions who were " of the circumcision." [5] Of his social position we know nothing, for his being a physician is compatible even with slavery; many slaves being educated by their masters for the learned professions and the arts. The supposition that he was also

[1] Gal. v. 7–10.   [2] Col. iv. 14.   [3] Philem. 24.
[4] 2 Tim. iv. 11.   [5] Euseb. Hist. iii. 4 ; Col. iv. 11, 14

an artist, rests only on the authority of authors who lived nearly a thousand years later,[1] so that the claim of likenesses of our Lord, and of some of the New Testament worthies, having been painted by him, is utterly worthless. *When* he became a Christian is not known, though tradition may possibly be right in regarding him as one of the Seventy. That he was not with Christ " from the beginning," is expressly stated by himself.[2] Yet he may have been won by the preaching of Christ, at a later period, and may, as some fancy, have been one of the two whom He accompanied to Emmaus; the incident being noticed only in Luke's Gospel. But, after all, he may just as probably have been one of the Antioch congregation, won by the preaching of Paul, or some other of the founders of the church there. That he met Paul at Troas seems implied in the abrupt introduction of the plural, " we,"[3] in the narrative, at this point, but what led him there is not said. Perhaps he was already working for the Master, either independently, or as an assistant of the apostle. He appears to have gone with him to Philippi, but the change of person on Paul's leaving that city, hints at his having been left behind in it. We next hear of him, on Paul's return to Philippi, on his third journey; as if he had been labouring there in the interval,[4] which was no less than seven years. Then, however, he accompanied his chief, from Miletus, to Tyre and Jerusalem.[5] On Paul's voyage to Rome as a prisoner, Luke would not leave him, but shared his dangers and shame. During the first imprisonment, his noble love and devotion kept

---

[1] Nicephorus, A.D. 980, is the first who mentions it.
[2] Luke i. 2.   [3] Acts xvi. 11.
[4] Acts xx. 5.   [5] Acts xx. 5 ; xxi. 18.

him by Paul's side,[1] and I have already spoken of his presence with him when the Second Epistle to Timothy was written, which seems to have been during his second imprisonment. From this the apostle was let go, only to be arrested, a third time, two years, at most, later, and handed over to the headsman's block. With his death, Luke virtually disappears from notice, for only the most confused and contradictory traditions of his future life remain. We know neither when he died, nor where, nor his age when he rejoined his martyred leader and friend. As with many other noble spirits to whom the world is indebted for the greatest bene-factions, Providence has seen fit to let his work be his only record, veiling personal details in impenetrable obscurity; as if to remind us, that fame on earth is not worth seeking; work for God carrying its high reward here, in the good done, and, hereafter, in the welcome accorded to the faithful servant.

[1] Col. iv. 14; Philem. 24.

CHAPTER XVII

ALEXANDRIA TROAS, or simply Troas, where Paul now was, lay on the coast of Asia Minor, opposite the south-east end of the island of Tenedos. When the apostle saw it, there was a large population. Originally built by Antigonus, one of the heirs of Alexander's empire, on the military road along the coast, it had been settled by sweeping into it the people of a number of neighbouring towns, and when incorporated in the Roman dominions, had been strengthened by a military colony, sent to it by Augustus; carrying with them the privileges which a colony enjoyed. Its modern representative, the village Eski, is nearly deserted, but many remains of former splendour tell what it must have been in Paul's day and later. These mementos cover a wide space, and include arches of a stone aqueduct, ruins of public baths, and fragments of walls, rising in a circumference of several miles. All the marble pillars and fine stones, however, have long ago been carried off to build edifices in Constantinople. The harbour from which Paul sailed is all gone; its docks and breakwaters having disappeared under the reign of Turkish barbarism, that has made the whole country, once one of the finest in the world, a mere waste and neglected "garden of God."

On my first visit to the East, I crossed the Archipelago from Cape Matapan; sailing, north-east, towards the Dardanelles. Beyond Lemnos, as we came near the land, Mount Athos rose six thousand four hundred feet high, far in the north. Presently, the coast of Ionia appeared on the east; the shore, low and bare, reaching back to more or less distant hills and mountains, or to the table-land of a high plateau. The light had all things for its own. The air, the hills, the sea, and the rolling coast plain, were all, alike, bathed in splendour. Far and near, the waters quivered like white flame, pouring, as if from some sea-like lake, in a broad river of trembling fire, towards the east. Flocks of sea fowl skimmed the glittering surface, and settled here and there, as one has seen on some inland loch.

Anchoring off Troas for the night, I had before me the landscape on which Paul looked out, when he reached the old city. Tenedos lay about eight miles off on the west, swelling up like a shield from the waters; a round hill forming a boss in the centre. Lemnos, forty miles off, still west, showed a fine outline of romantic heights. Twenty-five miles north-west, rose the hills of Imbros, and far beyond them, but in the same direction, towered up the still higher mountains of the island of Samothracia. The plain of Troy begins at Troas, reaching, in low swampy undulations, to distant hills and table-land; Mount Ida rising in stately majesty above a sea of hills, fifty miles off, to the east. Ten or twelve miles due north, was the sharp bend into the Dardanelles, across which, low banks, covered with verdure, revealed the first glimpse of Europe.

Paul looked out on this view, across waters white with the sails of numberless boats and vessels, hailing from the

strange wondrous regions of the great western world,—
the queen continent of the earth,—from which had come
—by the puny hand of unaided Greece, at Marathon and
Salamis,—the first shattering blows at the claims of Asia
to put Europe under Oriental despotism;—from which,
like a radiant war-god, the Macedonian Alexander had
led his host, in the following century; overthrowing, from
the Mediterranean to India, the empire of the Great
King;—from which had then followed, in the track of
his victorious standards, the art, the culture, the commerce, the philosophy, of Greek civilisation; creating, in
all Western Asia, a reflection of Greek life and manners,
—and from which, finally, had appeared the colossal
power of Rome, mistress of the habitable globe, whose
proconsuls and governors, whose laws, and whose language,
were supreme among all nations and tongues, from the
Atlantic to the Indus, and from the scorched depths of
Africa to the snows of the frozen north. No wonder that
a soul capable of such lofty imaginings as that of Paul,
kindled at the possibility of its being permitted to him, to
plant the Cross on the shores of the western world, and
thus take possession of it for his Lord; the crucified and
risen Messiah; the destined Saviour of mankind. To bow
the head of imperial Rome to the Prince of Peace,—to
found, in a truer sense than Israel had ever dreamed, that
world-empire of its God, Jehovah, which his countrymen,
in all lands, were working, night and day, to bring about,
by the tortuous arts of political ambition, and vain pre-
parations for violent revolution; was a grand conception.
He, too, would revolutionise the existing state of things,
but it would be by winning over the hearts of men to
willing obedience to One whose kingdom rose high above

earthly thrones; in the far nobler sphere of truth, and peace, and love. Full of such splendid visions, the dreams of sleep reproduced them in a living embodiment, which seemed to beckon him irresistibly on. Macedonia was the province of the great Roman Empire nearest Troas,—for Thrace was not made one till the reign of Vespasian— A.D. 69–79,—and as Paul lay sleeping, a Macedonian stood before him, entreating him, in the touching words—" Come over into Macedonia and help us,"—to preach the Gospel in Europe. The die was cast. He would, forthwith, turn his face westwards, to conquer a new world for Christ.

Neapolis, or as we should now call it, Naples, " the new city," was the port to which Paul resolved to sail, on this magnificent crusade. It lay about a hundred miles north- west of Troas, and would be easily reached, by any of the cloud of vessels which must have been constantly passing to or from Europe, in established " lines" of this or that company, or by private " service."

White sails specked the waters thickly when I saw them, and no doubt they were much more numerous nineteen hundred years ago. It took Paul four days to sail from Nea- polis to Troas on the return voyage, but the little company of evangelists were more fortunate now; for the first day brought them under the lee of Samothracia, which is little more than a great mountain, towering out of the blue sea, and the second night saw them safe at their destination. We can infer the appearance of the port, in some measure, from that of Levantine coast-towns now. There would be the same mixture of East and West, the same pro- vision for harbourage, and the same style of houses; but also, I fear, a little of the neglect which seems to mark all places in the East or near it.

Philippi, to which the travellers were going, lay about ten miles inland, but was easily reached from Neapolis, as that town was the coast-ending of the great Egnatian Road, which crossed Macedonia and Thrace, on the one hand, and stretched away, on the other, to Thessalonica, on the west. Climbing a defile through the hills which lie close behind Neapolis, by the massive squarely paved causeway of that military highway, between precipices almost overhanging the sea, the missionaries would have a glorious view behind them on gaining the crest; if they chose to interest themselves in anything but their errand. Yet it is doubtful if they did; for Nature calls forth no enthusiasm in any of the Epistles. So far as Paul was concerned, its charms appeared to have been overlooked by a mind so entirely absorbed in other attractions, and perhaps without the poetical sensibility which marks the human side of Christ. Looking down before them, towards Philippi, a plain, level as the sea, lay at their feet, framed, in the nearer and further distance, in a background of mountains, of which some, within a sweep of thirty miles, rose to a height of from four to eight thousand feet.

The beauty of this wide-stretching landscape has been famous in all ages, when the brooks have not, by their spring floods, converted its hollows into marshes, or winter stripped it of its verdure. In the cold months, snowy peaks look down on it; in summer, the slopes are hidden with roses, and every loveliness of shrub and flower. Philippi had been virtually built by the father of Alexander, who had chosen for it the site of an old Thracian town, and given it his name. It had been created, to form a border fortress, for the protection of Macedonia from the Greeks on the south, and the Thracians on the north; a purpose for which it was well suited, from its lying on a steep height which commanded all approaches, either from the hills or the sea. On the west it was defended by swamps; on the north and east, by the gold-bearing chain of Pangaeos; and, on the south, by marshes, which extended to the sea-shore. The only stream, however, near it, was the rivulet Gangas; the comparatively navigable Strymon, being more than a day's journey to the west.

On the wide plain beneath the town, the great battle known by its name, had decided the fate of the world, a little more than a hundred years before Paul's visit; for here, in B.C. 42, Octavian and Antony had revenged the murder of Cæsar, by the rout of the so-called republican leaders, Brutus and Cassius. Behind the marshes, as the least defended point, Antony had made the first unexpected onset on Cassius, whose legions had been drawn up along the course of the streamlet, on whose now quiet banks Paul was, presently, to meet with some pious women who had chosen it for their place of prayer. Here, Cassius had sought escape from a worse fate, by voluntary death; an example followed by Brutus twenty days later; the two despairing of their own star and of that of Rome. Philippi had been famous for its gold mining, for ages, but the industry had latterly flagged. The great battle, however, secured it a new and higher prosperity, for Octavian, that is, Augustus, presently made it a Roman colony, with colonial rights; shrewdly settling it with disbanded soldiers of Antony, whom he naturally wished to keep out of Italy. Proud

Coin of Philippi.

of its having Roman citizenship for all its burghers, the
city became more Latin than Greek ; Latin even becoming
the local tongue; the gods of Latium, also, being set up
with all their rights, and the plain dotted with towns,
which made it seem a Roman county reproduced on the
borders of Thrace. The population seem to have been industrious, quiet and orderly; honest, thoughtful, and gentle;
following the old worships of their forefathers in a more or
less rude simplicity. Round them, the rich plain, abundantly watered and carefully irrigated, grew everything,
from grain to vegetables and flowers. Tall poplars, still a

Macedonian Coin.

favourite tree in Asia Minor and the south-east of Europe,
stood out against the sky; willows bent over the banks of
springs and rivulets led from them ; figs cast their broad
shadow in the orchards and along the paths; cherries
abounded, and wild vines more than equalled the luxuriance of their cultivated rivals in the numerous vineyards. As at the upper end of the Lake of Galilee, the
broad marshes offered a perennial joy to the great, heavy-
eyed, black buffalo, with great horns bent flat backwards,
along the sides of the head, which alone was to be seen
above water, and we may be sure there were bees in

abundance and many coloured butterflies, **for the** young
to chase and every one to admire.

This new field chosen by Paul was in every way more
hopeful and cheering than his last. He had no longer to
do with effeminate Syrians or fickle Phrygio-Galatians,
but had come to a more manly race. They might be
harder to win, but the work done was enduring.
Partly rough miners, partly old legionaries, partly men
engaged in different occupations, who found a living in
such a military but peaceful inland town; those of them
who listened favourably to Paul and his fellow-mission-
aries became, not only their faithful personal friends, but
showed themselves true-hearted and constant in their
devotion to Christ. The fidelity of the Macedonian
character, which was proverbial in the ancient world,
shone out in the converts who yielded to the new faith.
Hard-working, conservative by instinct, utterly opposed
to the restless turbulence of the loquacious, disputative,
Greek municipal town-life, the race was the soundest and
most noble of the old world, and hence proved itself,
on the one hand, the most stubborn opponents, and, on
the other, the truest upholders of Christianity. From
first to last, the relations of the apostle to the Philippian
congregation were those of tenderest friendship. They
had none of the fickleness and inconstancy of their Asia
Minor brethren, and nothing of the self-conceited factious-
ness, and light instability, of the Greek congregations; but
were, at all times, true, obedient, helpful in the " work,"
and sympathetic.[1] Nothing was more anxiously avoided
by Paul than the taking contributions towards his support, from the churches; but he had no scruples about

[1] Phil. i. 5 ; ii. 12.

accepting money-help from the Philippians, all through
his journeys; feeling sure that there was no risk of misconception, or abuse of his confidence, in their case.   Even
when he lay in bonds in Rome, indeed, we find their " messenger, and minister to his need," at his side,[1] and, even
then, when he was old, and worn out, and in chains, he
" trusts in the Lord that he would once more come back
shortly," to a people he loved so well.[2]   It is touching,
moreover, to notice the glimpses of local colouring which
this affection throws into his epistles to them ; whether at
Thessalonica, on the west of Macedonia, or at Philippi, on
the east.   Writing to a city full of old legionary veterans,
in a province always famous for its military spirit, the
camp and the battle-field supply his imagery.   He sees, once
more, " the man of Macedonia," in full armour, and exhorts
his converts to " put on the breastplate of faith and love,
and for a helmet, the hope of salvation."[3]   The Philippians were his " fellow-soldiers " who had " fought, with
him, for the faith of the Gospel."[4]   Amidst the " crooked
and perverse generation" of Greek populations round
them, they were to be like torches, " holding forth the
word of life,' or " like sentinels on their watch,"[5] and to
" stand firm," as fellow-combatants, with himself, " in one
spirit, with one soul fighting for the faith ; having no fear
of their adversaries."[6]   He cheers them by the good news
that the grounds of his imprisonment are already known
favourably through the whole camp of the Prætorian
Guard, at Rome.[7]   They had public games and chariot
races at Philippi, as everywhere else, and these he uses to

[1] Phil. ii. 25.   [2] Phil. ii. 24.   [3] 1 Thess. v. 8.
[4] Phil. i. 27 ; ii. 25.   [5] Phil. ii. 15 ; 1 Thess. v. 6.
[6] Phil. i. 27, 28.   [7] Phil. i. 13.

urge them to zeal in running for a heavenly crown.[1]
They had the Roman citizenship, and were proud of it;
he reminds them that Christ had made them citizens of
the heavenly Jerusalem, which was far better.[2]   His whole
soul goes out to them.   " Their names are written in the
book of life;" they are " his joy and crown." [3]   Like himself they may well hold out, bravely and meekly, for ' the
Lord is at hand."   Their triumph and his, will soon be
proclaimed by the voice of the archangel and the trump
of God, as the Crucified One descends in the clouds, with
power and great glory.[4]

Philippi, which was honoured, like some other towns
elsewhere, with the title of a " first city " of Macedonia,—
though Amphipolis was the political capital, and, in other
respects, the first city of the district,[5]—had, apparently,
attracted Paul and his companions from its seeming likely
that they would find a Jewish community there.   For
Jews liked to settle in towns where there was a Roman
garrison—as at Antioch, Iconium, Ephesus, and Troas;
the presence of Rome securing them from the hatred of
the native races.   It was, moreover, attractive to Roman
citizens, like Paul and Silas, as promising personal safety.
But the number of local Jews must have been very
small, since there was no synagogue; though, as it was
obligatory that even if there were no proper building,
synagogue service should be established wherever there
were ten Hebrews; there was a place for public prayer,
outside the city, on the banks of the Gangas.   Only a few
Jewesses, however, attended it; drawn to the town, we
may suppose, by trade, like Lydia, or selling " purple " cloth,

---

[1] Phil. iii. 12–14.   [2] Phil. iii. 20.   [3] Phil. iv. 1, 8.
[4] 1 Thess. iv. 16.   [5] Eckhel, i. 4, 282.

of which thirteen shades were not prohibited as royal; so
popular was it, in one tint or other, all over the Empire.
The missionaries had reached the city in the early part
of the week, and employed the interval till the Sabbath,
our Saturday, came, in surveying their new ground, and
planning their future work. It proved that their only
chance of meeting a gathering of what Jews there were
was at their "place of prayer," chosen, as I have said, at
a quiet spot, outside the town, on the small local stream,
which bursts out of a hillside, about a league and a
half from Philippi, in a strong fountain, like those in
the bed of the Dog River in Syria, or that of the Jordan
at Dan. On this rivulet, away from the noise of the town,
and the risk of unfriendly or light interference from their
heathen neighbours; in a slight enclosure, open above, or
even in the open air, a small band of women, assembled
at least each Sabbath; perhaps Jewesses married to
Gentiles; perhaps only proselytes of Gentile birth;
"devout women" who, not satisfied with heathenism,
had turned to the worship of Jehovah, though not in
other respects "Jews." The brook at hand was, indeed,
a special attraction, from the facilities it offered for the
many ablutions connected with almost all worship, in
antiquity. Hither, the little company of preachers betook
themselves, when Sabbath came, and, sitting down with the
women, spoke to them, through Paul, of the great tidings
that the Messiah had actually come, in the person of the
crucified, risen, and glorified Jesus. Among the group,
we are told, sat Lydia, the dealer in purple fabrics, who
was originally of Thyatira, in Asia Minor, a place which,
curiously, has yielded in late years, an inscription recording the great dyeing trade carried on in it. She is

expressly described as a proselyte, that is "one that worshipped God," so that she was not a Jewess, but, by birth,
a heathen Her heart, "the Lord opened, to give heed to
the things spoken by Paul." There and then, it may be,
she sought baptism, with her household; the waters of the
Gangas offering all that was needed for the rite. Nor was
her acceptance of Christ only a passing emotion. From
its first beginnings, she became the mother of the little
congregation which soon confessed the faith of the Nazarene in the town. It is more probable, however, that some
interval elapsed, between her first hearing Paul, and her
admission to the Christian communion, for we are told
that when she and her household had been baptized, she
pressed the missionary band to be thenceforward her
guests, "if they had judged her to be faithful to the
Lord,"—which implies her having proved her sincerity in
a longer or shorter probation. At a later date we learn
the names of some others, who were, like her, won to
Christ, from her fellow-worshippers at the river-side;
Euodia, and Syntyche, then loving enough no doubt, but,
alas for human nature, afterwards far from being of one
mind; though when Paul was at Philippi "they laboured
together, with him, in the Gospel." [1] Before long, men
joined the Christians; among others, Syzygus, on whose
name, which means "yoke-fellow," Paul plays, by calling
him a true "Syzygus,"—all that his name conveyed—a
true fellow-worker with himself, in heart and deed. There
was Epaphroditus, also, whom we meet with Paul, in his
imprisonment at Rome, whither he had brought kind
gifts from the Philippian Church, and whom he calls his
"brother and fellow-soldier, as well as their messenger

[1] Phil. iv. 2, 3.

and minister;" who had "come nigh unto death, hazarding his life" to do all for him that, as he knew, the brethren would like to have been done.[1] We, further, read of one Clemens, otherwise unknown, and, finally, of a number of faithful souls whose names are not given, though they are honoured as "the rest of my fellow-workers, whose names are in the book of life."[2]

How long Paul remained at Philippi is not told, but such a band as he gathered, could not have been won except gradually; nor could the close affection, which bound the apostle and the Philippians in fondest tenderness till his death, have been called forth, except by the endearments of prolonged intercourse. At the close of his life, indeed, he could say, "I thank my God upon all my remembrance of you,—for your fellowship in furtherance of the Gospel, from the first day until now," and that "God was his witness, how he longed after them all."[3]

But the peaceful weeks or months of his stay were, ere long, to be rudely interrupted. The place of prayer had become that of the Christians' gathering, and one day, as Paul and Silas were going to it, perhaps with their comrades, a poor slave girl met them, whose highly nervous temperament, exciting her brain, and joined to a power of ventriloquism, had led her to be regarded, according to the superstitious notions of antiquity, as possessed by a spirit; whose utterances were found in the words issuing from her while her lips were closed; as in the case of ventriloquists generally. She may have been consciously a cheat, but she may, also, have been honest, as some of the "mediums," her counterparts in our day, no doubt are.[4] We may regard her, in fact, as a clairvoyante, whose

[1] Phil. ii. 25-30. [2] Phil. iv. 3. [3] Phil. i. 3-11. [4] Acts xvi. 18.

mental condition, under whatever mysterious laws, led her
to claim insight into the distant or future. She was the
property of a number of persons, who had, we may suppose, bought her as a speculation, getting payment from
the people who consulted her, believing in her powers.
Day after day, the poor creature, able, in her half imbeci-
lity, to feel something of the force and truth of what she
had heard fall from the lips of the preachers, or of what
some one had reported them to her as saying, followed
the little band, calling out, "These men are servants of
the Most High God, who proclaim to you the way of
salvation." That he and his work should run the risk
of being supposed such as demons were pleased to patro-
nise and wish God-speed, troubled Paul greatly ; for like
Christ, when in the same way acclaimed by the "possessed,"
he recognised "unclean spirits " as the real speakers in such
cases.[1] Turning round, therefore, to the girl, as she kept
crying out, behind him, he "said to the spirit, I charge
thee in the name of Jesus Christ, to come out of her."
That moment she was calmed, and the "possession " was
gone. What this really means, is impossible for us, with
our utter ignorance of the spirit world, to tell ; but if only
the therapeutic aspect be regarded, may it have been that,
as the girl looked on Paul as a servant of the Most High
God, and as clothed with power from Him, her hallucina-
tion of being inspired by some "demon " passed off when
she heard it adjured in the name of a far Higher, to leave
her; her mind being thus suddenly cleared, and restored to
a natural and healthy condition ? However it happened,
her being cured was the immediate cause of the first persecution of Christianity by the heathen. Her masters

[1] Mark iii. 11.

seeing at once that their hitherto heavy profits were annihilated, were furious, and setting the rabble on Paul and Silas, who may have been the only two present at the moment, dragged them into the market-place, and fiercely denounced them before the prætors, or duumvirs of the town, then holding their open-air court. "These men," said they, "being Jews, exceedingly trouble our city, and set forth customs which it is not lawful for us to receive or observe, being Romans." It was a dexterous thrust, to speak of them as of that most hated of all races, the Jews, while they, themselves, the aggrieved, were as dignified as the offenders were the reverse; "being Romans!" Claudius had expelled the Jews from Rome in A.D. 48, some years before this, and both people and magistrates would know this; if, indeed, it was not the reason of only women being found at the place of prayer. The introduction of foreign religious usages and rites, in opposition to the legalised public faith, was a great offence among the Romans. To add to the trouble, the infuriated slave-owners had stirred up the worthless idlers always hanging about the market-place, ready to make a tumult to order, on promise of pay, and these, now gathered in numbers, set up wild howling, and began to fall foul of the accused. Disturbance of the peace was, with the Romans, as with us, a serious misdemeanour,[1] especially, when, as in this case, it threatened any industrial interests, the riots against Paul at Thessalonica, and at Ephesus, springing, as, now, at Philippi, from these grounds. The town was in an uproar, whoever was to blame, and these men were of the everywhere detested Jews. The duumvirs, had they been cool and self-possessed, would have demanded proof

[1] Acts xvii. 7; xix. 26.

of the charges made, but they lost their heads, and, without hearing the case at all, or justifying their decision
by evidence, ordered the prisoners to be stripped, and
scourged on their bare backs by the lictors, with their
stout flogging - sticks, there and then, in the public
street. Among the Jews, only thirty-nine blows could
be given, but there was no such merciful limitation
among the Romans, so that "many stripes were laid
upon them." They might have claimed exemption from
this torture, as Roman citizens, but the hideous uproar
very probably made it impossible for them to get a
hearing, try as they might. It was not unlawful to beat
Roman citizens with rods, but to beat them "uncondemned" was a very different matter.[1] Besides, they
seem to have been beaten, not with the lighter ones,
with which even Roman citizens might be scourged in
certain cases, but with the heavier rods used on provincials or slaves. At best, however, it must have been
a terrible punishment, for after their backs had been
bared, they would be tied to a frame, and beaten, in
presence of the magistrates, with as many blows as these
officials thought fit to inflict; death under the rods being
not unknown. Josephus speaks of the very bones being
sometimes exposed.[2] But this was only the beginning
of the torture of the Christian preachers. They were,
further, committed to prison; the jailer being specially
charged to keep them safely. Prisons were arranged on
very much the same plan over all the empire. They
were generally connected with the municipal or government buildings, and consisted of two parts. Of these, the
outer, was a chamber opening from the prætorium, and

[1] Winer, *Leibesstrafen;* Pauly, *Verbera.*   [2] *Bell. Jud.* vi. 5, 3.

surrounded by cells, which enjoyed the light and what air
could reach them from the external chamber. It was here
that Paul was confined at Cæsarea, where the prison was
in the "prætorium of Herod." From this outer ward,
however, there was a passage to the "inner prison," called
robur or lignum, from the bars of wood which formed
the "stocks" in which prisoners were secured, in bad
cases, or from the walls having originally been of oak. It
had no window or opening, except the door, which, when
shut, absolutely excluded both air and light. Into this,
Paul and Silas were thrust, though the magistrates who
thus maltreated them, were only local justices; without
authority to act summarily, or otherwise, in criminal
matters. To protect himself from their possible escape,
they were, here, set by the jailer with their feet in the
stocks, or lignum. The horrors of this "inner prison" are
often dwelt upon in the story of the early Christian confessors. Its awful darkness, its heat, and stench, were
fearful, as may be well supposed; for prisoners were confined in it, night and day, without either exercise or
renewal of the air. But there was a still worse dungeon,
the Tullianum, so called from the original prison at Rome,
on the back of the Capitoline Hill, facing the Forum, to
which a steep flight of steps leads from it. A narrow stair
goes down to this dismal pit, from the level of the prison
entrance, but, long before I saw it, water had risen in the
lower depths, and cut off all access to them. The upper
prison is only some rough stone arches, but the dungeon,
below, must have been beyond description horrible. A
round hole in the floor was, in antiquity, the only entrance
to it; prisoners being, we may suppose, let down into it, as
Jeremiah was into his prison in the miry pit. "There is a

place in the prison," says Sallust, " called the Tullianum "
—from the king of Rome who added it to the prison
above,—" sunk about twelve feet under ground. Strong
walls line all sides of it, and, overhead, there is a vaulted
roof, bound together by stone arches; but its condition,
from neglect, darkness, and stench, is foul and horrible." [1]
Such a deepest depth there would, in all probability, be,
underneath the midnight blackness of Paul's dungeon;
the pestilential terrors it hid rising in deadly effluvia, to
poison still more the already putrid air.   But

> The mind is its own place, and, in itself,
> Can make a heaven of hell, a hell of heaven.

The first generation of Christian missionaries, like some
of the early representatives of similar tidal waves of religious enthusiasm in later ages, were so filled with a lofty
conception of the glory of their Master, and held it such
honour to suffer for His name, that it transfigured and
illuminated their lives, as light glorifies all on which it
shines. The dark pestiferous cell was so transformed,
by their spiritual exaltation, that the gloom around only
heightened the light within. As, in the natural world,
the stars kindle the heavens with their glory, only when
night has veiled all things below; the splendours of
eternity shone down on these confessors, now, when all
temporal interests were blotted out, as they had never
done when their life had been brightest.   Does not God
dwell in thick darkness?   Did not the Psalms declare that
the darkness and the light are both alike to Him; the
night shining before Him as the day? [2]   So—cramped, as
they were, in the galling stocks, tortured by the wales

[1] Sall, *Cat.* 55.   [2] Ps. cxxxix. 12.

and cuts of their scourging, now stiff and swollen, and
clotted with blood, there, as they sat, or lay, on the foul
rough floor, "fast bound in misery and iron, in darkness and the shadow of death," Paul and Silas "cried to
the Lord in their trouble." Assured, moreover, that He
would hear, and that this "light affliction," which, at
worst, was "only for a moment," was His will, for some
gracious purpose, they alternated their prayers with rejoicing hymns, probably from the old Psalms,—already, for
ages, the "songs in the night" of all the afflicted children
of God. Other prisoners were shut up with them; the
usual tenants of a Roman jail; runaway or delinquent
slaves, debtors, thieves, robbers, roughs of all kinds; but
even such company did not abate their fervour. Prayers
and hymns, amidst the horrors of an inner prison, seemed
strangely out of place, but even the outcasts among whom
they lay dropped their loud ribaldry and wickedness, to
listen. And now, we are told, "suddenly, there was a
great earthquake, so that the foundations of the prison-
house were shaken : and, immediately, all the doors were
opened, and every one's bands were loosed." Roused out
of sleep, in a moment, by the heaving shock, and the
wild clamour of universal alarm, and seeing the prison
doors open, the jailer assumed that the prisoners had
escaped, and knowing that, whatever the cause, and however unworthy he might be of blame, he would certainly
be put to death, and preferring anything to such disgrace, he drew his sword, to kill himself. But, at that
instant, a loud cry from Paul saved him. The apostle,
even though he could see nothing, knew what might be
expected. Shouting out, "Do thyself no harm : for we
are all here," he made the terrified man put his sword

back into its sheath. "Lamps and torches, here," cried
he, to his warders, and, when these came, sprang through
the open door, trembling for fear, and fell down before
Paul and Silas. Their bearing from the first, their very
looks, their prayers and hymns, which he may have heard;
the cry of Paul, which had saved his life, and the story of
their power over the slave girl's demon, which he would
know, combined to fill him with awe; and, that an earthquake should have followed their imprisonment, showed
that they were, assuredly, in alliance with the gods.
Bringing them, therefore, to the outer ward,—no doubt
locking the door behind them, on the other prisoners, as he
did so,—the thought of what he had heard of their preaching, about the end of all things being at hand,[1] and, of
the earthquake, a moment before, took form in an eager
cry—"Sirs, what must I do to be saved?" "Believe on
the Lord Jesus, and thou shalt be saved," answered his
prisoners, "thou and thy house." He could know nothing,
or next to nothing, about Christ, but he believed in those
who spoke of Him, and accepted their counsel. At most,
he could only, for the time, have been eager to hear about
Jesus, and disposed to receive what they advanced as
reasons which should make him believe in One, in whom
they themselves trusted so implicitly. For belief can come
only from conviction, and conviction must rest on adequate
grounds. They, therefore, "spoke the word of the Lord
unto him, with all that were in his house," for they had
all gathered into the ward, and, there, with the lamps and
torches for light, the great truths, of there being only
one God, of man having sinned, of Jesus having lived,
and died, and risen again, to satisfy the broken Divine

[1] 1 Pet. iv. 7 ; Rom. xiii. 12 ; Phil. iv. 5; 2 Thess. ii. 2.

law; of His resurrection, and of His speedy return, in the clouds of heaven, to judge the living and the dead, were, no doubt, recited, with all the impressiveness of deep sincerity and assured conviction. How could the wondering listeners hesitate, at such a time, with such divinely accredited preachers? Then and there, the jailer and all his household declared themselves Christians. This change of relation brought, forthwith, change of bearing towards the prisoners. They must be confined till formally set free, but the jailer could at least get their wounds dressed;—for they had been too much absorbed in their message of love, to think about themselves, and still endured all the increasing misery and pain of their yesterday's maltreatment. Now, however, in "the same hour of the night" their convert "took them and washed their stripes." But he and his needed another washing, still more beneficent, as the symbol of their having broken with their heathen and sinful past, and of their having become "new creatures, in Christ Jesus." The jailer and "all his" were, therefore, we are told, baptized immediately. The whole scene had passed very quickly, and, now, all was changed with the household and its head. Bringing the missioners "up into his house, he set meat before them, rejoicing greatly, with all his house, having believed in God."

We may be sure that men to whom the keeper looked up with so much loving reverence would suffer no more indignities while in his charge, and that they were allowed to remain his guests till day. Then, however, the prætors having come to themselves, and feeling the danger of their illegal conduct, in ordering them to be scourged while nothing had been proved against them, sent the lictors to the jail, with an order that they should be let go. Glad at heart, the jailer forthwith led the messengers to them, and the official permission to leave was announced. But Paul could now repeat his words of yesterday, which the uproar had kept the magistrates from then hearing, and was resolved to make them feel the legal trouble they had brought on themselves, by their cowardly yielding to the mob. "We are Roman citizens," said he, and "they have beaten us publicly, uncondemned, and do they now think of casting us out in this private way? No, verily; they must themselves come and bring us out." It was enough. To have beaten men that were "Romans" was a very serious offence, and entirely beyond their legal authority. Hurrying off, therefore, to the jail, in person, on hearing this, the justices besought them to pardon the unfortunate mistake, and having brought them outside, which they would not have stooped to do, had they not been thoroughly humbled, they begged them to leave the town. To do this would, on their own account, be safer, at least till matters had calmed down, and, therefore, they resolved to go. The house of Lydia, their hostess so long, was none the less lovingly open to them, than it had been when all was quiet, and thither, therefore, they first went; sorely in need of the peaceful rest it offered, after the excitement and physical tortures of the past twenty-four hours, and the horrors of the inner prison. But even the refreshment of sleep would hardly have fitted them for starting on a journey at once. They must have lain in the friendly shelter of this hiding-place for some time; the infuriated owners of the "pythoness" slave, and the mob, thinking, perhaps, they were safe in the tender mercies of the jail. Meanwhile, word was passed round to the "brethren," to meet them in Lydia's house, and hearty, indeed, would be the mutual greetings, when souls bound together by such true affection, on both sides, once more, after such troubles, could look in each other's face. How deeply Paul felt what Silas and he had endured, is touchingly shown in his reminding the brethren in Thessalonica, at the other end of Macedonia, in his first letter to them, written about two years after this, how, as they had heard,—for the story had probably been told them already by himself, as well as possibly by visitors from Philippi,—he and Silas had "suffered" in that city, before coming to Thessalonica, and had been "shamefully entreated." Long and frequent discourse would be held with the little band, with due exhortations and counsels, and their organisation into a "church." This, in these earliest days of Christianity, meant virtually their being formed into a Christian synagogue, or as it would be called in Macedonia, an *ecclesia*, both words meaning "an assembly," "gathering," or "meeting," though our word "church," the usual translation of "ecclesia" in our Bibles, has now, largely, acquired a different sense.[1]

In the letter of Paul to the Philippian Church, written about ten years after this, he addresses its "bishops" or overseers,—elsewhere called, from their age, instead of from their office, "presbyters" or elders,—and "deacons,"[2] the two grades of officers needed for the effective management of the congregation, from the first. These may, therefore, very probably, have been set apart by Paul, with the concurrence of the members, as usual. The pres-

---

[1] The only case in which it is rendered, in its natural sense, "an assembly," is in the account of the uproar at Ephesus. Acts xix. 32, 39, 41.   [2] Phil. i. 1.

byters or bishops, in this elementary stage of the development of the Church, were, as already stated, the counterpart of the "elders" or "rulers" of the synagogues,[1] elected by vote of the members; a custom from which, doubtless, the popular vote, in elections to office, in the earliest Christian assemblies, was taken; a right formerly enjoyed by the Jews among them, necessarily being continued when these became Christians. The "deacons," by parity of reasoning, we may regard as the counterparts of the inferior officials of the synagogue—"the ministers," or, to use English for Latin, "the servants,"—who attended to details connected with the building, and the lesser offices of public worship, besides carrying out the orders of the rulers, generally. We must carefully avoid transferring to these simple days, the developed institutions of later ages, if we would see things as they were in the apostolic times.[2]

A few days' rest having, in a measure, restored the late prisoners, they, at last, no doubt secretly, started for the West. As, however, Luke, apparently, had not been compromised in the riot, he remained in Philippi, to continue the good work. Nor did he see Paul again, it would seem, for about six or seven years.

[1] Acts xiii. 15 ; Luke vii. 3.

[2] It is pleasant to see, in these days of traditional fancies, that Bishop Ellicott, and some others, following Jerome and Chrysostom, recognise that in the Epistles to Timothy and Titus and in the New Testament generally, "bishop" and "presbyter" are used interchangeably. See, especially, Hatch, "On the Organisation of the Early Christian Churches," passim.

CHAPTER XVIII

SECOND MISSIONARY JOURNEY (*continued*)—THESSALONICA AND BERÆA

A.D. 52—SPRING A.D. 55 ; PAUL'S AGE, *c.* 42–45

THE three missionaries, Paul, Silas, and their young companion Timothy, when leaving Philippi, travelled along the great military "Egnatian" road, called so, perhaps, from the town Gnatia or Egnatia, on the south-east coast of Italy, a little north of Brundissium; a place much frequented in antiquity, from the Appian Way running to it from Beneventum, a little south. This coast road continued round the head of the Adriatic, through Epirus, to Thessalonica, and thence, through Philippi, to Byzantium, the modern Constantinople.[1] It was, throughout, paved with the massive squares, or cubes, of stone, still seen on the Roman military road down the coast of Syria, and in the wonderful paving of some of the streets of modern Naples. Always very narrow, according to our ideas, these military roads were, otherwise, admirable, so that, even now, the causeway laid by Rome along the promontory north of Beyrout, though in sad disrepair, is the only road, in these parts, north and south. Along the Egnatian, the legions of Cassius and Brutus had marched to their doom at Philippi, and other hosts, before and after them, had borne or were to bear their standards, this way or that, over its vast length.

[1] Pauly iii. 58.

The first stage of the Christian missioners was to Amphipolis, the chief town of a district, and the nominal capital of Macedonia as a whole; a much larger and much more important place than Philippi. The road to it ran south-west, through a broad valley, behind the range of mountains which roughened the coast-line, and it was a long day's journey from Philippi. At Amphipolis they were again near the sea, for the town lay about three miles from the mouth of the Strymon, on the banks of which it was built. They only rested here, however, for the night; passing on, next day, over the same great road,—which here crept along the narrow fringe of coast plain,—towards Apollonia, about thirty miles farther on.

Two days would, probably, be spent in reaching it, and they would take at least one night's rest, when they got thus far; the end of their present journey being Thessalonica, which lay another thirty-six miles off. But Orientals never travel quickly, and we may feel sure that at least

Sandals.

four or five days passed,—perhaps more—before they at last ended their toils. The city lay on the sea, in an amphitheatre of hills, its streets rising one above the other from the waters, on the north-east corner of the Gulf of Therme. Mountains fill the landscape whichever way you look, but the eye turns with special emotion to the jagged peaks of Olympus, white, till late in the year, with snow, rising in the south-west, on the other side of

the great gulf, about 10,000 feet above the neighbouring sea. These rough heights, poetry and superstition
had fabled as—

"The gate of heaven, guarded by the Hours
To whom the heaven and also Olympus were entrusted,
That they should now open wide, now close, the veiling
    clouds." [1]

But nature, in spite of all its glories, was apparently
without special interest to Paul, and he was not likely
to turn with any eagerness to the rocky throne of the
gods of Greece which, to him, were only "devils," [2]
the ghostly foes of the Eternal Father, zeal for whose
glory was the consuming passion of his heart His road
thus far, had been in great part through a succession
of wondrous visions of great valleys sleeping at the
feet of shadowy mountains. Picturesque villages had
looked out from the folds of the hills; the slopes and
wide straths were, ever and again, shaded with rich woods,
or dotted with park-like clumps of all manner of trees,
and uncounted orchards; the clearest waters had threaded
the fields or meadows all the way to Amphipolis. And,
when he set out, once more, from that town—not making
any stay in it from its being a purely Greek city, without
a Jewish population,—after leaving the estuary of the
Strymon behind him, he had passed through a region of
noble woods and open fields, between the sea and the
mountains; skirting the shore, with its glorious landscape
of deep blue waters; and had then crossed the deep gorge
where the Arethusa drains off the waters of the great
lakes behind. Nothing could exceed the beauty of the
woodlands, or the wealth of shrubs and ferns of all kinds,

[1] Iliad v. 749-751.   [2] 1 Cor. x. 20, 21 ; 1 Tim. iv. 17.

on the slopes, or the deliciousness of the air, and the charm of the countless brooks, as he travelled on to Apollonia,—a little town, with no synagogue to invite delay at it. And now, following the great paved track along the south of long, beautiful lakes, with the Mygdonian hills on his left, he reached the heights which round the east of the bay of Thessalonica. The top of these gained, Olympus had risen far away, before him, in all its majesty, its peaks white with untrodden snows, easily lending themselves to the fancies of an early race, as the seat of the gods. But of all this beauty and sublimity of nature there is not a word in the narrative of the Acts. Man, to Paul, was, as Chrysostom calls him, "the true Shekinah," and it was his absorbing life-aim to restore this Divine image, now all but faded out, to more than its original glory, by the many-coloured light of the knowledge of the glory of God, in the face of Jesus Christ revealed in the Gospel. Even the physical world was, indeed, in a very literal sense, crucified to him, and he to it. He was so habitually expecting "the appearing of the glory of our great God and Saviour, Jesus Christ," that nothing else could attract more than a cold and evanescent interest, in his thoughts. Besides, he was a man of the city; not like his Master, of the country, and early surroundings united with his riper tastes, to make man and all things human, indefinitely more to him than any charms of inanimate nature.

Thessalonica, the busiest trading place of Macedonia, had a large population of Greek and Roman shopkeepers and merchants; but many thousand Jews, also, had been attracted to it, at once for its prospects of money-making, and for the security it offered, as the seat of the

II.   2 C

Roman proconsul. Hebrews seem, indeed, to have formed a large part of the citizens, as they do still. A simple place of prayer had sufficed for those of Philippi, but here there was a great synagogue; the rendezvous, perhaps, of any stray Jews there might be in Amphipolis and Apollonia, as well as the sanctuary of those in Thessalonica. Nothing could better suit the plans of the apostle. To deliver his message to such a concourse of Jews, secured its being spread far and wide. The city had become one of the greatest commercial centres on the Mediterranean; its position on the Egnatian Way, no doubt, contributing to its prosperity. This road, stretching from Brundusium, the chief port on the east of Italy, through two provinces, touching the Ægæan Sea at Thessalonica, and then reaching on across Thrace to Byzantium, linked together Asia Minor and the West, and even the Black Sea and the Adriatic. Thanks mainly to it, Thessalonica had obtained so high a position, that it dreamed of, finally, being the head of the whole province. But amidst all the stir of a great city, Paul knew only the road to the synagogue. There he could meet not simply multitudes of his own race, but large numbers of Greek proselytes, with many " devout women " of the higher Greek society; the worship of Jehovah having, here as elsewhere, led not a few of the more thoughtful among the heathen population, to attend the public services on the Sabbath, and to make the sacred books of the Hebrews their study. The old mythology, had, in fact, lost its hold on the better class of minds. With Cicero, they felt that the summits of Olympus were only forbidding rocks and snows; most unfit for the seat of the gods! The once holy mountain now looked from afar, on a city whose best women betook themselves, for their spiritual good, to the prayer-house of the despised Jew, and many of whose men were soon to be won, by the preaching of Paul, to "turn unto God from idols, to serve a living and true God, and to wait for His Son from heaven."[1]   On three Sabbaths, Paul got an opportunity of speaking in the synagogue; "reasoning with the congregation, from the Scriptures"—it may be, the Psalms, or, perhaps, the Prophets, especially Isaiah —"that it behoved the Messiah to suffer, and to rise again from the dead; and that this Jesus whom he proclaimed to them was He."

But Paul was speedily to realise that the violent opposition which his nation had displayed from the first, to the new faith, as an innovation on their traditional belief, that the Messiah would be a national political deliverer from their past subjugation to the heathen; not, as Paul affirmed, a suffering and even crucified Saviour from sin, and the founder of a purely spiritual kingdom; was as active in Thessalonica as elsewhere.   He was, moreover, to feel bitterly, that his presentation of Christianity as a religion for all mankind, was resented strenuously and with wild fierceness by his brethren.   To understand the troubles that beset him, we must keep in mind the attitude of even the Jewish-Christians, from the moment that his admission of heathen converts into the Church, without previous circumcision, had been clearly shown, by his course in Asia Minor, during his first missionary journey. Till then, the new faith had been practically a Jewish sect.   The Jewish converts held, indeed, that Jesus was the Christ, and practised Christian morality, but admission to the Church was strictly confined to Jews by birth,

[1] 1 Thess. i. 9, 10.

or by formal acceptance of the distinguishing Jewish rite of circumcision. Christ had certainly commanded His faith to be preached to all nations; Stephen had counselled a wide charity; Philip, and even Peter and John, had preached to Samaritans; Cornelius had been baptized at Joppa, and, at Antioch, a church had been gathered largely from Gentiles. Yet all this might be exceptional; not a universal rule. If delayed, circumcision might be insisted upon afterwards, and, moreover, as long as the mass of Christians were Jews, a few, who were not, did not practically divorce the new faith from the Judaism of the nation.

But reports had spread before long how Paul and Barnabas, sent out by the Antioch congregation, had gathered whole brotherhoods of Gentile converts, in Asia Minor, and how they "had turned to the Gentiles" as their future care, after seeing how, to use their own words, the Jews "had thrust the word of God from them; thus judging themselves unworthy of eternal life;" how, moreover, Paul spoke of himself as "intrusted with the Gospel of the uncircumcision, even as Peter with the Gospel of the circumcision," God equally honouring both,[1] —and these tales, if true, proved beyond question, that, instead of being a Jewish organisation, with a sprinkling of Gentiles in it; the Christian society, unless this revolutionary movement were stopped, would soon be a virtually Gentile community, including in it, a pitiful minority of Jews. The birthright of the Kingdom of God, bestowed on His ancient people as their exclusive dignity, would thus be filched from them, and transferred to the abhorred heathen. Fierce hostility at once broke out, as we have

[1] Gal. ii. 8; Acts xiii. 46.

seen, and the cry rose in the Jerusalem Church, in reply
to the story told by Paul and Barnabas, of "God having
opened the door of faith to the Gentiles," that the watch-
word for the future must be, "Except ye be circumcised
after the manner of Moses, ye cannot be saved." Hitherto,
in the Holy Land, loyalty to the Temple and its services
had been the great external bond of union among the
brethren—the necessity of circumcision never having been
questioned. But Christianity had now been carried into
outside countries, far from the Temple, and the observance of the Law was the natural link of nationality among
all the scattered Hebrew race, whether of the synagogue
or "the upper room." But, of the many observances,
honoured everywhere by all Israel, one claimed the supreme
place. Festivals and Sabbaths, clean and unclean meats,
were doubtless of high importance, but, as before, these,
the sign of the covenant made by God with Abraham—
the rite of circumcision—was the one distinctive, indispensable mark of the Jew. It could not, then, be
tolerated, that any one who outraged the fundamental
condition of national unity, by wanting that divinely
prescribed sign, should be accepted as a member of the
kingdom of the true Messiah, the Prince of the People
of God, which meant,—in the opinion of the Jews,—of
their race and no other. They shrank from meeting as
a brother one whom their forefathers, in all ages, had
held in abhorrence, as outside God's favour, and even the
object of His curse.[1] They might grudgingly assent to a
compromise on other points, but, on this one, they were
immovable. Paul, however, saw that the whole question
of Christian liberty was involved in this matter, and

[1] Gen. xvii. 14 ; Exod. xxxi. 14 ; John vii. 49.

hence, would not give way to their demand; "no, not for an hour." [1] Indeed, he even went so far as to declare, when, at a later time, the controversy had become fierce, that "if any were circumcised, Christ profited them nothing, they were fallen from grace." [2] Nor was he left unsupported by the Apostles at Jerusalem, for, in their final decree, they emphatically announced that "they gave no such commandments" to those who went out from them asserting, "Ye must be circumcised and keep the Law." [3]

Though foiled at Jerusalem, the zealots for the Law would not yield, but determined to fight for their opinions wherever the Gospel was carried. We consequently find them, from this time, labouring as a distinct party, in every place over the world, to which Christianity spread. This they could the more easily do, by the vast numbers of their race scattered in every land, with their contingents of proselytes, who had become so countless that Seneca, in the reign of Nero, could say that "the conquered had given laws to the conquerors." [4] In all, or nearly all, the cities which Paul visited, he found a synagogue, and in all except Philippi, his troubles rose from the hold of the Jews on the local population. All the Epistles, moreover, even when addressed to those who had originally been heathens, imply a familiar acquaintance with Jewish practices and with the Old Testament. Every facility was thus offered to the Hebrew Christians,— whom, from their subordinating Christianity to the Law, we call Judaisers,—to urge their doctrines, and thus check the admission of the heathen, while uncircumcised, into the Church; to what they deemed its pollution,

[1] Gal. ii. 5.　　[2] Gal. v. 2.　　[3] Acts xv. 24.　　[4] Neander i. 93.

and to the destruction of its Jewish character, which they regarded as vital.

This furious crusade, roused by the loving catholicity of Paul, as soon as he began his independent career, as the apostle of the Gentiles, continued till his death, and even after it. To undo his work, and neutralise his influence, was the one great aim of the Judaisers. He must be utterly effaced. They might win over the other Apostles, but in him they had an uncompromising opponent. Unless he were crushed, the narrow nationality of the new faith must perish. Christianity would be a universal, not a Jewish religion. Hence, nothing that could excite suspicion or distrust of him was left unused. Judaism was sanctioned by law, but, from the moment when Paul separated Christianity from it, there were possibilities of alarming the Roman authorities, by denouncing it as new, and dangerous to the existing order of things. The interested owners of the slave girl at Philippi had raised this cry already, and the Jews at once took the hint; repeating the charge so furiously at Thessalonica, Paul's new sphere of action, that the missionaries had, forthwith, to leave the city.[1] Henceforth emissaries, always abundant and zealous among the restlessly wandering Hebrews, passed ceaselessly from ghetto to ghetto, along all the track of the apostle, stirring up similar trouble.

But other modes of attack were peculiar to the Jewish-Christians. "Who was this Paul?" As to themselves they came from the great Mother Church of Jerusalem; they knew the Galilæan Apostles, the companions of Christ; some of them had even seen Christ Himself.[2]

[1] Acts xvi. 20, 21 ; xvii. 6, 7.
[2] Gal. ii. 9 ; xii. 14 ; 1 Cor. i. 12 ; iii. 22 ; ix. 5.

Claiming to be followers of Cephas and the other pillar Apostles, they "trusted to themselves," from this, and from their having seen and heard Jesus, that they were peculiarly His party, and boasted of being so.[1] They vaunted of having proofs of His speaking in them, and called themselves Apostles, and ministers of Christ; even assuming apostolical authority, as legates *a latere*, to say the least; bearing rank, in this subordinate, derivative way, with the very chiefest Apostles; "letters of commendation" exhibited by them attesting their commission. Nor did they fail to magnify their office, in the airs they assumed, claiming to live "of the Gospel," lording it over the converts, and bringing them into bondage, while they exalted themselves; acting, in short, not as the servants, but as the masters of the brethren.[2]

But who was this Paul? Confessedly he had not seen Christ during His lifetime. His authority was, therefore, only by man, and through man; whether the prophets at Antioch, or Ananias at Damascus. He was only a Jew of Tarsus, not of the Holy Land, like the Twelve chosen by Christ, and he held no letters of commendation from the Jerusalem authorities.[3] Even his personal infirmities, the "weakness" of his bodily presence, and the alleged "contemptibleness" of his speech, were urged to his discredit. He was charged with vacillation in his plans, so that, to-day, he was "yea, yea;" to-morrow, "nay, nay;" and it was maintained, that he was "lowly" enough "when with them," and of "good courage" only when he was

[1] 1 Cor. i. 12.

[2] 2 Cor. xiii. 3; xi. 3; vi. 13, 23, 21, 20, 18; xii. 11; iii. 1; v. 12; x. 12, 18; ix. 14, 2; i. 4, 5; Matt. x. 11.

[3] 1 Cor. ix. 1; Gal. i. 1, 17; 2 Cor. ii. 22; Phil. iii. 5; 2 Cor. iii. 1, x. 12, 18.

"absent." As to his vaunt of working for his personal support, it was insinuated that he did so, because, not being really an apostle, he had not "power to eat and drink" at the cost of the brethren, and that he remained single, only because "he had not power to lead about a sister or a wife," like true Apostles, such as "the brethren of the Lord and Cephas." Moreover, this affected humility was only a cover for selfish ends! He boasted that he could "become all things to all men," and the exhortations of such a person might well be "of deceit, and uncleanness, and guile;" "flattering words and a cloak for covetousness;" the tricks of "fleshly wisdom," "dealing in the hidden things of dishonesty," "walking craftily, and handling the words of God deceitfully;" employing "secret meanings," and "writing other things than would be read or acknowledged" by him—speaking, in fact, in an apparent, and a secret sense. Nay, in the very matter of self-support, was he not "catching them with guile," by making "a gain of them by Titus, and those he had sent" to collect money, ostensibly for the poor brethren in Judæa, but really to be used for his own benefit?[1] Thus assailed, and thus depreciated, in comparison with the other Apostles, and with his haughty opponents, Paul had, indeed, a sore battle to fight. To add to his difficulties, there was the painful but indisputable fact, that while the majority of his accusers were, no doubt, sincere in their Jewish fanaticism, jealous for what they regarded as the claims of their Law and their race, however crafty and slanderous; there were others whom he was able to convict of being

[1] 2 Cor. x. 10; xi. 30; xii. 10; x. 1; i. 17; xi. 10; i. 12; ii 17; iv. 2; iii. 12; i. 13; xii. 20; ix. 20, 21; ii. 1, 3; 1 Cor. ix. 4, 6; ix. 5, 22; 1 Thess. ii. 3, 5.

"deceitful workers of their own interest," who made "a trade of the word of God," siding with the Judaisers, to escape persecution as Christians, by identifying themselves with a "permitted religion"—men whose praise was not of God but of man.[1]

How sadly these rancorous detractors succeeded in raising trouble in the churches which Paul, at such cost of self-devotion, had gathered, is seen in all his epistles. Wherever he went, they followed, to wrest to their party, the fruits of his toil and prayers.[2] We have seen how they appeared at Antioch, immediately after the supposed compromise at Jerusalem; in the hope of remodelling the Antioch Church on a narrow Jewish basis. In Galatia, they, ere long, carried away "to another Gospel," converts who, at first, would have "plucked out their eyes, had it been possible, and given them" to the apostle. A little leaven had so entirely leavened the whole lump, that he had come to be regarded by them as their "enemy."[3] Even at Thessalonica, after his sufferings through the heathen slave-owners at Philippi, he had to defend himself from base charges, urged by these inveterate foes.[4] At Corinth, to which he went soon after, the Judaisers, known as the party of Cephas, presently began to question his apostolic authority,[5] and had, in the end, and that very soon, a majority among the teachers of the congregation; forming "the many," and "corrupting," or "making merchandise, of the word of God."[6] Injurious reports of many kinds had, moreover, been so widely spread, that he had, in his second letter

---

[1] 2 Cor. ii. 29; xi. 13; Gal. i. 10; v. 11; vi. 12; iv. 17, 18; Rom. ii. 29.
[2] 2 Cor. x. 14.   [3] Gal. ii. 12; iv. 15; v. 9; i. 6; iv. 16; + 4
[4] 1 Thess. ii. 3–6.   [5] 1 Cor. ix. 1–7.   [6] 2 Cor. ii. 17.

to Corinth, to clear himself, in detail, from them.[1]   There
was even a plot of the old Jews to kill him, before he
left the city, and we may well believe, from the blind
fury of sectarian hatred,—as seen, for instance, in the
ferocity of the lower Romanists in Ireland, against any
attempt, however uncontroversial on the part of Pro-
testant clergymen to address the people,—that the wilder
Jewish-Christian fanatics would think it a service to God,
to get such a "heretic" as Paul out of the way.   Sympa-
thising, as they did, intensely, with the old Jews, on what
these regarded as the most vital matters, we can hardly
question that some of them were concerned, in the succession of attacks and plots against one so hated, which
threatened him, at Ephesus, in Greece, in Jerusalem, and
on the way between that city and Cæsarea.[2]

The results of this persistent malignity would, we may
be sure, seem to his enemies a visible sign of God's
approval of their hostility, for, at Jerusalem, it finally
wrecked the hopes of the apostle, that his zeal for his
poor Jewish-Christian countrymen there, in bringing
them the money so laboriously collected for their needs,
would finally prove his loyalty to them, and secure their
future confidence : an aim and service which his opponents bitterly misrepresented, lest it should be accepted
as a peace-offering.[3]   Still more, the Jerusalem outbreak
against him destroyed all his designs of visiting Western
Europe, and shut him up in prison for four of his best
years; cutting him off from that missionary work in
which he so much delighted, and in which he was so

---

[1] 2 Cor. i. 13–18; iii. 1; iv. 7; x. 13.
[2] Acts xvii. 5; xix. 23; xx. 3; xxi. 20.
[3] Rom. xvi. 25–27; 1 Cor. xvi. 10; 2 Cor. vii. 9; Acts xxiv. 17.

supremely efficient. Nor did he escape similar persecution even in his closing days, for during his imprisonment at Rome, we read of Judaisers who " proclaimed
Christ of faction, not sincerely, thinking to raise up
affliction for him in his bonds." [1] Even then, he had to
tell the Philippians to " beware of the dogs "—a name
of deepest contempt in the East, as implying all uncleanness—" to beware of the evil workers," to " beware
of the concision "—not merely circumcised, but mutilated
and unmanned ; language showing the bitterness of Paul's
soul respecting them. [2] How, indeed, could he speak
otherwise than with fierce anger, for, before this time,
he had heard himself, full as he was of love to all men,
zealous for the Law in its moral integrity, devoted to
his Master with a unique loyalty, denounced everywhere
as an apostate, and false teacher, and as, having originally
been a heathen converted to Judaism, and then, on being
disappointed and rejected in his love of a daughter of a
high priest, turning to Christianity, to wreak his revenge
through it, by a furious zeal against circumcision, the
Sabbath and the Law. [3] We must keep this state of
affairs in mind at every step of his life, to understand its
tragic story. [4]

The bitterness of religious jealousy and hatred very soon
broke out in Thessalonica, among the old Jews, against the
new preachers from Philippi ; and was raised to additional
intensity, after a time, by the added ill-will of Judaisers
and their supporters. The addresses of Paul in the syna-

---

[1] Phil. i. 17. [2] Phil. iii. 2.

[3] Irenæus, Eusebius and Epiphanius, quoted by Grætz, iii. 451.

[4] I have been much indebted in this sketch to the essay of Stanley, on
the Judaisers, in his Sermons on the Apostolic Age.

gogue on the three successive Sabbaths, had disclosed his
apparently revolutionary teaching respecting the Messiah,
whom he painted as having been crucified and then rising
from the dead; to be a sin-offering on the cross, and an
advocate in the heavens, for the sins of all mankind.   To
a race whose most cherished passion it was, to look forward to the "Anointed of God" as a national hero,
destined to raise "the fallen tent of David," and make the
Jew the lord of the whole earth, nothing could be more
hateful; for the increasingly furious nationalism of recent
years had spread from Palestine, through all lands, and
was growing into a mad frenzy, which, ere long, was to
break out in the great revolt through which Jerusalem
perished; a revolt which simmered even after that appalling catastrophe, to burst into flame again, over the empire,
under Trajan, and, once more, under Hadrian; bringing
with it, in each case, an awful punishment.

As was to be expected, therefore, Paul found a much
more ready hearing from the Greek proselytes, who were
only Jewish in having accepted Jehovah, and repudiated
idolatry, and among the Greek women, who, in the same
way, had learned to think well of the synagogue.   Very
few born Jews listened favourably to him, the names of
only two being mentioned, one Jason—the same name as
Jesus,—who offered him and his companions hospitality,
and Aristarchus, who shared his last imprisonment with
him.[1]   This worthy, indeed, showed an abiding and truly
Macedonian fidelity, for we find him at Ephesus, when the
tumult rose in the theatre; in Troas, waiting for Paul
after he was driven out of Corinth; at Cæsarea, when the
apostle was sent prisoner to Rome; and he even managed

[1] Col. iv. 10 ; Philem. 24 ; Acts xix. 29 ; xx. 4 ; xxvii. 2.

to secure a passage thither, in the same ship, so that he might still be with him. Two other names appear later, Secundus of Thessalonica, who was one of the faithful friends at Troas, along with "Gaius of Derbe."[1] The large majority of the converts were, thus, Greeks, and included quite a number of women, some of whom were wives or daughters of prominent Greek families. As a whole, however, the adherents gained to the new faith seem to have been of humble position; for in all the later epistles we read of the "deep poverty" of the Macedonians. Most of them, in fact, appear to have been mechanics;[2] willing in too many cases, to look to the brethren for support, when they should have been earning their own bread.[3] But though the converts thus gathered, consisted, virtually, of non-Jews, the success of the missionaries was more than the Jewish quarter could stand; for, besides a vigorous abhorrence of heresy, its population had the same jealousy at the progress made by the new preachers as we too often see, in our own day, between competing churches and chapels. The Jews, however, always turbulent, did not confine themselves to bad feeling. At all times ready to air their troubles in public, by tumult and violence, they bribed a number of the town rabble to make a riot, and create alarm in the city; whetting their fury by telling them, that Paul and his companions were setting up a new religion, contrary to the decrees of Cæsar, which forbade the preaching of unlicensed religions, and, still worse, were stirring up treason, saying that there is another king, one Jesus. We might think that the authors of these cries, must have heard from some

---

[1] Acts xx. 4. [2] 1 Thess. iv. 11.

[3] 2 Thess. iii. 7–12 ; 2 Cor. viii. 2.

who had been in Palestine, the accusations shouted out, at
the instigation of the priests, against our Lord. In any
case, news of the disturbance at Philippi, where the same
cry had been raised with disastrous effect, had evidently
reached Thessalonica. Nor was it less successful now, for
the Jews, heading the mob, led it to the house of Jason,
where the missionaries were lodging, to drag them out and
hand them over to the rioters, by whom they would have
been killed forthwith. All this in the name of God! Fortunately the missionaries had been warned in time, and
could not be found, but Jason, and some of the brethren,
were seized, and dragged before the politarchs, or town
magistrates, and accused of the ominous offences that
had been invented. The Jew leaders of the mob were
the accusers, and created great excitement by their
assertions. Those whom they had caught, however, could
not be charged with having taken active part in the
alleged revolutionary propaganda, though friendly to Paul
and his companions, so that the magistrates were satisfied
by requiring bonds from them, that nothing should be
attempted against the Roman majesty, and then letting
them go. Nothing more could be done, for the time, in
Thessalonica, and their safety demanded that Paul and the
others should leave the city at once. They were, therefore, sent off, without delay, when night fell, to Berœa, a
town about forty miles off, to the west, on one of the lower
ridges of mountains running towards the north. Here
they were still in Macedonia, and here also, the Jews
were numerous enough to have a synagogue. Berœa is
even now a town of about 2000 families, and traces may
yet be seen of its ancient walls and citadel. A river
makes its way through a deep gorge near, to the great sea-

coast plain, which stretches from the east slopes of the range on which Berœa stands, to the Archipelago. The local Jews were fortunately of a nobler character than those of Thessalonica, listening readily to Paul, and examining the Scriptures daily, to see if they supported his statements. The result was, we are told, that many of them believed, besides a number of the Greek proselytes, both men and women; the women, it is said, being "of honourable estate."

But the Jewish ghetto at Thessalonica had no mind to let the good work go on. They seem, indeed, to have been malevolent beyond common, for, in all the apostolic notices of Macedonia, in the next five years, we read of the continued persecution of the local churches.[1] Their first onslaught must, indeed, have been specially violent, since it spread the name of the Christians from ghetto to ghetto, through all Macedonia and through Achaia, which included the lower part of Greece and the whole of the Peloponnesus.[2] But even the after-claps were violent enough. Yet Paul always looked fondly back on his stay at Thessalonica. Before he withdrew from the synagogue, to gather his converts round him in some more peaceful spot, he must have had wild times, in his disputes with the excited mob of synagogue zealots; for what Jews were, when roused by religious fanaticism, had been shown only too often in their fury from first to last, against Christ, and in even the dignified Sanhedrim so losing self-control at the address of St. Stephen, as to "gnash on him with their teeth.[3] But though, in looking back on these typhoons of rage, and clamour, and

[1] 1 Thess. iii. 3; 2 Cor. vii. 5; viii. 2.   [2] 1 Thess. i. 7.
[3] Acts vii. 54.

threatened personal violence, Paul could only compare
what he had undergone to the "agony" of the struggle
in the arena, with wild beasts, or gladiators still more
ferocious,[1] his confidence and victorious joy had never
been more assured than on these days. A year or two
later, he writes, that, though "he had suffered before,
and been shamefully entreated at Philippi, he waxed bold
in his God, to speak to them"—the Thessalonians—"the
Gospel, in much conflict." [2]   The eagerness with which
the proselytes listened to him, was, in fact, an earnest
of success, helping him to speak "with power," in the
assurance that the Holy Ghost was with him; [3] as shown
by their "receiving the Word, in spite of much persecution, with joy of the Holy Spirit, and by their Christian
virtues, the report of which had spread far and wide." [4]
The howling mob of the synagogue, or before the doors
of Jason's house, had not shaken their belief, that Paul's
words were not of man but of God. His converts, indeed, were soon so many that he looked forward to a
protracted stay among them, and, for this end, sought
and obtained work, no doubt in the handicraft he best
knew, and toiled day and night, though living in a brother
Jew's house; that he might not burden any one.[5]   He
lived, in fact, as a common working-man, preaching in
the evenings when his day's labour was over, to the new
brethren, and then, when they left, resuming his ill-paid
toil, far into the night.

His first letter to this loved band, gives a delightful
picture of his intercourse with them in these chequered
times. As he writes, they are once more before him.

[1] 1 Cor. iv. 9 ; xv. 32.   [2] 1 Thess. ii. 2.   [3] 1 Thess. i. 4, 5.
[4] 1 Thess. i. 7, 8.   [5] 1 Thess. ii. 9.

sitting, in Eastern fashion, at his feet, while he taught
them. He feels that he is bereaved by being away from
them, though it is only in the body, not in heart, and has
been trying " with great desire " to return; longing, " once
and again," to do so, but has been hindered by Satan. And
why should he not? For are they not his hope, and joy,
and crown of rejoicing, before our Lord Jesus at His
coming?[1]　He tenderly reminds them, "how he dealt
with each one of them, as a father with his own children,
exhorting, and encouraging them, and entreating them to
walk worthily of God, who was calling them to His own
kingdom and glory.[2]　He had been " gentle " among them;
bearing himself as tenderly to them as a nurse does to
her own children; fondly cherishing them in her loving
arms. Yearning, just so, towards them, he had not only
been eager to impart to them the Gospel of God, but
willing to sacrifice even his life, had it been necessary,
because they were become very dear to him.[3]　The Epistle
not only, however, brings before us Paul's sweet relations
with them, but lets us hear the burden of the discourses
he delivered, in the quiet of Jason's house; shut in from
the bustle and noise of the busy port. The violence of
the town mob, from which they had suffered so much,
may well be borne patiently, he tells them, for it is only
what his other congregations have had to bear from " the
Jews (and Judaisers), who are contrary to all men; forbidding us to say to the Gentiles, that they may be saved
(without becoming Jews);" language which shows the
struggle he had to make, for a Christianity which should
be more than a mere continuation of Rabbinism. For
the rest, the preaching was essentially an announcement

[1] 1 Thess. ii. 17–19.　　[2] 1 Thess. ii. 11, 12.　　[3] 1 Thess. ii. 7. 8.

of the approaching wrath of God. To use the language
of the Baptist, Paul proclaimed that the axe was at the
foot of the trees, and that every tree that did not bear
good fruit, would be hewn down, and cast into the fire.
The Lord was at hand, about to be revealed from heaven
with a shout, with the voice of the archangel, and with
the trump of God. They must, therefore, take heed to
live as sons of light, and thus escape the sudden destruction that might peal forth, at any moment, from the skies.[1]
Such an awful culmination of human affairs, so close at
hand, might well fortify them, to endure the utmost that
man could do against them. Startled, as if from sleep, by
the announcement that they were, possibly, on the brink
of the day of judgment, they might well "watch and be
sober," "waiting for God's Son from heaven."

The "signs of the times," moreover, seemed to support
the warnings of the apostle, for it was now almost the
end of the reign of Claudius; a period marked, in the
heathen world, by an alarming succession of omens and
prodigies. An accidental concurrence of exceptional
phenomena may, actually, have marked the last year of
the emperor, but more probably, the excitement and
mortal anxiety of the nations, at the position of affairs,
made them see omens in what they otherwise would have
overlooked. The rule of the vile Agrippina, the adoption of her son, Nero, and the sinking life of Claudius,
cast such a shadow over the empire, that the superstition
of the age, as was natural in such circumstances, saw,
or imagined evident wonders in nature which proclaimed
the wrath of the gods. A comet stretched its great
scourge-like tail over the nightly heavens; bloody rain

[1] 1 Thess. i. 10 ; ii. 16, 19 ; iii. 13 ; iv. 13–17 ; v. 2–11, 23.

fell; a swarm of bees settled on the top of the Capitol;
misbirths of man and beast roused the terror of Rome;
a sow had been farrowed, with the talons of a hawk.
The monument of Drusus was struck by lightning; the
temple of Jupiter the Conqueror opened of itself. Already,
on Nero's official coming of age, the heavens seemed in
flames, and a nocturnal earthquake shook Rome. Everything pointed, as men thought, to a change of affairs for
the worse, and the strange fact that each of the holders
of the five highest offices of the State, died, one after the
other, seemed to speak of the Fates being let loose on
men. Moreover, while Paul was preaching at Thessalonica, the near coming of Christ the Messiah, the Jews
of Rome had been discovered plotting a very different
appearing of their own Messiah, which resulted in their
being banished from the city; to plot treason more harm-
lessly at a distance. In days of such universal tension, the
trumpet call of the apostle to the Thessalonian proselytes,
to prepare to meet the Judge of the living and dead, fell
on hearts open to hear it. But such a proclamation of
the coming of the Christian Messiah, was likely to paralyse
the Jewish dream of proselytising the heathen world; to
get its help, when the hour arrived for their universally
planned rising against Rome, in installing their own
Messiah, on His appearance, as King of the whole earth,
on Mount Zion. Affecting with smooth hypocrisy, as in
the case of Christ, to charge the missionaries with being
the enemies of Rome, when their not being so was the
very ground of the fury of the synagogue against them;
alleging that they sought to overthrow Cæsar, when
it was because they had no thought of doing so, they
had been dragged before the politarchs,—their foes had

driven them from the city. Before long, however, the news that Paul was preaching once more in Berœa reached them. Fancying himself, at last, safe, the apostle was, meantime, fondly wondering whether matters might not have so calmed down in Thessalonica, as to let him re-visit his converts, there, when a number of Jews from that city appeared in Berœa, "stirring up" and troubling the town with renewed charges, of political and revolutionary aims, on the part of the preachers. Once more, flight alone could save the apostle, and the brethren therefore at once sent him off to the nearest port, which was not far distant; in accordance, no doubt, with his wish to go on to Athens, at least three days' sail off. Some of them, however, went with him all the way, but he left Silas and Timothy behind, at Berœa. Finding himself lonely, however, when he reached his new resting-place, when thus separated from his fellow-workers, he reluc-tantly allowed the kind friends who had escorted him so far to return home, but not till he had begged them to send his two old companions to him, with all speed.

The authorities for the omens and prodigies said to have been noticed in these years, are Cass. Dio. lx. 6, 35 ; Sueton. *Claud.* 25, 46 ; Plin. *Hist. N.* ii. 25 ; **xxiii.** 92 ; Seu. *Quæst. Nat.* vii. 17, 2 ; Tac. *Ann.* xii. 52, 59, 64.

CHAPTER XIX

THE coasting vessel which bore Paul to the south had to skirt the mountainous shores of Thessaly, and the equally mountainous island of Eubœa, and then strike south-west, to the lovely promontory of Sunium. Here the southern point of Attica was reached; a lovely spot, still crowned by the ruins of a temple, from which the eye ranges over a wondrously beautiful view of shining waters, picturesque islands, famous in story, and a romantic succession of mountain peaks, girdling the shores of the Isthmus of Corinth and of the Peloponnesus. The bluest of skies overarches a still bluer sea, while the whole landscape, of island, mountains, and waters, lies bathed in a sunshine which heightens their charms while it half conceals them. Then, turning north, thirty miles more sailing brought Paul to the Piræus, the port of Athens. The beauty of the bay as one approaches—is perfect. On the west is the island of Salamis, where the destruction of the Persian fleet, in the year 480 before Christ, finally established European liberty, and, driving back Oriental despotism, transferred the centre of political power from the Euphrates, to the then new-born West. Farther off, rises the hilly loveliness of Egina, hardly less famous, and in the still farther distance, the lofty Acropolis of Corinth guards the mass of hills and mountains of the Peloponnesus. On the mainland, the range of Cithæron stretches, east and west, in the background, and the eye rests on Pentelicus, from which the white marble of statues and temples innumerable has been quarried, and on the seemingly bare slopes of Hymettus, from the aromatic growths on which, clouds of bees then, as now, suck exhaustless stores of honey; for the sweets gathered by them were the delight of Plato and Socrates, and are the glory of Athenian tables still. From the top of Pentelicus you look down on Marathon, and over to Eleusis, and away to Parnassus; shining waters stretching afar, at every point, on both sides of the isthmus, away to the south. Nor is Athens, itself, less ideally romantic. On the platform of the Acropolis, a steep height, nearly in the centre of the Athens of St. Paul, and just outside the Athens of to-day, stood the grandest of temples made with hands — the Parthenon—the name given the "virgin" goddess Athena. It now looks down on the city, as if mourning departed glories;—its friezes, rough with immortal sculptures, gone; its once snow-white marble pillars, yellow or softly brown with age; its marble floor and courts broken into a wide confusion of fragments. Near it, on the north side of the platform, stood the Erechtheium, now strewing the ground with marble heaps, but then the most holy of Athenian sanctuaries; enshrining the olive-wood statue of Athena believed to have fallen from heaven. The approaches to this sacred height, from the city, were in those days glorious with the vast accumulated splendours of architecture known as the Propylæa or entrances; built by Pericles; over which, Paul daily saw the colossal bronze figure of Athena, by Pheidias—showing her armed for battle, spear in hand—towering, with the pedestal seventy feet high, the point of the spear and the crest of the helmet glittering afar, so that ships saw them as they rounded Sunium, thirty miles off. At the foot of this mountain of wonders lay the outcrop of hard red lime-stone, or we might say marble, famous as Mars Hill, or Areopagus; the judgment-seat of the Supreme Court of Athens; rising, next the city, perhaps two storeys high, but much less where it breaks out of the slope, on the side next the Acropolis. Its whole surface is still, as then, in its natural roughness, but for some steps leading to a rudely levelled space, round which the rock forms the equally rude seat once occupied by the Areopagi, when Paul stood before them, and spoke to the venerable dignitaries and the motley crowd, of Jesus and the Resurrection. Forty or fifty yards off, between Mars Hill and the Acropolis, there is still seen the wide chasm in the rocks, with a spring bubbling up from its depths: the dreaded subter-ranean abode and temple of the Furies, in the time of Paul. A quarter of a mile off, in the opposite direction, the semicircle of the Pnyx, or Ecclesia—our word "church" in the New Testament—the place where the Athenian people assembled for public business and affairs, is still as when Paul saw it. Even the steps remain at the middle of its arc, from which Demosthenes, Pericles, Themi-stocles, Aristides, and Solon; but, alas, also, pestilent demagogues like Cleon, and heresy hunters like the accusers of Socrates, addressed the citizens from the raised Bema, or tribune.

The Agora, or market-place, in which Paul reasoned day by day, with the ever-ready talkers of the town, looks up to this by a gentle slope, so that he saw it constantly;

THE ACROPOLIS OF ATHENS.

[*See explanation on back.*]

EXPLANATION OF WOODCUT.

In front are the great mounds of rubbish removed in uncovering the remains on the slope and at the foot of the hill. Below, on the left, is the Odeium of Herodes' Atticus, of the time of the Antonines, and thus non-existent in the days of Paul. It was large enough to accommodate 3000. Next, to the right, are the remains of the Stoa Eumeneia (good will), and the stone theatre of Dionysius, which could seat, it is said, 30,000. Above, on the left, are the great buildings of the Propylæa (entrances): then, the remains of various temples, &c. Next, in front, the Parthenon, and at an angle to it, the wonderful Erechtheium. The platform on which these great buildings stood is girt round with the ancient walls. Mount Lycabettus rises behind : now the site of an observatory. The trees in the front of the picture, line the high road. The south side of the Acropolis is shown. Mars Hill is outside the picture, a short way to the left ; in fact, just below the Propylæa. The view is from a photograph I got in Athens.

the " painted Stoa " or " porch," from which the " Stoics "
took their name, rising just outside it, towards the Pnyx,
behind a row of superstitiously venerated four-cornered
stone posts, known as the Hermae, from ending, a-top,
in a bust of Hermes, our Mercury ; the god of traffic
and markets. On the north side of the Agora stood a
row of statues—a sample of the " idols " with which he
grieved to see the city so " full." Under the shadow of
the old walls, which hold up the platform of the Parthenon, we still see, on the south side of the Acropolis,
the open-air theatres for music and the drama, cut out in
the rock, familiar to Paul. Away to the north-west, the
temple of Theseus, still wonderfully perfect, rose in all its
glory before him. A little south-east of the enormous
rock-hewn theatre there, sixteen pillars are still erect out
of a hundred and twenty, partly raised in Paul's time,
towering sixty feet high, with a diameter of more than six
feet, along the sides of the great temple of Jupiter ; then
awaiting its finishing in the next century, by Hadrian.
Every here and there, indeed, one comes even now, on
monuments, and remains of temples, on which the eyes of
the apostle must have rested. All, however, are only reminiscences of what they once were. The glorious pillars
of the temple of Jupiter, once snowy white, rear their heads,
brown with age, and in part pitted with bullet-holes, the
memorials of Mussulman domination, and one lies fallen.

As the apostle entered the city he would pass by, or
through, the cemetery,—even now, after so many centuries,
wonderfully touching in its monuments, many of which
were ancient when Paul was in the city. I remember
one, on which a lady is wistfully looking at the jewels she
feels she must leave behind her, and is handing to the girl

slave standing by. On another, are a child with a pet little dog, a youth with a tame bird, and a husband and his wife ; she, bidding him an eternal farewell.

The cities of antiquity were adorned to an extent we cannot realise, with statues of men and gods, and Athens, above all others, had, in its best days, been embellished, in endless profusion, with the masterpieces of the finest sculpture the world ever boasted. When Paul saw it, its highest splendour was long past, but, even then, the "excess of glory" was only "obscured," and left it, still, a dream of architectural and artistic perfection. But, even in its decay, eighteen centuries ago, long lines of colonnades, countless statues, and a world of monuments, and ideally beautiful temples and public buildings, adorned spaces where there are now only patches of barley or lentils, or banks of grass, sheets of scarlet anemones, or spots of asphodels and aloes. Men live in the open air, much of the year, in such a climate, so that they were building an open-air theatre on the banks of the Ilissus, a mere thread of a brook, when I was there. Over the Parthenon and its great courts, as over all the landscape, the heavens are still filled with ethereal brightness; yet all is solitude, but for the finches and little birds, that fly where they choose, over marble floors once filled with awe-struck crowds, and for the clouds of hawks, of which I counted seventeen in the air close by, at one time, which make the birds, the lizards, and mice, their quarry.

The twenty years of civil war which introduced the emperors, had wasted the earth beyond any former parallel, but no province showed their terrible results so much as did the Grecian peninsula. The three great decisive battles of that awful time—Pharsalia, Philippi, and Actium

—had been fought on virtually Grecian territory, or on its coasts, and the military operations of both parties in connection with their campaigns, had demanded a sacrifice of human life and property greater than any other region had suffered. Plutarch, indeed, tells us, that he heard from his grandfather, how the officers of M. Antony compelled the citizens of Cheronea, to carry the last of their grain. on their own shoulders, to the nearest port, to ship to the army; their slaves and beasts of burden having already been taken. The local decay, previously begun, was so accentuated by such requisitions, that Greece remained half desert from that time. Cæsar and Augustus had both tried to stay the great depopulation, so alarming to rulers, by introducing Italian colonists, but Corinth and Athens, in which, mainly, they were settled, remained the only two towns of Greece of any importance. The national spirit, also, fell, with the general deterioration of the country. Youths and men gave themselves to athletics, fancying the greatest glory for boys was in gymnastics, and for men, in boxing; so that while no province gave so few soldiers to the army, none boasted so many wrestlers and pugilists. The citizens of Athens, like their forefathers, were restless, serious, and light, in turn; delightful to-day, and hateful to-morrow. Even half-Italian Corinth only allowed fights of gladiators at a very late period, and Athens tardily sanctioned them, not to be behind its rival. In no land of antiquity were slaves so kindly used as in Greece, for no one would sell those he owned to any but a Greek, and thus the slave-trade, in the ordinary sense, was not known. There was, indeed, much in Greek life which was attractive. If the communities were poor, they bore their poverty gracefully; enjoyed free speech among friends; made leisure for intellectual pleasures; in short, brightened life by a greater or less fulness of quiet enjoyment. "How could you," asks one Greek of another, in Rome, "leave the light of the sun, Greece, with its happiness and its liberty, for this crowd?"

Cheerful, as becomes the people of so bright a sky, and poor as the inhabitants of a country of bare hills must always be, even when it has not been wasted by war and extortion as Greece had been, the race, then, as now, was forced largely to live by its wits, with all the scheming and chicanery this involves. Athens, itself, was in permanent straits for existence. Once and again, its Council offered this or that island for sale, to get money. For the noble buildings which continued to be added to the attractions of the city, it was indebted to the liberality of strangers, such as Herod the Great, and, above all, Hadrian; who among other gifts, finished the mighty temple of Jupiter Olympus, begun seven hundred years before. Athens itself, had not even funds to keep its port in repair. In the time of Augustus, the Piræus was only a poor village of a few houses, though it had temples, from the old time, adorned with masterpieces of painting. There was no longer almost any trade or industry in the city, and for the burgesses and common townsmen alike, the only flourishing occupation was begging. Nor did it at all times bear its poverty quietly. If there was peace over the world. there was often the reverse at A'hens. Bread riots and risings against the city authorities, not infrequently disturbed it. Yet its pride was as great as its poverty, and amidst all its impotence it occasionally acted with so high a hand, as to give great trouble to the Romans. When Paul visited Athens, it depended on

imperial grants, and the money spent in it by the concourse of tourists and students, and the endowments made
to this or that foundation, by Roman nobility or foreign
princes.[1]

The Piræus, at which Paul landed, is a fine harbour
with a narrow entrance, the sides broken by moles from
which, in antiquity, chains were stretched across, to exclude enemies. The vessels and steamers, of which there
are not many, anchor out in the deep water, not at the
landing,—a stone quay, running along the edge, on the
two sides of the angle occupied by the town, which boasts
of some fine public buildings, good streets, and nice boats.
Soldiers are, now, seen everywhere. Hymettus and Pan-
telicus rise in the distance behind. As you come in, the
bare rocks of Salamis, and some other islands, powdered
here and there with low shrubs, are close at hand. Inside
the harbour, the side opposite the town rises in low
heights, without peaks, wooded in parts, but mostly grey
rock; snow-crowned mountain tops standing up in the
distance, when I saw it.

The size of Athens was never very great, but the
crowded, narrow streets, seem to have given shelter to
a population somewhere about 150,000. The meanness
of the houses was in striking contrast to the splendour
of the public buildings. Latterly, some private dwellings
had become pretentious, but the bulk of the citizens appear to have lived in low houses of unburnt brick, with
no windows to the road. Few of the streets were paved,
and they were not kept clean even in dry weather. Nor
were they lighted; so that Aristophanes could raise a

[1] I am indebted, for this sketch, in great measure to Mommsen, vol. v
chap vii.

laugh, by describing a party picking their steps, by night, through the mud, by the help of a lantern.[1] Even the water supply seems to have been poor, and, as a whole, we may, perhaps, compare Athens, for its want of wholesome municipial arrangements, to some of the sordid towns of southern Italy, in the present day.

But such as it was, so different, in much, from our imaginary conceptions, Athens was the metropolis of culture in the time of Paul, and it was an incident of sublime significance, that he, a Jew, passing beyond the narrow limits of his own nationality, should have so united in his person the religious training of Judaism, with the wide sympathies, and all embracing charity of the New Faith, as to have recognised in Christianity a gospel for the Gentile as well as the Hebrew: a mental and moral equipment uniquely fitting him to be its representative in this centre of the highest expression of Gentile religion and philosophy.

As everywhere else, there were Jews at Athens, and in the home of some of their number, he, doubtless, found shelter, while waiting, all alone, for the coming of Silas and Timotheus from Berœa. He had seen "idols" in every Gentile city he had visited, but his spirit was "provoked within him," to see the number there were in Athens, for "the city was full" of them. All the way from the Piraeus, the road had been lined, from point to point, with monuments to famous men, or statues of heroes or of gods, and every open space in the city obtruded on him its idolatry, so intensely hateful to a Jew; the great brazen image of Athens, cast from the spoils of Marathon, looking down on him, as I have already said,

[1] Aristoph. *Vesp.* 248.

in its gigantic size, spear and shield in hand, from above all the wondrous buildings on the Acropolis, as the tutelary divinity of Athens and Attica. The number of statues in Greek towns, everywhere, was, indeed, amazing, in spite of the systematic plundering of them by the Romans, for two hundred years. The conquerors of the world had even stooped to empty the market-places of small spots like Andros, to fill the temples and the forum of Rome. So late as under Vespasian, Rhodes, which seems to have escaped the spoilers, had three thousand statues, and yet the number at Athens, Olympia, and Delphi,—places which had been sorely robbed, was estimated as not fewer. Hence, even after Paul's death, the aggregate of such "idols;" for to Paul as a Jew, the likeness of anything in heaven, or earth, or sea, was an "idol;" could hardly have been less, in the petty mainland of Greece, and its islands, than from 20,000 to 30,000.[1]

As usual, the apostle betook himself, first, to the synagogue which even Athens possessed, and there reasoned, in support of the Messiahship of Jesus, with the Jews and the "devout persons," for there were, it seems, here, as elsewhere, numbers of heathen so dissatisfied with the old paganism, as to have turned to the worship of Jehovah, though not identifying themselves any further, with Judaism. Not contented, however, with this restricted activity, he went out daily to the market-place, a favourite resort of the disputatious Athenians, to argue with such as might gather round him, in favour of the One God, and against idolatry. Philostratus, in his sketch of Apollonius, gives a picture of his experience, about the same time as the visit of Paul, which may help to bring back the

[1] Friedländer, iii. 131.

surroundings of the apostle, in this respect. Having landed
at the Piræus, the "prophet" went on to the city, meeting
numbers of philosophers and philosophisers, making for
Phalērum, the western harbour of Athens.   Some of them
sunned themselves, their outer garment off; some were
immersed in their book; some were practising speechify-
ing to an imaginary audience, as they went on; others
disputed with their fellow-travellers. No one frankly
identified himself with him, as a teacher, but all gave him
to understand that they had heard of him, and turned
back a space with him, or went on with him, amidst
friendly greetings. Propertius sets the Athens of those
days no less vividly before us. "I will improve my mind,"
says he, "there, by the doctrines of Plato, or indulge my
fancy in the garden of Epicurus, the Wise. Or I will
diligently cultivate oratory, the weapon of Demosthenes.
And thy salt, O wise Menander, attracts me to thee, or
many a fine picture enchains my eyes, or statues of
ivory or bronze."[1]   Vain, conceited, clever, frivolous, the
Athenians were fond of nothing so much as displaying
their smartness in arguing; to show, as they fancied,
that they were worthy of philosophical Athens,—much
as even a peasant, in Scotland, is often a keen theolo-
gian. No sport pleased them more, than to chop logic
with any one, while the appearance of a stranger, advancing new ideas, was a delightful ripple on the monotony of
an idle or idly busy life. It gave them something to talk
about, and drew round them a circle of eager quidnuncs,
all attention, to listen to the latest gossip.   In this, all
Athenians, and even the temporary visitors in the city,
were, we are told, alike; "spending their time in nothing

[1] Philostr. *Apoll.* iv. 17; Prop. *Eleg.* iii. 22, 24 ff.

else, but either to tell or to hear some new thing." [1] The
poor Jewish weaver was free of the Agora or market-
place;—the favourite lounging quarter for all classes; and
of the halls, or rather colonnades, along its south and
western sides; the headquarters of the different professors
of philosophy, as we may call them, and of their disciples.
Teachers and students used these porches,—which were
only portions of longer colonnades, bordering the streets
leading to the Agora,—as the rabbis of Jerusalem used the
arcades round the Temple courts. About a hundred years
after Paul's visit, Pausanius describes this continuous line
of pillared arcades, on both sides of the street; adding that,
under them, were entrances to private houses and sanc-·
tuaries.   One of these stoai, known as the Painted Porch,
from its pictures, was the gathering-place of one of the
two chief schools of philosophy of the day,—that of the
Stoics—so called from this place of meeting; the headquarters of the rival school—the Epicureans—being at the
gymnasium of Ptolemæus, some distance off, to the north-
west.   The account of the Painted Porch brings before us
its appearance to Paul.   " In approaching it, is a bronze
Mercury, and near it, a gate on which is a trophy of the
Athenians, commemorating a cavalry triumph.   Before
it, stand brazen statues of Solon and Seleucus.   In the
Agora is an altar of Pity, to whom the Athenians alone,
of Greeks, give divine honours."   The " porch " or stoa
had three walls, covered with paintings; a middle wall
with two large paintings, and a wall at each end.   The
subjects were battles,—among others, that of Marathon,—
and a meeting of the Greek chiefs after the fall of Troy,
and were all by famous masters.

[1] Acts xvii. 21.

Adherents of both schools—the Epicurean and the Stoic—soon got into discourse with the clever Jew, who had made his appearance of late, day by day, in the market-place, and they soon drew others round them. Both schools had risen soon after Alexander the Great, and flourished till the time of the Antonines, as the repre-sentatives of the opposite aspects of philosophic thought, by which the sinking old world sought to extricate itself from the wreck of the ancient popular religions, and supply a key to the riddle of existence. The Epicurean system was essentially materialistic. Perception by the senses was the only source of knowledge. The world was traced back to atoms, by the chance aggregation of which, all existence was formed; even the soul being a substance created by the union of air and fire-like atoms. Hence, immortality was a dream, freedom of the will a self-deception, and the gods superfluous; though Epicurus, illogically, allowed them to remain, while denying them any part in the government of nature, or any influence on the fate or fortune of men. The highest good of man, endowed with the five senses, and with no aim beyond life, was pleasure; ideal wisdom lay in attaining the highest measure of this, and virtue was a life guiding us to the same end.

The Stoic philosophy, on the contrary, was essentially pantheistic. It recognised two principles in the universe; Matter and Energy, calling the latter, in relation to the All, by the apt names of Reason, Providence, and God-head. This Divine principle, however, they conceived to be only an impersonal Something, without independent existence, and hence not a true spiritual essence, but rather, an all-forming, all-quickening fire, which, by an

iron necessity, brought all beings and worlds into existence, and after a time consumed them.   The human soul,
a spark of this impersonal divinity, and hence without
personal immortality, had, according to the Stoics, its
highest good in virtue.   But virtue was a life agreeable
to nature; the harmony of the human will with the eternal
laws of the world; and therefore, above all, resignation
to the Fate that governed all things.   It is curious to see,
in these doctrines of the Epicureans and Stoics, the early
anticipation of much that characterises modern thought;
but it must be so, for the mind has only a limited sphere
in which to move, and create its theories, and the old
must return, when its place in the circle has again come
round.

The discussions of representatives of these two systems,
then so important, with the apostle, would lead them,
with Greek politeness, and the condescension of supposed
superiority, to see in the Gospel he proclaimed,—in spite of
any differences in its theory of the world and of morals,—
a new Oriental fanaticism, of which one feature, at least,
was fit only for a smile, as ridiculous folly—the declaration that there would be a resurrection of the dead.   It
had all the charm of a new sensation.   "Do you think
there's any meaning at all," asked some, "in what this
ranter is jabbering?"   "He seems to be a setter forth
of foreign gods," said others—"this Jesus, the waker of
the dead, of whom he speaks, especially."   In any case, it
would amuse, and pass away an hour, to hear more fully
what he had to say.   Taking him kindly by the hand,
therefore, they led him, nothing unwilling, to Mars Hill,
or Areopagus; the seat, as I have said, of the highest
court; their object not being, in any way, to put him

on his defence before the judges, but simply, to gratify
the curiosity of the crowd, by supplying him with a platform from which he could freely address any number
gathered on the slope below, looking down on the Agora.
I have already described Mars Hill, but a fuller notice of
it will bring Paul's address to the multitude from it, more
vividly before us. Though mainly hard red limestone,
or coarse marble, yet, in parts, it is rather a conglomerate.
Lying east and west, it crops out at its west end from the
slope towards the Acropolis, and very soon sinks in the east
in a low, perfectly bare, reddish, rough crag. Goats were
asleep in the shadow of this when I first saw it. The
north side has been scarped, and a cross cut out on it;
marking the remains of an ancient church. There are also
other cuttings, as if of primeval cave houses. On the
south side very shallow steps, rudely cut—eleven still
remaining, but eight or nine gone—lead to the flat top—
the platform from which Paul spoke. The steps do not,
however, run up any rock-face, for there is none, but turn
squarely to the west, half way. On the south side, indeed,
the word "hill" is quite a misnomer; the rock breaking
out from the level of the ground, and rising only in a
rough, lava-like bulge, so modest, that even on the north
side, where the slope is, of course, greatly increased, the
height, to the top of the "hill," is not more than from
twenty to thirty feet. The bench hewn in the rock, of
which I have spoken, is cut along the two ends and the
back, or north side, and was the "bench" on which the
Areopagites sat, as judges, in the open air. Time, that
gnaws all things, has strewn the ground with fragments
—some of a good size; fallen, in the course of ages; and
has roughened out of shape, two blocks of the hard marble,

MARS HILL (*from a Photograph*).

one at each end of the platform, on which, apparently, stood the accuser and the accused.

On this shelf of rock, so insignificant and yet so famous, Paul had before him a spectacle which might have stirred him to enthusiasm by the historical glory it recalled, had not his whole soul been absorbed by thoughts infinitely greater. On his right, as he looked south, a little way off, was the low rostrum in the native rock—the Pnyx— on the semicircular area before which, the Athenians, as I have said, had listened to the oratory of Demosthenes; at his feet lay the Agora, and the "Porches" of the schools of philosophy, with their wealth of statues, and architectural triumphs; beyond them rose the hill which took its name; from being the burial-place of the poet Musæus; its sides covered with houses, and its top crowned by monuments; on his left, close at hand, rose the Acropolis, with its aggregate of temples such as no spot on earth ever saw; the mighty figure of Athena rising above the whole; its very material, the bronze of the spoils at Marathon, an epic of patriotism and lofty heroism; while below, in the city, rose altars, temples, and statues at every point.

The apologist for Christianity in such a unique theatre was, as I have said, uniquely fitted for his task. No one could have been more perfectly a connecting link between the East and West; representing the loftiest religious ideals of Hebrew prophets and psalmists, but in full sympathy with mankind of every race. He showed, more-over, the characteristics of Western intellect as no Ori-ental had ever done; in his subtle reasoning power, in his habit of impassioned appeal, and even in the complicated sentences into which his fervour hurries him. He has no

Jewish austerity, or contemptuous pride. Between him
and Jews of his day, there is a wide gulf, in the treatment of subjects common to both. He probes the heart
in that practical, individual spirit, which marks Western
minds. He shows, in his mingled self-respect and defe-
rential respect to others, what we honour as one of the
most precious creations of Western culture. He who,
before his arrest on the way to Damascus, had been only
a Jew of the narrowest type, had caught, from the
great commission given him by his Master, who then
appeared to him, a Divine enthusiasm for humanity.
Henceforth this glowed in his soul towards the whole race,
like a grand realisation of the noble sentiment of the
Roman slave, Terence, "I am a man; I think nothing
connected with human interests foreign to me"—that
is, as "not my concern." To Paul, whatever belonged
to man, as such, belonged to himself. He could even
wish that he "were anathema, for his brethren's sake,"
though they were his bitter enemies.[1] And, as he felt,
thus, ready to show entire self-negation and even self-
sacrifice for his fellow-Hebrews, he could write to the
Greeks of Corinth that "he would most gladly spend and
be spent for their souls."[2] "Love," said he, "is the fulfilling of the Law." "The greatest of all heavenly graces
is love."[3] Like his Divine Master, his heart went forth to
all the world, recognising a brother in Jew and Greek,
Barbarian, Scythian, bond or free, alike. With him,
Christianity was no local, or national, Jewish sect, but the
religion of all mankind, without distinction of race; the
one fold, into which regenerated humanity was, one day,

[1] Rom. ix. 3.　　　　　　　[2] 2 Cor. xii. 15.
[3] Rom. xiii. 10 ; 1 Cor. xiii. 13.

to be gathered, under One Shepherd,—the Eternal Son of that one and only God, whose name was Love. To see a Jew standing on Mars Hill, and appealing to an Athenian audience, as children of the same Divine Father, and, though unconsciously, worshippers of the same God as himself, proclaimed a new era in the spiritual history of the world. It was this grand charter of heavenly charity, which he announced to the Gentile everywhere, that has created the Christendom of these last eighteen hundred years, and bears, in its all-embracing sweep, the ultimate divine manhood of the race.

From the Agora, where Paul held discourse with pro-

Scythian Warriors, from a Vessel found in a Grave.—*Rawlinson.*

fessional and would-be philosophers, native and foreign, it was a very short way to Mars Hill, which stood out, slightly to the north of it. Eight paths, forming a double-cross, like that on the Union Jack, ran across the market-place; the shortest to the proposed place of further discussion being the middle one. Along this he would go, in the company of his new friends, of the Painted Porch and the Gymnasium of Ptolemy. As he passed under the triumphal arch in the centre of the open space, with a famous bronze statue of Mercury beside it, he would have on his

left the row of Hermæ—the mutilation of the phallic sym-
bols on which, here, and elsewhere, in the city, just before
the sailing of the disastrous Sicilian expedition, caused
dismay in Athens, in B.C. 415.   On his right, would be the
court-house of the city, and the round hall in which the
monthly magistrates—the fifty prytaneis, or presidents of
the city wards, held power actually, for thirty-five, or thirty-
six days,—met to dine.   Just outside the Agora, on his
right was the temple of the daughters of Leos—sacrificed,
according to the legend, to deliver the city, from plague or
famine ; on his left, a long row of twelve statues, beyond
which stood the altar of the twelve gods, and the statues
of Harmodius and Aristogeiton ; two great friends, who,
having plotted the death of Hippias, the " tyrant "—that
is, one who had made himself ruler of a hitherto free
democracy—by misadventure murdered his brother ; their
high purpose, however, making them famous in all the
future story of Athens, as patriots, heroes, and martyrs.
A little farther on, in the middle of the path, rose the
temple of Mars, a few steps before he reached the platform of the Areopagus ; where, on his right, as he looked
south, he was within a few yards of the cleft in the rock,
revered as the sanctuary of the Furies.   No wonder that
he felt himself in the midst of "idols."

Taking his place, on one of the two rough pedestals of
rock, used as a tribune ; that he might be seen and heard
to the best advantage, the pale-faced, weakly, insignificant-
looking Jew ; most probably in Jewish dress,—his bald
head protected by a turban or mortar-cap,—his person
covered with a long closed sack, under a shorter tunic,—
having separated himself from those round, began his
address, unconsciously showing, in its wise dexterity of

topics and treatment, and in its eloquence, how admirably and yet honestly, he could become "all things to all men;" to the heathen Greeks he was now so liberal and widely human, as to engage their interest and disarm their opposition ; as, in addressing Jews, he suited his language to Jewish feelings; his one object being in either case that he "might by all means"—by every worthy adaptation of speech—"save some."[1] Stretching out his hand, as we may suppose, from his ordinary habit, and beckoning his audience to stillness—a special necessity in a concourse of loquacious Greeks[2]—he began :

"Ye men of Athens, I see the proofs round me that you are, in all respects, specially given to religious reverence."

This was, indeed, admitted to be a characteristic marking the Athenians, in comparison with other Greeks.

"For, in my going through your city and closely noticing the objects of your worship,—your temples, altars, Hermæ, and the like,—I found among them an altar with this inscription, TO AN UNKNOWN GOD."

There were several such in Athens, raised on the occasion of some public misfortune which could not be ascribed to any known god. I saw an altar with this inscription on the Palatine Hill at Rome.

"That which you, therefore, according to this inscription, worship, without knowing it ; even this unknown Divine object of your worship, *I* disclose to you."

He proceeds to reveal this hitherto unknown God, and does it in a way which incidentally exposes the vanity of the polytheism which deified the powers of nature. HE is

"The God who made the world, and all things in it."

---

[1] 1 Cor. ix. 22.   [2] Acts xiii. 16 ; xxi. 40.

In these few words he gives a delicate contradiction to the system of Stoic and Epicurean, alike.

"He, being Lord of heaven and earth, does not dwell in temples made with hands—not even in the wondrous temples of your Acropolis, or of your city—for He is far too great to inhabit less than immensity.—Neither is He ministered to by men's hands, as your gods are, as though He needed anything from you ; He Himself giving to all men life itself, and the breath that sustains it, and all things needed for it. And, further, He has made from one blood every nation of mankind to dwell over the whole face of the earth, and has ordained both how long they shall occupy the regions in which He has placed them, and also the bounds they shall be allowed."

This origin of all men from one stock and their spread over the earth, he now declares had for its end

"That they should grope for, and seek after God, so that they might somehow find Him out and come to know Him ; though, indeed, He is not far from any one of us. For in Him we live and move and have our being ; as, indeed, some of your own poets have said,—For we are also His offspring, —words used by Aratus of Cilicia three hundred years ago, and repeated almost literally by Cleanthes of Troas, the disciple of Zeno, at least as long ago.[1] Being, then, in the opinion of your own poets, 'the offspring of God,' it does not become us, conscious, thus, of our relation to the Divine, to think so degradingly of it, as to imagine that it has anything in common with gold or silver, or with stones graven or sculptured by the skill and art of a man, or to think that it can be in any respect like them."

Having thus left it, with infinite delicacy and force, to

[1] Aratus and Cleanthes both lived about B.C. 300 or 270. The quotation introduced by the apostle may be found in Fabric. Bibl. Gr. iv. 87 ff., and iii. 550.

their own consciousness, to admit the violence done to
the Divine, by attempting to materialise it, as polytheism
did, Paul glides to the Christian application, which would,
alone, in his eyes, give his words any worth.

"**Thus, in the past, God has not become the Known, but
has remained the Unknown God ; a blindness you may justly
think reprehensible, and exposing us to the Divine wrath.**
But these bypast ages of ignorance of Him, God has graciously
overlooked. However, **His long-suffering forbearance being
wearied out,** He commands men that they should all, everywhere, repent, since He has appointed a day, **and that near
at hand,** in which He shall judge the world, in **unswerving**
righteousness, by the Man whom He has ordained **to act
as His representative, and in His stead;** of whose appointment **to this august office** He has given all men a convincing
proof, **in** the fact that He has raised Him from the dead."

As yet Paul had not once mentioned the name of Jesus,
seeking, before he did so, to rouse the interest of his
hearers, so as ultimately to direct it to Him supremely.
But at the mention of the resurrection of the dead, there
broke out, at once, from some, jeering laughter—the thing
was so ridiculous! while others, equally repudiating such a
mad idea, but more polite in their mode of doing so, interrupted, and closed, his address, by telling him they would
hear him again about this, some other day. Paul, therefore, thus stopped, could only bow assent, and leave the
assembly. His words, however, had not been entirely
. lost, for some men identified themselves with him ; with
the result that after further enlightenment they became
Christians. Of these, we only know the name of one,—
Dionysius, a member of the Court of Areopagus—the
"Upper Council" of Athens,—the "upper house" in fact

—created, originally, by Solon, to be a check, with the senate, on the democracy; that the State, to use his words, "riding upon them as anchors, might be less tossed by storms." They were the censors of public morals, "the overseers of everything, the guardians of the laws," [1] and the supreme judges in both religious and criminal cases—and were held in the highest respect, as "most righteous and venerable." It was a great matter, therefore, to win a convert from such a body. We know nothing of Dionysius, however, beyond this mention of him, though legend has it, that he became "bishop of Athens," and died a martyr. [2] "A woman named Damaris" is also named as a convert, but we know nothing more than this respecting her.

It is clear, however, that Paul found it especially hard to secure an entrance for Christianity among the self-important citizens of Athens, where "what is truth" was a subject of daily wrangling in the Schools; the self-exalting Sophists and their disciples—of whom all the citizens delighted to be the lunar reflections—being the last persons likely to accept light on the true wants of the human heart. He had, we may hope, greater success in the lowly chambers of his fellow-Jews, in the back lanes of the town. But his stay in the city was only brief. The Greeks everywhere were so intellectually restless, so given to rhetorical display, so irrepressible in their talking and disputing, so incapable of forgetting their individuality; so vain, so contentious in every sense, that, with all their cleverness, they were very unsatisfactory material out of which to build up the new faith; the same qualities which had raised their native Greece, and then wrecked

---

[1] Plutarch, *Solon* c. 22.   [2] Eus. Hist. iii. 4; iv. 23.

it, going far to produce the same trouble in early Christianity.

Paul had been waiting at Athens for Silas and Timothy, whom he had requested the brethren from Berœa to send to him, on their return, with all speed. He started, however, before they could get so far, and first met them in Corinth; whither, some " brother" in Athens had told them, he had gone. Whether he went to the Peloponnesian city by land or water, is not told. I, myself, went the one way and returned the other. The road skirts the bay of Salamis, to Eleusis—the chief seat, when Paul went by, of the worship of the goddesses Demeter and Persephone; the " mysteries" celebrated in honour of whom, were known as the Eleusinian, and continued, down to the fall of paganism, to be regarded as the most sacred of any in Greece. It stood on a swell, in a very fertile plain,—a rare phenomenon in so barren a country, and is quite near the sea. About twelve miles south-west from it, he would reach the town of Megara; the road to it passing between, and over, hills, grey and bare, though its site was judiciously chosen in a specially large plain, where it stood about a mile from the Archipelago, which is, however, concealed behind the ever-present hills. It is strange to think that a place which must have been so small and insignificant, had been the scene of endless notable events in Grecian history; had a school of philosophy all its own, and its famous games and festivals. Here, probably, Paul rested for the night, for Megara was reckoned a day's journey from Athens. Thence, to Corinth, was a further journey of about thirty miles, hilly all the way, with little exception, till the isthmus was reached.

This neck of land, joining the Peloponnesus to Greece,

is only about five miles from east to west, and was, in
Paul's day, the busiest part of Greece; offering, as it did,
an easy escape to sailors and travellers, from the then
dreaded perils of sailing round the Morea. Cargoes were,
largely, transhipped from one side of it to the other, for
it had a flourishing port on both its eastern and its
western shore; the former, Cenchrea, now Kenchries;
the other, Lechæum. In the harbour of the former, now
almost deserted, only some parts of the old quays remaining—Paul had to make his way, when he sailed from it,
at a later day,—through lines of great corn-ships from Asia
Minor and Alexandria, and between row after row of
smaller vessels, coming, or going, from, or to, all parts of
the Levant; while, in the western port, he must often have
seen the clouds of ships and boats, trading to and from
Italy and all parts between, which created the bustling
many coloured life, of a thriving seaport. But, both east
and west, where seafaring men, and the trades which
supply maritime wants of all kinds, gave both ports their
character, there is now only comparative solitude, for the
green low hills with their clumps of firs, which gird the
old haven of Cenchrea, look down on still waters, and
at Lechæum, there was neither any sign of a port, nor any
vessel of any kind, when I was there, and I could not
find even the humblest lodging for the night, in any of
the few wooden houses which now do duty for the ancient
town. The waters laving the shores of the fine " Bay of
Corinth," with its picturesque hills on the north side, and
its fertile plain on the east and south, ran up an idle
beach. At Cenchrea, indeed, there was a gathering of
store-houses, and some lodgings for sailors, from time
to time visiting its bay, now that of " Kalamaki," but

they were only the pale ghost of long vanished prosperity;
though, it is hoped that commerce may soon revive, both
east and west, by the completion, in these years, of the
canal across the isthmus, projected so long ago as the days
of Nero.   Anciently, passengers landed from the west, at
Lechæum, and walked, or rode to Cenchrea, where they
took a new ship, for the east; as when, for example,
Ovid bought or hired there, the *Minerva*, to carry him on
towards his place of banishment at Tomi.   Light boats
were often, however, carried bodily, on wheels, across the
isthmus, and launched again at the side from which they
were to set out again.[1]   But Corinth was the attraction of
Paul to these parts, and thither we must accompany him.

[1] **Friedländer,** ii. 21–24; Hausrath, iii. 215.

CHAPTER XX

INTENSELY a townsman, Paul was once more in his element when he found himself in the crowded streets of Corinth, the seat of the Proconsul and of the local and imperial authority, and the capital of Greece; now known, under the Romans, as Achaia. It was, moreover, the headquarters of Grecian Jewry, boasting the chief synagogue of the province; a prime attraction to one whose journeys were not so much, from city to city, as from one synagogue to another. The Roman Corinth was not indeed, that of the famous past, for the old city had been utterly destroyed in the year B.C. 146, by the Roman consul, Mummius. How surpassing its glory had been could not be forgotten, since the triumph of its conqueror was the most magnificent Rome had ever seen. So rich had it been in all the master works of Grecian art and civilisation, that long before its fall, it had been the source from which the Roman nobility had obtained their marbles, paintings, and statues, for the adornment of their villas and palaces, while even after this long continued exploitation, the mass of gold, silver and bronze, melted down, when Mummius gave the city to the flames, was so great, that the amalgam thus formed, when afterwards dug up, formed

what was known as "Corinthian brass;" worth more
than its weight in gold. Corinth had become, in its later
years, the head of Greece, and its importance, as such,
was marked by the dispersion of its disarmed inhabitants,
and the pall of desolation under which it was left buried.
It had lain for a hundred years, mere heaps of rubbish;
a few temples, and the citadel on the mountain above
them, having alone escaped the fury of the Roman
barbarian. Its successor, after years, had been only a
wretched hamlet, when the genius of Cæsar, realising the
advantages of its position, used his power as dictator, in
the year B.C. 46, to cause it to be rebuilt. He owed it,
he said, to Venus, the mother of the Julian race, whose
favourite he had always been, to restore her most ancient
home. His grand energy had swiftly carried out his will;
the city rose once more, and was colonised by veterans
and descendants of freemen, sent to it by him. The
treasures found in digging the new foundations—the
melted lumps of precious metal, and the costly jewels,
created an instant source of trade for the settlers, and
developed special arts in manufacturing a continuous
supply of the new metal, and in reproducing the artistic
triumphs of antiquity, for which the many examples dug
up, and even the lessons of exhumed potsherds gave them
models. So much of the former local grandeur was,
indeed, disinterred, that the old soldiers built their houses
of carved stones, ancient columns of polished syenite and
marble, and splendid wreck of all kinds, from former
public halls, temples, and mansions; as Cairo has been
built largely from the ruins of Memphis and Heliopolis,
and mediæval Rome from those of the city of the Cæsars.
Thatched roofs covered rude, motley walls, which, within,

were adorned with costly rarities, yielded by the soil. In our own times, indeed, in a less splendid way, the site of the Corinth of Paul's day, is an inexhaustible quarry of antiquities, more or less valuable; rings, jewels, seals, coins, pottery, and at times smaller or larger statues, in metal or marble; so that we can imagine what was the state of things in Cæsar's Corinth.

The new Corinth, like its predecessor, became the capital of the southern division of the Roman province of Greece, known, as I have said, as Achaia, and was thus, really, the capital of Greece proper; the northern half of the Roman "Greece," which included Thessaly and the northern section of Macedonia, never having become really Grecian.

The name given his new creation by Cæsar, Julia Corinthus, marked, however, its wide departure from strictly Grecian characteristics. As a Roman capital, the seat of a proconsul, the home of Roman veterans, with a Roman garrison and Roman fortifications, it was rather a Latin than a Greek community, or, at least, a very mixed one; its position and its ports flooding it with representatives of every nationality, and making it so largely foreign, that it was long looked at askance by the pure Greeks. So Latin was the public feeling, that Corinth boasted a temple to Jupiter Capitolinus, and another to Octavia, the sister of Augustus, and monstrously ill-used wife of Marc Antony. Gladiators' shows, and fights with wild beasts, which Greece would not tolerate, found a home in Corinth. Even the names of Corinthians, in the Epistles, seem to carry us to an Italian town, rather than to belong to a Greek one—Titus Justus, Caius, Crispus, Tertius, Quartus, and Fortunatus.

Yet, if not all Greek, but largely Roman in many
ways; Corinth and its isthmus were not without a dash
of Oriental colour, from being on the route of travel
and commerce between Asia Minor and the West. A —
busy intercourse between Western Asia and Europe had
followed the conquests of Alexander, and this, naturally,
made itself felt, in a business place such as Corinth.
Syria, as the hot-bed of every form of frivolity and
vice, sent out a steady emigration of jugglers, dealers in
the black arts of all kinds, astrologers, magicians, sooth-
sayers, conjurers, dancers, actors, singers, courtesans, and
every other variety of ministers to the folly, amusement,
or sins of the rich provinces of the Western Empire, and
if, as Juvenal tells us, incredible numbers of these worthless parasites of society came to Rome, many must, no
doubt, have stopped, on the way, at such places as Corinth.
The Jews had, moreover, been expelled from Rome in
A.D. 48, by Claudius, as disturbers of the public peace by
their plottings and internal factions. But, as no fewer than
8000 had accompanied a deputation of their countrymen to
Augustus, and 4000 Jewish freedmen had been banished
from the city in A.D. 19, "for Egyptian and Jewish superstition," to the mines of Sardinia, the numbers driven out
under Claudius must have been large, and of these, as
we know, Corinth received its share.[1] Trade, so active in
it, was, moreover, enough to secure the presence of multitudes of the money-making race. Hence, rose the great
synagogue, with its rulers, and so effective a proselytism
by the restless ghetto, that we find the Gentile converts of Paul familiar with the Old Testament. There
was, besides, a floating population of men of all nations,

[1] Acts xviii. 2

in a city half-way between Rome and Ephesus; as we see in the case of Aquila and Priscilla, of whom we hear, successively, at Rome, Corinth, and Ephesus.[1] Phœbe of Cenchrea passes from Corinth to Rome; others go from Corinth, to Paul, at Ephesus.[2] Now, however, a few columns here and there in the fields, old coins dug up from the soil, pottery, fragments of pillars, and carved stones, are all that remain to tell where Corinth once stood. Yet where I found only a few poor sheds and equally poor houses; the streets, markets, and great buildings, temples, and mansions, of a magnificent metropolis, spread out, far and wide, in the days of Paul. The city lay at the foot of the lofty Acropolis, a hill 1886 feet high, crowned with fortifications. Up the steep bare sides of this, rose mansions, temples, and sumptuous public buildings, and they extended in all directions from its base. From the far visible top, the seas on both sides of the isthmus are seen, dotted with innumerable islands rising from the blue waters, of old whitened by countless sails, and laving the shores of both East and West, to which, alike, they offer an open pathway. To the north, rise the hills of Greece, and to the west, on the coast of Attica, the eye catches the glitter of the ruined temples on the Acropolis of Athens; while to the south, it wanders over the tangled confusion of the mountains of the Peloponnesus, which, having no towns in Paul's day, had no attractions for the apostle. The rich plain of the isthmus, far below, then surrounded the gay city with waving fields, luxuriant vineyards, and far-famed orchards. Its climbing sides and its broken gullies, are still, in spots, green with the low pine

---

[1] Rom. xvi. 3, 4; Acts xviii. 1, 2; 1 Cor. xvi. 19.
[2] Rom. xvi. 1; 1 Cor. xvi. 17.

from the emerald green of whose fronds the garlands for
victors in the Isthmian games were made; contrasted by
Paul with the unfading crowns of the Christian com-
batant. On its eastern slopes are still visible the traces
of the stadium, or racecourse, over which the Corinthians
often saw the crowd of competitors pressing with a
universal eagerness, which he holds up as an example for
themselves, in their Christian zeal. Near this, are the
remains of the open-air theatre, and near the site of the
old forum, in the city, those of the huge amphitheatre—

Corinthian Coin, with the Crown given in the Isthmian Games.

290 feet long by 190 feet broad; a subterranean vomitory
in it, at one end, for the entrance of wild beasts or
gladiators, realising to us the vividness, to a Corinthian
church, of the apostle's allusions to "fighting with
beasts," or of his being "set forth as the last of all" in
the file of combatants "doomed to death." [1] The gold,
and silver, and precious marbles of temples and palaces,
and the thatch of reeds or straw on the poorer dwellings,
may well have suggested to him, the figure of a noble
spiritual development, which would withstand the terrors

[1] 1 Cor. iv. 9.

of the approaching judgment, when what might be compared to wood, hay, or stubble, perished in the flames.[1]

This Liverpool of the Levant—the centre of a world commerce—a sailor town, without an old settled citizenship to give it a healthy public opinion : without an aristocracy ; rich, full of adventurers, and constantly changing a large proportion of its population ; was naturally low in morals. Harpies of all kinds and of both sexes, abounded, with every temptation of the East or West, to plunder the seamen, the tourists, and the travelling commercial men, of their pay, their gains, or their purses. The city was appropriately under the protection of Poseidon, the god of the ocean, and Venus, the goddess of love. Her oldest and most sacred temple stood on the Acropolis hill, and maintained no fewer than a thousand slave-girl prostitutes, whose gains were a large part of the priestly revenues ; new bands of girls being constantly added to the throng consecrated to the goddess, and following their revolting traffic as part of the temple staff. Proverbs in all languages warned men of the dangers of this Greek Sodom. A "Corinthian" was the phrase for a loose woman ; "to Corinthise" was to surrender to immorality. No wonder that, in writing his Epistle to the Roman Church, on his third visit to such a place, Paul felt overwhelmed at the wickedness around, which so vividly illustrated the foulness of heathenism.[2] All the horrors of vice he there recounts were, indeed, so universal in Corinth, that when he required his converts to have no company with the impure, they frankly avowed that to obey him, would require that they must needs go out of the world altogether.[3] Nor was sensuality confined to

[1] 1 Cor. iii. 12.   [2] Rom. i. 21-32.   [3] 1 Cor. v. 9.

one form. The drunkenness of the town was so proverbial, that Corinthians were always represented as
drunk, when introduced in plays, on the stage.[1]

Yet Corinth was especially fitted for a centre of
Christian propagandism, for so great was the intercourse
between it and other parts, that a letter sent by the
apostle to the Corinthians, could fitly contain his greetings to "all the saints in the whole of Achaia."[2] Here,
therefore, he settled down, not, as usual, for a few weeks,
but for eighteen months. His first consideration, we may
assume, was to find work at his trade, by which to support
himself, and, in seeking for this, he was fortunate enough
to discover a brother Jew, who was not only, like himself,
a tent-maker, but, also, with his wife, a Christian. They
had come from Rome to Lechæum, having been among
those driven from Rome by the edict of Claudius, and had
settled down for the time in Corinth.[3] Both,—especially,
it would seem, Priscilla,—were energetic in all Christian
activity, and, indeed, it is not improbable that their zeal
for Jesus, as the Messiah, in the Roman ghetto, had
identified them with disturbances in it on this question,
which, with other party conflicts, had brought on the
collective Jewry a sentence of expulsion. Aquila was of
Pontus, the province of Asia Minor reaching along the
east half of the southern side of the Black Sea; so widely
had Jews wandered. He and his wife must have taken a
prominent part in the affairs of Corinthian Christianity,
for they are mentioned in four different New Testament
writings. A "church" or assembly of Christians, met in
their house, and Paul not only calls them his "fellow-
workers in Christ, who for my life laid down their own

---

[1] Ælian, *V. H.* iii. 15.   [2] 2 Cor. i. 1.   [3] Acts xviii. 2.

necks," but says, that "all the churches of the Gentiles"
also "give them thanks." [1] With this worthy couple, Paul
forthwith took up his abode, joining them in their humble
craft; working "day and night" to earn, at his badly paid
toil, the modest cost of his food, and thus keep himself
independent. His preaching could, hence, only have been
in the evenings, when men were free to gather to hear
him. Through the day, he was at his goat-hair web, or
sewing; then, as a poor working-man, when the day was
closing, he spoke to the friends who came to him, or to
whom he went at their place of assembly; returning to
resume his toil again, far into the night. So modest
were the first princes of the Church. But when Silas
came, with a gift of funds from the Philippians, and
brought Timothy with him, not only were his wants
supplied, but the way was opened to more active labours
for the Faith. A few adherents, of whom Stephanas
and his house were the first, had, apparently, been
already gathered,[2] and showed such splendid devotion
in "ministering to the saints," that Paul desires the
brethren to "be subject to such, and to every one who
helped in the work and laboured." [3] With this larger or
smaller band of assistants, including Silas, Timothy, and
Aquila and his wife, Paul now felt that he could come
more publicly forward. He must, till now, have been
much depressed, for he writes to the Thessalonians, that
when Timothy and Silas came, bringing good news of
the faith and love of the Thessalonian brethren, "he was
comforted in all his distress and affliction." [4] Now, however, he could give himself more fully to his special work;

[1] Rom. xvi. 3, 4.   [2] 1 Cor. xvi. 15.
[3] 1 Cor. xvi. 15–18. [4] 1 Thess. iii. 7.

going to the synagogue, and reasoning with the congregation there, every Sabbath, that Jesus was the Messiah, in the hope of winning over to Him, both Jews and Greek proselytes.

As I have said, he did not affect to be more than a working-man; coming to the services from the poor workroom of Aquila—and we may judge what a poor Jew's dwelling would be, from what it is to-day, even in London. We can hardly imagine that he had the use of a loom for weaving the goat's hair, unless he and Aquila had found work with some local master-weaver; but if he had been cutting, and shaping, and sewing tent-covers, all day, it was nothing against him; for all rabbis earned their own living, apart from their religious profession as "doctors of theology," by some handicraft, or by small trading, unless they had private means. Paul only acted as the rabbi he was, by education and Jewish feeling, when he laboured as he did, to maintain himself without cost to his converts; for the rabbi was required to do so, either by working as a common labourer, by some handicraft, by field-work as a peasant, or by trade. Thus, the great Hillel was first a day-labourer, and then a wood-splitter. The most famous rabbis might be seen carrying loads as common porters. One was a perfumer, another a baker, a cooper, a shoemaker, a gravedigger, a miller, a leather-worker, a blacksmith, a scribe, a potter, a tailor, a stone-mason, a sandal-maker, or a fisherman.[1] Paul would have ruined his influence with his countrymen, if he had, as a Christian doctor, been less disinterested in his teaching, than their own rabbis. When, therefore, he rose to address his audience, after a day's work, the

[1] Hamburger, ii. 288.

audience would honour him, as illustrating the national
feeling in such cases, embodied in the recorded greeting
of a rabbi who was employed in menial labour,—"Great
is work, it honours the Lord."

That Paul, in Corinth, as elsewhere, made it the burden
of his addresses, that the Scriptures had foretold the Messiah as doomed to a life of suffering, and to a shameful
death, is seen from his own references to his teaching.
"I delivered," says he to the Corinthians, "first of all,
. . . that Christ died for our sins according to the Scriptures." [1]   Indeed, he sums up his one theme, as "preaching
a Messiah crucified; which the Jews regarded as blasphemy,
and the Greeks mocked as folly." [2]   As an ambassador of
Christ, announcing, as the mouthpiece of God Himself,
the atoning death of his Master, we find him calling out
to the congregation in the synagogue, "Be ye reconciled
to God." [3]   The result, as elsewhere, was that the Jews at
once rose in violent passionate opposition, not only against
the "scandal" of the cross, but, also, against the extending
of the Messianic prophecies to the heathen.   They railed
and stormed, indeed, so wildly, that he tells the Corinthians
"he was with them in weakness, and in fear, and in much
trembling," [4] and wrote to the Thessalonians, that "he was
appointed to affliction," and had endured much "distress
and suffering;" [5] breaking out into bitter words against
the Jews, as bearing themselves, towards the preaching
of the Gospel by him, as they had borne themselves,
years before, against Jesus; persecuting His Apostles as
they had persecuted Him and the Prophets, "driving us
out, pleasing not God, and being contrary to all men

---

[1] 1 Cor. xv. 3.   [2] 1 Cor. i. 23.   [3] 2 Cor. v. 20.
[4] 1 Cor. ii. 3.   [5] 1 Thess. iii. 4, 7.

forbidding us to speak to the Gentiles that they may be saved" without becoming Jews.[1]

But Paul was determined not to be forced away from such a promising field as Corinth; the ruler of the synagogue and all his house, with many townsmen who had frequented the synagogue, having encouraged him by accepting his message. Of these first converts, Crispus, Gaius, and Stephanas, with his household, were baptized by the apostle himself, as if they had joined him before the later accessions, whom he left to be baptized by Silas and Timothy; then, apparently, arrived.[2] The tumult at the synagogue having, however, at last, grown intolerable, Paul turned against his opponents, and shaking out his clothes, to rid himself of the very dust of a sanctuary so profaned, he declared aloud that, henceforth, he would leave them. "Your blood be on your own heads," said he, "I am clean" (of responsibility in the matter); "from this time I will go to the Gentiles." He had, indeed, an offer of accommodation close at hand; one Titus Justus, a worshipper of Jehovah, and, so far, a member of the synagogue, — a devout heathen, in fact, — putting his house, which was beside the synagogue, at his disposal, for his meetings But his mental excitement must have been intense, for it broke out even in his sleep; raising visions, sent, we may be sure, in the gracious Providence of God, in one of which he heard Christ saying to him, "Not to be afraid, but to speak, and not hold his peace: for He was with him, and no one would harm him, for He had much people in the city."[3] Emboldened thus, he remained in Corinth eighteen months, "teaching the Word."

That the president of the synagogue, who had so often

[1] 1 Thess. ii. 15, 16.   [2] 1 Cor. i. 14, 15.   [3] Acts xviii. 9, 10.

read the lessons and expounded them, should have gone ovei to Paul, was equally, a mortification to the Jews, and a great success to the apostle. Gaius, another of the seceders from the synagogue, was a man in good position, for Paul lived at his house during his last visit to Corinth, when the Jewish-Christians had raised trouble. Nor was he Paul's "host" only, but, from time to time, that of "the whole church."[1] After a while, other persons of substance joined the apostle; Erastus, the treasurer of the city, Quartus, and the useful Tertius, who wrote, at Paul's dictation, the Epistle to the Romans; men apparently descendants of the old veteran fathers of the Julian Corinth. To these, three Jews added themselves— Lucius, Jason, and Sosipater; "kinsmen" to Paul in their nationality,[2] and among the most faithful of his flock. These, with Titus Justus, and "those of the household of Chloe," whether slaves or connections is not said,— appear to have been the central nucleus round which others soon gathered; spreading the faith in the city, so that it was ere long embraced by some of the middle class, including some Jews, by some proselytes, and a number of heathen. The great majority of the converts, however, were, seemingly, heathen of the lower classes; not a few being even slaves.[3] Overhead, there were not "many wise, or mighty, or well-born" in the brotherhood.[4] The rich merchants and influential officials, as a rule, stood aloof. The Christians could boast of no illustrious names; the scribes of the synagogue, and the Sophists of the Schools, kept away. God had chosen the weak, the base, the despised, and those who were counted nothing in

---

[1] Rom. xvi. 23.
[3] 1 Cor. vii. 21 ; xii. 13.
[2] Rom. xvi. 21 ; ix. 3.
[4] 1 Cor. i. 26.

the eyes of the world.[1]   Paul and his fellow-labourers
seem, in fact, to have gone, in their zeal, to the veriest
slums, where the sailors and slaves herded, who so
abounded in Corinth; for the slaves amounted, even a
hundred and fifty years later, to as many, it was reckoned,
as 460,000.   He must have often found himself among
the hovels beside the docks, where Egypt delivered its
corn and papyrus, Lybia its ivory, Syria its Oriental
products, Phœnicia its countless wares, Eubœa its fruit,
and Phrygia its slaves; in the roughest dens of the
roughest of the population; to have gathered such converts as he describes in his First Epistle: men who had
been "fornicators, idolaters, adulterers, cravens, sodomites,
thieves, covetous, drunkards, revilers, and extortioners."[2]
An ideal missionary, he penetrated the most abandoned
quarters of this wickedest of cities, to seek the almost
effaced traces of the Divine image in the blasphemer
and profligate, whom all others had left to their fate as
hopeless; to rake in the ashes of fallen humanity, for any
spark still by chance glimmering, that he might kindle it
to a flame.   This must be kept in mind, to enable us to
comprehend how things afterwards happened, in the
Christian community, in sad contrast to the title of
"saints" with which Paul honours the converted and
baptized.

That a great many women, perhaps the majority of the
"church," were among the converts, may be assumed from
the many counsels Paul gives to virgins, wives, divorced
women, and widows.[3]   Catching the exceptional manners
of the town, the weaker sex even affected to take part in
the public services of the congregation; contrary to all the

---

[1] 1 Cor. i. 26–29.   [2] 1 Cor. vi. 9, 10.   [3] 1 Cor. vii., xi.

apostle's ideas of propriety, and brought down on themselves the warning, "Let the women keep silence in the
churches."[1] Yet the names of only two females are preserved to us; that of Priscilla, the wife of Aquila, and of
Chloe, a deaconess, active in Christian work at Cenchrea,
who had been a "succourer of many," Paul, himself, among
others.[2]

How many members the Christian community finally included, through the united labours of Paul, Silas, Timothy
and the local brethren, may, perhaps, be conjectured ap-
proximately, from the fact that they met in a private
house, and that there were few such upper chambers in
Greek dwellings, as in Oriental, permitting the gathering
in them, of large numbers.[3] The rooms, indeed, were
usually very small, as we see in Herculaneum, and on the
Palatine; life being spent largely in the open air. Yet
the atrium and peristyle, the two principal chambers, were
often spacious, and would allow of comparatively large
meetings, nor have we to forget the room on "the third
storey," at Troas; from which Eutychus fell into the street.[4]
But, in any case, the Christians must have been counted by
scores rather than by hundreds. Three years, or nearly so,
after Paul's leaving, we still find common meals possible;
the whole community being present. The many allusions
to individuals, moreover, in the Epistles, imply a close
intimacy between all the membership; else the apostle
would not have touched on so many private details, to
the collective body. Every one, evidently, still knew the
affairs of all. Yet the rise of such an organisation as
a "church," in a state of society so degenerate as that of
Corinth; worn out in its religion, philosophy, and morals,

[1] 1 Cor. xiv. 34.   [2] Rom. xvi. 1, 2.   [3] Acts i. 15.   [4] Acts xx. 8.

was so startling, that all eyes in the scattered assemblies
of Christians, everywhere, were soon fixed on it. The
change wrought on the lives of converts formerly so un-
attractive, by the intense earnestness of the new preachers,
and especially of Paul, arrested attention, far and near.
The commanding position of Corinth, moreover, made the
interests of its local church so important, that, after Paul,
it commanded the services, not only of Silas and Timothy,
but of one after another of the leading brethren of the
apostolic times—Titus, Aquila, Apollos, Sosthenes, and
disciples who could claim to have seen Christ; though
their names have not come down to us.[1] Indeed, within
perhaps three years, the restless love of speculation and
discussion; the individuality, in fact, of the Greek mind,
fed by vanity and conceit as well as by higher considerations; had split the Church into as many as four parties, or
factions, which wrangled and contended keenly with each
other; but the very simplicity of their church organisation
forbids us to think that these various fissures were, even
after years, very numerous.

The new community, however, was an aggravation to
the old Jews which they could not endure. Not only
was it made up, largely, of seceders from the synagogue,
meeting almost next door to the Jewish place of worship;
luring, week by week, fresh deserters from it, and thus crip-
pling its pecuniary resources; but it was, also, spreading
the pestilent heresy, that the Messiah was a crucified
man, not a national hero, and that heathen might enter
the kingdom of the Messiah without becoming Jews. To
think of proselytes setting up an independent synagogue
in which they aped the Jewish services, was to make an

[1] 1 Cor. i. 1, 12; 2 Cor. i. 19; viii. 23; iii. 2.

insolent parody of them.   Judaism was one of the "per-mitted" religions of the empire, but this travesty of it was unauthorised, and would surely be put down, on that ground, by the law.   In the end, the whole ghetto, having agreed that it could reckon on support from the Roman magistrates, rose, Jewish fashion, in wild excitement, and rushing to Paul's humble quarters in Aquila's house, dragged him off, not, we may be sure, without tumult and roughness, to the official residence of the proconsul; to demand his punishment as the leader of the new illegal faith; as their brethren in Jerusalem, had led Jesus to Caiaphas and Pilate.

The high office of proconsul of Achaia was held, from April 53 to April 54, by Lucius Junius Gallio, originally known as Annæus Novatus, elder brother of the philo-sopher Seneca, and brother, also, of the famous geographer, L. Annæus Mela.   Their father, a knight and professional rhetorician, of Corduba, now Cordova, in Spain, M. Annæus Seneca, had carefully educated his three splendid sons, and then sent them to Rome; where Annæus Novatus won the affection of the then noted rhetorician L. Junius Gallio, who, having adopted him, was repaid by his hence-forth taking the name of L. Junius Annæus Gallio.   His character, as painted by his brother the philosopher, must have been admirable.   "Nobody," says Seneca, "is so delightful to one, as he is to all." [1]   Under Claudius, the brothers, who till then had been in favour at court, fell into disgrace, an intrigue of Messalina causing Seneca to be banished to Corsica, whence he was ultimately brought back by Agrippina, as tutor to her stepson, the future Emperor Nero, on Messalina's fall.   Gallio now became

[1] "Nemo mortalium uni tam dulcis est quam hic omnibus."

consul, but had to leave Rome when his term expired,
to seek recovery from a spitting of blood, for which he
went to Egypt. In the last year of Claudius, however,
he was able to accept, from the Senate, the proconsulship
of Achaia.

Some years before this, the spread of Christianity had
caused the same disturbance in the ghetto at Rome, as
had now broken out at Corinth—disputes respecting the
Messiah having roused the bitterest feuds between opposing Jewish factions. Stirred up by "Chrestus,"—possibly
a Roman mistake for Christus—the Hebrew quarter on
the Tiber was in perpetual ferment; to abate which the
emperor, in the end, expelled the most troublesome from
Rome, and prohibited the rest from opening the synagogues which had been the centres of disturbance.[1] But
the strife put down in Rome, was carried by the banished
Jews wherever they went, and had flamed up in Corinth,
when Paul and his friends, including Aquila, who apparently had been active in the controversy at Rome,
appeared in the Corinthian synagogue. Things came to
a head, we may suppose, on the defection of Crispus, the
ruler of the synagogue, and, now, the crowd of heated
fanatics clamoured round the judgment-seat of Gallio, to
have Paul condemned for bringing in a new religion.
But the accusation was too vague for the cool head of the
proconsul. Had the apostle been formally indicted as
setting up an unlicensed religion, Gallio must have gone
into the matter, but the preaching of Jesus as the
Messiah had not, apparently, as yet, been considered by
the Jews as more than a corruption of Judaism. As such,
Gallio would regard it only as a local outbreak of the

[1] Suet. *Claud.* 25 ; Dio Cassius, lx. 6.

feuds in the synagogues, which had created so much tumult at Rome; a strife about "words and names and their own Law." Indifferent to such sordid disputes among a race universally detested, Gallio refused to interfere, and ordered his lictors to clear the court; leaving the contending parties to settle the matter, as they had power to do, by synagogue law, but forbidding neither Jews nor Christians from holding their meetings. As against municipal or Roman law, there was no ground of action.[1] But the tenacity of the race would not submit to this rebuff. Still vociferating, therefore, and raising an uproar, Gallio had them driven away by force; a turn of affairs which gave the heathen rabble a welcome opportunity for showing their Jew-hatred. Seizing Sosthenes, the successor, as ruler of the synagogue, of the so-called apostate, Crispus, they beat him in the basilica itself, under the eyes of Gallio, without his interfering: a climax which finally moved the accusers of Paul to think discretion the better part of valour, and make a hurried retreat to the safe shelter of the ghetto.

Gallio, like Paul, lived on after Claudius had been poisoned by Agrippina his wife, to make way for her stepson Nero, and was weak enough to seek favour with the new emperor by bitter words against his predecessor, whom he described as taken up to heaven with hooks, because the corpses of criminals were dragged away by hooks to be burned or buried. The three brothers for some years basked in the sunshine of imperial favour, but only by stooping to unworthy services. Gallio, for example, acted as herald at the theatrical performances of Nero, Seneca standing at his side as prompter, in case he should forget

[1] Acts xviii. 12–17.

any of the prearranged flatteries.   In the year 62, strange
to say, Paul once more crossed his path, when brought to
Rome as a prisoner.   It is possible that while thus in the
capital when Gallio was at court, Paul may, as an old
legend asserts, have met Seneca.   In any case, Gallio and
Seneca were still at court when Nero set fire to Rome, and
then charged the crime on the Christians, whom Gallio
had learned to know at Corinth, if not earlier, and to the
horror of Seneca burned them, in pitch coats, in his gardens,
to illuminate them.   Ere long, the imperial monster laid
his hands on Gallio.   In the year 64, the year before Paul
was beheaded, the old proconsul's nephew, Lucan, the poet,
a son of Mela, had been put to death, ostensibly as involved
in Piso's conspiracy, but, really, through the jealousy excited in Nero by the great success of the victim's poem,
Pharsalia.[1]   A little later, Seneca was allowed to kill himself.   Gallio in terror, then fled to the senate, and implored
their protection against the creatures of the emperor, and
for the time received it.   Soon after, Mela perished, and
finally, among the last victims of Nero, Gallio was put to
death ; for though, in agony at the proscription of all his
house, he degraded himself to every form of abasement,
nothing could save him.[2]

The defeat of the Jews, at Corinth, in their appeal to
Gallio, broke down active opposition to the apostle, so
that he was able to finish an eighteen months' residence
in the city ; from which, as his Epistles show, he, meanwhile, went out from time to time, to neighbouring towns
founding small churches in a number of them.

But even the district round Corinth was not enough to
exhaust Paul's energies, in these eventful months.   The

[1] Tacitus, *Ann.* xv. 70.   [2] Tacitus, xvi. 17 ; Dio Cassius, lxii. 25.

news brought from Thessalonica, by Silas and Timothy,
showed that questions had risen among these dear ones,
on which it was desirable he should write to them, since he
could not go to them in person.   Ill-will and outrage had
tried their fidelity; old sins, like old wounds, had broken
out afresh, and misconceptions respecting the resurrection of the dead called for additional instruction, to quiet
their fears and comfort them.   Paul had been anxious to
return to the city, as soon as the persecution which had
driven him from Thessalonica broke out, against his converts, shortly after his flight; not only for love and sympathy, but lest they should give way before their trials.[1]
With that true affection which never thinks of itself, he
had twice resolved to go back and see them all, again,
though it would, of course, take him into the midst of the
enemies from whose malignity he had narrowly saved even
his life, so lately; but circumstances had, in both cases,
hindered his carrying out his purpose.[2]   Timothy, however, not having been mixed up with the troubles of the
past,[3] was sent by him to them, from Athens, to obtain
information for him, of the position of the Christians,
and at once to cheer them, and to animate them to bear
up against their enemies.   The return of Timothy, and
the news he brought, which were on the whole encouraging, now determined Paul, as he could not safely visit
their city, at least to write them.[4]   In spite of trials and
sufferings, they had remained so firm in their new faith,[5]
that their fidelity had been reported, from one church to
another, through all Macedonia and Achaia; setting an
excellent example how Christians should bear themselves

---

[1] 1 Thess. ii. 14; iii. 3; i. 6; ii. 17 ff.; iii. 5.   [2] 1 Thess. ii. 18.
[3] 1 Thess. iii. 1, 2.   [4] 1 Thess. iii. 6.   [5] 1 Thess. vi. 2, 14

in such circumstances.[1]   Still more, they were praise-
worthy for active brotherly love,[2] and, as a whole, for
their observance of the rules of conduct which Paul
had inculcated.[3]   Moreover, they cherished the tenderest
memories of the apostle,[4] and their church life had
already developed so healthily, that "gifts of the Spirit"
and "prophecy" had appeared among them.[5]

Timothy had, nevertheless, found it necessary to disclose some painful wants and imperfections.[6]   They were
still, to some extent, tainted with the two cardinal sins
of heathenism—lust and covetousness;[7] they did not, in
all cases, show due respect and obedience to their presbyters;[8] and, by turning their thoughts too exclusively
to the presently expected Coming of Christ—the Messiah,
—they had fallen, in some instances, into an unhealthy
moral condition, giving up their occupations and living in
idleness.[9]   Finally, the community was morbidly anxious
as to the fate of their dead Christian friends; wondering
whether the felicities of Christ's coming, were to be
enjoyed only by those who were still living when He
appeared, or whether those who had died in Him would
also share in them.[10]   On this matter, indeed, the Thessalonians seem to have, themselves, asked information
from the apostle.[11]

The use of written communications had been familiar
to the Jews from an early period, as in the case of the
shameful letter, sent by David to Joab, when he wished
the bearer, Uriah, to be put out of the way.[12]   This use

[1] 1 Thess. i. 7, 8.   [2] 1 Thess. i. 3; iv. 9, 10.   [3] 1 Thess. iv. 1.
[4] 1 Thess. iii. 6.   [5] Thess. v. 19, 20.   [6] 1 Thess. iii. 10.
[7] 1 Thess. iv. 3 ff.   [8] 1 Thess. v. 12.   [9] 1 Thess. iv. 11 ff.
[10] 1 Thess. iv. 13 ff.   [11] 1 Thess. iv. 13.   [12] 2 Sam. xi. 14.

of epistolary correspondence, naturally became greatly developed by the wide dispersion of the race, in after centuries: intimate relations being maintained between the scattered Hebrew communities and the mother country, especially in connection with their common religion; for Jerusalem was the universally acknowledged seat of authority in things spiritual, as Rome is, now, in the Roman Catholic world, or as Babylon was, in old times, in Western Asia. Jeremiah could thus, as a "prophet" write a letter to the exiles in Babylon, which reads like an early anticipation of the "Epistles" forming so large a part of the New Testament.[1] Official correspondence of the central authorities with all synagogues in every part of the world was, moreover, as much a part of Judaism, long before Christ, as similar correspondence between the Curia in Rome, and all Roman Catholic bishops or clergy, is to-day. A similar absolute centralisation issued its commands in the one case to the Jewish, and, in the other, to the Roman Catholic world; though the encyclicals of the Curia at Jerusalem were never questioned, or in the least detail evaded; while, in Ireland, at least, we have seen those of the Pope, in recent years, treated by Irish bishops and people, alike, with indifference, where the sins denounced were too popular to be forbidden. Of such letters, we have illustrations in the New Testament, as when Paul received missives from the high priest and his official council at Jerusalem, directed to the synagogues of Damascus, to arrest and send to Jerusalem for trial, any Christians found in that city, and when the Jewish synagogue rulers at Rome stated to Paul, that they had received no letters from Judæa respecting him.[2]

[1] Jer. xxix. 1, 2.   [2] Acts xxviii. 21.

Nor were the letters sent from Jerusalem, or elsewhere,
to Jewish communities, confined to official rescripts. In
the century before Christ, the Second Book of Maccabees
shows us a letter—said to have been sent by the Jews of
Jerusalem to "the Jews throughout Egypt,"—which is a
narration of the gracious ways of God with the nation,
and, in fact, "an epistle," in the New Testament sense.
We have, besides, in Baruch, written after the fall of Jerusalem, a long letter, said to have been sent by Jeremiah
to the captives in Babylon; embodying just such a religious exhortation as the Apostles wrote to the Christians.
It was natural, therefore, that St. James should write to
the small Jewish-Christian "synagogues" "of the twelve
tribes," and that, a little later, the Apostles at Jerusalem
should write a letter to "the Gentiles, that is, heathen-
Christians in Antioch, Syria, and Cilicia,[1] conveying to
them the decision of the heads of the Jerusalem Church,
and of some at least of the apostolic college, respecting the
exemption of the heathen-born Christians from the Mosaic
Law. Nor can we suppose that this letter was, by any
means, the only one received by Jewish-Christian communities, in Syria and elsewhere, in the first years of the
faith. They must often have applied to the Mother Church
for counsel, as they had applied to the Temple authorities
before they became Christians, and, in both cases, this
involved correspondence. When, therefore, Paul had
founded mixed churches, partly of born Jews, but, more
or less largely, also of heathen-born converts, he instinctively followed the custom of his people and the example
of the other Apostles, by writing to these communities
when he could not visit them. A letter like that of

[1] Acts xv. 23, 32.

James, and a series like those of Paul, were felt to be
even more effective means of edification than spoken
addresses, as they could be preserved; and they were.
hence, greatly valued. Paul himself, indeed, set their
authority as high as his spoken words,[1] and required
them to be read before the assembled churches;[2] while
some were designed as " circular letters," to be sent to a
number of churches, one after the other.[3] The letter to
the Ephesians, for example, and even that to the Romans,
appears to have been intended for this general perusal.
The Sunday after the receipt of such an apostolic missive,
would, therefore, be a red-letter day in the little communities, nor would the interest in such correspondence
cease with a single reading. Preserved by a special official, it would be read time after time, as a sacred treasure,
yielding permanent instruction and comfort. Apostolic
letters were, thus, the distinctive form of the earliest
Christian literature, for, though documents embodying
the substance of our Gospels were, we may suppose, more
or less widely circulated and copied, there is no allusion
to them in the "Epistles;" the story of our Lord's life
and death being, as yet, rather handed down by oral tradition, than by formal written narratives such as we now
possess. In Paul's day, the Scriptures of the Old Testament were still the basis of apostolic argument and proof,
and the time had not come for connected writings independent of them. The universal belief that the end of
all things was at hand[4] would, indeed, in itself, make
such a literature appear unnecessary. Jesus had come to
fulfil the ancient Scriptures by returning, presently, to

2 Thess. ii. 2, 15 ; iii. 14.   [2] 1 Thess. v. 27.
[3] Col. iv. 16 ; 1 Cor. i. 2 ; 2 Cor. i. 1.   [4] 1 Pet. iv. 7.

ΟΤΙΤΟΠΝΑΕΠ
ΗΑΛΗΘΕΙΑ ΟΤΙΤΡΕΙϹΕΙϹΙΝΟΙΜΑΡ
ΤΥΡΟΥΝΤΕϹ·ΤΟΠΝΑΚΑΙΤΟΥ̅Α̅ωΡ
ΚΑΙΤΟΑΙΜΑ ΚΑΙΟΙΤΡΕΙϹΕΙϹΤΟ
ΕΝΕΙϹΙΝ

347 Cod Alexand   (1 John v 7).

ΜΙϹΘϹΘΕΘΥΛΟΓΙΖΕΤΑ
ΚΑΤΑΧΑΡΙΝΑΛΛΑΚΑΤΑ
ΟΦΕΙΛΗΜΑ̅ΤωΔΕΜΗ

ΚΑΛΥΜΜΑΕΠΙΤΗΝΚΑΡ
ΔΙΑΝΑΥΤωΝΚΕΙΤΑΙ·ΗΝΙ
ΚΑΔΑΝΕΠΙϹΤΡΕΨΗΠΡ
Κ̅Ν̅ΠΕΡΙΕΡΕΙΤΑΙΤΟΚΑ

348 Cod Vatican. (Rom iv. 4 : 2 Cor iii. 15, 16)

ΚΑΙΟΜΟΛΟΓΟΥΜε
ΝωϹΜΕΓΑΕϹΤΙΝ
ΤΟΤΗϹΕΥϹΕΒΕΙΑϹ
ΜΥϹΤΗΡΙΟΝΟϹΕ
ΦΑΝΕΡωΘΗΕΝϹΑΡ
ΚΙ· ΕΔΙΚΑΙωΘΗΕΝ
Π̅Ν̅ΙωΦΘΗΑΓΓΕΛοιϲ
ΕΚΗΡΥΧΘΗΕΝΕ
ΘΝΕϹΙΝΕΠΙϹΤΕΥ
ΘΗΕΝΚΟϹΜω·
ΑΝΕΛΗΜΦΘΗΕΝ
ΔΟΞΗ

349 Cod Sinair. (1 Tim. iii. 16).

Examples of New Testament Manuscripts—the Alexandrine—Vatican—and Sinaitic
The Epistles of Paul would be just such as these in their appearance.

close the story of the world. Letters which met the questions of the moment, and exhorted to patient fidelity till the Lord came, cheering the brethren, meanwhile, by the hopes and consolations of His promises, were all for which there seemed any occasion.

Nor could Paul, in the circumstances of his wandering life, have found opportunity for settled compositions, even if he had been disposed to sit down to them, which his restless, eager, nature forbade. Writing was painful to him. It required a sedentary inactivity which his ardour could not bear. Even his letters, indeed, were dictated to an amanuensis, as if he could not stand the drudgery of the stylus, and only spoke what others must put down.[1] His Epistles show an indifference to anything like care for their finish or even connection, and the rapid transitions of a mind passing from thought to thought, and from one mood to another, in what was virtually a rush of ideas and emotions such as marks the glow of fervent speech. Very probably we are indebted to Timothy for the embodiment of many of the Epistles, though Tertius and others helped in some cases.

The letter once written out, with all its mountain-stream-like variety of course,—now smooth and limpid, now wheeling in sharp angles, now white, in its rush over hindrances, now boiling in eddies, now calm and mirror-like for a space,—Paul seems, at times, if not always, to have had it read over to him, when finished, and to have inserted, where he thought desirable, additions occurring on the moment, often without any care as to their effect on the continuity of the sense; parentheses detached and independent, often interrupting the flow of the argument

[1] Rom. xvi. 22 ; 1 Cor. xvi. 21 ; Col. iv. 18 ; 2 Thess. iii. 17.

or exhortation, and even, apparently, breaking it off abruptly.[1] By turns, tender, delicate, stern, sarcastic, or even bitter; disjointed, closely reasoned, obscure, luminous, homely, or rising into outbursts of eloquence dignified and sublime; lighted up, throughout, by inner fires of an almost heavenly love, and breathing, at all times, a spirit of the noblest catholicity of mind and heart, the letter, once on the papyrus sheet, was signed by the apostle himself, as "the token" of its genuineness; a precaution necessary, from the fact that "epistles as from him,"[2] were circulated by his opponents. Sometimes, indeed, he added quite a postscript, as when he bids the Galatians notice "with how large letters he had written to them with his own hand,"[3] as if he wrote the Greek characters with difficulty, or as we might say, as if he wrote "a bad hand;" not small and regular like that of the brother who had written the rest of the letter.[4] The due sealing up of the roll having been finished, the letter was sent, by some trusty hand, to its destination; for there was no institution in the Roman Empire like our post; the only approach to it being the arrangements for conveying official correspondence of the government.

How many letters to the churches Paul wrote, cannot be settled, for it seems clear, from allusions in those that have come down to us, that there were perhaps many others which have not been preserved.[5] The priceless value of his communications was apparently realised only by degrees, for even Justin Martyr, in the next century, does not allude to them. His fierce

---

[1] Rom. ii. 14, 15; 1 Cor. viii. 1–3; Gal. ii. 6, 7.   [2] 2 Thess. ii. 2.
[3] Gal. vi. 11–18.   [4] 2 Thess. iii. 17; 1 Cor. xvi. 21; Col. iv. 18.
[5] 1 Cor. v. 9; 2 Cor. x. 9 ff.; Col. iv. 16.

persecution by the Judaisers seems, indeed, to have well-nigh effaced recognition of this greatest of the Apostles, for he had sunk so completely below the horizon of mediæval Christendom, that the prominence assigned him by Luther was a virtual resurrection.

CHAPTER XXI

PAUL'S LETTERS TO THE THESSALONIANS

A.I. 52 OR 53, AND A.D. 53 OR 54; PAUL'S AGE, *c.* 42–44.

THE Epistle or Letter now sent from Corinth to the Thessalonians ran as follows; amplifications being inserted where necessary to elucidate the text :—

The greeting.

I. 1. Paul, and Silvanus, and Timothy, to the church (*ecclesia*) of the Thessalonians in God the Father and the Lord Jesus Christ: Grace to you and peace.

Thanksgiving for Timothy's good report of them.

2. We thank God always for you all, making mention of you in our prayers; 3. Remembering constantly your work of faith, and labour of love, and patience of hope in our Lord Jesus Christ, before our God and Father;—the three cardinal virtues;[1] your faith, begun and maintained energetically, amidst all difficulties; your self-sacrificing love to the brethren; your assurance of hope in the promises of Christ. 4. Knowing, as you do, brethren beloved of God, how you became Christians—by your election by Him. 5. For our gospel was announced to you not in word only, but with power, and with the Holy Spirit, and with the confidence of firm conviction on our part; as, indeed, you are aware, for you know how we bore ourselves toward you—having been made what we were by God—for your sake—that He might

---

[1] 1 Cor. xiii. 13.

win you to Himself.   6. Through this divine impulse ye
became, moreover, imitators of us, and of the Lord, having
received the word into your hearts even while much affliction
of persecution was raging, with the joy which comes from the
Holy Spirit.   7. So that you became an example to all who
believe in Macedonia and in Achaia—the two provinces of
Roman Greece.   8. For from you has sounded forth, far and
near, the word of the Lord—that is, the Gospel, so that not
only in Macedonia and Achaia, but in every part, the report
of your faith towards God has penetrated, by traders and
others; in such fulness that we need say nothing on this
matter, since your lesson of fidelity is already so well
known.   9. For, instead of our needing to do it, they themselves report concerning us, what kind of time we had with
you; with what power and fulness of the Holy Spirit, with
what inner confidence, and contempt of all dangers, we
preached the gospel to you; and how you turned from *dead*
idols, being till then heathen, to serve a *living* and true God, 10.
And to wait for His Son from the heavens, whom He raised
from the dead, thus, by a mighty proof, proclaiming His
Sonship [1]—even Jesus, who, by our union with Him delivers
us even here, on earth, from any fear of the wrath to come.

He can, however, appeal to their own knowledge, respecting his stay among them.

II. 1. For you yourselves know, brethren, that our bearing
among you was not feeble and spiritless: 2. But though we
had suffered before, and been shamefully treated, as you know,
at Philippi, we had such confidence in our God, that He would
stand by us, as to preach the gospel of that God to you, as I
have said, in power, and in the confident assurance of its
truth which the Holy Spirit gives,[2] even amidst manifold sufferings and persecutions.   3. For *this* enabled and pledged us to
act thus fearlessly, that we know our exhortations, in whatever form, were not the preaching of what rested on error, or

[1] Rom. i. 4.   [2] Chap. i. 5.

fancy of our own brain, but on reality ; being, in fact, divine truth—and that we had no unworthy motive, either of vanity, or covetousness, or any similar impure impulse, or any crafty ulterior object.   4. But, in keeping with the fact that we have been reckoned fit by God, to be intrusted with the preaching of the gospel, so we speak ; not as we might, if we wished to please men, but as men who seek to please God, who searches our hearts and tests our sincerity.   5. For neither at any time were we found using words of flattery, as you know, nor making our preaching a cloak under which to hide covetousness ; God is witness ; 6. nor seeking honour and distinction by it, from men, whether you or others ; though we might, without doubt, have secured both, as apostles of Christ ; for Silas and Timotheus, like Barnabas, are in a sense apostles.[1]   7. But instead of standing on our dignity, we were tender and gentle among you, like a nursing mother, when she folds her own children in her bosom.   8. So we, filled with love to you, found delight in giving you not the milk of the gospel only, to sustain your feeble spiritual infancy, but were ready to give up for you even our lives, if needs were, because you had become very dear to us.

The Apostle reminds them of proofs of this.

9. For ye remember, brethren, our working and toil : labour ing night and day ; in the dark hours and bright, from sun-set to sunset,[2] in a poor workplace, with the short wool, or hair of Cilician goats ; rank smelling enough ; to weave it into the stuff for tents, horse-cloths, tarpaulins, and the like ; or cut out that was already woven into such things, and make them up, that we might not be a burden on any of you for our maintenance ; preaching, meanwhile, to you without money and without price, the gospel of God.   10. You are witnesses, moreover, as also is God, how holily we lived towards Him, and how righteously and blamelessly towards you, our

[1] Acts xiv. 14.
[2] The Jews, like the Athenians, reckoned the day thus. Gen. i. 5, &c.

converts.   11. This you know, for you recollect how we dealt with each one of you, making no distinction of rank or gifts, as a father with his own children, exhorting and encouraging you, and beseeching you earnestly   12. to walk worthily of God, who calls you to His own kingdom and glory.

If, however, the preaching of the Gospel by the Apostolic missionaries had been enthusiastic and self-sacrificing, so also had the reception of it been on the part of the Thessalonians.

13. Since therefore, God has called you to such a glorious future, we thank Him without ceasing, that when you heard from us God's message to you, you accepted it not as the mere word of us men, but as what it really is,—the word of God, of whom we are simply the ambassadors [1]—*that* God who, Himself, is the real worker who brings about such a result in you that believe.   14. For, under the same circumstances of persecution you became imitators of the heroism of the churches of God which are in Judæa in Christ Jesus : for you also suffered and bore up nobly under the same things from your own countrymen, as they endured from the Jews : 15. who both killed the Lord Jesus and the prophets, and have chased us from city to city, and are displeasing to God and enemies of all men; since they hinder us by opposition, calumny, and plots against our lives from preaching to the heathen that they, as well as Jews, may be saved ; to fill up the measure of their sins. now, as always,—before Christ ; in His time ; and now, after Him :—but the wrath of God is come upon them to the uttermost,—for their final ruin is already surely foreshadowed in their restless conspiring, everywhere, against Rome.

The Apostle now passes to speak of the anxiety he had felt respecting them, of his sending Timothy to them, and of the comfort he had received from the report his messenger had brought back.[2]

[1] 2 Cor. v. 20 ; Eph. vi. 20.   [2] Chap. ii. 17–iii. 13.

17. But we, brethren, as your spiritual parents, having been torn from you for a short time, but only in presence, not in heart, have, ever since, yearned more than we can tell, to see you face to face, once more. **18.** On this account, therefore, we, that is, I, Paul, would fain once and again, have come to you ; and, lo! Satan hindered us, by raising difficulties. **19.** For what is our hope, or joy, or crown in which we glory ? what but your own selves, before our Lord Jesus at His coming ? **20.** For ye are, indeed, our glory and our joy.

III. **1.** Therefore, as you were all this to me; when I could not bear the anxiety I felt about you, any longer, I thought it best to be left behind at Athens alone ; **2.** and sent Timothy, our brother and God's minister in the gospel of Christ, to strengthen you to bear up under persecution, and to stir you up to growth in faith ; **3.** That no man be shaken by these trials ; for ye yourselves know, both from our words and from your own experience, that they are our appointed lot. **4.** For, indeed, when we were with you, we forewarned you that we must needs suffer afflictions; as, to your knowledge, has come to pass. **5.** On this account—the actual outbreak of persecution—I, myself, when I could no longer restrain my anxiety, sent, that I might know how your faith held out; lest by any means the tempter had tempted you, and our labour should be in vain. **6.** But, now, when Timothy has come back to us from you, and brought us the glad news of your unabated faith and love, and that you have an abiding fond remembrance of us, wearying to see us, as we ourselves, weary to see you,—**7.** by this news, brethren, I repeat, we were comforted about you, in all our own straits and distresses, here, in Corinth,—the opposition we meet, my feeble health, my poverty, and my heavy daily toil with my hands, for bread,—**8.** For now, in spite of all these troubles, we shall not die of them, as we must have done had bad news been added about you, but live, if ye stand fast in the Lord. **9.** For what possible thanks can be enough to render to God, in connection with you, for all the joy we have on your account,

before our God ; 10. since we **hang on you with such fatherly
love that we** pray, beyond words, earnestly, night and day,
that we may **once more** see you face to face, to perfect what
may be still wanting to **the full completeness of** your faith **!**
11. But may our God and Father, Himself, and our Lord
Jesus, make plain our way to you ! 12. And the Lord make
you, **meanwhile,** to be rich, and to have overflowing fulness,
in love toward each other, and toward all men ; such fulness
of love, in fact, as we have towards you, 13. That **by this
love, which is the fulfilling of the law, and the bond of per-
fectness** [1] He, **the Lord Jesus,** may stablish your hearts **so
that they shall be** unblamable in holiness, before our God and
Father, at the coming of our Lord Jesus with all His saints—
**that is, with His holy angels, and the spirits of the righteous
dead.**

The Apostle is now approaching the end of his letter.
There are still, however, some matters on which he would
like to speak. If they are to advance in the Christian
life, they must flee sensuality ; a sin grievously familiar
to them in their past heathenism.

IV. 1. As to other matters, brethren,—**as friends,** we
beseech you, and, **as apostles,** exhort you,—**being, like yourselves,** in the Lord Jesus, **as members of His mystical body,** [2]
that, as you were taught by us how you ought to live so as to
please God,—which indeed you are striving to do—you do so
more and more. 2. For you know what injunctions we gave
you **on this point**—the Lord Jesus speaking by us.—3. For
the **sum of these injunctions is this :**—the will of God—**that
is, Christ's command**—is, that you keep yourselves holy ;
which implies that you keep from unchastity ;—4. that each
of you know how to live with his own wife in purity and honour,
5. not giving the reins to lust, like the heathen, who do not
know God ;—6. that no man **covet his neighbour's wife, and**
take advantage of his brother in this matter : because the

[1] Rom. xiii. 10 ; Col. iii. 14.   [2] Col. i. 24.

Lord, who will presently come to judgment, is an avenger in all these things, as I have already told you plainly and pressed on you when I was in Thessalonica. 7. For God called us not that we should be impure, but that we should be holy. 8. Therefore he who rejects these counsels, rejects not *man*,—that would be bad enough, considering who gives them,—but *God*, whose supreme command these counsels embody,—that God who, moreover, has shown you the unspeakable grace of having given His Holy Spirit to you !

A word about brotherly love !

9. But as to love of the brethren there is no need to write to you: for ye yourselves are already taught of God to love one another; 10. For, indeed, your love extends beyond your own circle; showing itself toward all the brethren throughout all Macedonia. But we exhort you, brethren, to abound in this active love more and more; 11. And that you make it your pride to live quietly, and to attend to your own concerns, and to work at your handicrafts as we charged you while in Thessalonica; 12. that you may live honourably, in good credit with those outside the church, whether Jews or heathen, and have need of nothing from any one; your own labour maintaining you.

Anxiety had been felt by many respecting Christian friends who had died, lest they should not share in the glory of the unexpected coming of Christ, and this Paul now seeks to allay.[1]

13. But we would not have you ignorant, brethren, concerning those of your number who fall asleep in Jesus ; that you may not sorrow respecting them as the rest of men do—the heathen and the Sadducees—to whom death is an eternal sleep, and who therefore have no hope of passing, through death, to be for ever with the Lord. 14. For if we believe, as we do, that Jesus died and rose again, even so, them also

[1] Vers. 13–v. 11

that are fallen asleep in Jesus will God raise from the dead, and bring from the heavens, with Christ, at His coming. 15. For this, that follows, we say to you by the " Word of the Lord," so that it rests not on what we think, but on the infallible authority of Christ, from whom we received it— that we who are alive, and remain on earth till the Lord returns, shall in no way have precedence of them who have before then fallen asleep, or advantage over them. 16. For the Lord Himself shall descend from heaven, with the loud shout of a commander to his host—that is, with the mighty call of the archangel to the slumbering dead, to rise and meet their Lord, and with the trumpet blasts of God's angels, amidst the armies of whom Christ shall return to earth:[1] and the dead in Christ shall rise first, 17. and then, we who are still alive, and remain on earth, shall, together with them, be caught up in chariot clouds, to meet the Lord in the air, as He approaches, and so shall we be for ever with the Lord. 18. Wherefore comfort one another with these words.

The near-approaching return of Christ was known to all; yet it would burst on them suddenly and unexpectedly.[2]

V. 1. But as to the time and hour of the coming again of Christ, ye have no need that anything be written to you. 2. For ye yourselves know fully, from what I told you by word of mouth, that the day of the Lord will come as suddenly and unexpectedly as a thief comes in the night.[3] 3. When they are saying, Peace and safety, then destruction will burst on them—the unbelieving—in a moment, as her labour on a woman with child; and they shall in no wise escape.

Let all, therefore, be ready, as befits Christians—enlightened from on high.[4]

---

[1] Chap. iii. 13 ; 2 Thess. i. 7 ; Matt. xvi. 27 ; xxiv. 30, f. ; xxv. 31 ; Mark viii. 38 ; xiii. 26, f. ; Luke ix. 26 ; Exod. xix. 16 ; Ps. xlvii. 6 ; Zech. ix. 14 ; Isa. xxvii. 13 ; 1 Cor. xv. 32 ; Matt. xxiv. 31.

[2] Chap. v. 1–3.   [3] 2 Pet. iii. 10 ; Mark xxiv. 43 ; Luke xii. 39.   [4] Vers. 4–11

4. But you, brethren, are not in darkness, **like the unbelieving**, that the day should come upon you, as a thief **on men asleep**: 5. for you, all, are sons of light, and sons of day: we are not of the night nor of darkness. 6. Therefore **let us** not sleep. as others—**the unbelieving**—do, but let us watch and be sober. 7. For they who sleep, sleep in the **night;** and they that are drunken are drunken in the night.

Due preparation, means the putting on that spiritual armour, which will secure their having the watchfulness and sobriety needed. Paul delights to picture the Christian as a soldier, required to fight a good fight.[1]

8. But let us, since we are of the day, be sober ; putting on the breastplate of faith and love, and for a helmet, the hope of salvation. 9. For God has not ordained us to **come under His** wrath, but to obtain salvation through our Lord Jesus Christ, 10. who died for us, that, whether we wake or sleep—**that is, live or die,**—we should live together with Him, **partaking His glory.** 11. Wherefore exhort one another, and **build** each other up ; as, indeed, ye do.

The Apostle closes with various counsels, and the prayer that God will in all respects sanctify the Thessalonians, in anticipation of the impending coming of Christ.

12. But we beseech you, brethren, to recognise **the worth, and honour the position of** those who labour among you, and are over you in the Lord,—**the presbyters or episcopoi, whom we appointed to preside in the church.**[2]—and to **instruct and** admonish you ; 13. and to esteem them exceeding highly in love for their work's sake— **its weary labour, and the fact of its being that of appointed** ministers of Christ. **And while bearing yourselves thus to those over you, take heed to** be at peace among yourselves. 14. And we exhort you **all,** brethren, admonish the disorderly—**the idle and the**

---

[1] 2 Cor. x. 4, ff. ; Rom. vi. 13 ; xiii. 12 ; Eph. vi. 11, ff. ; 2 Tim. iv. 7.
[2] Tit. i. 5, 7 ; Acts xx. 17, 28.

unsettled [1]—encourage the faint-hearted, support the weak, be longsuffering towards all. 15. See that no one pay back evil for evil to any one; but always strive to do good, both to each other and to all. 16. Rejoice always, whatever happens, for all things work together for good to you, as the children of God.[2] 17. Pray constantly for heavenly grace; 18. but, also, give thanks, alike in joy and sorrow: for that you should do so is the will of God, declared through Christ Jesus to you. 19. Quench not the flame of the Holy Spirit, which kindles the soul to prayer, and is the source of all the graces which constitute the spiritual life, as well as of all those extraordinary graces,—the gift of tongues, prophecy and much else—vouchsafed to the church; 20. Despise not the utterances inspired by the Holy Spirit, called prophesyings, which fervently enlighten and exhort the brethren, as well as at times foretell things to come; 21. Test all things whether they be of God or not; hold fast that which is good, rejecting whatever does not stand the test; 22. Keep aloof from every form of evil.

But to secure all this needs God's help, and therefore Paul appends a prayer on their behalf.

23. And the God of peace, Himself,—He who gives us peace, through Christ—sanctify you wholly; and may your spirit and soul and body be preserved perfect in all respects, at the coming of our Lord Jesus Christ. Faithful is He who calls you. He will fulfil my prayer. 25. Brethren, pray,—in turn,—for *us*,—that our work may prosper. 26. When this epistle is read before the congregation, salute all the brethren with a holy kiss; the kiss, always, as you know, being part of a greeting, especially where Eastern manners are recognised as with us. 27. I adjure you by the Lord, that this epistle be read to all the brethren. 28. The grace of our Lord Jesus Christ be with you.

---

[1] Chap. iv. 11 ; 2 Thess. iii. 6, 11.   [2] Rom. viii. 28 ; v. 3 ; 2 Cor. vi. 10.

This letter was duly sent to Thessalonica by some trusty hand; opportunities, doubtless, constantly offering, at such a great centre as Corinth; especially in a community which, like the Christian, included many Jews, who, then, as now, were largely "tribes of the wandering foot and weary breast." After a time, Paul had the gratification of hearing anew, respecting the far away converts, and that, to a large extent, pleasantly. The church was keeping on steadily in the Christian course; their faith was more confirmed; their brotherly love wider and deeper, and their steadfastness, under a renewed outbreak of persecution, had shown itself most encouragingly.[1] Anxiety about the coming of Christ had, however, created fresh excitement and much disquiet. The earlier concern, as to the fate of those of their number who might have died before the Lord's return, had indeed, subsided, after the receipt of the Apostle's letter. But the idea had now risen, that Christ might be expected at any hour; the result being, on the one hand, terror and dismay; on the other, an impatient, wild anxiety as to the moment, when the kingdom of God would thus be formally inaugurated. The minds of all were unsettled, and, as was inevitable, restlessness and excitement had risen higher than ever, causing a lamentable increase in neglect of the every-day duties of life. This paralysing belief that the coming of Christ was imminent, had, moreover, been strengthened by the fact of some persons maintaining that they had received revelations confirming it; indeed, it was even asserted that the Apostle had said as much when with them, and an epistle, alleged to have been written by him, had actually been concocted, as still further proof of its

[1] 2 Thess. i. 3, 4.

correctness.[1] It is, in fact, possible, that even the statements respecting Christ's coming in Paul's genuine epistle, afforded colour for the prevailing state of feeling, since, although nothing is said in it of the immediate nearness of the great event, that awful crisis is described as breaking on the world with appalling suddenness, at a moment when it was not expected, and that while Paul and the existing generation were still alive.[2] This dangerous condition of feeling could not be overlooked, and hence the Apostle had to write a second letter to the church, from Corinth, a few months after he had sent off the first. This second epistle ran as follows :—

SECOND EPISTLE TO THE THESSALONIANS.

Address and greeting.[3]

I.   1. Paul, and Silvanus, and Timothy, to the church of the Thessalonians in God our Father and the Lord Jesus Christ ; 2. Grace to you and peace from God the Father and the Lord Jesus Christ.

Pleased recognition of their growth in grace, and steadfastness under trial.

3. We owe it you to give thanks to God continually, on your account, brethren, as is meet, because of the very great increase of your faith, and for the overflowing love of each of you all toward one another ; 4. so that we, ourselves, speak highly of you among the churches of God, for your steadfastness and faith, under all your persecutions and afflictions which you are enduring ; 5. which is a sure presage of the righteous judgment of God at the appearing of Christ,—the result of which will be, that you will be counted worthy of

---

[1] Chap. iii. 2.   [2] 1 Thess. v. 2, 3 ; iv, 15, 17.   [3] Chap. i. 2.

the kingdom of God; in the hope of obtaining which, indeed, you are now suffering :

The recompense of the Christian, and the wrath on the unbelieving, when Christ comes.

6. If so be, as we know it is, right in God to give back, in turn, tribulation, to those who now inflict it on you, 7. and to grant you who are now suffering, rest, with us, who, like you, have a load of trouble, at the revelation of the Lord Jesus from heaven, with the angels who proclaim and execute His power 8. in flaming fire,—so great will be His majesty and glory;—rendering, as He will do, vengeance on the heathen who do not know God, and on all, Jews and Gentiles alike, who will not hearken to the gospel of our Lord Jesus : 9. who shall receive their righteous doom, even everlasting destruction, flaming forth from the sunlike countenance of the Lord, and from the glory which is the symbol of His awful might—10. in that day when He shall come to be glorified in His saints, and to be gazed at with wonder in His glory, to which He has caught up all them that have believed in Him— of whom you will be part,—for our testimony was believed among you.   11. To which end we also pray constantly for you, that our God may count you worthy of the call He has vouchsafed you, to future bliss, and, by His Almighty power, carry out to its completeness every impulse in you to good- ness, and every work of faith ; 12. that the name of our Lord Jesus may be glorified in you, and that you may be glorified in Him, according to the grace of our God and the Lord Jesus Christ.

The Apostle passes on to correct their ideas respecting the coming of Christ.

II. 1. But respecting the coming of our Lord Jesus Christ, and our gathering together to Him, we beseech you, brethren, 2. that you be not readily shaken from your soberness of mind, nor frightened, by excited addresses, wrongly supposed

to express the mind of the Spirit, or by alleged language of
ours, or by any pretended letter of ours; so as to fancy that
the day of the Lord is close upon us.   3. Let no one lead you
astray by any lure : for before that day, The Apostasy—the
falling away from God and the true religion—must first have
come, and the man of sin be revealed, the son of perdition :
4. who opposes himself and exalts himself against all that is
called God, or is an object of worship ; even seating himself in
the temple of God, and openly setting himself forth as God.
For has not Christ said that the abomination of desolation,
spoken of by Daniel the prophet, must come before His return,[1]
and does not Daniel speak of the great enemy of God who is
thus to reveal himself, in language such as I have used ?[2]
This is the Antichrist—the Man of Sin, and Son of Perdition,
whom all our people expect at any moment ; all our books, as
you may know, and all our rabbis, agreeing in this rendering
of the prophet's words.[3]   5. Do you not remember, that, when
I was with you, I repeatedly told you these things ?   6. And
now you know what hinders the appearing of this Antichrist,
and that he is thus kept back, that he may be revealed only
when the time arrives appointed by God.   7. For indeed the
mystery of revolt against the law of God is already working, but
He who now hinders the open appearing of Antichrist, will continue to hinder it till he be taken out of the way.[4]   8. And

[1] Matt. xxiv. 4–41 ; Mark xiii. 5–27 ; Dan. ix. 27 ; xii. 11.

[2] Dan. viii. 23, ff. ; xi. 36, ff.

[3] The Sibylline Oracles, iii. 657–668 ; the Book of Enoch, xc. 16 ; the
Fourth Ezra, xiii. 531–34 ; the Apocalypse of Baruch xl. and the
Targums, agree in looking for an enemy of the Messiah who will appear
before He comes to set up His kingdom, and who will be destroyed by Him
at His appearing, as Paul describes.

[4] The Fathers, apparently rightly, understood by " that which restrains,"
the Roman Empire, and by the "one who restrains," the Roman Emperor.
Remembering that the Apostle believed he would, himself, in his lifetime,
see the coming of Christ, he seems to have looked for the breaking up of
the Roman power within a very short time ; the hideous corruption of the
central government at Rome, with its proscriptions, its imperial favourites,
raised from the slave-bench to rule the world, its murders in the circle of

then shall be revealed the impious one, whom the Lord Jesus
will blast with the breath of His mouth, and bring to naught
by His mere approach : **He will, I say, blast and destroy** him
whose appearing will be an output of all the energy of Satan's
working, with all **the resources of his diabolical** power, and
with signs, and false wonders, 10. and with every form of deceit **which can seduce** to unrighteousness, those who are in the
way of perdition, **as their doom**, because they have not received **into their hearts** the love of the truth, that **thus** they
might be saved. 11. On this account, God sends **into** them an
active principle of delusion, **in order** that they should believe a
lie : 12. That they all might be condemned, who have not
believed the truth, but have taken pleasure in unrighteousness.

Passing from doctrinal subjects, the Apostle speaks of
practical details of the Christian life.

13. But we feel bound, brethren, beloved of the Lord **Jesus,**
to give thanks to God continually for you, because He chose
you from the beginning,[1] to salvation, in **granting you** sancti-
fication of the Spirit and belief of the truth : 14. To which
He called you through our **preaching of the** gospel, that you
might obtain **a share in** the glory of our Lord Jesus Christ.
15. Therefore, brethren, **since such a future awaits you**, stand
fast, and hold firmly to the teachings which have been delivered to you, whether by word **of mouth** or by our letter.

the imperial family, its insecurity of succession, and moral vileness of
every kind, probably appearing to many, in those days, to make a huge
catastrophe inevitable.   But this belief, which was one of the current
Jewish ideas of the time, does not seem to have been long retained by
Paul, when the expected end of the world did not come at the death of
Claudius, and the probability of a speedy destruction of the Roman
Empire receded.   Though still at a later period confident that he would
yet be alive when Christ returned; and though he speaks and writes on the
consummation of human affairs, he makes no reference whatever, after
this, to Antichrist, as we see in the grand picture of the Resurrection-
glory, in the fifteenth chapter of the First Epistle to the Corinthians.

[1] *Sept.* Gen. i. 1 ; John i. 1, 2 ; Heb. i. 10, &c.

That they may do so is the prayer of the Apostle.

16. And now, our Lord Jesus Christ, Himself, and God our Father, who has loved us and given us a consolation which is everlasting, whatever our trials, and a sure hope, through His grace, 17. comfort your hearts, and stablish them in every good work and word.

As he has prayed for *them,* he asks them to pray for *him* and his associates.

III. 1. Finally, brethren, pray for us, that the word of the Lord may hold on its onward course, and be glorified in others, as it has been among you; 2. and that we may be delivered from wrong-headed and wicked men ; for all men have not faith. 3. But the Lord is faithful, and He will keep you steadfast, and guard you from evil.[1] 4. But if the Lord be faithful to you, so also must you be to Him. And, indeed, we have confidence in you, as brethren in Christ, that you are now acting and will continue to act as we enjoin. 5. And the Lord lead your hearts to the love of God, that you may be filled and may glow with it ; and into the patiently steadfast endurance of all trials, which the example of Christ shows.

Meanwhile, they must be specially strict in suppressing disorder and idleness that have appeared among them, from their fancies respecting the coming of Christ.

6. Now we enjoin you, brethren, in the name of our Lord Jesus Christ, not on my own authority only, to withdraw yourselves from every brother who breaks from your ranks, and walks disorderly, and not according to the teaching he received from us. 7. For you yourselves know, from our example, how you ought to act ; for we did not behave thus disorderly among you. 8. nor did we live on any one's bounty, but earned our bread by our own labour and sore exertion, toiling night and day, that we might not burden any of you : 9. not because we have not the right to be maintained by you ; for, as

---

[1] Or, from the evil *one,* but not so well.

apostles, we are entitled to support from you; but that we
might make ourselves a pattern, for your imitation. 10. For
even when we were with you, we often repeated, as our own
command, the Jewish proverb—"If any man will not work,
neither let him eat." 11. For we hear of some who walk
among you disorderly, doing no work at all, but idly busy in
useless, superfluous things. 12. These we enjoin and exhort,
as united with them in the Lord Jesus Christ, that they work
at their callings with quiet steadfastness, and eat their own
bread; living at no one's cost, as they have been doing. 13.
See, however, that ye, brethren, who have not given way to
this course, be not weary in doing good, though you may have
been imposed upon in some cases. 14. But if any one fail to
obey our command, as given in this second epistle, note that
man, and keep aloof from him, that he may be ashamed. 15.
Yet cherish no hostile feelings towards him, but admonish him
to change his ways, as a brother.

Now, the Lord of peace, Jesus Christ, who is our peace,
Himself give you peace in Him, at all times, in all ways. The
Lord be with you all.

17. So far I have dictated this letter, but I, Paul, now add
the closing salutation with my own hand, which is the token,
in every epistle, that it is really from me. See my hand-
writing; this is it. 18. The grace of our Lord Jesus Christ
be with you all.

These two letters to the Thessalonian converts incidentally throw light, in a striking degree, on the direction
of thought in the Apostolic age, among both Jews and
Christians. The one supreme subject filling all minds,
was the appearance of the Messiah; Christians looking
for His second appearance; Jews, for His first. All, however, were substantially agreed as to the events that
would herald His approaching advent. The "distress of
nations" predicted by Christ Himself, as overshadowing
all mankind before He returned, had its counterpart in

similar expectations of the Jews, in connection with their
Messiah's coming.[1]   The "abomination of desolation" in
the Book of Daniel was quoted by Christ and also by the
Jews, with similar meaning.   Paul only repeated the
Jewish belief, when he spoke of the "man of sin," in the
words of Daniel, as exalting himself above every god,
and blaspheming the God of gods, the God of his fathers,
and polluting the sanctuary, and setting up in it "the
abomination." [2]   The rabbis also taught, like him, that
this awful Antichrist would be slain by the Messiah at
His coming.   Thus, the Apocalypse of Baruch, dating
from soon after the fall of Jerusalem, tells us that the
Messiah will slay "the impious one," after convicting
him, to his face, of all his impious deeds,[3] while the
Fourth Ezra "saw how he (the Messiah) sent out of His
mouth, as it were, a wave of fire, and from His lips spirits
of flame, and from His tongue sparks of tempest; and all
these were mingled together, waves of fire, and spirits of
flame, and a multitude of tempest,—and suddenly nothing
was perceived of the innumerable multitude, save only
dust of ashes, and an odour of smoke." [4]   Paul, thus, only
repeated to the Thessalonians the universal belief of his
race, in his disclosures respecting Antichrist; and Peter,
in his speech at Pentecost, showed that the anticipation
of terrible troubles, symbolised by the blood, and fire,
and vapour, of smoke, of burning cities, and the slaughter
of vast hosts; the sun itself being turned into darkness
and the moon into blood, before the coming of the day of
the Lord; was shared by him, also, and of course by the
Apostles at large.   The fact is, that the rabbis had elabo-

---

[1] Luke xxi. 25 ; 4 Esdras xiii. 5 ; Sibylline Orac. 669–697, &c.
[2] Dan. xi. 31, 36, 37.   [3] Chaps. xxxv.-xl.   [4] Chap. xiii. 35–38.

rated a detailed account, from the Prophets and Psalms, of all that would precede the revelation of the Messiah. Joel had spoken of all nations being assembled by God in the valley of Jehoshaphat, to meet their doom at His hands, as the enemies of His people.[1] Zechariah had painted a similar gathering of all nations to fight against Jerusalem, and their destruction by God.[2] Isaiah had described the day of the Lord in similar language.[3] Ezekiel had discoursed of the attack by Gog—the future "Antichrist"—on the people of God, and his fall on the mountains of Israel, with awful slaughter of his hosts,[4] and passages were quoted from the Psalms filling in the picture. In the hands of the rabbis, all this had supplied material in abundance; for the assured conviction of every Jew of Christ's time, and of succeeding generations; that before the Messiah appeared, Antichrist would rise against the saints; that awful calamities would burst on the world, and that, at the time appointed of God, the Messiah would be revealed, and would consume the Wicked One with the breath of His mouth, smite the heads over many countries, and tread down and break in pieces the rule of the heathen. Then, they held, in the words of Daniel, "the kingdom and dominion, and the greatness of the kingdom under the whole heaven, would be given to the people of the saints of the Most High," whose kingdom, thus introduced, "would be an everlasting kingdom, and whom all dominions would serve and obey." Thus, in the near future, how near no one could tell, both Jew and Christian expected the "end of all things," and the setting up of a heavenly kingdom upon

[1] Joel ii. 31; iii. 2, 11, 16.   [2] Zech. xiv. 2, 3.
[3] Isa. xiv. 9.   [4] Ezek. xxxviii., xxxix. 4.

earth; the Jew, however, making no doubt that it was to be a great Jewish world-empire, erected by God on the ruins of the Roman Empire, whose days even Paul, as we have seen, held to be numbered. A thinly veiled conspiracy, therefore, bound together every Jew over the world, as the army of the saints, in preparation for a universal revolt, to break out on the instant when the Messiah appeared, to lead them against Antichrist and Rome, and set up the everlasting, universal reign of the Jew. It is easy to imagine, therefore, the rage of the ghettos at the preaching by Paul, that their belief in this confidently expected temporal glory of the race was a delusion, and the hatred they would feel towards him, for maintaining that men who were not Jews, but " unclean " heathen, could be members of " the Kingdom of God."

But the political results of the Messianic expectations which engrossed the whole race of Jacob, from beyond the Euphrates on the east, to the Atlantic on the west, and from north of the English Channel, to the slopes of the Atlas, and the recesses of Ethiopia, were destined to affect Christianity, to its sore hurt, from its connection, at its rise, with the Jews. The wild fanaticism of a race, which regarded itself as the divinely appointed heir of the world, kept from its own by the heathen, whom God abhorred, and whom He had sworn, by His prophets, to trample under the feet of His saints, had been intensifying for generations. Now, at last, under the cruel oppressions of the Roman procurators, it had broken out into sputterings of fierce revolt, which grew bolder after each temporary suppression in blood, and proved the first gusts of that tempest, which in a few years was to rise to the hurricane storm of the last war, overthrowing temple, city, and state in a common ruin.

Jerusalem, the focus of this revolutionary movement, was dear to all Jews, and its Temple-junta the one government they all owned. Romanism, in its days of strictest obedience to the Vatican, never exerted so absolute an authority over its communion, as that of the council of priests, elders, and rabbis, which issued its orders from a chamber in the Temple courts. Jewry, throughout the world, moreover, was not only one great secret society, spreading, like a net, its innumerable meshes over all the earth; but was, also, an aggregate of carefully organised communities, with their own laws and self-government, able to act, as a whole, in any direction. The Jew was thus, everywhere, in effect, if the central authorities so ordered, a soldier, ready at any moment to fall into his place in the armies of Israel. All that could appeal to human passions made him loyal only to his own secret government, and fanatical pride made him equally fearless and resolute. For was not the Law, by the declared will of Jehovah, to go forth from Jerusalem? Were not the riches of the Gentiles to flow to it? Were not the suppliant kings of the nations to come to its light, and to the brightness of its rising? Were not the dromedaries of Midian and Ephah, the flocks of Kedar, and the rams of Nebaioth, to stream to it? Were not its gates to be open continually—all kingdoms and nations fearing its power so abjectly, that only peaceful submission would mark them? The spirit of revolution was thus in the air, in the Jews' quarter of every town and city of the world, and with this Christianity had to contend wherever it came. Nor was this all. The wild expectations

of the Jew gravely influenced his morality, and, as time
wore on, led to the grossest corruptions in his religious
ideas, which tended naturally to superstition : and the
deadly effect of these, in their reaction on the Christian
communities, is seen in the later New Testament writings.
It was in such a disturbed, storm-laden atmosphere, that
the new religion had to make its way.

How long Paul remained in Corinth, after the defeat of
the Jews before Gallio, is not mentioned.   He stayed, in
any case, long enough to prove that, as had been told him
in his vision, Christ had " much people " in the city, and
that no man would be allowed to harm him.[1]   How earnestly he and his companions toiled in their Divine aims,
we may imagine.   Night after night, when the slave and
the working man were free, he and his co-labourers, with
Aquila, Priscilla, and other lay helpers, would meet in the
house of Titus Justus; sometimes one, sometimes another
leading their devotions, or exhorting, or teaching them.
The organisation was still, in effect, a synagogue—all the
brethren taking part in the services, more or less.   But,
whereas the Jew wore the tallith on his head at worship,
Paul decided to follow the Greek practice of the head being
uncovered;[2] the women, however, keeping their heads
modestly veiled, as they sat apart in Eastern fashion, in
their own place.[3]   As in the synagogue, their humble
worship consisted, mainly, in reading the Scriptures, exposition, and discussion.   The spirit and matter of Paul's
addresses may, no doubt, be assumed from those of his
letters.   The topics handled in the letters to Thessalonica,
written from Corinth, would be those of his intercourse
with the flock which met in the house of Justus, for the

[1] Acts xviii. 9   [2] 1 Cor. x. 4.   [3] 1 Cor. x. 10; 2 Cor. iii. 18.

Corinthians were hardly less excited about the coming of Christ than the Thessalonians; "the time" before it "being so shortened," even in his opinion, that it was not worth while to marry, or to trouble about trade, or indeed about anything.[1] Here also, the ground seemed to be giving way under men's feet. The great white throne might be set up at any moment, and all things earthly, in anticipation of this, were of little interest. This one wept at the thought that a departed friend might lose his part in the coming glory, and had himself baptized in his stead, if possible to bring him within the blessed number; others thought of the great day as that of their exaltation to sit as judges of the world at large, and even of angels.[2]

Meanwhile, the general spiritual development of the converts gave the Apostle much encouragement, though, necessarily, among a body with such mixed antecedents, some shadow mingled with the light. The new religious life grew in enthusiasm. A fruitful rain seemed to have fallen on their natures, calling forth, in the smile of the heavens, the germs of everything good and gracious. There was, moreover, a bursting forth of all the special gifts which marked the high spiritual fervour of that age. Eloquence, thoughtfulness, capacity to teach, showed themselves, to Paul's delight, in men who, till lately, had followed the crowd which streamed like an unthinking herd to dumb idols—themselves as dead and without thought as they. These men, neither mighty nor noble, but from the classes despised as foolish, weak, contemptible, and indeed not worth naming at all,[3] now, under the influence of the new spirit bestowed on them from above,

---

[1] 1 Cor. vii. 25-40. [2] 1 Cor. vi. 2, 3; xv. 29. [3] Cor. i. 26-28.

cheered him by their bright individuality, peculiar endowments, and original eloquence. He saw that they came
behind in no gift,[1] and thanked God that they were enriched, in Christ, in all utterance and all knowledge,[2]
so that they could carry on the worship of the Church, in
all its temporary peculiarities, even without needing the
presence of an Apostle.[3] The early community of goods
had shrunk, apparently, to the joining in a common meal,
we do not know at what intervals; each who was able
contributing to the general provision for it; this "love-
feast" closing by a distribution of the bread and cup
which had been appointed by Christ Himself, as a
memorial of Him and of His death till He returned.[4] But
even so faint a survival of the first enthusiastic union of
the new society, soon showed that selfishness has a deeper
root in human nature than religious fervour; the richer
brethren leaving the poorer to remain hungry, while they
themselves, in too many cases, turned the scene into one
of gluttonous feasting and debauch.

Uniform customs, like this, in its original form, and
regulations of various kinds, had been sanctioned, or
appointed, by the Apostle in all the churches.[5] The
internal organisation of each assembly, however, seems
to have been a continuation of that to which Paul, and
all the Jewish brethren and proselytes, had been accustomed in the synagogues; yet not as a final and binding
form, but, rather, subject to such modifications as circumstances demanded. Thus we read of "The house of
Stephanas," and of "them of Chloe," and of Phœbe of
Cenchrea, as devoting themselves to the wants of the

---

[1] 1 Cor. i. 7.   [2] 1 Cor. i. 4, 5.   [3] 1 Cor. i. 4–6; xii. 1–12.
[4] 1 Cor. xi. 20–34.   [5] 1 Cor. xi. 16.

poor and sick, but it would be too much to speak of them
as deacons and deaconesses, since the Greek word is constantly used in the general sense of "minister," in whatever way; except in the Epistle to Titus, which dates from
almost the close of Paul's life. The offices distinctly
mentioned are that of the Apostle, the prophet, and the
teacher, but there is no word of presbyters or of a president.[1] "Subjection" is enjoined towards such as the
house of Stephanas, and to "every one that helps in the
work, and labours," and, therefore, to such as the Apostle's
hosts, Justus and Gaius, and to all like Stephanas, and
Fortunatus, and Achaicus, who aided in founding and
building up the infant Christian community.[2] It seems,
indeed, as if Paul had been less definite in his organisation of the Corinthian than he had been of the church
among the military veterans of Philippi, for he speaks
of "bishops and deacons" as in office there. Was it
that the strong individualism of the Greeks, so instinctively given to extreme democracy, made them indisposed
to submit to any central authority—so that matters were
left in the hands of the brethren as a whole, more than
elsewhere? That their being so resulted badly, is seen
in the turbulent and divided condition of the Corinthian
Church in a very short time.

Paul had stayed in Corinth longer than he usually
remained in one place, but not long enough, as it proved,
to establish things so fully as to prevent future trouble.
At last, however, he felt himself compelled to leave, having
determined to return to Syria, for what special reasons,
beyond, no doubt, a desire to report the progress of his

---

[1] Rom. xvi. 1; 1 Cor. xii. 27–29; xvi. 15; i. 11.
[2] 1 Cor. xvi. 15–18.

mission to those from whom he had been sent out and
to the other Palestine churches, we have no means of
knowing. We may imagine his farewell, from that which
is recorded on the similar case of his leaving the elders of
the church of Ephesus, at Miletus.[1] He could truly say
that he had served the Lord with all lowliness of mind,
and with tears; and, amidst trials from enemies, had not
feared to say whatever he had thought for their good;
teaching them not only publicly, but from house to house.
And we may be sure that there were some who, as at
Miletus, fell on his neck and kissed him, fearing they
should see him no more.

Crossing the isthmus to Cenchrea, where, apparently,
he had already gathered a little band, of whom Phœbe,
a "servant of the church," had endeared herself to him
as a "sister,"[2] he sailed from that port for Ephesus, as
a stage on the way to Syria. He took with him his two
friends, Aquila and Priscilla, of the former of whom St.
Luke notes that, having some time previous taken a vow,
to let his hair grow for a fixed period, and that period
having expired while he was at Cenchrea, he now absolved
himself from it by enjoying the luxury of having his head
shaved; Orientals keeping their head cool by regularly
shaving it; their thick turban protecting it out of doors.
The occasion of the vow is not told, but was probably
his escaping some danger. Paul would assuredly have
abstained from becoming a Jew in this way, but to Aquila,
it was a natural thing to act as he had done.[3]

The voyage to Ephesus was one of over 200 miles, past
island after island of the Archipelago, but no particulars

---

[1] Acts xx.   [2] Rom. xvi. 1.
[3] See Vulgate; "Aquila, qui sibi totonderat in Cenchris caput."

of it are given.   As in our own times, with sailing vessels
it may have taken only two or three days, or, it might be
as many weeks: instances of both occurring.   The great
city lay at the north-west corner of the bay bearing the
name of the river Caystrus, the mouth of which then
offered a harbour for trading vessels plying to or from
Ephesus, though it has long been dry, partly from the
deposits of the river, but, also, from the gradual elevation
of the coast; a change of level common to all the shores
of western Asia Minor.   The immense commerce of the
port made it easy for Paul to find a vessel sailing thence
to Cæsarea, which he reached safely.   From this he seems
to have started forthwith for Jerusalem, where, however,
he appears to have stayed only till he had met the
Christian congregation, with its leaders, and "saluted"
them.   He had perhaps, after all his trouble, arrived too
late for the feast he had proposed to attend, and had,
therefore, no more attraction to keep him in the Holy
City.   For it is not to be forgotten that the Jerusalem
Church was the headquarters of the Judaisers who had
so bitterly opposed him at Antioch, and all through
his mi-sionary journey; seeking to counterwork and undo
all his efforts to spread the Gospel among the non-Jewish
races.   Possibly on this ground, or from news of a state
of things at Antioch which made his presence there
desirable, or from a wish to be in the Syrian capital
again before his enemies at Jerusalem could send down
a fresh deputation to raise new disputes, or revive those
of the past, he turned northwards, towards the Mother
Church of his own school of Christianity, by which he
had been sent out on each of his missions, amidst prayers
and tearful loving adieus, to carry the Gospel to the

Gentiles as well as to the Jews. The free atmosphere of
Antioch suited a nature like his, immeasurably better
than the twilight bigotry and insolent pride which
claimed for the Jew what was meant for mankind at
large. The Syrian capital, moreover, was, practically,
more the metropolis of the new faith than Jerusalem,
since the influx of so many heathen proselytes to its
membership, without becoming Jews, and the extension,
under the sanction of the local church, of the same com-
prehensive charity, by the missions of Paul; to which it
stood almost in the relation of founder. Jerusalem, to
him, had become the slave-mother Hagar, who, with her
children, was in bondage;[1] the churches founded on the
Antioch model were his Isaac, the free-born son of promise,
rejoicing in the freedom brought them by Christ, and
determined not to be entangled again by any Judaisers,
in a yoke of bondage.[2]

To reach the northern city, Paul would have to take
the Roman road to Cæsarea, by Antipatris, which he was,
hereafter, to travel as a prisoner. Antioch lay about
three hundred miles north of Jerusalem, and if, as seems
probable, Paul went by land, would take well-nigh a
month's travel on foot; occasional temporary rest being
inevitable, alike to refresh him, and to enable him to
see and fraternise with the little groups of brethren at
different points. Supposing he was ten years older than
our Lord, though it is only supposition, he would now,
in the spring of the year 55, be between forty and fifty,
though perhaps nearer the former than the latte since
Christ was born we hardly know how many year before
the received date. Travelling on foot, for one so roken

[1] Gal. iv. 25.   [2] Gal

by frequent illness, would be no light undertaking, but
there would be only the alternative of an ass, which he
may have used, if one so self denying could bring himself
to afford even so small an indulgence.   In any case, the
road led on, along the coast, round the promontory of
Carmel and the bay of Acre, past Tyre and Sidon, both,
in those days, and for long after, "illustrious and splendid
cities;"[1] Tyre, indeed, being described by Jerome,[2] more
than three hundred years later, as that "most noble and
most beautiful city."[3]   But these places would, doubtless,
be most attractive to Paul, from their containing, each,
a Christian community, we do not know of what size.[4]
Beyond Beirout, he would pass the tablets on which I, in
common with all travellers, have looked with profound
interest, carved on the rock, at the side of the narrow
road overhanging the sea, by Rameses II., the oppressor
of the Hebrews in Egypt, and by Sennacherib, the As-
syrian; all, alike, memorials to Paul, as a Jew, of the
mighty arm with which God protects His people, and
delivers them from all their distresses, and a pledge to
him, as a servant of Christ, that the same outstretched arm
would defend the cause of the risen and glorified Saviour.
About two hundred miles of weary advance still remained,
along the shore, as far as Laodicea, and then, behind the
shore mountains, he would go straight north to Antioch,
through delightfully fertile regions of varied beauty;
valleys and slopes and hills alike offering a continual
panorama of loveliness.   We may imagine with what joy
the great church in the free Gentile city would welcome
one who had gone so far, and braved so much, to carry to

---

[1] Strabo (d. between A.D. 21 and 25), xvi. p. 756.   [2] A.D. 331–420
[3] Comment. on Ezek. xxvi. 7.   [4] Acts xxi. 3-7 ; xxvii. 3,

their Gentile brethren the message of love, offered, for
the first time, in his preaching, as much to them as to
the hitherto favoured Jew.   St. Luke mentions the visit
of the Apostle to Jerusalem in the single expression
that "he went up"—the usual phrase in those day, for
visiting the Holy City—"and saluted the church."   Of
Antioch, on the other hand, he tells us, that Paul "spent
some time there,"—apparently from the spring of the
year 55, to the late summer.   The metropolis of Christianity was no longer the Hebrew Jerusalem, but the
Gentile Antioch ; the new faith was no longer a Jewish,
but had become a universal religion, and of this, Paul was
the Apostle, specially chosen and consecrated by Christ
Himself, on the way to Damascus, when, from amidst
the revelation of His Divine glory, He told him, he was,
henceforth, to bear His name far thence to the Gentiles.

INDEX